OXFORD IB DIPLOMA PROGRAMME

CONFLICT AND INTERVENTION

COURSE COMPANION

Martin Cannon

OXFORD
UNIVERSITY PRESS

OXFORD
UNIVERSITY PRESS

Great Clarendon Street, Oxford, OX2 6DP, United Kingdom

Oxford University Press is a department of the University of Oxford. It furthers the University's objective of excellence in research, scholarship, and education by publishing worldwide. Oxford is a registered trade mark of Oxford University Press in the UK and in certain other countries

© Oxford University Press 2015

The moral rights of the authors have been asserted

First published in 2015

British Library Cataloguing in Publication Data

Data available

978-0-19-831017-4

1 3 5 7 9 10 8 6 4 2

MIX
Paper from responsible sources
FSC® C007785

Paper used in the production of this book is a natural, recyclable product made from wood grown in sustainable forests. The manufacturing process conforms to the environmental regulations of the country of origin.

Printed in Great Britain by Bell and Bain Ltd, Glasgow

Acknowledgements

The publishers would like to thank the following for permissions to use their photographs:

p15: Stocksnapper/Shutterstock; p15: Stocksnapper/Shutterstock; p16: REX; p13: Universal History Archive/Universal Images Group/REX; p19: Punch Limited; p22: Robana/British Library/REX; p23: Stock Montage/Getty Images; p25: INTERFOTO/Alamy; p26: Sueddeutsche Zeitung Photo/Mary Evans; p27: akg-images/Newscom; p30: Howard Davies/Corbis; p31: AP Images; p33: Graphi-Ogre; p38: Peter Stuckings/Getty Images; p39: Sipa Press/REX; p40: WWF/Altor IGCP, Goma/HO/EPA; p42: STR New/Reuters; p44: Photos 12/Alamy; p46: Kangura Archives; p41: Universal History Archive/Getty Images; p53: Scott Peterson/Liaison/Getty Images; p59: Corinne Dufka/Reuters; p62: Bettmann/Corbis; p65: Inyenzi/Andrew Brown; p68: Jean-Marc Bouju/AP Images; p69: Digital Globe; p73: Pascal Le Segretain/Sygma/Corbis; p71: Alexander Joe/AFP/Getty Images; p77(L): Scott Peterson/Liaison/Getty Images; p77(R): Antony Njuguna/Reuters; p87: Sam Kiley/Sygma/Corbis; p84: Ricardo Gangale/Africa 24 Media/Newscom; p90: United Nations Photo; p98: Corbis; p102: Pat Oliphant/Universal Uclick; p106: Benoit Gysembergh/Paris Match/Getty Images; p109: Peter Turnley/Corbis; p110: David Turnley/Corbis; p113: Howard Sayer/Alamy; p104: Jean-Marc Bouju/AP Images; p121: GM/KM/Reuters; p126: Thomas Coex/AFP/Getty Images; p129: Carl Wilkens; p135: David Brown/The Independent/British Cartoon Archive; p136: Bettmann/Corbis; p139: Punch Limited; p141: Kukryniksy; p142: Bettmann/Corbis; p144: Bettmann/Corbis; p146: Punch Limited; p147: Sovfoto/Universal Images Group/REX; p149: Associated Newspapers Ltd/Solo Syndication/British Cartoon Archive; p150: Victor Weisz/British Cartoon Archive; p151: Artgraphixel/Shutterstock; p154: Associated Newspapers Ltd/Solo Syndication/British Cartoon Archive; p157: AP Images; p153: STR New/Reuters; p159: Joshua Trujillo/Seattle P-I; p160: Sean Gallup/Getty Images; p162: Peter Northall/EPA; p163: Romano Cagnoni/Getty Images; p164(T): Marco De Angelis; p164(B): Marco De Angelis; p167: Anja Niedringhaus/EPA; p169: Everett Collection/REX; p170(T): Fehim Demir/EPA; p170(B): Michael Evstafiev/AFP/Getty Images; p171: Marco De Angelis; p172: Wostok Press/MAXPPP/Newscom; p176: Steve Back/Daily Mail/REX; p178: Vadim Ghirda/AP Images; p179: Pool/Reuters; p181(T): Chris Priestley/British Cartoon Archive; p181(B): David Brown/The Independent/British Cartoon Archive; p182: Express Syndication Ltd/British Cartoon Archive; p184: Reuters; p185: News UK/British Cartoon Archive; p187: Louisa Gouliamaki/EPA; p191: Lionel Lourdel/Getty Images; p192: John Schults/AP Images; p194: Bill McArthur/British Cartoon Archive; p196: News UK/British Cartoon Archive; p197: Trouw and Tom Janssen; p202(L): Ivan Milutinovic/Reuters; p202(R): Dod/Getty Images; p203: News UK/British Cartoon Archive; p204: Reuters; p195: STR New/Reuters; p206: Usaf/Getty Images; p207: Phil Walter/Getty Images; p210: Reuters; p211: David Brown/The Independent/British Cartoon Archive; p213: Hektor Pustina/AP Images; p217: EPA; p220(T): Mike Forster/Daily Mail/REX; p220(B): US ARMY; p221: Hazir Reka/EPA; p222: Judy Ryan/Department of Defence; p223: Telegraph Media Group Ltd/British Cartoon Archive; p225: Andrew Wong/Reuters; p226: Adrian Raeside/Raesidecartoon.com; p232: Tom Stoddart/Getty Images; p235: Shinichi Murata/REX; p236: Adrian Raeside/Raesidecartoon.com; p237: STR/EPA; p241: Peter Schrank/The Economist; p242: Frederik Enneman/Demotix/Corbis; p246: Sipa Press/REX; p117 (B): Steve Bell; p248: Martin Rowson/British Cartoon Archive; p250: Chris Riddell/British Cartoon Archive; p251(T): News UK/British Cartoon Archive; p251(B): Telegraph Media Group Ltd/British Cartoon Archive

Cover artwork by Karolis Strautniekas, Folio Illustration Agency.

Artwork by QBS Learning and OUP.

We are grateful to the authors and publishers for use of extracts from their titles and in particular for the following:

Amnesty International: 'The truth behind the killings of 45 ethnic Albanians in Kosovo must be found', Amnesty International, 18 January 1999, copyright © Amnesty International Publications, 1 Easton Street, London WC1X 0DW, United Kingdom (www.amnesty.org), reprinted by permission.

Anonymous: extract from *Cahiers Lumière et Société Dialogue IV*, 1999, December issue, number 16, pages 33–38, reprinted by permission.

Kofi Annan: from 'Secretary-General deeply regrets Yugoslav rejection of political settlement; says Security Council should be involved in any decision to use force', New York, 24 March 1999, © 1999 United Nations, reprinted by permission of the United Nations.

John Catalinotto: 'Pretext for war in Kosovo was a hoax. Report finds no evidence of 'Racak massacre'', *Workers World* (www.workers.org), 8 June 2000, reprinted by permission.

Christophe Chatelot: 'Were the Račak dead really coldly massacred?' (translation of 'Les morts de Racak ont-ils vraiment été massacres froidement?') *Le Monde*, 21 January 1999, reprinted by permission.

William J. Clinton: from *The President's Radio Address*, April 3, 1999, from 'Public Papers of the Presidents, William J. Clinton, 1999 Vol. I' p.495 and found here: http://www.presidency.ucsb.edu/ws/index.php?pid=57358.

William J. Clinton: quotation from 'Remarks to the Military Community at Norfolk Naval Station April 1, 1999' from 'Public Papers of the Presidents of the United States' and found here: http://www.gpo.gov/fdsys/pkg/WCPD-1999-04-05/pdf/WCPD-1999-04-05-Pg564.pdf.

Continued on back page

Course Companion definition

The IB Diploma Programme Course Companions are resource materials designed to support students throughout their two-year Diploma Programme course of study in a particular subject. They will help students gain an understanding of what is expected from the study of an IB Diploma Programme subject while presenting content in a way that illustrates the purpose and aims of the IB. They reflect the philosophy and approach of the IB and encourage a deep understanding of each subject by making connections to wider issues and providing opportunities for critical thinking.

The books mirror the IB philosophy of viewing the curriculum in terms of a whole-course approach; the use of a wide range of resources, international mindedness, the IB learner profile and the IB Diploma Programme core requirements, theory of knowledge, the extended essay, and creativity, activity, service (CAS).

Each book can be used in conjunction with other materials and indeed, students of the IB are required and encouraged to draw conclusions from a variety of resources. Suggestions for additional and further reading are given in each book and suggestions for how to extend research are provided.

In addition, the Course Companions provide advice and guidance on the specific course assessment requirements and on academic honesty protocol. They are distinctive and authoritative without being prescriptive.

IB mission statement

The International Baccalaureate aims to develop inquiring, knowledgable and caring young people who help to create a better and more peaceful world through intercultural understanding and respect.

To this end the IB works with schools, governments and international organizations to develop challenging programmes of international education and rigorous assessment.

These programmes encourage students across the world to become active, compassionate, and lifelong learners who understand that other people, with their differences, can also be right.

The IB learner Profile

The aim of all IB programmes is to develop internationally minded people who, recognizing their common humanity and shared guardianship of the planet, help to create a better and more peaceful world. IB learners strive to be:

Inquirers They develop their natural curiosity. They acquire the skills necessary to conduct inquiry and research and show independence in learning. They actively enjoy learning and this love of learning will be sustained throughout their lives.

Knowledgable They explore concepts, ideas, and issues that have local and global significance. In so doing, they acquire in-depth knowledge and develop understanding across a broad and balanced range of disciplines.

Thinkers They exercise initiative in applying thinking skills critically and creatively to recognize and approach complex problems, and make reasoned, ethical decisions.

Communicators They understand and express ideas and information confidently and creatively in more than one language and in a variety of modes of communication. They work effectively and willingly in collaboration with others.

Principled They act with integrity and honesty, with a strong sense of fairness, justice, and respect for the dignity of the individual, groups, and communities. They take responsibility for their own actions and the consequences that accompany them.

Open-minded They understand and appreciate their own cultures and personal histories, and are open to the perspectives, values, and traditions of other individuals and communities. They are accustomed to seeking and evaluating a range of points of view, and are willing to grow from the experience.

Caring They show empathy, compassion, and respect towards the needs and feelings of others. They have a personal commitment to service, and act to make a positive difference to the lives of others and to the environment.

Risk-takers They approach unfamiliar situations and uncertainty with courage and forethought, and have the independence of spirit to explore new roles, ideas, and strategies. They are brave and articulate in defending their beliefs.

Balanced They understand the importance of intellectual, physical, and emotional balance to achieve personal well-being for themselves and others.

Reflective They give thoughtful consideration to their own learning and experience. They are able to assess and understand their strengths and limitations in order to support their learning and personal development.

A note on academic honesty

It is of vital importance to acknowledge and appropriately credit the owners of information when that information is used in your work. After all, owners of ideas (intellectual property) have property rights. To have an authentic piece of work, it must be based on your individual and original ideas with the work of others fully acknowledged. Therefore, all assignments, written or oral, completed for assessment must use your own language and expression. Where sources are used or referred to, whether in the form of direct quotation or paraphrase, such sources must be appropriately acknowledged.

How do I acknowledge the work of others?

The way that you acknowledge that you have used the ideas of other people is through the use of footnotes and bibliographies.

Footnotes (placed at the bottom of a page) or endnotes (placed at the end of a document) are to be provided when you quote or paraphrase from another document, or closely summarize the information provided in another document. You do not need to provide a footnote for information that is part of a 'body of knowledge'. That is, definitions do not need to be footnoted as they are part of the assumed knowledge.

Bibliographies should include a formal list of the resources that you used in your work. The listing should include all resources, including books, magazines, newspaper articles, Internet-based resources, CDs and works of art. 'Formal' means that you should use one of the several accepted forms of presentation. You must provide full information as to how a reader or viewer of your work can find the same information. A bibliography is compulsory in the extended essay.

What constitutes misconduct?

Misconduct is behaviour that results in, or may result in, you or any student gaining an unfair advantage in one or more assessment component. Misconduct includes plagiarism and collusion.

Plagiarism is defined as the representation of the ideas or work of another person as your own. The following are some of the ways to avoid plagiarism:

- Words and ideas of another person used to support one's arguments must be acknowledged.

- Passages that are quoted verbatim must be enclosed within quotation marks and acknowledged.

- CD-ROMs, email messages, web sites on the Internet, and any other electronic media must be treated in the same way as books and journals.

- The sources of all photographs, maps, illustrations, computer programs, data, graphs, audio-visual, and similar material must be acknowledged if they are not your own work.

- Works of art, whether music, film, dance, theatre arts, or visual arts, and where the creative use of a part of a work takes place, must be acknowledged.

Collusion is defined as supporting misconduct by another student. This includes:

- allowing your work to be copied or submitted for assessment by another student

- duplicating work for different assessment components and/or diploma requirements.

Other forms of misconduct include any action that gives you an unfair advantage or affects the results of another student. Examples include, taking unauthorized material into an examination room, misconduct during an examination, and falsifying a CAS record.

Contents

YOUR GUIDE FOR PAPER 1

The final years of the twentieth century saw one of the worst episodes ever witnessed in that tumultuous period. It also witnessed attempts by the international community to intervene in one region and prevent further ill treatment of a civilian population. The latter demonstrated an active will to take a stand in Kosovo, whereas in the earlier episode in Rwanda, little had been done to prevent genocide. The two episodes are linked both by what happened in these two distinct regions through conflict, but also by the role played by members of the international community that intervention could prevent bloodshed.

This book deals firstly with a case study of graphic brutality in a small African nation decimated by forces which lay within its own borders. It examines the causes of the conflict, looking at the ethnic tensions and other reasons such as economic issues and the legacy of colonial rule before dealing with the genocide itself, the response of the international community and the impact the genocide had on Rwanda and its neighbours.

The second case study examines the conflict in the tiny province of Kosovo in the context of the break-up of the former Yugoslav federation in Europe. It looks at how the international community played a different role compared to Rwanda and assesses the causes of the conflict in Kosovo as well as the impact that intervention had in the region. Both case studies examine the role of the International courts in dispensing justice.

Historical concepts

The content in this unit is linked to the six key IB concepts.

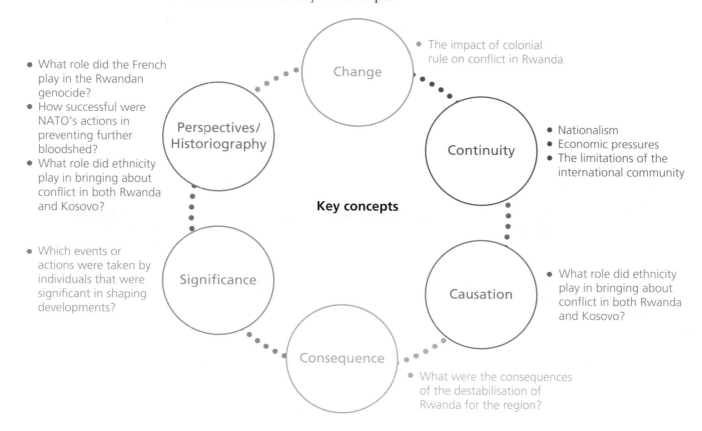

Key concepts

- What role did the French play in the Rwandan genocide?
- How successful were NATO's actions in preventing further bloodshed?
- What role did ethnicity play in bringing about conflict in both Rwanda and Kosovo?

Perspectives/ Historiography

Change
- The impact of colonial rule on conflict in Rwanda

Continuity
- Nationalism
- Economic pressures
- The limitations of the international community

Causation
- What role did ethnicity play in bringing about conflict in both Rwanda and Kosovo?

Consequence
- What were the consequences of the destabilisation of Rwanda for the region?

Significance
- Which events or actions were taken by individuals that were significant in shaping developments?

"Conflict and intervention" is a prescribed subject for Paper 1 of your IB History examination. This book focuses not only on helping you to cover and understand the content relating to this topic, but will also help you to develop the skills necessary to answer the source questions.

History is an exploratory subject that fosters a sense of inquiry. It is also an interpretive discipline, allowing opportunity for engagement with multiple perspectives and a plurality of opinions. Studying history develops an understanding of the past, which leads to a deeper understanding of the nature of humans and of the world today.

The content of this prescribed subject may also be relevant to the topics that you are studying for Papers 2 and 3.

This book includes:

- analysis of the key events in each case study
- activities to develop your understanding of the content and key issues
- links between the content and historical concepts (see previous page)
- timelines to help develop a chronological understanding of key events
- some relevant historiography
- a range of sources for each topic
- practice source questions along with examiner's hints
- links to theory of knowledge (TOK).

How to use this book

This first chapter will explain how to approach each question on the IB Paper 1; there will then be source exercises to try throughout the book which will give you the opportunity to practise your Paper 1 skills.

Where you see this icon, you will find extra help answering the question, either at the end of the chapter or next to the question itself.

Where you see this icon, go to www. oxfordsecondary.com/ib-history-resources to find extra help.

Preparing for Paper 1: Working with sources

As historians, our training and discipline is based on documentary evidence.

— David Dixon

When you work with sources you are practising a key component of historians' methodology. Paper 1 skills are the skills that historians apply when they research a question and attempt to draw conclusions.

In Paper 1 you will:

- **demonstrate** understanding of historical sources
- **interpret and analyse** information from a variety of sources
- **compare and contrast** information between sources
- **evaluate** sources for their value and limitations
- **synthesize** evidence from the sources with your own detailed knowledge of the topic.

ATL Thinking skills

Read the following comment on sources and then answer the questions that follow.

> The practice of history begins with evidence and with sources. The availability of sources is often the key determinant of what becomes most popular, because some areas, for example nineteenth-century France, benefit from a greater volume of documents than others, such as ancient Germany. Whereas historians of early modern and medieval popular culture face a constant battle to find material ... those concerned with modern political history face a veritable forest of official documents – more than any one person could marshal in a lifetime. It is vital, therefore, that students of history become aware of the scope of historical sources, and the methods which historians use to order them.
>
> Black J and Macraild, D M. 2007. *Palgrave Study Skills – Studying History*. 3rd edn, page 89. Macmillan. Basingstoke, UK

1 According to Black and Macraild, what makes certain historical subjects more popular than others?

2 What problems do contemporary historians face?

Following the catastrophe of the First World War the new Bolshevik government in Russia published all the Tsarist documents relating to the outbreak of the war. This led to other European governments publishing volumes and volumes of documents – in what became known as the "colour books" – but in most cases attempting to demonstrate how their country had **not** been responsible for causing the war. Historians have subsequently had vast quantities of documents to use as more government and military sources were declassified and released. However, as recent historiography has revealed, there is still no consensus among historians as to the key causes of the First World War.

3 In pairs discuss whether each generation of historian can move closer to "historical truth" and can be more objective because they are further away in time from an event and have more sources to work from.

4 Listen to this discussion on the historiography of the causes of the First World War: http://www.bbc.co.uk/programmes/b03srqz9?p_f_added=urn%3Abbc%3Aradio%3Aprogramme%3Ab03srqz9

What different interpretations do historians have on the causes of the First World War? What factors have affected their interpretations?

Following on from your discussions for question 3 and 4, get into small groups and consider *what is the role of the historian?* To what extent do you agree that the key role of historians is to bring us closer to historical truth? Or do historians, selection of evidence and use of language tell us more about their own eras and societies than those of the past?

What can you expect on Paper 1?

Paper 1 has a key advantage for students as the question format is given in advance; you can predict the nature and style of the four questions on this paper. This means that you can also learn and practise the correct approach for each of these questions and maximize the marks you attain technically. The majority of marks on this paper are awarded for skills.

This book deals with the prescribed topic of global war. As this is an IB prescribed topic you will need to ensure you have learned all of the content in this book which is linked to each sub-topic from the bullet point list set down in the syllabus:

Case studies	Material for detailed study
Case study 1: **Rwanda (1990–98)**	**Causes of the conflict** ● Ethnic tensions in Rwanda; the creation of the Hutu power movement and the Interahamwe; role of the media ● Other causes: economic situation; colonial legacy ● Rwandan Civil War (1990–1993); assassination of Habyarimana and Ntaryamira (1994) **Course and interventions** ● Actions of the Rwandan Patriotic Front (RPF) and Rwandan government; role of the media ● Nature of the genocide and other crimes against humanity; war rape ● Response of the international community; the United Nations Assistance Mission for Rwanda (UNAMIR); reasons for inaction; role of France, Belgium and the US **Impact** ● Social impact; refugee crisis; justice and reconciliation ● International impact; establishment of the International Criminal Tribunal for Rwanda (1994) ● Political and economic impact; RPF-led governments; continued warfare in the Democratic Republic of Congo (Zaire)

Case study 2: **Kosovo (1989–2002)**	**Causes of the conflict**
	• Ethnic tensions between Serbs and Kosovar Albanians; rising Albanian nationalism
	• Political causes: constitutional reforms (1989–1994); repression of the Albanian independence campaign
	• Role and significance of Slobodan Milosevic and Ibrahim Rugova
	Course and interventions
	• Actions of Kosovo Liberation Army, Serbian government police and military
	• Ethnic cleansing and crimes against humanity; significance of the Račak massacre
	• Response of the international community; response of the UN; NATO bombing campaign; Kosovo Force (KFOR)
	Impact
	• Social and economic consequences; refugee crisis; damage to infrastructure
	• Political impact in Kosovo; election of Ibrahim Rugova as president (2002)
	• International reaction and impact; International Criminal Tribunal for the Former Yugoslavia (ICTY); indictment of Milosevic.

The four sources on the examination paper will be a selection of both primary and secondary sources. The length of each source may vary – but the total length of the paper should not exceed 750 words in total. One of the four sources will be a "visual" rather than text-based source, for example a photograph, cartoon, table of statistics, graph or map.

This book will thus give you plenty of practice with a wide range of different sources on the topic of global war.

How to approach the source questions on Paper 1

Refer to the guidelines below when attempting the source-based questions in each chapter of the book.

First question

This is in two parts. It is made up of a 3-mark and a 2-mark component – giving you a possible total of 5 marks. It is assessing your *historical comprehension* of the sources. You do not need to give your own detailed knowledge in your response.

This is the only question that asks you to **explain** the content and meaning of the documents

Part a

The 3-mark question asks you to comprehend, extract and possibly infer information. Here are some suggestions for answering this question:

- Write: firstly …, secondly …, thirdly … to ensure that you make at least three separate points.

- Do not repeat the same point you have already made.

- Do not overly rely on quotes – make your point and then briefly quote two or three words of the source in support.

Part b

- You should try to make two clear points for this question.

- For each point, refer specifically to the content of the source to provide evidence for your answer.

For parts a and b you should not need to bring in your own knowledge; however your contextual understanding of the topic and sources should enable you to understand more clearly the content and message of each source.

Second question

As you know, historians need to use and evaluate sources as they research a historical era or event.

For the second question, you need to evaluate one source in terms of its "value" and "limitations" by examining its origin, purpose and content. This question is worth 4 marks.

To find the origin and purpose look carefully at the provenance of the source:

For origin	**Who** wrote it/said it/drew it?
	When did the person write it/say it/draw it?
	Where did the person write it/say it/draw it?
	What is the source – a speech/cartoon/textbook, etc.?
For purpose	**Why** did the person write it/say it/draw it?
	Who did the person write it/say it/draw it **for**?
For content	Is the language objective or does it sound exaggerated or one-sided?
	What is the tone of the source?
	What information and examples do they select or focus on to support their point?

From the information you have on the origins of the source, and what you can infer about the document's *purpose*, you must then explain the value and limitations the source has for historians researching a particular event or period in history.

The grid on pages 7 and 8 gives you an idea of the kinds of values and limitations connected with different primary sources.

Examiner's hint: *Note that value and limitations given in the grid are general or generic points that could be applied to these sources. However, your contextual knowledge and the specific provenance of any source that you get in the examination will allow you to make much more precise comments on the value and limitations of the source that you evaluate in a document question. Notice also that the value of the source will always depend on what you are using it for.*

What are the values and limitations associated with secondary sources?

The most common secondary source that you will have to deal with is one from a text book or historian. Again the key questions of "What is the origin of the source?" and "What is the source's purpose?" need to be addressed in order to work out the value and limitation of the source in question.

Here are some points you could consider regarding the value and limitations of works by historians and biographers:

Source	Values	Limitations
Historians	• are usually professionals or experts in field • have the benefit of hindsight which is not present in contemporary sources • may offer sources based on a range of documents; the more recent the publication, the more sources will be available	• might have a broad focus to their work or might have a very specific and narrow focus • might be an expert in a different region or era from the one they are writing about • may be influenced by their nationality, experience, politics or context
Biographers	• will have studied the individual in question in much detail • may provide sources that have value due to tone, use of language and expression • sometimes have the benefit of hindsight	• might have become too involved with their subject and have lost objectivity • may focus on the role of the subject of their biography at the expense of other individuals or factors • might not have direct access to the subject and/or other relevant sources (the place and date will be key here) • may have limitations due to tone, use of language and expression

ATL Thinking skills

Consider the following source:

Romeo Dallaire. *Shake Hands with the Devil* **(2003).**

1 Using the points above, consider the value and limitations of this source for a student analysing the events of the Rwandan genocide and the role of the UN in this period. [Remember to reflect on Dallaire's position as head of the UN force in Rwanda and his credentials as an historian.]

2 How would a school history textbook differ in value and limitations compared to the work of an eyewitness or a professional historian?

ATL Communication and thinking skills

Task 1

Find a biography of one key figure from the period of history that you are studying. With reference to the questions above, analyse the value and limitations of the source in providing extra insight into the role and impact of this individual.

Task 2

What questions would you ask about an **autobiography** to assess its values and limitations to your research

ATL Thinking skills

Read the following extract:

> Part of the problem for historians is defining what a source is. Although primary sources are usually closest, or indeed contemporary, to the period under observation, and secondary sources those works written subsequently, the distinction is actually quite blurred. Once we move away from simple cases [such as politicians' diaries, or cabinet minutes] which are clearly primary, difficulties do arise. Take Benjamin Disraeli's novel of 1845, *Sybil; or the Two Nations*. This is first and foremost a piece of fiction … For historians … however, Sybil is something of a primary source: it typifies the milieu [social setting] of the young Tory Radicals of the day [of whom Disraeli was one] …

Black J and Macraild, D M. 2007. *Palgrave Study Skills – Studying History*. 3rd edition, page 91. Macmillan. Basingstoke, UK.

Note: Disraeli was a 19th-century British Conservative Party leader, and British Prime Minister from 1874–80.

Question

What is the problem with trying to define sources as "primary" or "secondary"?

Examiner's hint: *Note that for the purposes of evaluation, a source has no more or less intrinsic value to historians just because it is primary or secondary.*

Always focus on the specific origins and purpose of a source – not whether it is primary or secondary. You do not need to give this distinction in your answer.

ATL Communication and thinking skills

Read the following statements. Why would these statements be considered invalid by examiners?

- A limitation of this source is that the translation could be inaccurate.

- This source is limited because it doesn't tell us what happened before or after.

- This source is limited because it is biased.

- This textbook was written over 70 years after the event took place so it is unlikely that the author had first-hand experience. This is a limitation.

- A value of this source is that it is an eyewitness account.

- This source is only an extract and we don't know what he said next.

- This is a primary source and this is a value.

- As it is a photograph, it gives a true representation of what actually happened.

Refer back to the Examiner's hint on page 5 regarding this table.

Source	Values These sources:	Limitations These sources:
Private letters (audience – the recipient) Diaries (audience – personal not public at the time of writing)	• can offer insight in to *personal* views or opinions • can indicate the affects of an event or era on an individual • can suggest motives for public actions or opinions • can, through tone, use of language and expression give insight into perspective, opinion or emotions	• only give individual opinion, not a general view or government perspective • may give an opinion that changes due to later events or may give a view not held in public • might have the motive of persuading the audience (in the case of private letters) to act in certain way • may have limitations because of tone, use of language and expression
Memoirs to be published (audience – public)	• can offer insight into *personal* views, suggest motives for public actions and might benefit from hindsight – an evaluation of events after the period • might show how the individual *wants* his or her motive or actions to be viewed by the public	• may revise opinions with the benefit of hindsight, i.e. now the consequences of actions are known • might be written because the author wants to highlight the strengths of his or her actions – to improve the author's public image or legacy • may have limitations because of tone, use of language and expression
Newspapers, television or radio reports Eyewitness accounts	• could reflect publicly held views or popular opinion • might offer an expert view • can give insight into contemporary opinion	• could be politically influenced or censored by specific governments or regimes • may only give "overview" of a situation • might only give a one-sided narrow perspective • could emphasize only a minor part of an issue • may have limitations because of tone, use of language and expression (Note that eyewitnesses are not useful just because they are at an event; each eyewitness will notice different aspects and may miss key points altogether, which could be a limitation)
Novels or poems	• could inform contemporary opinion • might offer insight into emotional responses and motives	• could provide a "dissenting" voice, i.e. not popular opinion • could exaggerate the importance of an event or individual • could have political agenda • may have limitations because of tone, use of language and expression

Statistics	• can offer insight into growth and decline • might suggest correlations between indicators, e.g. unemployment and voting patterns • might suggest the impact of an event or its results over time • make comparisons easier	• are gathered for different purposes (e.g. political, economic) and could be deliberately distorted • might relate only to one location or time period • might suggest incorrect correlations; there could be another causal factor not included in some sets of statistics
Photographs	• can give a sense of a specific scene or event • can offer insight into the immediate impact of an event on a particular place, or people's immediate response • might offer information on the environment	• are limited as we cannot see beyond the "lens" • might distort the "bigger" picture because of their limited view • might be staged • might reflect the purpose of the photographer; what did he or she want to show?
Cartoons or paintings	• can inform public opinion as cartoonists often respond to popularly held views • can portray the government's line when there is censorship	• could be censored and not reflect public opinion • often play on stereotypes (particularly cartoons) and exaggeration • could be limited to the viewpoint and experience of the cartoonist or artist (or the publication the cartoon or painting appears in) • may have limitations because of tone, use of language and expression
Government records and documents Speeches Memoranda	• might show the government's position on an issue • can offer insight into the reasons for decisions made • might reveal the motives for government policies • can show what the public has been told about an event or issue by the government • might be a well-informed analysis	• often do not offer insight into the results of policies and decisions • might not reveal dissent or divergent opinion • might not show public opinion • can be used to keep sensitive information classified for many years • may not explain the motives for a decision or political purpose • may have limitations because of tone, use of language and expression

ATL Research skills

Find primary sources of the types listed in the grid above for the topic that you are currently studying. Using the notes in the grid above, analyse the values and limitations of each of these sources.

For the sources that you have assessed, also look at the content and the language being used. How does the tone, style or content help you to assess the value and limitations of the sources?

Third question

This will ask you to **compare** and **contrast** two sources. Your aim is to identify similar themes and ideas in two sources, and to also identify differences between them. It is marked out of a total of 6 marks.

The key to this question is *linkage*, i.e. you are expected to discuss the sources together throughout your response. The examiner is looking for a *running commentary*. At no time should you talk about one source without relating it to the other. "End-on accounts" – where you write about the content of one source followed by the content of the second source – do not score well.

How do you approach this question?

You must find **both** similarities and differences. This is best presented as two separate paragraphs – one for comparisons and one for contrasts. Here are some tips:

- You could practice using highlighter pens – highlight the similarities in each source in one colour and the differences in another colour.

- You must make sure that you mention **both** sources in every sentence you write. The skill you are demonstrating is linkage.

- Always be clear about which source you are discussing.

- Find both the more "obvious" similarities and differences, and then go on to identify the more specific comparisons and contrasts.

- Deal with similarities in your first paragraph and differences in your second.

- Ensure that each point you make is clearly stated. If you quote from the sources, make this brief – quote only two or three words to support your point.

- Do not introduce your answer or attempt to reach a conclusion. This is not necessary and wastes time.

- Do not waste time explaining what each source says.

- Do not discuss **why** the sources are similar or different.

How to draw comparisons/show similarities

Both Source A and Source B …

Source A suggests … ; similarly, Source B suggests …

Source A supports Source B …

Like Source B, Source A says …

In the same way that Source B argues … , Source A points out that …

How to draw contrasts / show differences

Source A suggests … ; however, Source B says …

Source B disagrees with Source A regarding …

Source A claims … as opposed to Source B which asserts …

Source B goes further than Source A in arguing … while A focuses on…

Question Three will be assessed using generic markbands, as well as exam specific indicative content. The markbands are:

Marks	Level descriptor
5–6	• There is discussion of both sources. Explicit links are made between the two sources. • The response includes clear and valid points of comparison **and** of contrast.
3–4	• There is some discussion of both sources, although the two sources may be discussed separately. • The response includes some valid points of comparison **and/or** of contrast, although these points may lack clarity.
1–2	• There is superficial discussion of one or both sources. • The response consists of description of the content of the source(s), and/or general comments about the source(s), rather than valid points of comparison or of contrast.
0	• The response does not reach a standard described by the descriptors above.

Examiners will apply the "best fit" to responses and attempt to award credit wherever possible.

Fourth question

This is worth the most marks, 9 of the total of 25. It requires you to write a mini-essay. The key to this question is that an *essay* is required – not a list of material from each source. However, you are required to *synthesize* material from the sources with your own knowledge in your essay.

How do you approach this question?

It is recommended that you plan your answer as you would any essay question. The difference here is that you will use evidence from the sources as well as from your own detailed knowledge to support your arguments.

- First make a brief plan based on the sources and group them into either those which support the point in the essay title and those which suggest an alternative argument, or group them under themes if the question is open, e.g. "Examine the reasons for the changing alliances...". Add the sources to the grid as shown below.

- Then add your own knowledge to the grid. This should be detailed knowledge such as dates, events, statistics and the views of historians.

- When you start writing, you will need to write only a brief sentence of introduction.

- When using the sources, refer to the them directly as Source A, Source E and so on.

- You can quote briefly from the sources throughout the essay but quoting two or three words is sufficient.

- Use *all* the sources.

- Include own detailed knowledge

- Write a brief conclusion which should answer the question and be in line with the evidence you have given.

Sources that suggest X	Sources that suggest other factors
Source A	Source B
Own knowledge: events, dates, details	Own knowledge: events, dates, details
Source D	Source C
Own knowledge: historian	Own knowledge: events, dates, details
Source E	Source A makes more than one point, can be used to support more than one argument or theme
Own knowledge: events, dates, details	

▲ Planning grid for the fourth question – mini-essay

The Fourth question will be assessed using generic markbands, as well as exam specific indicative content. The markbands are:

Marks	Level descriptor
0	• The response does not reach a standard described by the descriptors below.
1–3	• The response lacks focus on the question.
	• References to the sources are made, but at this level these references are likely to consist of descriptions of the content of the sources rather than the sources being used as evidence to support the analysis.
	• No own knowledge is demonstrated or, where it is demonstrated, it is inaccurate or irrelevant.
4–6	• The response is generally focused on the question.
	• References are made to the sources, and these references are used as evidence to support the analysis.
	• Where own knowledge is demonstrated, this lacks relevance or accuracy. There is little or no attempt to synthesize own knowledge and source material.
7–9	• The response is focused on the question.
	• Clear references are made to the sources, and these references are used effectively as evidence to support the analysis.
	• Accurate and relevant own knowledge is demonstrated. There is effective synthesis of own knowledge and source material.

Examiners will apply the "best fit" to responses and attempt to award credit wherever possible.

Here is a summary of the key points for each question with the kind of language that is useful when answering each question.

First question, part a

Remember you have to show your understanding of the source and come up with three points. Here are some useful sentence starters:

> This source says that …

> Secondly …

> It also suggests that …

First question, part b

Always start with your key point.

> One message of this source is …

> This is supported by … *here refer to specific details in the source.*

> Another message of the source is …

> *You need to make a separate point, not an elaboration of the first point: you need two clear points about the message of the sources.*

Second question

This question is assessing your ability to analyse a source for its value and limitations by looking at its origin and purpose and content.

> Make sure that you use the words "origin", "purpose" or "content" in each of your sentences to ensure that you are focused on what the question needs, e.g.

> A value of the source is that its author …

> A value of the purpose is that it …

> The language of the content of this source indicates that …

> The content also seems to focus on, or use, examples which are …

> On the other hand, there are also limitations to using this source for finding out about … This is because (*explain here how origin and purpose can cause problems for the historian*) **or**

> A limitation of the origin is …

> A limitation of the purpose is …

> The content of this source makes it less valuable because …

Third question

This is designed to assess your cross-referencing skills.

When comparing two sources you could use the following structures:

> Sources A and B agree that …

> Moreover, the two sources are also similar in that … This is supported by … in Source A and … in Source B …

For a contrasting paragraph:

> Source A differs from Source B in that Source A says … while Source B argues that …

> Another difference between the two documents is that …

> Moreover, Source B goes further than Source A when it suggests/says that …

Fourth question

This is a mini-essay and is assessing your ability to synthesize sources with your own knowledge as well as your ability to give supported arguments or points that address the specific essay question.

Use your essay writing skills and vocabulary for this question.

In addition, as you are using sources as well as your own knowledge, you could use the following to help tie in the sources to your own knowledge:

> As it says in Source C …

> This is supported by the information given in Source …

> Source A suggests that … and this is supported by the fact that in the Soviet Union at this time …

> Historians have argued that … This viewpoint is supported by the information in Source E concerning …

How should I distribute my time in the Paper 1 examination?

A key issue for this paper is managing your time effectively in the examination. If you do not work through the questions efficiently you could run out of time. You must allow enough time to answer the fourth question; after all this is worth the most marks on the paper.

You will have one hour to complete the paper. At the beginning of the examination you have five minutes reading time when you are not allowed to write anything.

We recommend that you use your five minutes reading time to read through the questions first. This will give you an initial understanding of what you are looking for when you read the sources. Read through the questions and then begin to read through the sources.

How much time should I spend on each question?

Some examiners have suggested that the time you spend on each question could be based on the maximum number of marks that the answer could receive. The following is a rough guide:

First question, parts a and b	10 minutes	5 marks
Second question	10 minutes	4 marks
Third question	15 minutes	6 marks
Fourth question	25 minutes	9 marks

1.1 Africa in the late 19th century: European imperialism in East Africa

Conceptual understanding

Key concepts
→ Perspectives
→ Change
→ Consequence

Key questions
→ What happened to effect change in Africa?

Every morning in Africa, a gazelle wakes up. It knows it must run faster than the fastest lion or it will be killed. Every morning a lion wakes up. It knows it must outrun the slowest gazelle or it will starve to death. It doesn't matter whether you are a lion or a gazelle … when the sun comes up, you'd better be running.

— An African saying

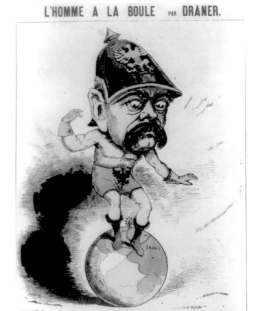

▲ Bismarck, the Iron Chancellor

Introduction

We penetrated deeper and deeper into the heart of darkness.

— Joseph Conrad, *Heart of Darkness and the Congo Diary*

Early in the morning of 7 April 1994, the killing began. For one hundred days as spring turned to summer in the tiny African country of Rwanda, the number of corpses rose into the hundreds of thousands before the rate of killing began to slow down and come to a halt. By the beginning of July, when much of the developed world were planning their vacations and basking in the summer sunshine, the people of Rwanda had been destroyed. In a small African republic, the rate of killing exceeded that of any other known event in history. Out of the original population of almost 8 million Rwandans, at least 800,000 people had been butchered; some estimates put the number of dead at over a million. The massacre of civilians, men, women and children eclipsed the genocide which had taken place in Cambodia in the 1970s and the slaughter of Bosnians in the 1990s. The speed of killing was approximately five times the rate of the extermination of the Jews by the Germans during the Holocaust. *"It was…"* wrote Samantha Power (2001), *"the fastest, most efficient killing spree of the twentieth century."* The Rwandan genocide was the result of a deliberate policy by an elite in the government to keep itself in power. This small faction, faced with losing power, altered a strategy of ethnic division into genocide, and seized control of the state and its machinery to carry out the bloody massacre which transformed Rwanda and the whole Great Lakes region for years to follow.

Background

The story of the conquest and partition of Africa took place over a relatively short time in the final decades of the 19th century. The majority of the takeover happened between 1880 and the end of the century.

ATL Research and thinking skills

Why did this rapid and largely (from the European perspective) easy takeover of the continent occur, and happen so smoothly?

The scramble for Africa in the mid-1880s took place largely because of changes of power in Europe. Some historians advocate economic reasons as the driving force in the opening up of the African continent; others suggest the crumbling of British power and growing European competition for the renewed interest in imperialism. As European states became industrialized, a result was a revolution in power driven partially by the creation of two new European states: Italy and, more significantly, Germany.

The world had experienced European imperialism for centuries but the takeover of the huge continent of Africa was virtually unparalleled in its scale and speed. In 1880, 10% of the landmass had been colonized; European powers controlled some coastal ports in a number of African countries but few Europeans had penetrated the interior. By 1914 only 10% of the continent remained out of European control. What had happened to effect this change? Why had this taken place and what was the impact on the countries concerned, both on the colonizers and the subjects who came under imperial control? These are *essential questions*, which need to be addressed in order to understand what happened in Rwanda as well as a number of other African countries over the course of the 20th century.

What had happened to effect this change in Africa?

A combination of reasons encouraged competition in the African continent. These elements were to be found in the power politics of Europe as well as in the technological advances which had taken place in the century. Certainly the growth of industrialization and the revolution in transport and communications laid the ground for possible expansion, and this was not limited to the African continent in this period. Earlier periods of European overseas expansion were driven by the search for commodities – spices, sugar, silks, slaves and precious metals, for example. In the latter half of the 19th century, instead of being primarily buyers of goods found overseas, the industrializing nations were increasingly becoming sellers, in search of markets for their own products. Progress made in medical knowledge enabled people to be better equipped to face the multitude of diseases and challenges to health. Among some was a growing awareness that the more developed nations could and should help other parts of the world to develop; in the vernacular of the day, bringing others into the "light of civilization". For the majority however, there were more egocentric and self-serving motives. Principal among these was Léopold II, the King of the Belgians, who in 1876 shamelessly said, *"I do not want to miss a good chance of getting us a slice of this magnificent African cake"*.

Why had this taken place?

One of the countries that was a driving force towards this change in Africa was Belgium, a small kingdom that had gained its independence from the Netherlands in 1830. The accession to the throne of Léopold II in 1865 transformed the country into a colonial power on the world stage and his reign galvanized relations between the European powers as well as having a devastating impact on central Africa.

In 1876, Léopold founded the International African Society and invited the journalist and explorer, Henry Morton Stanley to help him open up the continent. By 1871 Stanley achieved the fame he so desperately sought by leading an expedition into the interior of Africa to search for the missionary and explorer David Livingstone. Livingstone was a national hero in Britain and had been the first white man to cross the continent of Africa from coast to coast. Having been out of contact for four years, Stanley's meeting with Livingstone in Ujiji on Lake Tanganyika (in today's eastern Tanzania) on 10 November 1871 has become legendary. When Henry Stanley found Livingstone he uttered the famous words *"Dr Livingstone, I presume?"* This great publicity scoop in tracking down Livingstone overshadowed Stanley's later and greater achievement which was solving the last great geographical mystery of Africa by mapping the Congo River. The name given him by the Congolese, "Bula Matari", meant "Breaker of Rocks" in recognition of this great achievement in African exploration. Stanley exemplified the spirit of the so-called "New Imperialism". When he returned to England he gave a speech in 1884 saying:

> There are 40,000,000 naked people and the cotton-spinners of Manchester (England) are waiting to clothe them … Birmingham's factories are glowing with the red metal that shall presently be made into ironwork in every fashion and shape for them … and the ministers of Christ are zealous to bring them, the poor benighted heathen, into the Christian fold.

Stanley was one of the ways in which King Léopold planned to open up the region. Following Stanley's exploration of the Congo River in 1876–77, Léopold formed the International Congo Society in 1878 with the intent to exploit the resources and establish a number of trading post stations along the Congo River, including Léopoldville (now Kinshasa). Stanley negotiated treaties with local chiefs, getting them to sign away tracts of land (with a signature of an "X", as many of them could not read or write) and followed this up with a proposal to build a railway to exploit the Congo basin. King Léopold gathered a series of paper treaties with which he was able to justify a serious foothold on the Congo and its mighty river. *"The treaties must be as short as possible and, in a couple of articles, grant us everything"*, Léopold is

▲ The meeting of Stanley and David Livingstone in 1871

ATL **Communication skills**

▲ Henry Morton Stanley posing in 1872 with Kalulu, his adopted son

What does the photograph and the pose tell you about HM Stanley?

ATL **Research and thinking skills**

In order to understand the mindset of the Europeans, examine the various viewpoints offered at or around the conference. In addition, explain how and why they were able to come to some agreement over the division of such a large continent in a relatively peaceful manner.

reported to have said (Didier Gondola, 2002). The penetration of the African continent was to remain limited until the introduction of the railways and the arrival of steamships opened up navigable waterways. These developments stimulated the infiltration of the continent, but also exacerbated relations between competing states, creating further rivalries. A number of European powers agreed to meet in Berlin in 1884 to establish ground rules for the exploitation of the continent. No African representative was invited.

The Berlin Conference, 1884–85

The settlements established in Berlin represent the high point of imperialism in an age when the pre-eminence of the white race was clear for all to see. HM Stanley was the star attraction. He was the only man with any serious African experience.

The instigator and driving force behind the meeting, King Léopold, stayed in Brussels, receiving daily telegrams on developments. The new German state was the first to recognize Léopold's Association, fearful that the bigger colonial rivals France or Britain would extend their control.

The agreements reached at Berlin by greedy and competing powers would determine Africa's future for much of the next century. They account for much of the political fragmentation which helps to explain the problems experienced by Rwanda and other newly independent African countries in the latter half of the 20th century. The conference consolidated Léopold's web of agreements, and recognizing Belgium's pre-eminent position in the Congo basin granted him a personal colony greater in area than most of western Europe itself, and almost 80 times the size of Belgium. In return, Léopold permitted access to trade for all nations and allowed missionaries to enter for him to govern the estimated 15 million Black subjects. The slave trade was officially ended and, through the Principle of Effective Occupation, it was agreed that no power should be able to gain territory legally unless they were able to exercise actual control over the land. Léopold named his newly acquired territory and personal property, the Congo Free State. Hochschild commented that the Berlin Conference had been, *"the… expression of the age… whose enthusiasm for democracy had clear limits, and slaughtered game had no vote."*

In the next two decades the magnificent African cake was divided with a host of European powers each getting their slice. Aside from the Belgians, the lion's share went to the British and the French, colonial rivals both in Africa and elsewhere in the world. The Spanish, Italians and the Portuguese extended (or kept) territories in Africa and the new European powerhouse of Germany gained a substantial empire in Africa, achieving her "place in the sun". By the turn of the century, approximately 90% of the African continent was under European control. The conference in Berlin and the ensuing "scramble for Africa" were to have far-reaching

consequences in the creation of the Rwandan state which later resulted in the instigation of an ethnic divide with tragic consequences for the people of Rwanda. As a precursor to the Rwandan genocide, the Germans conducted their own African genocide between 1904 and 1907. Regarded by many as the twentieth century's first genocide, German policy in south west Africa (present day Namibia) resulted in the deaths of up to 100,000 Herero inhabitants.

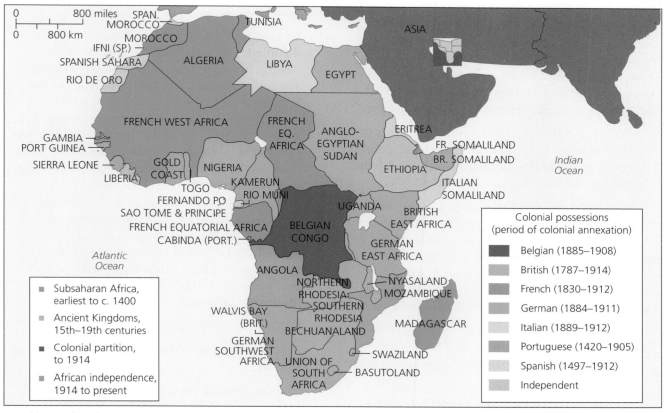

▲ Africa to 1914: Colonial partitions

ATL Communication and thinking skills

Students will need to be able to understand, interpret and address the demands of the questions asked in the IB examination. In order to do this, first you will need to:

- understand and acquire content knowledge – a solid base of factual knowledge
- develop concepts which are big, powerful ideas relevant to the discipline
- develop skills which can help you move from the acquisition of basic facts to an understanding of how and why historical skills can be applied.

In addition, concepts can provide a connection between knowledge and understanding, which is crucial for students to get to the heart of why they are studying history. Look at the following sources on imperialism.

Source skills

Source A

"How I Found Dr. Livingstone" by Henry Stanley, published in *The New York Herald*, 1871.

Henry Stanley, a well-known African explorer, started out as a reporter for the New York Herald. His paper sent him to Africa to search for Dr David Livingstone, a missionary and explorer who had been missing for years. Most believed he was dead. Stanley wrote accounts of his adventures, printed in The New York Herald, *which helped stimulate a popular interest in the exploration of Africa in Britain and America. When he found Dr Livingstone, Stanley reported this famous exchange.*

We were now about three hundred yards from the village of Ujiji, and the crowds are dense about me. Suddenly I hear a voice on my right say, "Good morning, sir!"

Startled at hearing this greeting in the midst of such a crowd of black people, I turn sharply around in search of the man, and see him at my side, with the blackest of faces, but animated and joyous … a man dressed in a long white shirt, with a turban of American sheeting around his woolly head, and I ask: "Who the mischief are you?"

"I am Susi, the servant of Dr. Livingstone," said he, smiling and showing a gleaming row of teeth.

"What! Is Dr. Livingstone here?"

"Yes, sir."

"In this village?"

"Yes, sir."

"Are you sure?"

"Sure, sure, sir. Why, I leave him just now."

"Now, you, Susi, run, and tell the Doctor I am coming."

"Yes, sir," and off he darted like a madman…

But, during Susi's absence, the news had been conveyed to the Doctor that it was surely a white man that was coming, whose guns were firing and whose flag could be seen; and the great Arab magnates of Ujiji … and others, had gathered together before the Doctor's house, and the Doctor had come out from his veranda to discuss the matter and await my arrival… My heart beats fast, but I must not let my face betray my emotions, lest it shall detract from the dignity of a white man appearing under such extraordinary circumstances.

So I did that which I thought was most dignified. I pushed back the crowds, and, passing from the rear, walked down a living avenue of people until I came in front of the semicircle of Arabs, in the front of which stood the white man with the grey beard. As I advanced slowly towards him, I noticed he was pale, wore a bluish cap with a faded gold band round it, had on a red-sleeved waistcoat and a pair of grey tweed trousers. I would have run to him, only I was a coward in the presence of such a mob … I would have embraced him, only he being an Englishman, I did not know how he would receive me; so I did what cowardice and false pride suggested was the best thing … walked deliberately to him, took off my hat, and said:

"Dr. Livingstone, I presume?"

"Yes," said he, with a kind smile, lifting his cap slightly.

I replace my hat on my head, and he puts on his cap, and we both grasp hands, and I then say aloud: "I thank God, Doctor, I have been permitted to see you." He answered, "I feel thankful that I am here to welcome you."

Source B

Rhodes wrote this on 2 June 1877, in Oxford, when he was 23 years old. In this he writes in support of imperialism, asserting that Britain has the right to conquer and control other lands. Rhodes moved from England to South Africa as a child and made a fortune in the diamond mine business founding the white dominated state named after him (Rhodesia – today, Zimbabwe).

"Confession of Faith" by Cecil Rhodes, 1877: http://www.pitt.edu/~syd/rhod.html

I contend that we are the finest race in the world and that the more of the world we inhabit the better it is for the human race. Just fancy those parts that are at present inhabited by the most despicable specimens of human beings what an alteration there would be if they were brought under Anglo-Saxon influence, look again at the extra employment a new country added to our dominions gives. I contend that every acre added to our territory means in the future, birth to some more of the English race who otherwise would not be brought into existence. Added to this the absorption of the greater portion of the world under our rule simply means the end of all wars … The idea gleaming and dancing before one's eyes like a will-of-the-wisp at last frames itself into a plan. Why should we not form a secret society with but one object – the furtherance of the British Empire and the bringing of the whole uncivilized world under British rule for the recovery of the United States for the making the Anglo-Saxon race but one Empire. What a dream, but yet it is probable, it is possible. I once heard it argued by a fellow in my own college, I am sorry to own it by an Englishman, that it was a good thing for us that we have lost the United States …

We know the size of the world we know the total extent. Africa is still lying ready for us; it is our duty to take it. It is our duty to seize every opportunity of acquiring more territory and we should keep this one idea steadily before our eyes that more territory simply means more of the Anglo-Saxon race, more of the best, the most human, most honorable race the world possesses.

Source C

A cartoon, "The Black Baby", published in *Punch* magazine in 1894.

THE BLACK BABY.

Source D

This is a powerful indictment of the evils of imperialism. At the end of the story Conrad tells us of a man named Kurtz, dying, insane, and guilty of atrocity and genocide.

J. Conrad. *Heart of Darkness* (1899).

I left in a French steamer, and she called in every blamed port they have out there, for, as far as I could see, the sole purpose of landing soldiers and custom-house officers. I watched the coast. Watching a coast as it slips by the ship is like thinking about an enigma. There it is before you … smiling, frowning, inviting, grand, mean, insipid, or savage, and always mute with an air of whispering, come and find out. This one was almost featureless, as if still in the making, with an aspect of monotonous grimness. The edge of a colossal jungle, so dark-green as to be almost black, fringed with white surf, ran straight, like a ruled line, far, far away along a blue sea whose glitter was blurred by a creeping mist. The sun was fierce, the land seemed to glisten and drip with steam. Here and there grayish-whitish specks showed up clustered inside the white surf, with a flag flying above them perhaps. Settlements some centuries old, and still no bigger than pinheads on the untouched expanse of their background …

Every day the coast looked the same, as though we had not moved; but we passed various places – trading places – with names like Gran' Bassam, Little Popo; names that seemed to belong to some sordid farce acted in front of a sinister back-cloth. The idleness of a passenger, my isolation amongst all these men with whom I had no point of contact, the oily and languid sea, the uniform somberness of the coast, seemed to keep me away from the truth of things, within the toil of a mournful and senseless delusion …

Now and then a boat from the shore gave one a momentary contact with reality. It was paddled by black fellows. You could see from afar the white of their eyeballs glistening. They shouted, sang; their bodies streamed with perspiration; they had faces like grotesque masks-these chaps; but they had bone, muscle, a wild vitality, an intense energy of movement, that was as natural and true as the surf along their coast. They wanted no excuse for being there…

It was upward of thirty days before I saw the mouth of the big river. We anchored off the seat of the government. But my work would not begin till some two hundred miles farther on. So as soon as I could I made a start for a place thirty miles higher up … At last we opened a reach. A rocky cliff appeared, mounds of turned-up earth by the shore, houses on a hill, others with iron roofs, amongst a waste of excavations, or hanging to the declivity … A lot of people, mostly black and naked, moved about like ants. A jetty projected into the river.

A blinding sunlight drowned all this at times in a sudden recrudescence of glare. "There's your Company's station," said the Swede [*the Captain*], pointing to three wooden barrack-like structures on the rocky slope. "I will send your things up. Four boxes did you say? So. Farewell."…

A slight clinking behind me made me turn my head. Six black men advanced in a file, toiling up the path. They walked erect and slow, balancing small baskets full of earth on their heads, and the clink kept time with their footsteps. Black rags were wound round their loins, and the short ends behind waggled to and fro like tails. I could see every rib, the joints of their limbs were like knots in a rope; each had an iron collar on his neck, and all were connected together with a chain whose bights swung between them, rhythmically clinking. Another report from the cliff made me think suddenly of that ship of war I had seen firing into a continent. It was the same kind of ominous voice; but these men could by no stretch of imagination be called enemies. They were called criminals, and the outraged law, like the bursting shells had come to them, an insoluble mystery from the sea. All their meager breasts panted together, the violently dilated nostrils quivered, the eyes stared stonily up-hill. They passed me within six inches, without a glance, with that complete, deathlike indifference of unhappy savages.

First question, part a – 3 marks

What, according to Source A, is the attitude of Stanley to the native inhabitants of the Congo? What evidence can you point out to support this observation?

First question, part b – 2 marks

What is the message of Source C?

Second question – 4 marks

Compare and contrast the view expressed in Source B, "*Africa is still lying ready for us; it is our duty to take it*", with that of the Punch cartoon in Source C.

TOK connections

From examining Sources C and D, consider:

- How can one gauge the extent to which a history is told from a particular cultural or national perspective?

- How does Source D contrast with Source B regarding the author's attitude towards the native Africans?

With reference to Sources B and D, consider:

- What is the relation between the style of language used and the history written?

- How can historical accounts be assessed?

- What distinguishes a better historical account from a worse one?

- Is it possible for historical writing to be free from perspective?

ATL Research skills

Conrad (see below) is one of the most famous writers of the period regarding Africa and imperialism. You may choose to discover more about Conrad as a man, his experiences and views on imperialism as well as examining the literary context of his writings.

Joseph Conrad (1857–1924)

Joseph Conrad was born in Poland but was granted British nationality in 1886. He wrote primarily in English becoming one of the greatest novelists at the turn of the 20th century. He published several stories and novels, many of them connected to the sea, trade and exploration. His themes illustrate the trials of the human spirit locked in the midst of an uncaring universe. Among his most famous novels is *Heart of Darkness*, written between 1898 and 1899. Conrad wrote to his publisher saying, "*It is a narrative after the manner of youth told by the same man dealing with his experiences on a river in Central Africa ... The title I am thinking of is 'The Heart of Darkness' but the narrative is not gloomy.*" (*Collected Letters* 2: 139–40).

Heart of Darkness has become one of the most widely read of Conrad's works, and it has provoked controversy for its depiction of Africa and Africans, and for its early twentieth century perspective on women. Based considerably on Conrad's own experiences, it is probably his most popular piece of writing and has inspired works by other artists, including TS Eliot's *The Waste Land* (1922) and "The Hollow Men" (1925), Graham Greene's *A Burnt Out Case* (1961), and VS Naipaul's *A Bend in the River* (1979). The film director Francis Ford Coppola used *Heart of Darkness* as the inspiration for his classic film based on Vietnam called *Apocalypse Now* (1979).

Explanations for imperialism

As Europe entered the industrial age Africa began to yield up its riches. Diamonds were discovered in the south in the late 1860s and gold soon afterwards – and imperialism began to shift gears. European powers had exercised control over some of the globe in the centuries before, but the extent and speed with which areas of the world were swallowed up has contributed to the term, "new imperialism" for what happened in South East Asia and Africa in the last years of the 19th century.

1 Economic forces

These are the most common arguments for imperialism in this period. The British economist Hobson suggested the shrinking of markets and surplus of capital in need of markets. This has been challenged by others who see the crumbling of British power as a more influential force (Sanderson). The long depression in the last 20 years of the 20th century is also seen as responsible. Lenin adapted Hobson's theory and contended that Imperialism was *"a direct continuation of the fundamental properties of capitalism in general"*. The imperialist powers had found a new proletariat to exploit.

Thinking skills

Conrad, J. 1899. *Heart of Darkness and the Congo Diary*:

The conquest of the earth, which mostly means the taking it away from those who have a different complexion or slightly flatter noses than ourselves, is not a pretty thing when you look into it too much. What redeems it is the idea only. An idea at the back of it; not a sentimental pretence but an idea; and an unselfish belief in the idea – something you can set up, and bow down before, and offer a sacrifice to …

1 According to this source, what were the motives for the expansion of imperialism in the late 19th century?

2 Examine some of the theories proposed for this expansion (see right). Come to conclusions about which were the most significant forces in driving these events.

2 Social forces

We can see something of the mindset of many Europeans at the turn of the century in the prevailing theories of social Darwinism. There can be little doubt that racial theories played a part in encouraging the New Imperialism. Herbert Spencer, the father of social Darwinism as an ethical theory, put forward the opinion that "might makes right" before Darwin published his own theory. It was Spencer who first used the phrase "survival of the fittest".

As social Darwinism and ideologies of racial hierarchy became widespread, some Europeans considered it their moral duty to bring their culture and morality to the rest of the world. In France, this was referred to as the "civilizing mission". In England it was known as the "White Man's Burden"; Rudyard Kipling created the term in reference to US actions in the Philippines in 1899. Both Cecil Rhodes and US President Theodore Roosevelt were among those who strongly advocated social Darwinism. Race theory was to have a major role to play in Rwanda later in the century.

3 Strategic and military forces

The scramble for Africa was also given impetus by the competitive spirit engendered by the need to keep ahead of rivals in the drive to secure empire. For Britain in particular, the need to maintain the country's empire pushed it to secure key bases at strategic points around the globe. The emergence of the new powers, including Germany and Italy as well as the USA, and Japan in the Far East, was certainly a contributing factor. The motivation came as much from the nature of European politics as from the drive of economic forces.

4 Individuals on the ground

The role played by individuals in encouraging imperialism is significant. These included missionaries, soldiers and explorers, all of whom in some form or another saw it as desirable that order was established out of what they considered to be chaos, or that the benefits of civilization and religion should be established. The men with the mission – such as Frenchman Pierre Savorgnan de Brazza, the German Karl Peters, Welshman Henry Morton Stanley or military men such as Charles "Chinese" Gordon – were all individuals who actively encouraged the opening up of parts of Africa previously ignored. They did this through independent actions on the ground, making deals with local rulers and by refusing or "misinterpreting" orders from their governments. The sources and nature of Imperialism in this period were diverse and complex and it seems unlikely that one theory can explain all aspects (see the sources below).

"THE WHITE MAN'S BURDEN."

▲ Cartoon by Victor Gillam published in 1899 by Judge Publishing Company, New York, USA

Source skills

Source A

A hymn, "Onwards Chartered Soldiers", written by Henry Labouchère in the late 1800s.

The 19th-century Liberal MP and radical journalist Henry Labouchère wrote this parody of the traditional triumphalist hymn, "Onward Christian Soldiers"; the parody is sung to the same tune.

> Onward Christian soldiers
>
> Into heathen lands
>
> Prayer books in your pockets
>
> Rifles in your hands
>
> Take the happy tidings
>
> Where trade can be done
>
> Spread the peaceful gospel
>
> With the Gatling gun.

From the 1984 documentary "Africa: A Voyage of Discovery with Basil Davidson", episode 5: "The Bible and the Gun" available at www.youtube.com/watch?v=oAK5gYRmfIl

Source B

A poem, "The White Man's Burden", written by Rudyard Kipling in 1899.

Sometimes called the "anthem of imperialism" this poem expresses the feelings of responsibility and paternalism at the base of British imperialism.

> Take up the White Man's burden –
>
> Send forth the best ye breed –
>
> Go bind your sons to exile
>
> To serve your captives' need;
>
> To wait in heavy harness,
>
> On fluttered folk and wild –
>
> Your new-caught, sullen peoples,
>
> Half-devil and half-child.
>
> Take up the White Man's Burden –

Source C

Edward Morel, a British journalist in the Belgian Congo, brought attention to the abuses of imperialism in 1903, in his response to Rudyard Kipling's poem, "The White Man's Burden".

It is [the Africans] who carry the "black man's burden". They have not withered away before the white man's occupation. Indeed … Africa has ultimately absorbed within itself every Caucasian and, for that matter, every Semitic invader, too. In hewing out for himself a fixed abode in Africa, the white man has massacred the African in heaps. The African has survived, and it is well for the white settlers that he has …

What the partial occupation of his soil by the white man has failed to do; what the mapping out of European political "spheres of influence" has failed to do; what the Maxim and the rifle, the slave gang, labour in the bowels of the earth and the lash, have failed to do; what imported measles, smallpox and syphilis have failed to do; whatever the overseas slave trade failed to do, the power of modern capitalistic exploitation, assisted by modern engines of destruction, may yet succeed in accomplishing.

Source D

A cartoon, "In the Rubber Coils", published in the magazine *Punch* in 1906.

IN THE RUBBER COILS.
Scene—The Congo "Free" State.

First question, part b – 2 marks

What is the message of Source D?

Third question – 6 marks

Compare and contrast the opinions of imperialism regarding the idea of paternalism that can be identified in Sources B and C.

TOK

What is the value of using contemporary literature to illustrate and understand history? What are the possible drawbacks or risks?

ATL Communication, thinking and research skills

1 What opinion of imperialism can be gained from reading Source A?

2 Examine the arguments and debate the issues in class or on paper, to construct reasoned arguments and to arrive at some conclusions.

3 Examine the role of individuals such as those mentioned above and assess their importance in the opening up of Africa.

Examiner's hints:

First question, part b – 2 marks

What is the message of Source D?

When you are asked "what is the message of the cartoon?", you need to study the cartoon itself, identify what you see, consider the title, the possible symbolism and the message you think the cartoonist may be trying to convey.

Example answer

The image in Source D shows a Congolese native being strangled by a snake. Behind the African, a primitive house and a mother and child are fleeing. The caption is significant in that it plays on the production of rubber, a major commodity produced in the Congo. However, the small print identifies the name of the Congo "free" state ironically in that, obviously, the man is not free. This political cartoon clearly shows the pain suffered by the people of Congo during this colonization period. The ferocious snake symbolizes King Leopold II, the leader of Belgium from 1865–1909 and the man, fighting for his life, symbolizes the common Congolese people.

A more sophisticated answer may include the following.

In the Western tradition, the snake has often symbolized "evil". In the Biblical case of Adam and Eve, the snake represented evil as it tempted Eve into eating forbidden fruit and God cursed the snake above all creatures. The snake, with its head replaced by Leopold's, is shown to be crushing the man to death and the man is helpless and unable to protect himself. It tells that out of helplessness the people of this country had to follow the orders of King Leopold II and if they could not satisfy him, the result was their death.

This cartoon was published by *Punch* magazine, a British weekly magazine of humour and satire, in 1906. We can see how this cartoon is trying to illustrate how colonisation often leads to exploitation. An interesting aspect of this cartoon is the fact that although many of the nations were expanding their empires by force, many still tried to justify their motives as acting in the interests of the people they colonised. Britain showed Belgium as a country that mistreated and murdered in Africa as a counterpoint to England as a country that "helped" African nations.

References and further reading

Conrad, J. 1899. *Heart of Darkness*. Blackwood's Magazine, UK

Didier Gondola, C. 2002. *The History of Congo*. Westport, CT, USA

Pakenham, T. 1992. *The Scramble for Africa: White Man's Conquest of the Dark Continent from 1876 to 1912*. Avon Books. New York, USA

Power, S. 2001. "Bystanders to genocide", *The Atlantic,* 1 September, 2001. www.theatlantic.com/magazine/archive2001/09/bystanders-togenicde/304571

Rhodes, C. 1877. *Confession of Faith.* http://www.pitt.edu/~syd/rhod.html

Stanley, H. "How I found Dr. Livingstone", in *The New York Herald,* 1871

http://www.archive.org/stream/addressofmrhmsta00stan/addressofmrhmsta00stan_djvu.txt
http://www.historywiz.com/africanimperialism.htm

1.2 Colonial Rwanda, 1884–1962

Conceptual understanding

Key concepts

→ Change

→ Causation

→ Consequence

Key questions

→ In what ways did the arrival of European imperialism impact the existing social, economic and political equilibrium of Rwanda and its neighbours?

▲ The German explorer, Gustav Adolf von Götzen

Colonial Rwanda, 1884–1962

Berlin Conference: Germany gains control of the area constituting present-day Rwanda	**1885**	
	1894	First European explorers arrive in Rwanda – Gustav Adolf von Götzen
In Brussels, the frontiers of Belgian Congo, British Uganda and German East Africa (including Ruanda-Urundi) are determined	**1910**	
	1919	The former colony of Ruanda-Urundi is made a League of Nations' mandate and given to Belgium.
The Belgians introduce ethnic identity cards	**1926**	
	1931	The Rwandan King Musinga deposed by the Belgians and replaced by his son, Mutari III
Identity cards became mandatory with the ethnicity of the bearer	**1933**	
	1945	The Belgium mandate of Ruanda-Urundi becomes a United Nations Trusteeship territory
The Hutu Manifesto is published, and the Party for the Emancipation of Hutu (PARMEHUTU) is formed.	**1957**	
	1959	Tutsi King Mutari III dies. The Hutu rise against Tutsi aristocracy. Thousands of Tutsi are killed and thousands become refugees
The monarchy is formally abolished and Rwanda becomes a republic	**1961**	
	1962	Rwanda gains independence from Belgium on July 1st. PARMEHUTU comes to power under the first president, Gregoire Kayibanda.

▲ King Yuhi V Musingi of Rwanda

General Paul Emil von Lettow-Vorbeck (1870–1964)

Paul Emil von Lettow-Vorbeck has become something of a legend in Germany. He was the commander of Germany's small African army during the First World War in German East Africa and was responsible for pinning down a large number of allied troops in the region through resourceful use of guerilla tactics.

For four years he held in check much larger forces of allied soldiers with a force composed of less than 3,000 German soldiers supported by 11,000 native Africans. His most notable victory was achieved at the port city of Tanga late in 1914, when he repelled a naval assault by the British. From then on he conducted successful guerilla campaigns disrupting British communications and tying down a far greater number of colonial troops for the remainder of the war.

He has been portrayed in popular culture in an episode of the "Young Indiana Jones Chronicles" and featured as a character in at least two historical novels set in East Africa.

German rule 1884–1919

Following the Berlin Conference in 1884–85, Kaiser Wilhelm's Germany occupied the area known as German East Africa. This consisted of the present-day countries of Tanzania, Rwanda and Burundi. Colonisation of the area was largely due to the actions of one individual, Karl Peters, an ambitious pioneer who created the Society for German Colonisation in 1885, following which Bismarck's government established a protectorate in East Africa. Later that year, (backed up by German gunboats) the local sultan acquiesced to the annexation of territory, and the British and Germans agreed to delineate their own spheres of influence (a term first used in the conference of Berlin).

In 1894, the German explorer Gustav Adolf von Götzen (pictured at the start of the chapter) was probably the first European to explore the modern-day country of Rwanda, reporting on the fertility of the eastern area near Lake Kivu. Following the tenets of the Berlin Conference, which set out the Principle of Effective Occupation, Germany tried to establish its control through Indirect Rule, using the existing Rwandan monarch, King Yuhi Musinga (King Yuhi V, 1896–1931).

In 1905 a rebellion broke out in the German colony, largely caused by the Kaiser's attempt to force the locals to grow a cash crop – cotton for export. The so-called Maji-Maji rebellion was precipitated by a drought in the region, combined with opposition to the government's policies, and led to open rebellion against the Germans in July 1905. Most of the trouble took place in southern Tanzania and was eventually put down by modern weaponry and discipline under the command of the now governor of East Africa, Count Gustav Adolf von Götzen. His deliberate policy of "slash and burn" helped create a famine, paralleling an act of genocide in Germany's other colony in South West Africa when the Herero rebellion was put down with great force between 1904 and 1907. It showed the German government's preference for solving political problems with extreme violence. On the eve of the First World War, Germany was the third largest colonial power in Africa.

▲ Map of German East Africa in 1892

By the end of the Great War, Germany could claim strategic victory in Africa, but the Allies had won the war. In 1914, neither side had many troops in their colonies nor did they wish to treat this as a new theatre of war, adhering to their original agreements from the late 19th century. However, the British were the first to break the understanding and began skirmishes near Lake Victoria. In response, the German military commander General Paul Emil von Lettow-Vorbeck retaliated. He spent the rest of the war causing great disruption to the British troops in the region, achieving victory in one or two campaigns. Importantly, he succeeded in compelling England to commit significant resources to this minor colonial theatre throughout the war, as well as causing an estimated 10,000 casualties. After the war, General Lettow-Vorbeck was hailed as a German hero, with his troops celebrated as the only colonial German force in the First World War not to have been defeated. At the Paris Peace conference, the Treaty of Versailles took away all Germany's colonies in Africa and gave the bulk of German East Africa to Britain and the north-western area to Belgium, as Ruanda-Urundi. Thus Rwanda came under Belgian rule in 1919.

Belgian rule 1919–1962

Following the signing of the Treaty of Versailles in 1919 and the establishment of the League of Nations, the mandate system was created. This was a compromise between the allied desire to appropriate former German colonies for themselves, and their pre-Armistice declaration that annexation of territory was not their intended aim. Mandates were divided into three groups, A, B or C, on the basis of their location and their level of political and economic development. Class B mandates consisted of the former German colonies of Tanganyika, parts of Togoland, the Cameroons and Ruanda-Urundi. Allied powers were to be responsible for the administration of these mandates and were obligated to protect the rights of the native peoples. It was under these conditions that Ruanda-Urundi (today, Rwanda and Burundi) was given to Belgium.

Whereas the Germans had not been closely involved in running the area of Rwanda, the Belgians were to become more active in shaping the politics of the country. The Germans found the established pre-colonial kingdom and social classes to be functioning effectively, and the Belgians followed this practice. It is here the problems lay for the future genocide. The social structure consisted principally of a small Tutsi ruling class, controlling a mostly Hutu population. The Belgians believed that the Tutsi were superior and deserved power; besides which, it made the governance of the mandate more efficient. Belgian rule thus reinforced the ethnic divide between the Tutsi and Hutu, and supported Tutsi political power. The character of indirect rule established by the Germans shifted to one of direct rule by the Belgians. They wanted the colony to be profitable for the mother country and introduced coffee as a commodity crop in the region's rich volcanic soils, promoting a system of forced labour for its cultivation. Belgian treatment of Rwandans was known to be exceedingly cruel even by European colonial standards, and this reliance on the Tutsi elite helped widen the rift between ethnic groups. It is clear that the unequal exploitation of Rwanda's resources damaged the cooperative working environment already established between Hutu and Tutsi.

The seeds of conflict – ethnicity in Rwanda

Twa
From the Bantu word, meaning "pygmy".

Historical evidence indicates that the first inhabitants of the area were the **Twa**, who were hunter-gatherers. Between the 5th and 11th centuries, successive migrations predominantly from the east and the north brought in the Hutu, whose principal means of living was farming and cattle. Around the 14th century the Tutsi arrived from somewhere around the Horn of Africa; a clan that eventually consolidated its power and, at the same time, absorbed much of the culture of the Hutu.

The ethnic divide in Rwanda is essentially a myth cultivated by the early Europeans and used as a means to exercise control. There had been integration between Hutu and Tutsi for centuries including marriage, culture, a working economic partnership and a common language, Kinyarwanda. There is no denying that there was a sense of inferiority experienced by the Hutu as the minority Tutsi gained power and influence through control of cattle – identified here, as in other parts of the world, with wealth. But the two groups shared much in common, including language and, after the arrival of the Europeans, their Christian faith.

Early European visitors observed the ethnic groups, and how the Tutsi appeared to be generally taller and slimmer. John Henning Speke (who searched for the source of the Nile and named Lake Victoria) described them as displaying an "intelligence and refinement of feelings". Some blame the colonizers for creating the race theory that the Tutsi had "invaded" the country. This was the version of history that was used by the Hutu extremists at the end of the 20th century.

It suited the colonists to foster the myth of the superior Tutsi so that they could use them to enforce their rule. It was not the first nor the last time that physical appearance would be used to distinguish between ethnic groups, and the Tutsi rulers were content to be used by the Europeans in this way to strengthen their racial superiority. Racial theories were prevalent in the late years of the 19th century but the Germans had not been as active as the Belgians in reinforcing the social divide in Rwanda. Europeans, the most advantaged minority, established control over all others. They promulgated a version of history that emphasized the supremacy of the Tutsi, and reinforced social stereotypes. This laid the ground for genocide and the racist ideology that underpinned government policy in Rwanda at the end of the 20th century.

Although Belgium pledged its mandates would have freedom of speech and religion, and be brought into the modern world, it largely ignored these guarantees. Instead, the Belgians exercised power by introducing a system of forced labour and heavy taxation on the people of Ruanda-Urundi, many of whom were subsistence farmers who used a barter system rather than money. As a result, many fled to neighbouring countries such as Uganda and Congo, where they found work. In 1931, the Belgians replaced King Yuhi V with his more compliant son, who became King Mutari III and continued to use the Tutsi to administer the country.

The Belgians did introduce some new crops, as well as extending education. They offered special treatment to the Tutsi, who were taught mathematics in elementary school. Hutu children were offered singing classes and natural sciences, which were compulsory for the Tutsi but optional for Hutu children. Tutsi children were educated in French but Hutu children in the local language, Kinyarwanda. It was all part of helping the Tutsi in their social advancement – and serving the needs of the Belgian colonial masters in the administration of their mandate. Such segregation only served to reinforce ethnic division and resentment, which built up over the years to culminate in the genocide. In addition, Belgium also made Christianity compulsory for the Tutsi elite and used them in the civil service to administer its rule.

In Kinyarwanda, the word **Hutu** actually means servant or subject, and the word **Tutsi** means someone who is rich in cattle.

Significantly for the future genocide, following a census in 1933, the Belgians imposed an identity card system which classified the ethnicity of each person. After this, a person's ethnic identity was designated for life – or death.

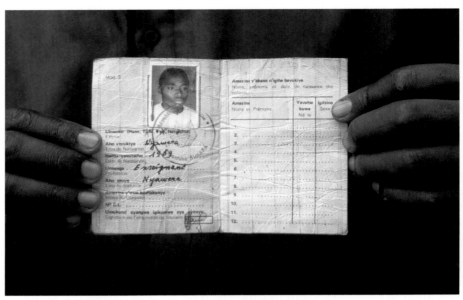

▲ Rwanda National Identity Card circa 1994. Note the "Ethnicity" category below the photograph

ATL Thinking and self-management skills

Historical extracts in the colonial period

The following sources are examples of the views of some missionaries and colonialists of Rwandan "ethnic groups" and of ethnicity practised by the Belgians.

Source A

Concerning Hutu or Tutsi leadership, Bishop Classes told President Mortehan the following in 1927.

If we wish to be practical and look for the true interest of the country, we have in the Tutsi youth an incomparable element of progress that anybody who knows Rwanda cannot underestimate. Eager to know and to learn whatever comes from Europe and to imitate Europeans, they are entrepreneurs. However, they conserve ancient political sense and the skills of their race to conduct people. These young men have the required potential for the country's future economic well being. Ask Bahutu [Hutu] if they wish to be led by commoners or nobles, the answer is simple; they prefer Batutsi [Tutsi] and for a reason. Chiefs by birth, they have the sense of ruling … It is the secret of their settling in the country and their domination upon it.

Quoted in Lacger, L (de), 1959: 523

Source B

R Kandt wrote the following in 1905.

If I can analyse and define honestly my feelings, I can say that they [Tutsi] impressed me very much. I have even today the same feelings … those people are barbarian with an intellectual level a bit lower than mine. Hutu have a strange behaviour. In presence of their bosses, they are reserved and raise issues. But when we are alone with them, they tell us almost everything we want and even what we do not ask them. I understand their difficulties and question them when they complain about their oppression and their lack of rights. Most of the time, I tell them to use their elbow and remind them that, their number is 100 times bigger than that of (Ba)Tutsi and they are only capable of complaining like women.

Lugan, B. 1980: 132

The favouring of the Tutsi as the dominant governing class solidified the already existing divisions within Rwanda and it is not a surprise that ethno-nationalist sentiments began to develop, becoming internalized by the Rwandans themselves – with drastic consequences in the years to come.

After the dissolution of the League at the end of the Second World War, the region became a United Nations (UN) trust territory in 1946, heading toward independence. The Trusteeship Council sent five missions to Rwanda between 1948 and 1962 and on each occasion criticized the lack of progress made by Belgium towards ensuring a smooth transition to democracy. The Hutu majority saw an ideal opportunity to finally assume the mantle of power in their own country. For the Belgians however, Rwanda was now a French speaking colony that sat on the fault line of Francophone and Anglophone Africa. In the 1950s an independence movement arose in neighbouring Belgian Congo and, as a consequence, political parties were permitted in Ruanda-Urundi in the late 1950s. The Belgian finally recognised that they may need to shift their support to the majority Hutu and this was manifested in the events that followed the death of the King Matari III in 1959.

The Rwandan revolution and independence, 1959–62

In 1957 the Hutus formed PARMEHUTU, the largest party for Hutu emancipation. In 1959 the Tutsi formed the National Rwandese Union (UNAR), trying to put distance between themselves and their former colonial rulers. After Mutari III died in July 1959, a period of ethnic violence broke out, following the beating of a Hutu politician by Tutsi groups. What followed was a foretaste of what was to come three decades later. Hutu masses staged an uprising under PARMEHUTU direction. The would-be king (Kigeli V) was deposed and fled the country along with thousands of Tutsi refugees, and a provisional Hutu government was installed. Estimates of the dead in this period vary from 10,000 to 100,000, nearly all of them Tutsi, and this became Rwanda's first ethnically driven conflict. Presaging events in 1994, rivers were filled with bodies as tens of thousands were clubbed and stabbed to death. Many Tutsi fled to refugee settlements in the neighbouring countries of Zaire, Uganda, Tanzania and Burundi and from these exiled groups rose Tutsi rebel movements (the "children of '59"). One of these rebel groups was the Rwandan Patriotic Front (the RPF) later to be led by Paul Kagame. The Belgian government was subsequently accused by the Tutsi of assisting the Hutu in the violence. The colony became independent on 1 July 1962 and divided along traditional lines as the new nations of Rwanda and Burundi.

ATL | **Research skills**

UK Prime Minister, Harold Macmillan's speech in February 1960 contained the following.

The wind of change is blowing through this continent. Whether we like it or not, this growth of national consciousness is a political fact.

Investigate the "Winds of Change" which characterised the gaining of independence by many African countries in the period from 1960 to 1970.

▲ Rwandan school children celebrate independence from Belgium in 1962

Name of territory	Date of Independence	Former colonial power
Cameroon, Republic of	1 January 1960	France
Senegal, Republic of	4 April 1960	France
Togo, Republic of	27 April 1960	France
Mali, Republic of	22 September 1960	France
Madagascar, Democratic Republic of	26 June 1960	France
Congo (Kinshasa), Democratic Republic of the	30 June 1960	Belgium
Somalia, Democratic Republic of	1 July 1960	Britain
Benin, Republic of	1 August 1960	France
Niger, Republic of	3 August 1960	France
Burkina Faso, Popular Democratic Republic of	5 August 1960	France
Côte d'Ivoire, Republic of (Ivory Coast)	7 August 1960	France
Chad, Republic of	11 August 1960	France
Central African Republic	13 August 1960	France
Congo (Brazzaville), Republic of the	15 August 1960	France
Gabon, Republic of	17 August 1960	France
Nigeria, Federal Republic of	1 October 1960	Britain
Mauritania, Islamic Republic of	28 November 1960	France
Sierra Leone, Republic of	27 April 1961	Britain
Tanzania, United Republic of	9 December 1961	Britain
Burundi, Republic of	1 July 1962	Belgium
Rwanda, Republic of	1 July 1962	Belgium
Algeria, Democratic and Popular Republic of	3 July 1962	France
Uganda, Republic of	9 October 1962	Britain
Kenya, Republic of	12 December 1963	Britain
Malawi, Republic of	6 July 1964	Britain
Zambia, Republic of	24 October 1964	Britain
Gambia, Republic of The	18 February 1965	Britain
Botswana, Republic of	30 September 1966	Britain
Lesotho, Kingdom of	4 October 1966	Britain
Mauritius, State of	12 March 1968	Britain
Swaziland, Kingdom of	6 September 1968	Britain
Equatorial Guinea, Republic of	12 October 1968	Spain

What impacts did the colonial era have on Ruanda-Urundi?

The impacts included:

- the weakening and limitation of the power of the king and the local chiefs

- close collaboration between Belgian colonial authorities, the church and missionaries

- political power being given largely to the Tutsi

- the introduction of identity cards with ethnicity designated

- the large-scale conversion of the people to Christianity

- the establishment of formal education and the construction of schools along Western lines

- the creation of political parties

- the introduction of new crops such as cassava and a forced labour system

- refugee Rwandans fleeing to Uganda and elsewhere

- elections in 1961 and independence on 1 July 1962.

ATL Communication and thinking skills

1   How many countries gained independence in this period in Africa?

2   Which countries did not?

3   Was the path for independence for many African countries peaceful or more troubled and violent?

4   How did the transition to independence for colonies differ among other European colonial rulers?

1.3 Rwanda from independence to civil war, 1962–1990

Conceptual understanding

Key concepts
→ Change

→ Causation

→ Significance

Key idea
Democracy introduced in 1962 caused radical change and upset the balance of the status quo which had existed since the arrival of the Europeans.

▲ The original flag of Rwanda from independence in 1962. It was changed after the genocide in 2001

Events in Rwanda: From independence to Civil War 1962–1990

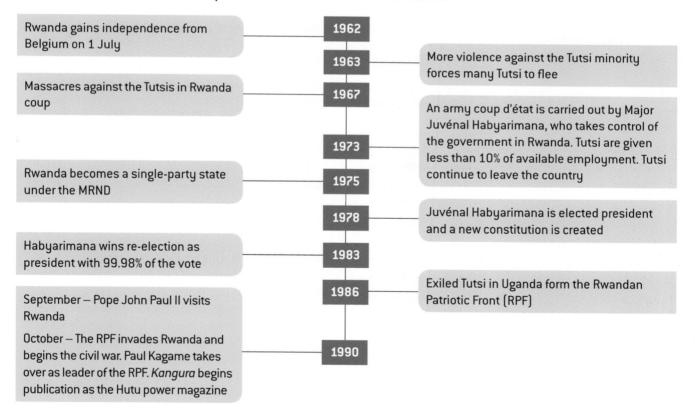

1962 — Rwanda gains independence from Belgium on 1 July

1963 — More violence against the Tutsi minority forces many Tutsi to flee

1967 — Massacres against the Tutsis in Rwanda coup

1973 — An army coup d'état is carried out by Major Juvénal Habyarimana, who takes control of the government in Rwanda. Tutsi are given less than 10% of available employment. Tutsi continue to leave the country

1975 — Rwanda becomes a single-party state under the MRND

1978 — Juvénal Habyarimana is elected president and a new constitution is created

1983 — Habyarimana wins re-election as president with 99.98% of the vote

1986 — Exiled Tutsi in Uganda form the Rwandan Patriotic Front (RPF)

1990 — September – Pope John Paul II visits Rwanda

October – The RPF invades Rwanda and begins the civil war. Paul Kagame takes over as leader of the RPF. *Kangura* begins publication as the Hutu power magazine

The First Republic, 1963–73

The political climate that emerged in Rwanda in the years following independence continued to divide along ethnic lines. The two groups in Rwandan politics consisted of the majority Hutu, which included hardliners, some moderates and the army. They held political power under the First Republic, which lasted until 1973. **Ethnic racism** occured against the Tutsi, as political restructuring and representative democracy had transformed the government and put power in Hutu hands. This meant that the Tutsi were discriminated against politically and in the work force. Finally, another group (not ethnically based) which had negligible impact on the Rwandan political scene, were the 2,500 UN peacekeepers and diplomats who were in the country largely for economic reasons and to maintain stability.

The Tutsi leaders represented later by the Rwandan Patriotic Front (RPF) were living in exile, many of them in Uganda.

In the 1960s, Kayibanda's regime was subject to attacks from the so-called **Inyenzi** refugees outside the country. In response to the Inyenzi attacks, many Hutu attacked the Tutsi inside Rwanda. In a speech given in March 1963 President Kayibanda said,

> *Some of you are causing trouble for your brothers who live in peace in democratic Rwanda ... suppose you take Kigali [the capital] by force, how will you measure the chaos of which you will be the first victims? ... it will be the total end of the Tutsi race.*

Later that year, massacres took place in Gikongoro near the southern border with Burundi. The official government version was that the Hutu population had run amok, and the authorities had temporarily lost control. Officially, they put the number of dead at 500; the UN estimated the figure to be 3,000, but the World Council of Churches believed that between 10,000 and 14,000 people had been massacred. Accusations against the Kayibanda regime of organized genocide were never officially proven.

Meanwhile, regional divisions within the country created further difficulties. These were problems common to emerging regimes: widespread corruption, social divisions and a one-party state. It was a new world for the dominant Hutu majority and Kayibanda promoted the concept of the superior status of being Hutu, the importance of following a Christian lifestyle and the significance of hard work to better the country. A Hutu slogan said, *"A Hutu knows how to cultivate the land. So let the Tutsi too learn how to cultivate; Rwanda has got its true owners – the Hutu, so let the Hutu dominate."* It was not an auspicious start for a new African nation.

The Second Republic under Habyarimana, 1973–90

In 1973 further disturbances followed a **purge of Tutsi** among the staff and students in universities, resulting in the army taking power and establishing the Second Republic under the army's chief of staff, Juvenal Habyarimana. During the same year in neighbouring Burundi, the

Inyenzi

"Cockroach" in Kinyarwanda. The term was first used by the Tutsi themselves to label their secret resistance group. The word was taken over by the Hutu and used as a derogatory term against all Tutsi.

minority Tutsi succeeded in retaining power after an abortive Hutu coup and the death of 200,000 Hutu. In Rwanda, this gave the army leave to impose further control – instigating violence and then stepping in, a favourite tactic of dictators around the world – and Habyarimana did just that. Once in power, however, Habyarimana went some way to encourage national unity, at least to the world. His main aim was to secure his own power in the PARAMEHUTU, and to gather vast wealth for himself and his cronies from the north. His own political party, the only one permitted to function in the country, was the National Revolutionary Movement for Development (MRND) formed in 1974, and soon became rich at the expense of the Rwandan people. All other political parties were banned and political opposition silenced. Former president Kayibanda and his wife died, amid rumours that they were starved to death or at the very least had medical treatment withheld. Habyarimana's international reputation was quite good though, certainly in comparison to that of other African single-party despots; he was a professed Catholic and on the surface, lived a modest, simple lifestyle. Rwanda appeared to be moving slowly in the direction of positive change.

In regard to addressing the imbalance between Hutu and Tutsi in Rwandan society, Habyarimana recognized the importance of education. More secondary schools were built and school enrolment increased. Acknowledging that it was a cornerstone of development, Habyarimana spent a larger percentage of the national budget on education than was spent in many other countries. His emphasis on educating the Hutu was not seen as trying to make a level playing field by the Tutsi, but as something which was unjust, and encouraged discrimination against their ethnicity. However, the system continued to remain discriminatory in this period, just as it had done under colonial rule, only this time, in favour of the Hutu against the Tutsi. Quotas were introduced and admissions to educational facilities put in place based not on merit, but on numbers. This was advertised as the programme of social justice; nevertheless, it served to reinforce the divisions within Rwandan society and laid the ground for the genocide.

The most dangerous ideas are the ones that tell people they are different …

— Laura, a genocide survivor

> ## ATL Self management and research skills
>
> You need to be able to identify and recognize ideas within a society which pose a threat to stability. You should recognize that ideas are significant social driving forces; the case of Nazi Germany and other 20th century societies can be examined in this context. You can also examine discrimination in Rwandan society prior to the decade of the genocide.

Source skills

Source A

The Story of the Two Cows: A Rwandan folk tale.

Once upon a time, there were two cows, one with horns and another without horns. Both of the cows looked across the lake from where they were and saw that the grass on the other side was rich and lush. The cows then said to each other that they were going to the other side of lake to eat some fresh grass. They had to cross the lake to get to the grass, but in the lake there lived some crocodiles. In the middle of their journey across the lake, the two cows started to quarrel and then they fought. Kungu, the cow without horns, said that the reason he had no horns was because the ancestors of the cow with horns, whose name was Nyambo, had knocked off Kungu's ancestors' horns because he was jealous of them. As a result, the descendants of Kungu were all born without horns. So for Kungu, it was time, in the middle of the lake, to seek revenge for that act. When the two cows were still fighting, they both saw a crocodile swimming towards them in the lake. The cows saw sense, and decided to

35

reconcile and live peacefully together. As a way of thanking the crocodiles for inadvertently bringing them together, the cows threw a big party inviting them and all the animals who lived in the lake area.

Source B

A Tutsi student recalls her school days.

I think that education contributed a lot [to violent conflict] because from primary school, from the youngest age, you had to differentiate the Hutu and the Tutsi. Every time Tutsi were the minority in relation to the Hutu. We were also taught in history that the Tutsi had in some way been exported, that they came from the north near the Nile river, that they met Twa and Hutu here [in Rwanda] and that they sort of colonized the country. They said all this and we learned it from a very young age. I think that it is normal that there be hatred between Hutu and Tutsi starting from this very young age.

... My little sister would tell me that at primary school they asked you to stand up (because even in class they would ask "Hutu get up, Tutsi get up") and from a certain moment, my little sister didn't want to get up because she found that there were just two [Tutsi] in class. Every time she would ask, "Why aren't I like everyone else?" She felt a bit marginalized. And then, as you grow up, you don't feel comfortable at school with the other students. And the Hutu were proud because they were the majority, and moreover that they were the indigenous, those that should be in the country. The others [Tutsi] shouldn't be in the country.

Even from the youngest age you learned that ... [Tutsi] found Rwanda and thought it was a nice country, so they settled, and little by little they took the land of the Hutu who were there. Well, they taught us that in primary school. They taught us that in history. And you had to learn it by heart because you were asked it on an exam. Imagine what that does in the head of a child. Yes, I think [education] really contributed [to conflict].

King, E. 2013. *From Classrooms to Conflict in Rwanda*

Source C

A story from an anonymous Tutsi author in 1999.

I was born in January 1968 during one of the most suicidal attacks of Inyenzi in Nshili. I am very sure of this. My mother told me this twice. She remembered it very well, because, when she was coming from her antenatal consultation, she met a military lorry carrying dead bodies and wounded soldiers. At that time, she wanted to know what was on the lorry, the driver stopped and asked her why she was curious and she ran away. It was probably 10 years after the 1959 revolution.

I began primary school at my parish. It was there that I learnt that Tutsi had oppressed Hutu for centuries and they had to pay for it. I also learnt that I was a son of a Tutsi from Ethiopia. Hutu classmates were the sons of poor Hutu who earned their living by doing hard labour and therefore justice had to be done for Hutu sons and daughters. I grew up with that shame of being one of the oppressors – the Tutsi. My social surroundings identified me as a "Tutsi".

At secondary school, I was constantly reminded that I was a Tutsi. This awareness was done through ethnic check-up done on regular basis in the classroom to remind us that we belonged to a "group of outcasts". During the check up, Hutu were proud to raise their hands, but for us, we could raise ours hesitantly and some could hide behind desks. We preferred to be Twa who had no traumatizing experience. Unfortunately, it was impossible to change to Twa. We were obliged to live the fate of our group.

First question, part a – 3 marks

According to Source B, what was one of the myths taught in Rwandan schools about the origins of the Tutsi people?

First question, part b – 2 marks

What is the message of Source A?

Second question – 4 marks

With reference to its origin and purpose, assess the values and limitations of Source C for historians studying the reasons for ethnic conflict in Rwanda.

Examiner's hints:

Here are some ideas for Source C. You should be able to identify the following origins, purpose, value and limitations for this.

Origin

Source C is a personal recollection from a Tutsi man recorded after the genocide in 1999.

Purpose

To recall the events almost thirty years before during his childhood, through his educational experiences.

Value

A value of the source is that it gives insight into the personal experiences of a Tutsi survivor of the genocide as a young student in the country during the Habyarimana years. It helps us understand how ethnic differences were taught and highlighted in schools.

Limitations

A limit of the source is that it is anonymous, we know nothing else about the author. This may be due to a number of factors and can lead historians to question the validity of a source.

ATL Research communication and thinking skills

1 How and why are myths important to a culture? How can they be used to teach people?

2 Relate your partner or the group a simple myth from your own culture or religion.

3 What lessons can be learned about segregation and cooperation from both Sources A and B?

4 In Source B what does the student mean when she says that the Hutu "were the indigenous"?

Rwanda: Economy and society

The country Habyarimana ruled was one of the smallest countries in the world. With a land area of a little over 10,000 square miles (26,000 square kilometres) it is one of the most densely populated countries on earth. This is largely due to its location, elevation, numerous lakes, fertile soil and its wonderful climate. Sometimes called "the Land of a Thousand Hills", Rwanda is a country of natural wonders, containing dense mountain forest and savanna grasslands. Situated in the Great Rift Valley, the lowest point in the country is 950 metres above sea level and its highest point is Mount Karisimba, a little over 4,500 metres high. Most of the country lies on a series of plateaux which were once covered by forest and have now been cleared for farming; Kigali, the capital, is located in the centre of the country.

As in many developing countries, the birth rate in Rwanda grew rapidly. The census for 1978 indicated that the total population was close to 5 million, with the Tutsi comprising almost 10% of the total (see below). The majority of people lived in poverty, with a population density on the arable land of about 800 inhabitants per square kilometre, making its density the highest in Africa. The World Bank estimated the annual population growth rate to be 3% per annum – Rwandan women were averaging over six children each, with an average life expectancy in the low 50s. The major cash crop was coffee, accounting for over 75% of the country's exports. However, the export of coffee was heavily dependent on world prices outside of local control so, when the prices plummeted in 1989, it had a major impact on

Class discussion

Nelson Mandela called education, "the most powerful weapon to change the world". Using the sources above, and your own experience, how important a vehicle do you think education is, as a force for change?

▲ View of Rwanda's fertile hills and volcano region

Ethnic group/ nationality	Total (in hundreds of thousands)	%
Hutu	4,295,275	89.7
Tutsi	467,587	9.77
Twa	22,140	0.46
Naturalized	3,567	0.07
Subtotal	4,788,567	
Expatriate	41,911	0.8
Total	**4,830,480**	

▲ Number of population by ethnic group or nationality in 1978

Figures from the 1978 census sponsored by the United Nations Food and Population Agency (UNFPA)

the Rwandan economy. The link between environmental factors, especially in population growth and land pressure, coupled with unsustainable agricultural practices, contributed to the outbreak of violence in 1994. However, the factors contributing to the genocide had been sown in the Habyarimana period of rule – seeds which his political party had planted.

The figure mentioned in the table on the right, rounded to 10%, was used to calculate ethnic quota for labour as follows:

- Tutsi: 9.8%

- Hutu: 89.8%

- Twa: 0.4%

The fall in the international coffee price coincided with other problems. The country's over-reliance on one crop, the lack of diversity in agriculture, growing population pressure and declining land yields made the situation dangerous. These upheavals made many Hutu peasants fearful for their future and willing to listen to the propaganda disseminated to them by the Habyarimana regime. This brew of uncertainty, mixed with populism, already seen in the periods between 1959 and 1963, and again in 1973, simmered below the surface. It was into this potent atmosphere that the Tutsi-dominated Rwandan Popular Front, the exiled organization dedicated to returning refugees to Rwanda, launched their offensive in 1990.

Gorillas in the Mist

One of the reasons why people might have been able to locate Rwanda on a map in the later years of the 20th century was due to its fame as the home of the vanishing species, the mountain gorilla. Gorillas were brought to the attention of many in the West through the thrilling scenes in the 1933 film "King Kong", one of the most iconic films in the 20th century. The gorilla was a focus of the WWF (World Wildlife Fund) in the 1970s and their important work on this creature (that shares 98% of our DNA) helped make people aware of Rwanda. The world's largest collection of mountain gorillas (the numbers of which are now thought to be less than 500) is found in a mountainous region known as the Virungas, bordering Rwanda, Uganda and the Democratic Republic of Congo. The mountain gorilla was unknown to Western science until the beginning of the last century, when two were confronted by a German explorer who shot them dead. In the last century, the numbers of the gorillas have dropped dramatically, largely owing to encroachments on their habitat by deforestation and their killing by poachers, to the point of extinction. In 1985, their greatest champion, a US scientist named Dian Fossey, was killed by poachers, at which point the number of gorillas were estimated to be less than 300.

Fossey brought the world's attention to the plight of these creatures and the 1988 film, "Gorillas in the Mist", helped to disseminate not only the dangers to endangered species, but to the country of Rwanda itself, prior to the genocide in 1994. Today, the Karisoke Research Center, run by the Dian Fossey Gorilla International Fund in Volcanoes National Park, is the world's most important facility for studying the mountain gorilla.

Fossey's book, *Gorillas in the Mist*, published in 1983, is her own account of the extraordinary struggles during which time she possibly saved the creatures from extinction. Murdered by poachers in 1985 in her cabin at Karisoke, Dian Fossey is buried next to Digit, a young male gorilla she habituated by constant visits to his group in the mountains. When poachers killed Digit in 1977, she founded the Digit Fund (after her death its name was changed to the Dian Fossey Fund)

to help raise awareness of the plight of the mountain gorillas across the world.

Dian Fossey is a controversial figure however. To some she was a single-minded obsessive who grew immensely protective of what she began to see as "her" gorillas. At times she fell out with some of the locals who saw the need to encroach on the habitat of the mountain gorilla, and with others who were drawn by the large sums of money to be made from killing gorillas and selling their body parts. For others she was a driven eco-warrior whose personal relationships were often difficult. The Rwandans called her Nyiramachabelli meaning, *"the woman who lives alone on the mountain"*. Dian Fossey undoubtedly advanced scientific knowledge of the mountain gorilla (which has never bred in captivity), and is remembered throughout the world for her heroic struggle to preserve, protect and study the creature. The gorilla programme coordinator at the Karisoke Research Center commented, *"Studying Dian Fossey, it's really clear how one person can really make the difference."* Today, the income generated by tourism is an important part of the local economy and has continued to help many to know Rwanda – for good reasons.

▲ Dian Fossey with gorillas

Thinking and research skills

Go to https://player.fm/series/witness/witness-the-murder-of-dian-fossey

Listen to a 10- minute podcast on the life and death of Dian Fossey.

Research the life of Dian Fossey and evaluate her contribution to the preservation of the gorilla species.

You may also wish to look at the work of Jane Goodall, and her work with chimpanzees in East Africa.

▲ In July 2007 one silverback male and three female mountain gorillas were killed in the Virunga National Park in the eastern Democratic Republic of Congo.

TOK

In essence, Dian Fossey was prepared to value the existence and preservation of mountain gorillas over the needs of humans.

Questions

1 What knowledge should precede value judgment or opinion?

2 What responsibilities do you think you have to preserve the world?

The IB Learner Profile states that "*[students should show] empathy, compassion and respect towards the needs and feelings of others. They have a personal commitment to service, and act to make a positive difference to the lives of others and to the environment.*"

3 What does this IB Learner Profile statement mean to you, and how far does your study of Dian Fossey and her work in the preservation of the mountain gorilla species support the statement?

4 How important is it to be aware of your own personal perspective, including its implications for how you think and act? Does your knowledge bring responsibility?

5 Read Dian Fossey's book, or watch the film, "Gorillas in the Mist". From either of these sources, consider how bias may come into the account and the interpretation of a character and their actions.

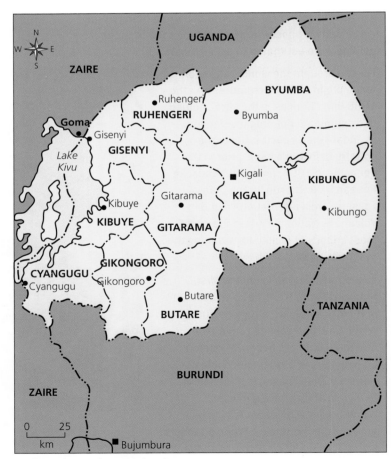

▲ Rwanda: provinces and major towns

1.4 The last years of the Habyarimana regime: Civil War, 1990–94

There's one way out.

Look around you.

We're all digging our graves.

— Taken from the poem "No More Tears" by Colleen Ruiz

▲ President Juvénal Habyarimana of Rwanda, taken in 1980

1991

January – Further massacres of Tutsi in the provinces

June – A new constitution is adopted to include multi-party representation

December – The Rwandan government begins to equip civilian militias, including the Interahamwe

1992

Local massacres of Tutsi are carried out

May – The RPF meets with the Organisation of African Unity (OAU)

August – Peace negotiations begin in Arusha, Tanzania

1993

January – Hutu and RPF leaders negotiate a power-sharing agreement at Arusha

March – A new cease-fire is agreed. The UN Security Council meet and the UN peacekeeping mission is discussed

July – Radio Milles Collines (RTLM) is launched and begins to broadcast anti-Tutsi propaganda

August – The Arusha Accords signed between the Rwandan government and the RPF rebels

October – 18 US soldiers are killed in Mogadishu, Somalia. The UN Security Council adopts Resolution 872 creating the UNAMIR, under the command of Canadian General Romeo Dallaire

December – UNAMIR peacekeepers arrive in Kigali

1994

January – Dallaire sends a genocide fax to the UN. Rwanda takes seat as non-permanent member of the UN Security Council

6 April – Presidents Habyarimana and Ntiriyamira are killed when their plane is shot down in Kigali. Killings began that evening.

When members of the RPF attacked Rwanda from their base in Uganda in October 1990, they were attacking a regime that had started to lose legitimacy among its own people. The civil war that ensued enabled the Habyarimana government to present itself as a unifying force against an external enemy, and it did so by continuing to encourage the concept of a superior Hutu identity. This ultimately contributed to the ensuing genocide. With the Rwandan economy and people already experiencing major problems, it was somewhat of a relief to Habyarimana that the RPF invasion caused some concern abroad, and helped to reinforce his own position in Rwanda as the legitimate government. In addition, the initial invasion by the RPF forces failed, not because of resistance by the Rwandan army but through the help it was given by the government's allies in Zaire and French troops, who blocked the RPF's advance on Kigali.

It was the coming to power of Paul Kagame, as commander of the RPF forces, which rescued the rebels from collapse. At this stage, the RPF was still a ragtag army of less than 2,000 men, but in a short time Kagame helped to consolidate this into an effective fighting force of 15,000 men. Kagame and other RPF leaders had helped the Ugandan president Yoweri Museveni take power from the former Ugandan leader Milton Obote in 1986 and so he, in turn, helped the RPF.

Kagame, a US-trained military man, believed that using the tactics of guerrilla warfare would defeat the Hutu regime. The regime reacted violently to the rebels and, early in 1991, attempted to wipe out the Bagogwe, a group of pastoralists (said to be of Tutsi descent) in Ruhengeri province in northern Rwanda, using methods virtually identical to those which would be employed three years later across the whole country.

Hundreds were massacred, many by their own neighbours and by government forces. Amnesty International later estimated that over 2,000 people were killed. It was a pattern that was to be repeated over the coming years; reprisals by the majority Hutu against any incursion by the Tutsi, or any perceived threat to their own position.

Genocide, after all, is an exercise in community building.

— Philip Gourevitch, 1998

Yoweri Museveni

Yoweri Museveni, born in 1944, took over the presidency of Uganda in 1986 following a campaign against the incumbent Obote, the man who had led Uganda to independence from Britain in 1962. Museveni was elected to the post in 1996 and again in 2001 and 2006, making Uganda a relatively stable economy after the chaos of the Obote and Idi Amin years.

▲ Major Kagame on military training in the USA at Fort-Leavenworth, KS, in 1990.

Ethnic tensions in Rwanda; the Hutu Power movement

In Rwanda, we have seen that since colonial times, one group has been favoured over another – a recipe for disaster in the long term. We have also seen that, after the inception of the Second Republic in 1973, Habyarimana aided the Hutu cause politically, socially and economically. Following the RPF invasion in October 1990 a series of meetings were held which set in motion the mobilization of the civilian population on an unprecedented scale. Self-defence groups had been used in 1963 to aid civilian security in the country, and to carry out genocidal measures against the Tutsi; but the scale after 1990 was much greater. The Rwandan army had increased in size, although the calibre

of the soldiers was generally poor. In response to the rebel advance, a meeting was called in Kigali in December 1991 of all government officers to determine policy and, (although no complete copy of the meeting has yet been found) this gathering was important in identifying the enemy in a particular way and determining their fate. Some present at the meeting believed that Habyarimana's power had eroded, forcing him to give way to Hutu hardliners.

It was in this situation that the Hutu Power Movement developed. There had been groups of Hutu who had committed acts of terror in the past against their neighbours, largely Tutsi and any moderate Hutu who opposed them. However the ideology of the movement under Habyarimana quickly took shape. In the same month, December 1991, the President's own party, the MRND, formed a youth wing that became known as the **Interahamwe**.

In 2015 (at the time of writing) many of the Interahamwe leaders are still at large after the defeat of the regime. A number of them fled, they mingled with the Hutu refugees and were given shelter in the neighbouring countries, including Zaire, now Democratic Republic of Congo, Tanzania and Sudan.

After 1991 the Interahamwe became the nucleus of the Hutu power movement and the arm of the regime, responsible in the following years for much of the genocide. Others in the Hutu power movement included the **Impuzamugambi** paramilitary militia and politicians in the **Akazu**.

Hard liners in the MRND formed the Coalition for the Defence of the Republic (CDR) in February 1992, but the largest, most notorious and best-organized militia representing Hutu Power were the Interahamwe.

The importance of the role of education has already been indicated from the colonial period onwards. Schooling was a key instrument of the state in defining and strengthening an awareness of different ethnic groups in Rwanda and justifying their inequality – all factors that underlay the conflict and facilitated the genocide. In many single-party dictatorships, the part played by youth groups, usually a thinly veiled collection of militia and disaffected thugs, has been crucial. The Interahamwe were spread across the country and given military training in the use of weapons and explosives, how to organize roadblocks and how to kill their victims. The training also included propaganda, which we shall come to later. In March 1992, following a news broadcast on Radio Rwanda about a supposed plot to kill some Hutu leaders, a directive went out for the Interahamwe to go and "clear the bush" – a euphemism to kill Tutsi. What followed was a massacre of innocents in Bugusera by groups of Interahamwe, together with soldiers supported by the authorities.

Finally, the Hutu power movement had infiltrated the government, many areas of society and the ruling elite. This group was bent on the destruction of the Tutsi by encouraging racism and division. It went by the name of Network Zero, so called because of its determination to eliminate all Tutsi – to bring their numbers down to zero. Membership of these groups was reasonably fluid, with the maintenance of Hutu power and the eradication of Tutsi influence being common goals. All of these formed the base of the Hutu Power movement and their beliefs were codified in the Hutu Ten Commandments.

Interahamwe

Kinyarwanda, meaning "those who work together".

The Impuzamugambi

Meaning "those who have the same goal" and was another branch of the Hutu Power movement. Formed a year after the Interahamwe in 1992, this group was technically controlled by the other radical party, the Coalition for the Defense of the Republic (*Coalition pour la Défense de la République*, or the CDR) with its members recruited from the CDR's youth wing. Less well organized, it was regarded as even more ethnically extreme than the MRND, and together with the Interahamwe, it was responsible for most of the deaths of Tutsi and moderate Hutu during the Rwandan Genocide of 1994.

The Akazu

The term given to the inner circle or elite in the Rwandan government who supported the president and his policies. Literally translated as "little house", it consisted of the northern Hutu, centred on the powerful clan of Agathe, the president's wife. The Akazu contributed to the development of Hutu Power identity and were determined to hold on to power through advocacy of an ideology of genocide.

A group of supporters of Hutu Power. Note the bright colours of the followers, the Rwandan flags and other banners

Kangura magazine and the Hutu Ten Commandments

First published in 1990 after the initial RPF invasion, *Kangura* was a magazine designed to promote the cause of the Hutu in Rwanda. Reminiscent of the work done by Josef Goebbels and his propaganda machine in Nazi Germany, the magazine named *Kangura* (meaning "wake it up" in Kinyarwanda) became a vital tool for the Hutu government's promotion of inter-racial hatred and vilification of the minority Tutsi. Although fewer than 3,000 copies per month were published (the magazine came out twice a month up to and including the period of the genocide), *Kangura* fanned the flames of hatred and furthered the ideology of Hutu Power.

The magazine was a direct counter to the RPF-sponsored newspaper *Kanguka*, having adopted not only a similar name, but a comparable informal tone and format to deliberately confuse readers. *Kangura* went on to become far more successful under the leadership of Hassan Ngeze, the editor of the new publication.

In December 1991, after President Juvénal Habyarimana had issued a call for ideas on how to defeat the enemy, Ngeze's strategy to disseminate racial hatred was given the green light by the government and *Kangura* became an important mouthpiece of Hutu power. The Hutu Power movement's ideology idealized all things Hutu. It emphasised Hutu superiority and targeted Tutsi as outsiders, bent on restoring Tutsi-dominated rule and taking over the country.

Previously, in 1990, the **Hutu Ten Commandments** had been in the December issue of *Kangura*. These reaffirmed the supremacy of Hutu in Rwanda, calling for the elimination of Tutsi from all public institutions and an exclusively Hutu leadership over Rwandan institutions and public life. Warning of the devious ways the Tutsi might employ to gain power, the Commandments urged Hutu women to "be vigilant" and declared that any form of relationship between Hutu men and Tutsi women is forbidden. In addition, the Commandments state that any Hutu who *"marries or befriends a Tutsi woman"* or *"employs a Tutsi woman as a secretary or a concubine"* will be a "traitor" to the Hutu cause. The Commandments declare that Tutsi are "dishonest" in business and their *"only aim is the supremacy of [their] ethnic group"*; asserting that any Hutu who does business with a Tutsi will also be a traitor to the Hutu people. *"Hutu must stand firm and vigilant against their common enemy who were the Tutsi"*. Perhaps the most clear-cut and simple injunction among the Commandments is number 8, which declares *"The Hutu should stop having mercy on the Tutsi"*. The Hutu Power movement and its ideology was strikingly similar to that of Nazi Germany 70 years before, and was to become even more effective in the country.

The Hutu Ten Commandments

Kangura magazine, issue 6, published in December 1990

1. *Every Hutu must know that the Tutsi woman, wherever she may be, is working for the Tutsi ethnic cause. In consequence, any Hutu is a traitor who:*

    *   *Acquires a Tutsi wife*

    *   *Acquires a Tutsi concubine*

    *   *Acquires a Tutsi secretary or protégée.*

2. *Every Hutu must know that our Hutu daughters are more worthy and more conscientious as women, as wives and as mothers. Aren't they lovely, excellent secretaries, and more honest!*

3. *Hutu women, be vigilant and make sure that your husbands, brothers and sons see reason.*

4. *All Hutu must know that all Tutsis are dishonest in business. Their only goal is ethnic superiority. We have learned this by experience, from experience. In consequence, any Hutu is a traitor who:*

    *   *forms a business alliance with a Tutsi*

    *   *invests his own funds or public funds in a Tutsi enterprise*

    *   *borrows money from or loans money to a Tutsi*

    *   *grants favours to Tutsi (import licenses, bank loans, land for construction, public markets …)*

5. *Strategic positions such as politics, administration, economics, the military and security must be restricted to the Hutu.*

6. *A Hutu majority must prevail throughout the educational system (pupils, scholars, teachers).*

7. *The Rwandan Army must be exclusively Hutu. The war of October 1990 has taught us that. No soldier may marry a Tutsi woman.*

8. *Hutu must stop having mercy on the Tutsi.*

9. *Hutu wherever they be must stand united, in solidarity, and concerned with the fate of their Hutu brothers. Hutu within and without Rwanda must constantly search for friends and allies to the Hutu Cause, beginning with their Bantu brothers.*

    Hutu must constantly counter Tutsi propaganda.

    Hutu must stand firm and vigilant against their common enemy: the Tutsi.

10. *The Social Revolution of 1959, the Referendum of 1961 and the Hutu Ideology must be taught to Hutu of every age. Every Hutu must spread the word wherever he goes. Any Hutu who persecutes his brother Hutu for spreading and teaching this ideology is a traitor.*

The complete list of *Kangura* articles is available online at http://www.rwandafile.com/Kangura/ (see "Rwanda file – primary sources from the Rwandan Genocide").

ATL Thinking skills

The Nazis also had 10 commandments (some sources say 12). Find out what these were and compare the elements of those with the Hutu Commandments. Are there similarities regarding, for example, race?

Goebbels mentioned reducing propaganda to *"a few points and [to] repeat them over and over"*. Identify some of the points which Kangura seemed to stress (Inyenzi, for example).

ATL Thinking and communication skills

There is enough material in *Kangura* to warrant a good deal of research by students, not only to examine some examples of propaganda in this context but also to search for bias, both obvious and more subtle.

Consider the following statements by Nazi Minister for Propaganda, Josef Goebbels, who wrote:

The essence of propaganda consists in winning people over to an idea so sincerely, so vitally, that in the end they succumb to it utterly and can never escape from it.

He also said:

The most brilliant propagandist technique will yield no success unless one fundamental principle is borne in mind constantly – it must confine itself to a few points and repeat them over and over.

With a partner or in a small group, discuss how effective propaganda might have been in Rwanda during this period.

1   Does propaganda only work on the uneducated? If not, why not?

2   Why might propaganda also be effective in society in general?

3   The first and most basic element in all hate propaganda is the dehumanization of the target because, if the perceived enemy is considered to be non-human, the concept of killing enemies ceases to be a series of murders and instead becomes simple, necessary extermination. How might this be achieved?

4   To gain influence over the youth of a country, do you think it is more important for a government to manipulate the teachers or the curriculum?

5   Can you see any obvious exemplars used in advertising, not just political propaganda but in everyday examples?

Source A

The cover of Kangura, issue 26, November 1991.

Below is a translation of elements of the cover and questions relating to it.

Translation

Vertically on the left: "*What weapons shall we use to conquer the cockroaches once and for all?*"

Vertically on the right: "*We figured out the problem between Nzirorera and the Tutsis.*"

Horizontally at the foot of the cover: "*If we relaunched the 1959 Hutu Revolution or triumph over the Tutsi cockroaches.*"

Questions

1   How effective do you find this as a cover?

2   What is the connection to the genocide?

Source B

"A cockroach (Inyenzi) cannot bring forth a butterfly",
Kangura,
issue number 40, July 1994

Genetic scientists tell us that intra-Tutsi marriages are responsible for their minority status (wherever they are found). Can you imagine people from the same family getting married to each other and procreating! However, they should know that if they are not careful, this segregation could lead to their total disappearance from this world. If such were the case (and such will be the case), they should not take it out on anyone, for they will be solely responsible. Would it then be the Hutus who eliminated them with machetes? In fact, they propagate everywhere that their minority status was the work of the Hutus who eliminated them with machetes …

From the outset, we said that a cockroach cannot bring forth a butterfly, and that is true. A cockroach brings forth a cockroach. I do not agree with those who state the contrary. The history of Rwanda tells us that the Tutsi has remained the same and has never changed. His treachery and wickedness are intact in our country's history. Administratively, the Tutsi regime has been marked by two factors: their

women and cows. These two truths have kept the Hutus in bondage for 400 years. Following their overthrow during the 1959 social revolution, the Tutsis have never given up. They are doing everything possible to restore their regime by using their vamps and money, which has replaced the cow. In the past, the latter was a symbol of riches. [*A definition of "vamps": females who use their beauty, charm and sexual allure to achieve their purpose.*]

We are not wrong to say that an Inyenzi brings forth another Inyenzi. And in fact, can a distinction be made between the Inyenzi that attacked Rwanda in October 1990 and those of the 1960s? They are all related since some are the grandchildren of others. Their wickedness is identical. All the attacks were meant to restore the feudal-monarchy regime. The atrocities that the Inyenzi of today are perpetrating against the population are identical to those they perpetrated in the past, namely killings, plundering, rape of young girls and women … etc.

The simple fact that the Tutsi is called a snake in our language is enough and indeed says a lot. He is smooth-tongued and seductive and, yet, he is extremely wicked. The Tutsi is permanently vindictive. He does not express his feelings. He even smiles when he is in great pain. In our language, the Tutsi bears the name cockroach (Inyenzi), because under cover of darkness, he camouflages himself to commit crimes. The word cockroach again reminds us of a very poisonous snake. It is therefore not accidental that the Tutsi chose to be called that way. Whoever wants to understand should understand. Indeed, the cockroach cannot bring forth a butterfly. At close examination, the Tutsi treachery of today is not at all different from that of the years gone by. The history of Rwanda which bears witness teaches us that the Tutsis had enslaved the Hutus for a long time by using their women and cows. Following their overthrow in 1959, they again used their vamps and money (cows in the past) to subject the Hutus once again to slavery … While the Hutus were engaged in community development activities, the Tutsis were preparing the attack to regain power …

Questions

1 Look at the use of the term "inyenzi" (cockroach). Why is it an effective expression to use against a minority?

2 Explain what you think the writer means by repeating "*a cockroach cannot bring forth a butterfly*".

3 What is the connection between cows and the Tutsi?

4 What are some other points which, as Goebbels recommended, are repeated "over and over"?

Source skills

A cartoon from Kangura, published in January 1992.

Go to: http://i.imgur.com/bRL42cT.jpg to view the cartoon and then answer the questions below.

Translation

"*I am sick doctor!!*"

"*What is your sickness?!*"

"*The Tutsi… Tutsi… Tutsiiiiiii…*"

First question, part a – 2 marks

Who is the patient, and what is wrong with him?

First question, part b – 2 marks

What is the message of the cartoon?

Examiner's hint: *When you have a visual source, annotating the cartoon or photograph can help you to pick out the key points or features. In this case, you should be able to identify the following as the message.*

Example answer

The cartoon shows a doctor seated and a man resting on a bed. The doctor is asking the patient his problem to which he replies, "the Tutsi". The message portrays the problems of Rwanda as seen from the Hutu standpoint. The simple but powerful message shows how deeply divided Rwandan society has become. The message is reinforced by the authority of the doctor and the red cross symbol on his white coat.

The arm of Hutu Power: Radio broadcasts

Radio Television Libre des Mille Collines (RTLM)

Taking another weapon from the armoury of single party dictatorships, the Habyarimana government established a new radio station in 1993, named **Radio Television Libre des Mille Collines** (RTLM or Free Radio and Television of the Thousand Hills), which was to be intimately associated with the development of the genocide. Although short-lived, (the station operated for only a year, from 8 July 1993 until the end of July 1994) the radio station proved to be remarkably effective in disseminating Hutu power and its despotic ideology. It has been called, *"the most successful hate radio in history"*.

In a country where 60% of the population were illiterate, the radio represented a very important and effective tool for news. The journalist (and current US ambassador to the UN), Samantha Power said that, *"killers in Rwanda often carried a machete in one hand and a radio transistor in the other"* (Power, 2001: 89). From the moment they were formed, RTLM and *Kangura* magzine collaborated closely, inciting ethnic hatred and publishing lists of Tutsi and moderate Hutu who were to be exterminated. Editor-in-chief of *Kangura*, Hassan Ngeze, welcomed the formation of RTLM in the newspaper, describing it as, *"the birth of a partner in the fight for Hutu unification"*. Prior to the introduction of RTLM, the state had used Radio Rwanda to propagate government opinion but it was the introduction of RTLM and the circumstances in which it emerged which were to transform the situation in the country.

In a speech made in 1933, commenting on the significance of the role of the radio in propagating Nazi ideology, Propaganda Minister Goebbels called radio, *"the most influential and important intermediary between a spiritual movement and the nation, between the idea and the people"*.

He went on to say:

> *We intend a principled transformation in the worldview of our entire society, a revolution of the greatest possible extent that will leave nothing out, changing the life of our nation in every regard ... It is no exaggeration to say that the German revolution, at least in the form it took, would have been impossible without the airplane and the radio. ...[Events of great] social-political significance...reached the entire nation .... [and] was primarily the result of ... the nature of the German radio.*

In a similar way, RTLM broadcast anti-Tutsi propaganda, explicitly stating that the Inyenzi must be exterminated, even guiding those doing the killing by reading out known locations of Tutsi. Most of the broadcasts were done in Kinyarwanda, with many of the transcripts now available.

After the genocide, the International Criminal Tribunal for Rwanda (ICTR) charged four individuals related to RTLM with crimes against humanity, finding them guilty of genocide, incitement to genocide and complicity in genocide. The verdict of the court stated that the radio served as *"a drumbeat ... calling listeners to take action against the enemy ... heightening the sense of fear, the sense of danger and the sense of urgency giving rise to the need for action by listeners"* (Somerville, 2012: 205). For records of the ICTR go to http://unictr.org.

Its impact on listeners was tremendous, with almost every Rwandan home having a radio. George Ruggiu, one of the four found guilty by the ICTR, was indicted for genocide on charges identical to those levelled at the Nazi Julius Streicher, editor of the Nazi newspaper *Der Stürmer*. The radio and *Kangura* became the primary mechanisms through which the Hutu extremists could attack the Tutsi and spread the message of misinformation and slander. On the day that President Habyarimana was killed, RTLM clearly voiced the instruction: "Tutsis need to be killed."

Political reform, the civil war and the talks in Arusha

In the middle of 1991, as the civil war was being fought, Habyarimana and his followers contemplated political reform and the introduction of a multi-party system in an attempt to deflect both the RPF and international pressure for change. From 1975 until 1991, the MRND was the only legal political party in the country but the more extreme hardliners from within the MRND had formed the **Coalition for the Defence of the Republic (CDR)**, which became a separate party. While the President officially supported reform, in the background he was promoting Hutu extremism. However, international pressure for change and the success of the RPF in the fighting brought about preliminary talks in the summer of 1992 at Arusha, in neighbouring Tanzania.

The Arusha Accords and the introduction of the UNAMIR

The pressure for a settlement of the civil war in Rwanda came largely from external forces rather than from within the country. In Rwanda itself, there was certainly criticism of the Habyarimana government and his lack of action, but the solutions being put forward were becoming more radical. In a speech to the party, the vice president of the MRND, Leon Mugesera said, "*The fatal mistake we made in 1959 [w]as to let them [the Tutsi] get out. They belong in Ethiopia and we are going to find them a shortcut to get there by throwing them into the Nyabarongo river … We have to wipe them all out*" (quoted in Melvern, 2004: 39).

The reason why members of the RPF had been able to force an agreement from the Hutu regime had been their military superiority and determination to fight despite their obvious numerical disadvantages. When peace negotiations began to stall they mounted new offensives and, in February 1993, they succeeded in reaching to within 20 kilometres of the capital Kigali. Had it not been for the support of French troops in holding the line, it is likely that the RPF would have taken the capital and the genocide may have been avoided. French policy during this time, although officially neutral and aiming to bring the two sides to the negotiating table, was essentially to prop up the Habyarimana government. The Organisation of African Unity (OAU) condemned the French for prolonging the conflict, but the pro-Habyarimana lobby in Paris was led by Jean Christophe, the son of the French President François Mitterrand, who wanted to maintain Rwanda as a Francophone African state. One of the gifts given by the French to the Rwandan president was the personal jet whose shooting down in April 1994 was to precipitate the genocide. The relative success of the RPF hardened the position of the Hutu extremists in Rwanda. It weakened the government,

> **ATL Thinking skills**
>
> What was to happen on the night of 7 April in Kigali?
>
> Who, according to the announcer, is the source of his information about the RPF?

and meant that agreements reached at Arusha were viewed as a victory for the Tutsi-led RPF instead of a fair settlement for both sides.

Meanwhile, a series of meetings held outside of Rwanda led to a cease-fire between the Habyarimana government and the RPF who agreed to terms in the Accords signed in August 1993 in Tanzania. The OAU supported the negotiations between President Habyarimana and the chairman of the RPF, Alexis Kanyarquenge, and many observers thought it would be a textbook resolution to an African conflict. The two sides had seemingly come to agreement on issues which had been afflicting Rwanda for years – namely, how to share power between ethnic groups, the integration into the army of the Tutsi, and the repatriation of refugees from other countries. A price the RPF had to negotiate was to insist that the extremist CDR party would be excluded from the talks. This failure to include the extremists in the process allowed some to argue that it encouraged a harder line amongst Hutu radicals. Others contend that Habyarimana had no real intention of standing by an agreement which would share power more evenly and see his own power base weakened. It is clear that with hindsight, the hardliners were not handled properly and this was eventually to be significant in the sabotage of the **Arusha Accords** and the whole peace agreement.

The Arusha Peace Agreement, August 1993

The Arusha Peace Agreement set out terms for:

- a cease-fire between the two sides
- reduction in powers of the president
- the establishment of the rule of law
- the establishment of a broad-based transitional government, to include power-sharing between Hutu and Tutsi
- the repatriation and resettlement of refugees
- the integration of the RPF into the armed forces (50% of the officers were to be Tutsi)
- the establishment of a national assembly (to be formed about a month after the signing of the Arusha Accords)
- elections to be held within two years
- a UN force to oversee the transition.

Until the outbreak of civil war in 1990, outside pressure on Rwandan politics had been negligible. However, the influence of the OAU and the role of the Tanzanians in bringing about a peace agreement at Arusha also signalled the formal introduction of the UN into the process. The international body sent missions in the early years of the civil war and the new **Secretary General of the UN, Boutros Boutros-Ghali** encouraged these efforts at peacekeeping.

Boutros Boutros-Ghali recommended to the Security Council the establishment of the **United Nations Mission for Rwanda (UNAMIR)** in August 1993, after the signing of the Arusha agreements. Created by **Security Council Resolution 872**, the principal function of the UNAMIR would be to assist in securing the capital city Kigali and

Boutros Boutros-Ghali

Boutros Boutros-Ghali is an Egyptian diplomat and politician who was the sixth Secretary General of the United Nations, serving from January 1992 to December 1996. He remains the only man in that position not to have been re-elected for a second term in office, partially due to his handling of events in Rwanda, Somalia and the former Yugoslavia.

to monitor the cease-fire, as well as to provide security during the transitional period and security for the repatriation of refugees. The head of the mission was to be the Canadian soldier, Brigadier General Romeo A Dallaire. He was to be a key witness to the events from 1993 and throughout the approaching genocide.

On the surface, the mission in Rwanda appeared to be a traditional peacekeeping mission: a relatively stable situation, two parties and a civil war. There had been a truce, there was a peace agreement, and UN personnel were going in to help implement that agreement. The period between the appointment of the UNAMIR and the death of the Rwandan president in April 1994 was filled with possibilities but little promise. As plans were being made to monitor the transition from a single-party state to a democracy in Rwanda, the country had amassed a large amount of weaponry. Hutu extremists considered that President Habyarimana had betrayed them at Arusha, and that fulfilment of the promises made there would sound the death knell for Hutu supremacy. It is clear that the time taken to establish the transition to multi-party rule, as well as the gap between the arrival of the UN peacemakers, fuelled the climate of insecurity in Rwanda. But the international community still paid little attention to the Rwandan situation, and no one wanted to spoil the positive atmosphere created by the Arusha Accords.

The "shadow of Somalia" and the UNAMIR, 1993–April 1994

For more than 40 years the UN had employed peacekeeping forces whenever it was able to do so, and the blue helmets of the UN troops have been a symbol of credibility in areas of conflict. With the ending of the Cold War, a new phase of UN operations developed and in the years between 1989 and 1994 there were 18 new missions, more than had been undertaken in all the years of the UN's existence. It is the debacle which occurred in Somalia exactly at this time which was to have a profound effect on events in Rwanda and, according to some, help to precipitate the conditions which allowed the genocide to happen. The trigger for the UN came in the anarchy which developed in the African state of Somalia in 1992, when US president George H Bush sent troops into the country. In 1993 the US operation was officially handed over to the UN but the mission went drastically wrong when, in June, 23 Pakistani peacekeeping troops were killed by angry mobs. The USA sent in special forces and tried to arrest Mohamed Aideed, the warlord responsible. The killings which ensued and the failure of the Americans to secure Aideed was made famous by the Hollywood film "Blackhawk Down".

The images of dead Americans being dragged through the streets of the Somalian capital Mogadishu were to have a major impact on the USA's position regarding the UN, and led directly to the US decision not to intervene in Rwanda. US troops attempted to capture local warlord Aideed in Mogadishu but their Black Hawk helicopter was shot down and **18 US Rangers died**. It was seen as, *the greatest military humiliation for America since Vietnam*" (Melvern, 2000: 80) and shortly

Brigadier General Roméo Dallaire (1946 to present)

I know there is a God, because in Rwanda I shook hands with the devil … I know the devil exists and therefore I know there is a God.

— Roméo Dallaire, 2003

Romeo Dallaire was born in the Netherlands in 1946, his father was a Canadian soldier and his mother a Dutch nurse. He spent his childhood in the city of Montreal in French-speaking Canada. Dallaire joined the Canadian army in 1963, and graduated from the Royal Military College of Canada with a Bachelor of Science degree in 1970, staying in the army where he was commissioned into the Royal Regiment of Canadian Artillery. He rose through the ranks to be promoted to the rank of brigadier general in 1989. In 1993 Dallaire was given command of the United Nations Assistance Mission for Rwanda (UNAMIR) and given the mandate to oversee the peace agreement, ending a civil war. Commanding a limited number of troops from various countries, he was in a very difficult position when extremist Hutu began to massacre the Tutsi population. As the situation worsened, Dallaire unsuccessfully pleaded for reinforcements. Dallaire concentrated his troops in some urban areas to protect civilians, but by the time the genocide had slowed, in July 1994, more than 800,000 people had been murdered. After the genocide, Dallaire returned to Canada and later suffered great stress from his experiences in Rwanda. He was released from the army in 2000 on medical grounds. In 2003 Dallaire published his autobiography called *Shake Hands with the Devil: The Failure of Humanity in Rwanda* which was later made into a documentary film. In 2005 he was appointed to the Senate, Canada's upper house of parliament. As a voice of conscience for global humanitarianism, Dallaire has advocated for Western military intervention in the Darfur region of Sudan. "*My soul is in Rwanda,*" he says. "*It has never, ever come back, and I'm not sure it ever will.*"

afterwards, the US withdrew its troops. Despite it being a US mission, President Clinton used the UN as a scapegoat; the effects of this incident have been called, **"the shadow of Somalia"**. For many in the new Clinton administration the "Somalia syndrome" could be characterized as a belief that the US public would not tolerate military interventions that endangered US lives. Members of the Security Council voted on the mission for Rwanda two days after the battle in Mogadishu and their subsequent unwillingness to give the UNAMIR a strong force and comprehensive mandate were to greatly hamper Dallaire's efforts in the months to come. On the day before General Dallaire landed in Kigali, on 21 October 1993 in neighbouring Burundi (a country with a similar ethnic mix to Rwanda), the Hutu President Melchior Ndadaye was assassinated by his own Tutsi soldiers . Rwandan Hutu extremists used this as an opportunity to portray the RPF and so-called "collaborators" (moderate Hutu inside Rwanda) as a threat to peace. The men of the UNAMIR were in for a baptism of fire.

In Rwanda, Dallaire and his small band of peacekeepers were ill-equipped and understaffed for a task which, on the surface, looked like a classic mission in the UN tradition. Speaking later, Dallaire said that he had not been properly briefed in advance of the mission; he had received neither detailed briefing documents nor had there been any mention of the human rights reports which had been presented to the Security Council the previous year. The original plans for the UNAMIR had been based on an estimated 8,000 troops; eventually, Dallaire received only 2,500 peacekeepers. Much of the promised equipment necessary for the mission did not arrive for months, and over 900 of the troops were from Bangladesh and had virtually no training for the task they faced. Between October, when a small ceremony welcomed the peacekeeping mission, and the New Year, a series of massacres took place which according to the evidence gathered by Dallaire and informants had been perpetrated by paramilitaries trained by the Hutu government. At the same time the RTLM radio station ridiculed Dallaire and the peacekeepers for failing to find the culprits of the massacre and for bias in favour of the rebel RPF. In a cartoon published in *Kangura*, Dallaire was depicted as being duped by Tutsi women (see Source A on page 56).

Dallaire began to receive warnings that a series of massacres were about to take place. These warnings came from officers in the Rwandan army and were made more credible by reports from human rights groups operating in the country. It was obvious to many that Habyarimana was unable, or unwilling, to make good his pledges signed at Arusha. At the same time, informers told the UN mission that the militia leaders of the Interahamwe were stockpiling weapons ready for an attack. Human Rights Watch, an independent NGO, presented evidence that the government was spending large sums of money buying weapons and distributing them among the Hutu population for what they described as "civilian self-defence". As guns and ammunition were relatively expensive, the government had ordered large numbers of machetes (provided by China and paid for with French loans). This was to be the most common weapon used to kill an estimated 55% of the victims in the coming months.

The "genocide cable", January 1994

Early in January 1994 Dallaire was contacted by a source, code-named Jean Pierre. The source was a member of the presidential security guard, who told him in detail how plans had been drawn up by members of the government to train the Interahamwe and others to kill the Tutsi at the rate of 1,000 people every 20 minutes, in a carefully orchestrated campaign. At the same time, members of the peacekeeping force would be killed, forcing their governments to withdraw their troops and enable a genocide to be carried out without hindrance. On 11 January 1994 Dallaire wrote a coded cable to New York giving the secretary general this information. This has since become known as the "genocide cable".

Dallaire began the cable as follows (he wrote all in block capitals) informing the council that the informant was a *"very important government politician … a former security member of the president… [and was] a top level trainer in the cadre of Interhamwe-armed militia of MRND"*.

▲ Machetes imported into Rwanda and used in the genocide

As documents also include evidence submitted to the International Criminal Tribunal for Rwanda (ICTR), it is now possible to piece together a better account of the informant who inspired the "Genocide cable". His name was Jean-Pierre Abubakar Turatsinze, a half-Hutu and half-Tutsi, who worked for the head of the Rwandan intelligence agency. A lot of information came through his wife and the ICTR in 2003, some of it still confidential. Students can research this man at the United States Holocaust Memorial Museum at http://www.ushmm.org and at the National Security Archive at http://www2.gwu.edu/~nsarchiv/NSAEBB/NSAEBB452/.

Dallaire went on to warn the council of the existence of weapon stores, and a plan to assassinate Belgian UN peacekeepers and Rwandan members of parliament, which would force the Belgians to withdraw and allow free rein for the Tutsi to be killed. Dallaire sought permission to protect the informant ("Jean Pierre") and to confiscate the weapons. However, the council refused permission for him to do this, stating that it was outside the UNAMIR's limited mandate and instead that he should inform President Habyarimana of his findings without revealing the identity of the informant. Less than four months later, the whole scenario as described by Jean Pierre would be played out following the deaths of the presidents of Rwanda and Burundi in a plane crash. Since 1994, the "genocide cable" has become a symbol of the failure of the international community to prevent the mass killings in Rwanda. In view of the significance of this document to the genocide, it is useful to see it in full here.

Burundi, Rwanda and the Hutu-Tutsi divide

It is hard to discuss what happened in Rwanda without some knowledge of events in the neighbouring state of Burundi. Both states had been taken over by European colonial powers and, after the Belgian mandate was awarded through the League of Nations, Burundi could be seen as a mirror image to Rwanda. It is often referred to as the "false twin" of Rwanda, its neighbour to the north, in that both countries have the same ethnic make-up of Hutu, Tutsi and Twa, both speak similar languages, and both share many cultural traditions. Significantly, their histories played out quite differently. Nevertheless, what happened in Burundi certainly had an impact on developments in Rwanda.

After independence in 1962, for the 30 years which followed, Burundi was ruled by military regimes whose leaders were drawn exclusively from the Tutsi minority. The oppression of the Hutu majority led to uprisings and frequent cycles of ethnic-based violence.

In 1993 Melchior Ndadaye was elected as the first member of the Hutu ethnic majority to rule, after his party gained a majority of the seats in the June 1993 elections. As president he supported national reconciliation but his rule was ended savagely when he was killed in a bloody coup in October 1993 led by the Tutsi Chief of Staff Jean Bikomagu and former president Jean-Baptiste Bagaza. The killing of Ndadaye marked the beginning of a series of deadly events which culminated in the genocide. This provoked renewed years of violence between Hutus and Tutsi in which thousands of people were killed. It reinforced claims among the extremist Hutu majority in Rwanda that power sharing between the two ethnic groups was an impossibility.

The "genocide cable"

Facsimile from Major General Romeo Dallaire, Force Commander, the UNAMIR, to Major General Maurice Baril, United Nations Department of Peacekeeping Operations, "Request for Protection for Informant", 11 January 1994.

1 Force commander put in contact with informant by very, very important government politician. Informant is a top-level trainer in the cadre of Interhamwe-armed militia of MRND.

2 He informed us he was in charge of last Saturday's demonstrations whose aims were to target deputies of opposition parties coming to ceremonies and Belgian soldiers. They hoped to provoke the RPF BN to engage (being fired upon) the demonstrators and provoke a civil war. Deputies were to be assassinated upon entry or exit from Parliament. Belgian troops were to be provoked and if Belgian soldiers resorted to force a number of them were to be killed and thus guarantee Belgian withdrawal from Rwanda.

3 Informant confirmed 48 RGF PARA CDO and a few members of the gendarmerie participated in demonstrations in plain clothes. Also at least one Minister of the MRND and the sous-prefect of Kigali were in the demonstration. RGF and Interhamwe provided radio communications.

4 Informant is a former security member of the president. He also stated he is paid RF150,000 per month by the MRND party to train Interhamwe. Direct link is to chief of staff RGF and president of the MRND for financial and material support.

5 Interhamwe has trained 1,700 men in RGF military camps outside the capital. The 1,700 are scattered in groups of 40 throughout Kigali. Since UNAMIR deployed he has trained 300 personnel in 3-week training sessions at RGF camps. Training focus was discipline, weapons, explosives, close combat and tactics.

6 Principal aim of Interhamwe in the past was to protect Kigali from RPF. Since UNAMIR mandate he has been ordered to register all Tutsi in Kigali. He suspects it is for their extermination. Example he gave was that in 20 minutes his personnel could kill up to 1,000 Tutsis.

7 Informant states he disagrees with anti-Tutsi extermination. He supports opposition to RPF but cannot support killing of innocent persons. He also stated that he believes the president does not have full control over all elements of his old party/faction.

8 Informant is prepared to provide location of major weapons cache with at least 135 weapons. He already has distributed 110 weapons including 35 with ammunition and can give us details of their location. Type of weapons are G3 and AK47 provided by RGF. He was ready to go to the arms cache tonight-if we gave him the following guarantee. He requests that he and his family (his wife and four children) be placed under our protection.

9   It is our intention to take action within the next 36 hours with a possible H hour of Wednesday at dawn (local). Informant states that hostilities may commence again if political deadlock ends. Violence could take place day of the ceremonies or the day after. Therefore Wednesday will give greatest chance of success and also be most timely to provide significant input to on-going political negotiations.

10 It is recommended that informant be granted protection and evacuated out of Rwanda. This HQ does not have previous UN experience in such matters and urgently requests guidance. No contact has as yet been made to any embassy in order to inquire if they are prepared to protect him for a period of time by granting diplomatic immunity in their embassy in Kigali before moving him and his family out of the country.

11 Force commander will be meeting with the very very important political person tomorrow morning in order to ensure that this individual is conscious of all parameters of his involvement. Force commander does have certain reservations on the suddenness of the change of heart of the informant to come clean with this information. Recce of armed cache and detailed planning of raid to go on late tomorrow. Possibility of a trap not fully excluded, as this may be a set-up against this very very important political person. Force commander to inform SRSG first thing in morning to ensure his support.

12 Peux Ce Que Veux. Allons-y.

Note: Peux Ce Que Veux. Allons-y' is the motto of Dallaire's old school in Canada. It translates as "Where there's a will, there's a way. Let's go." This was how Dallaire used to finish each cable sent back to the UN.

The period between the sending of the cable and the shooting down of the presidential aircraft in April was characterized by an increase of tensions and numerous examples of provocation by Hutu extremists. It was clear that the situation was building to a crisis. The failure of Habyarimana to implement his promises contained in the Arusha Accords resulted in increasing frustration among the RPF and growing confidence among the Hutu extremists, who continued to stockpile weapons and spit hatred using RTLM and *Kangura*. Habyarimana reneged on his agreement to exclude the hardline members of CDR from the transition and demanded that they be included in the new assembly. Members of the RPF were furious, believing he was retracting agreements already months overdue. Habyarimana had also lost much of his power and credibility with the Hutu; rumours were rife that he was about to be assassinated. Dallaire recalls that the RPF commander Paul Kagame warned that *"something cataclysmic is coming, (and) once it starts, no one will be able to control it"* (Melvern, 2006: 125). On Wednesday 6 April Habyarimana flew in his private jet to Dar es Salaam in Tanzania for a regional summit meeting. There, he agreed to carry out the Arusha Accords

ATL Thinking and communication skills

1   According to the fax, why did the informant come forward to the UN mission with this information?

2   What did he want in return for this?

3   What were the "certain reservations" Dallaire expressed in clause 11 regarding the reliability of using such a source?

4   With a partner discuss how significant and credible you think the cable was.

and signed a communiqué to that effect, before boarding his plane for the one-hour flight back to Kigali. He offered a lift to the Burundian President, Cyprien Ntaryamira, and the Dassault Falcon jet lifted up into the air for its date with destiny.

Source help and hints

Source A

A cartoon published by Kangura in February 1994. Issue number 56, page 15.

Go to: http://rwandafile.com/Kangura/k56c1. html and view the cartoon. The text reads, "*General Dallaire and his army have fallen into the trap of the Tutsi femmes fatales.*" Note the tattoos on the arm of one woman, and the badge on the breast of the other woman which reads "FPR" for the Tutsi-led Rwandan Patriotic Front.

> **Examiner's hint:** *You need to find two or three clear points in the source to answer the first question 1(a) on the document paper. It is a good idea to underline or highlight these points, when you first read the source, before writing your answer.* **If the source is visual, annotate the cartoon or photo.**

- The message of the cartoon is that the Dallaire is falling under the influence of the Tutsi by being seduced by their women.

- The UN is basically favouring the Tutsi side in Rwanda because of this.

- The Tutsi are willing to do anything to further their cause, including using their women as prostitutes.

- The Tutsi are tools of the RPF.

Source B

Extracts from the Hutu Ten Commandments, published in Kangura, Dec. 1990.

1 All Hutu must know that all Tutsis are dishonest in business. Their only goal is ethnic superiority.

2 Strategic positions such as politics, administration, economics, the military and security must be restricted to the Hutu.

3 A Hutu majority must prevail throughout the educational system (pupils, scholars, teachers).

4 The Rwandan Army must be exclusively Hutu. The war of October 1990 has taught us that. No soldier may marry a Tutsi woman.

5 Hutu must stop having mercy on the Tutsi.

6 Hutu wherever they be must stand united, in solidarity, and concerned with the fate of their Hutu brothers. Hutu within and without Rwanda must constantly search for friends and allies to the Hutu Cause, beginning with their Bantu brothers. Hutu must constantly counter Tutsi propaganda. Hutu must stand firm and vigilant against their common enemy: the Tutsi

> **Examiner's hint:** *The following values and limitations would be relevant in your answer.*

Values:

- This has high value for anyone studying the origins of the genocide as it shows the view of the Hutu extremists and some of their policies or commandments.

- The value lies in the specific nature of the commandments which identify Tutsi dishonesty in business, and recommend that all "strategic positions" be in Hutu hands.

Limitations:

- The origins of the Hutu commandments come from a well-known extremist magazine which is biased against the Tutsi.

- The publication, in 1990, does not necessarily represent the view of the majority of the Hutu population in Rwanda.

Source C

A radio broadcast made three days before the genocide began: RTLM broadcast, 3 April 1994 (Easter Sunday). *Genocide in Rwanda: A collective memory*, **pages 117–18.**

And now, the Tutsis, these who have eaten lion, and who are with the RPF, they want to take power. To take it by force of arms. They want to do a "small thing", they want to do this small thing during the Easter holidays, and they even say that they have dates. They have dates and we know them.

In fact, they would do better to calm down. We have agents, yeah, heh, ha! [voice rises until it breaks.] Our agents are there with the RPF, we have agents who send us information. They tell us the following: On 3, 4, and 5 April they say that there will be a small thing, here in Kigali, Kigali City. From today [3 April], Easter, tomorrow, and the day after tomorrow, a small thing is planned for Kigali City. And even on the 7 and 8 April. And then you will hear the sound of many bullets, you will hear grenades exploding.

But otherwise, to hold Kigali, we know how to do it, we know how to do it. On 3, 4, and 5 April, we expect this small thing will happen here in Kigali, and then they will follow up and rest on the date of the 6 April, and on 7 and 8 April they are going to do another small thing, using their bullets and their grenades. … But as for the date, my agent in the RPF] has not yet told me, he has not yet told me……..All of this will be the doing of the Tutsis, they are the ones that have caused us all of these problems! …

Source D:

Extract from the "genocide cable", sent by Major General Romeo Dallaire, UNAMIR commander to United Nations, 11 January 1994.

1 Force commander put in contact with informant by very, very important government politician. Informant is a top-level trainer in the cadre of Interhamwe-armed militia of MRND.

2 He informed us he was in charge of last Saturday's demonstrations whose aims were to target deputies of opposition parties coming to ceremonies and Belgian soldiers. They hoped to provoke the RPF BN to engage (being fired upon) the demonstrators and provoke a civil war. Deputies were to be assassinated upon entry or exit from Parliament. Belgian troops were to be provoked and if Belgian soldiers resorted to force a number of them were to be killed and thus guarantee Belgian withdrawal from Rwanda.

3 Informant confirmed 48 RGF PARA CDO and a few members of the gendarmerie participated in demonstrations in plain clothes. Also at least one Minister of the MRND and the sous-prefect of Kigali were in the demonstration. RGF and Interhamwe provided radio communications.

4 Informant is a former security member of the president. He also stated he is paid RF150,000 per month by the MRND party to train Interhamwe. Direct link is to chief of staff RGF and president of the MRND for financial and material support.

5 Interhamwe has trained 1,700 men in RGF military camps outside the capital. The 1,700 are scattered in groups of 40 throughout Kigali. Since UNAMIR deployed he has trained 300 personnel in 3-week training sessions at RGF camps. Training focus was discipline, weapons, explosives, close combat and tactics.

> **Examiner's hint:** *Don't spend any more time on answering a 3-mark question than is absolutely necessary – you receive 1 mark for each point that you make, not for the style of your answer.*

First question, part a – 3 marks

What is the message of the cartoon in Source A?

First question, part b – 2 marks

According to the broadcast, what was the origin of the information he received about Tutsi plans?

Here are two possible reasons you might give.

- *The origin of the information came from "agents" who are with the RPF and who send information.*

- *The radio commentator later identifies one agent, also working with the RPF*

Second question – 4 marks

With reference to origin, purpose and content, assess the values and limitations of Source B for historians studying the origin of the Rwandan genocide.

Third question – 6 marks

Compare and contrast the accounts provided of the origins of the genocide in Sources C and D.

Comparisons

- Both sources were contemporary to the year of the genocide.

- Both identify an individual; Source C refers to an agent while Source D identifies a "top level informant".

- Both sources are emotional and inflammatory.

Contrasts

- There are more contrasts between the sources; the first, Source C, is a radio broadcast by a Hutu, while Source D comes from a Canadian general and UN representative.

- Source C blames the Tutsi and the RPF for inciting the violence in Rwanda while Source D reports that the Hutu themselves were responsible.

- Source D identifies the Interahamwe and government forces as planning the genocide; Source C does not attribute any responsibility to the Hutus for the violence.

Examiner's hint: *You should attempt to find at least six points of similarity and difference in your answer. Ideally there should be three of each in your answer but it may not always possible to achieve this, so a breakdown of four comparisons to two contrasts, or vice versa, is acceptable. Try to maintain a clear running commentary between the two sources throughout your answer.*

Fourth question – 9 marks

Using the sources and your own knowledge, to what extent do you agree with the claim that the genocide was brought about by the failure of authorities to recognise what was happening in Rwanda between 1990 and 1994?

1.5 The assassination of presidents Habyarimana and Ntaryamira, April 1994

Conceptual understanding

Key concepts
→ Significance
→ Causation
→ Change
→ Consequence

Hell is empty and all the devils are here.

— Shakespeare, *The Tempest*, Act 1, Scene 2

▲ Wreckage of President Habyarimana's aircraft in the garden of the palace, Kigali

As the presidential jet circled above Kigali airport at 8.20 p.m., two surface-to-air missiles were launched, the first hitting the wing and the second hitting the tail of the aircraft. The plane was swathed in fire and crashed in a huge explosion. It is certain that the aircraft was deliberately shot down and that the passengers – 12 in total – were all killed. This is one of history's least investigated political assassinations. What developed after this was the already planned genocide. Partly because the killing began within hours, the actual details of the assassination of the two presidents have tended to become submerged in what followed. However, it was the catalyst that preceded the genocide. At the time, people speculated about who had shot down the aircraft with, initially, two groups being suspected. The first were Hutu extremists, fed-up with Habyarimana's "giving away the farm", as his deal with the RPF and his negotiation of the Arusha Accords was sometimes referred. The second accused the RPF rebels, mistrusting the government's prevarication and its failure to make good on its promises.

The shooting down of the aircraft was a bold act with the immediate result of 12 people dying, including two heads of state. RTLM radio immediately blamed the crash on Belgian troops. The part played by the French in the whole affair will be examined in more detail later, but it is reported that one of the first on the scene of the wreckage in the grounds of the presidential garden was the head of the French military mission to Rwanda, Lieutenant Colonel Gregoire de Saint Quentin. There were other French officers in the vicinity, reported by one witness to have been in the grounds to pick up the plane's black box. Within hours of the crash, Major General Dallaire stated that there would be an international inquiry into the death of the president but, in fact, it was not until later that an official inquiry was held.

Who shot down the aircraft?

The Belgians immediately concluded that disaffected soldiers of the Rwandan government, who wanted the peace talks to fail, had probably shot down the plane. Another report mentioned the possibility that Colonel Théoneste Bagosora, chief of staff in the Ministry of Defence in 1994 and leader of an extremist Hutu power group, was responsible for the assassination. He was a key figure and leader of an extremist Hutu power group opposed to any accommodation with the RPF. In August 1993 he is reported to have stormed out of negotiations over the Arusha Accords, declaring that he would return to Rwanda to "prepare for the apocalypse". Bagosora figured prominently in the days following the assassination and wielded considerable influence with both the presidential guard and the military hierarchy.

The French ambassador to Rwanda, Jean-Philippe Marlaud, initially believed that RPF rebels were to blame for bringing down the aircraft, arguing that they recognized that the deaths of the presidents and the army chief of staff would lead to a reaction by the Hutu government against the Tutsi, and that the RPF would then be able to defeat the government forces and take power.

The head of the MRND party Ngirutmpatse, believed that the assassination was an attempted coup d'état by Prime Minister Agathe Uwilingiyimana to seize power. Habyarimana's widow, Agatha Kanziga Habyarimana, supported this version of events and said that troops from the south of the country had attempted a takeover and the Belgians were implicated because they were responsible for security at the airport. She relayed this version of events from the safety of France, where she and her children were evacuated days after the shooting down of her husband's aircraft.

The man who took over the interim government the day following the assassination, Jean Kambanda, told his version of events following his escape and exile after the genocide, when he was given refuge in neighbouring Zaire by President Mobuto. The part played by the French government in events in Rwanda has come under increasing scrutiny from scholars in recent years; some questioned whether the Rwandan catastrophe would have occurred had it not been for policies shaped in Paris. From the early days of the civil war and before, France was proactive in supporting the regime that promoted Hutu superiority and opposed the RPF. Mobuto told Kambanda that he had warned President Habyarimana not to attend the meeting at Dar-es-Salaam on that day, and that the warning had come direct from a key figure in the French government. In the hours after the shooting down of the aircraft, a high-ranking minister and personal friend of French president Mitterrand, François de Grossouvre, was found dead in his office at the Elysée with two bullets in his brain; it was ruled as suicide. Known for his links to French intelligence circles and arms sales, the 76-year-old aristocrat left no suicide note. Meanwhile in Kigali, other eyewitnesses reported seeing white men on Masaka hill near the Kanombe camp where the presidential guard was stationed. Gerard Prunier, author of numerous books on Rwanda, reported this to the French senate, but its investigation in 1998 came to no conclusive findings.

An investigation was requested by numerous parties including the UN Security Council, the African Union and the International Criminal Court for Rwanda, but it was not until 10 years after the genocide that the

Agatha Habyarimana

Agatha Kanziga Habyarimana remained in France for almost 20 years along with other key members of her husband's government and was sheltered from investigation by the French for years. In 2007 she was denied political asylum in France, but still managed to stay there. Dubbing her "Lady Genocide", Rwanda broke off diplomatic relations with France in 2006 when a French court accused RPF leader Paul Kagame of shooting down the president's aircraft. Diplomatic relations were restored three years later and in the following year, 2010, Agatha Habyarimana was arrested, following French President Nicolas Sarkozy's visit to Rwanda. Sarkozy apologized to Rwanda and admitted that mistakes had been made by France regarding the genocide. To date, Habyarimana's widow remains in France pending investigation.

French began an investigation, (claiming jurisdiction, as the three flight crew who died in the crash were French). French investigators aggressively pursued those who may have been implicated, to the point where the government of Rwanda temporarily suspended diplomatic relations after a French judge issued arrest warrants for several Rwandan ministers. In 2007 the Rwandan government itself launched a formal investigation into the plane crash. This is known as the **Mutsinzi Commission**. Their results were released in January 2010 and indicated that the downing of the aircraft was almost certainly carried out by Hutu soldiers with the intent of wrecking the peace negotiations. Their report went on to say that the extremists then used the incident as an excuse to initiate acts of genocide against the Tutsi and moderate Hutu, started by the elite presidential guard, under the command of Bagosora. The Mutsinzi Report concluded that

> *by comparing eyewitness testimony against a range of scientific data, British experts determined that President Habyarimana's plane was hit by at least one surface-to-air missile fired from Kanombe, an area controlled by Habyarimana's own presidential guard.*

According to Sean Moorhouse, a British army captain, the UNAMIR (II) team concluded that

> *the Rwandan president's airplane had been shot down by three Whites with the help of the Presidential Guard and that the shots from weapons which brought down the airplane were fired from the Kanombe military camp*

— http://mutsinzireport.com

The actions of the Rwandan government

Immediate reactions

Hindsight is a wonderful possession in the case of history; but in order to apportion blame in a balanced way, we must try to evaluate how and why people reacted the way they did at the time. It is clear that some people had certainly predicted that events might spiral out of control in Rwanda. Below are some of the reports from significant players in the first days of the genocide.

Source skills

Source A

Prudence Bushnell, a State Department's official for African affairs (who led the State Department's initial efforts during the genocide) advises Secretary of State Warren Christopher of the assassination of the two presidents.

Bushnell alerts Christopher that "widespread violence" is likely, upon the death of the president. Members of the presidential guard assassinated the Prime Minister, Agathe Uwilingiyama, a member of the opposition MDR party, on the following day.

A plane crash near Kigali has apparently resulted in the death of the Presidents of Rwanda and Burundi. There are unconfirmed reports that the plane was shot down by unknown attackers …

The UN special representative in Rwanda [Booh-Booh] has organized a meeting between the military and Western diplomats at the U.S. Ambassador's residence at 9:00 a.m. tomorrow to discuss the transition …

The succession question will be difficult in Rwanda, The Arusha Accords provide that the

1

President of the Transition National Assembly assumes the presidency on an interim basis. However, the Assembly has not yet been installed. An armed forces delegation told UN Special Envoy that the military intend to take over power temporarily. Booh-Booh encouraged the delegation to work with existing authorities and within the framework of the Arusha accords; however, the military was very resistant to working with the current (interim) Prime Minister, Agathe Uwilingiyamana …

If, as it appears, both Presidents have been killed, there is a strong likelihood that widespread violence could break out in either or both countries, particularly if it is confirmed that the plane was shot down. Our strategy is to appeal for calm in both countries both through public statements and in other ways. We are also in close contact with the Belgians. The White House has requested that we prepare a presidential statement expressing condolences and urging calm.

Source B

SPOT reports are intelligence reports intended to "flag" severe problems for senior US Department of State officials. This report from the morning after the shooting down of the plane provided by US Ambassador David Rawson in Rwanda.

United States Department of State Bureau of Intelligence and Research

APRIL 7, 1994

RWANDA/BURUNDI: **Turmoil in Rwanda**

[…] told Ambassador David Rawson this morning that rogue Hutu elements of the military- possibly responsible for shooting down the plane carrying Presidents Habyarimana of Rwanda and Ntaryamira of Burundi. The Chief of Staff of the Rwandan military, two ministers from Rwanda and two ministers from Burundi were among those killed in the crash.

Military elements are also blamed for the subsequent killing of Prime Minister Agathe Uwilingiyimana and the seizure and or killing of several other Rwandan cabinet officials including the senior ranking Tutsi. The Prime Minister had attempted to reach the home of the US Deputy chief of mission, but fled when she heard gunfire in the area. She subsequently sought refuge in the UNDP headquarters, but presidential guard elements broke down the door and executed her, according to Ambassador Rawson.

[…] told the Ambassador that the military is attempting to bring the rogue elements under control and that a meeting-had been scheduled for 11.00 Kigali time. We have no readout on that meeting or whether it even took place. News reports indicate fighting in Kigali among various elements of the military, the presidential guard and the gendarmes. The fighting appears to be limited to the capital, Kigali.

Ultra conservative Hutus have been opposed to the peace settlement agreed to by the Hutu Rwandan government and the rebel Tutsi Rwandan Patriotic Front (RPF). One Rwandan official has accused the RPF of shooting down the plane, according to press reports; the RPF has denied responsibility.

Bujumbura [the capital of neighbouring Burundi] is reported calm according to the US Embassy there.

Source C

Very recently, French documents have been released and translated which are helping to shed some light on France's role – which has been criticized by many – in its relationship with the Habyarimana government.

A report from Bruno Delaye to French President Mitterrand.

FROM: **Advisor to the Presidency**
April 7, 1994

SUBJECT: **Attack against the Presidents of Rwanda and Burundi**

1) Yesterday evening, the airplane of the Rwandan president, Juvénal Habyarimana, with the President of Burundi, Cyprien Ntaryamira, also on board, crashed in Kigali near the airport. The plane was returning from Dar-es-Salaam, where a meeting had taken place of regional heads of state, dedicated specifically to Rwanda and Burundi, and, in its final approach, came under fire. According to the Belgians, it was either rocket or missile fire. **The two presidents are dead, as well as all other passengers (a dozen) including the Rwandan Chief of Staff and two Burundian ministers. The three crew members – all French – were also killed.** The attack is attributed to the Rwandan Patriotic Front (RPF).

2) In Kigali, the presidential guard threw itself into the hunt for the opposition. We have received information, not yet confirmed, of arrests of ministers and figures, Hutu or Tutsi, who are political adversaries of President Habyarimana. A clash between the Rwandan army and the RPF in the capital seems inevitable. For the time being, the interior of the country is calm. Transitional institutions have not yet been able to be put in place, and the president's death leaves the country without any recognized authority (the government and parliament had not been installed). **We fear a military coup d'etat.**

In Bujumbura the president of the Assembly has taken charge of the country, in accordance with the constitution. The situation in Burundi is calm and authorities are developing, in their public declarations, the view that what happened to the Burundian president was an accident. It seems that it was not planned for him to be on board President Habyarimana's plane on the return from Dar-es-Salaam …

Family of President Habyarimana –They are, for the time being, under the protection of the presidential guard. If they wish, they will be welcomed at our ambassador's residence, subject to your instructions.

Source D

Zaire, an important African country and a Cold War partner of the USA, played a significant role in the Rwandan situation. President Habyarimana and Zairean President Mobutu maintained a close relationship. US officials believed that Mobutu helped spoil potential agreements between the Rwandan government and the rebel RPF, and had facilitated arms shipments to those carrying out the genocide. This telegram, dated 15 April 1994, from the US Embassy in Kinshasa, Zaire, reports "muted" reaction in Kinshasa to events in Rwanda, but also Mobutu's fantastic claims that the president's plane crash "was part of a larger plot to destabilize the region".

A report by John M Yates, US chargé d'affaires in Zaire from March 1992 until September 1995.

Zaire reacts to Rwanda events **April 15th, 1994.**

Reaction in Kinshasa to events in Rwanda has been muted but Kinshasa is a thousand miles away from the conflict and communication with Zaire's eastern frontier is spotty at best. Mobutu has made vague dark charges that the plane crash, which killed the two presidents, was part of a larger plot to destabilize the region, and has called for an international investigation. He has sent his security adviser, Ngbanda, to Kenya, Uganda, and Tanzania to deliver messages concerning the crisis. Zairian TV has taken advantage of the crisis to stick it to the Belgians, the former colonial power here, by suggesting that Belgium might be behind the deaths of the two presidents, and by decrying the departure of foreign residents, leaving the Rwandans to their fate.

First question, part a – 3 marks

In Source D, what does the comment *"stick it to the Belgians"* mean? Why might President Mobuto want to do this?

The causes of the genocide

The immediate cause of the genocide in Rwanda was the plane crash that killed President Habyarimana and precipitated the mass killing. But at this point it would be useful to summarize the main issues that have arisen, and to examine some of the historiography concerning the causes of the genocide. We can divide the causes of the Rwandan genocide into three broad paradigms:

- The first comprises socio-economic factors: the lack of resources, poverty and the ethnic balance of the Rwandan people.

- The second theory puts the genocide down to political manoeuvrings by a small powerful elite which had gained power and wished to retain it – no matter the cost. This also includes an appeal to a racist ideology to preserve power.

- Finally, we should consider the paradigm of extreme poverty coupled with the actions taken by the colonial rulers which exacerbated the divisions in the country, and created the potential for conflict.

There is overlap between each of the above in addition to actions taken – or not taken – by individuals, which helped bring about the perfect storm that in 1994, brought destruction on an unprecedented scale to a small African country. It is certain that the genocide in Rwanda has deeply entangled roots. The first paradigm is favoured by economic historians and asserts that poverty, pressures on the availability of arable land and the rapid growth of population were all key factors in bringing about the conditions which made people receptive to the political and ideological ideas promoted by the leaders of the country.

Socio-economic factors

Rwanda is one of the most densely populated countries in the world as well as one of the smallest countries in area. As a contributing factor to causing genocide, the scarcity of economic resources coupled with one of Africa's highest population growth rates has considerable merit. The situation in Rwanda after independence created conditions where resources were becoming exhausted. This, together with competition for land, rising prices and overpopulation, made social violence a distinct possibility. The situation in Rwanda is often considered to be perfect example of Malthusian reasoning. Even those who do not advocate the harsh application of Malthus' economic theory see great significance in socio-economic factors and the competition for resources. Gérard Prunier wrote that *"the genocidal violence of the spring of 1994 can be partly attributed*

Thomas Malthus, 1766–1834

Malthus was an English economist famous for his theory of the Principle of Population. Simply, the theory proposes that population tends to increase proportionately quicker than the supply of food, and if this happens a crisis will develop.

Centred on the foundation that "food is necessary to the existence of man" and "that passion between the sexes is necessary". Malthus argued that population, when unchecked, increases in a geometrical ratio. Therefore, if it is not possible to maintain the production of food to satisfy the population, then the population must be kept down to the level of food; failure will result in deprivation and misery.

to the population density" (1995: 4). In the period after independence, new farming land was available but by the mid-1980s the possibility of this was reduced largely due to competition for land.

Prior to the outbreak of the civil war in 1990, over 85% of Rwanda's population lived below the poverty line. The drastic fall in coffee prices in the decade of the 1980s worsened the situation, as coffee was Rwanda's principal export. With the addition of other variables, population pressure and socio-economic shortages have to be considered as important factors in causing the Rwandan genocide.

The loss of political power

The second major paradigm attributes the principal cause of the genocide to the potential loss of power by the political elite. It is a reason as old as human nature itself and, in the case of Rwanda, the governing Hutus (the powerful Akazu clan who fed off Habyarimana) were prepared to do anything to retain control. Political power, once tasted, is an intoxicating brew. President Juvénal Habyarimana, after nearly two decades in power, was losing popularity among Rwandans for a number of reasons. When the RPF attacked from Uganda in October 1990, the Habyarimana ruling clique did not initially recognize the rebel Tutsi as that serious a threat. They saw the advantages in building-up the RPF as a danger in order to stir up nationalist sentiment and exploit the radical Hutu ideology which portrayed the Tutsi as "Inyenzi" (cockroaches), and those who supported them and the RPF as "Ibyitso" or "accomplices of the enemy"; effectively any Hutu opposed to Habyarimana.

▲ Inyenzi, the cockroach

Appealing to a warped ideology, the sense of righteous indignation at the perceived unfair treatment of the Hutu majority in the colonial period helped to fan the fires that capitalized on a racist ideology which was not new, and served the purpose of the government who was able to manipulate the masses to preserve their own power. The governing elite was able to blame the Tutsi for all of society's problems, and this reinforced the beliefs of a majority of Rwanda's Hutu population. Expressed through myths and proverbs, and transmitted through speeches both in schools and in the media, the ethnic divide was seen as a reality for all of Rwanda's population, and this was a fundamental cause of the genocide. By using the population's strong sense of solidarity and identifying a common enemy – the minority among them – the elite in the government and the army set out to deliberately destroy an antagonist to preserve their own dominance. *"Hutu extremism was essentially a useful tool by which the corrupt elite that ran the country could hold onto power"* (Keane, 1996: 28).

Roots in the colonial past

Finally, there was a hypothesis that a combination of extreme poverty, and ethnic divisions fostered by the colonial powers was the root cause of genocide in the country. The international community did not cause poverty in Rwanda (although outside pressures such as the price of coffee did not help the local economy). Both at the time and since the events of 1994, accusations have been levelled at foreign countries for being responsible to some degree for causing the genocide. Action and inaction prior to and during the genocide by outsiders have generated debate, but it cannot be claimed that the international community deliberately caused the genocide through their actions. The role of France in particular comes under the spotlight throughout this period. Its military support for the Habyarimana regime, the presence of French troops in the country, the financial, political and diplomatic support for the government from France all helped to create the conditions for the genocide to happen. Others contend that the genocide was caused by the failure of the outside world to intervene forcefully when the international community knew what might happen or was happening. It is clear that, particularly through the UN's unwillingness to act, the international community gave the government of Rwanda clear signals that it could get away with extremist policies.

Clearly there cannot be a single, simple cause of the Rwandan genocide in 1994. Like so many events in history there are a number of possibilities:

- the situation of racial division fostered by the colonial powers from the beginning of the century

- the highly organized nature of Rwanda's social structure

- the growth of population and pressure on the land

- the economic and political crisis of the last two decades prior to the outbreak of civil war in 1990.

All of these, allied to the Hutu political elite who gained power and were determined to hold onto it at all costs, created a situation where the implementation of a plan to exterminate an ethnic minority became a viable option. The causes of the genocide were political and not ethnic.

The immediate aftermath of the assassination

The assassinations of the two presidents of Rwanda and Burundi, who were travelling back from negotiating the Arusha Accords in Dar-es-Salaam, Tanzania in early April 1994, was a coup d'état. The shooting down of the plane precipitated the genocide in Rwanda, which began almost immediately in Kigali, and continued for at least 100 days. The people who brought down the plane have never been clearly identified – but the controversy continues to the present.

To add fuel to the mix, the interim government which took power after Habyarimana's death at first accused the Belgians of perpetrating the plane crash. Others suspected the French; the aircraft was a gift from the French president, Francois Mitterrand's son, the aircraft and the crew were French, and French diplomats were the first foreigners on the scene where the wreckage landed in the presidential garden.

However, members of the president's inner circle, including Théoneste Bagosora, viewed the Arusha Accords as a threat to a Hutu-dominated Rwanda as well as their own power. By that time in 1994, these people had the means, the motive and the opportunity to act. Colonel Bagosora

was familiar with the president's travel schedule and was in charge of the presidential guard, as well as the Anti-Aircraft Battalion (LAA). These units were located in Kanombe Camp, close to the international airport in Kigali and directly under the flight path of the aircraft (see the maps given in Source E on page 69).

The LAA, which Bagosora had commanded for several years, not only had at its disposal anti-aircraft missiles but was responsible for the security of the area and, specifically, for the airport. They also had anti-aircraft weapons and had been trained in the use of surface-to-air missiles in France, Libya, China, North Korea and the Soviet Union.

Numerous eyewitnesses reported seeing two missiles fired at the plane, one hitting its wing and the other the tail of the aircraft, bringing it crashing into the grounds of the president's Kanombe residence. The time was about 8.20 p.m. Twenty Belgian peacekeepers from the UNAMIR were on the airport perimeter and, shortly after the crash, found themselves surrounded by members of the presidential guard. Another group of Belgian peacekeepers tried to go to the crash site but were stopped at 9.35 p.m. and their weapons taken from them. A French-trained unit of commandos were ordered to the crash site to pick up the bodies. It wasn't until the following month that the UN gained access to the plane, by which time the black box had disappeared.

The events that followed in Rwanda made an investigation of the shooting down of the aircraft much more complicated. It was not until a French magistrate, Jean Louis Bruguiere, investigating the deaths of the three French aircrew, brought a case against the RPF in 2004 to try and discover who perpetrated the assassination. The findings from this report, which implicated not just the Kagame RPF rebels, but the CIA as well, stirred the Rwandan government into action. In 2007 a commission was ordered which came out with detailed conclusions called the Mutsinzi Report.

The report clearly indicated that supporters of the Hutu power movement were responsible for bringing down the aircraft. This, in turn, allowed diplomatic relations between France and Rwanda (which had been broken off for a short time) to be normalized. In 2010 Filip Reyntjens from the University of Antwerp in Belgium produced a working paper responding to the discrepancies in the accounts regarding the shooting down of the Falcon 50 aircraft. He commented that *"it would seem that both Rwanda and France, in their attempt to improve relations, are intent on sacrificing justice on the altar of political expediency. The Rwandan people deserve better"*. Nevertheless, he does not come to any conclusions as to who was responsible. In 2012 another French investigation found that the missile that probably downed the presidential aircraft came from the Kanombe army camp. This investigation cleared the RPF of responsibility. However, relations between the Rwandan government and the French became strained again in 2014 when the latter were not represented at a high level at the commemoration for the 20th anniversary of the genocide. To date, no specific individuals have been found to be responsible for the shooting down of the aircraft which precipitated the fastest genocide in history.

Class discussion

Refer to the background information on the left and then discuss the following question about the assassination of presidents Habyarimana of Rwanda and Ntaryamira of Burundi in 1994.

ATL Research skills

Who was responsible for the shooting down of the Presidential aircraft in April 1994, which precipitated the Rwandan Genocide?

Full document questions

Source A

Wreckage of President Habyarimana's aircraft.

Source B

Government of Rwanda, Committee of Experts, 2010. Extract from the Mutzini Report following the investigation of the 6 April 1994 crash of President Habyarimana's Dassault Falcon 50 Aircraft

According to Sean Moorhouse, a British Army captain, the UNAMIR (II) team concluded that: "the Rwandan president's airplane had been shot down by three Whites with the help of the Presidential Guard and that the shots from weapons which brought down the airplane were fired from the Kanombe military camp."

Source C

Taken from an article from the Global Researcher by Barrie Collins published in August 2008.

A former member of Paul Kagame's, rebels, Aloys Ruyenzi told French judge Jean Louis Bruguiere in 2004 that he was in the room when Kagame gave the order to shoot down the president's plane, and gave the names of all those who were present. The meeting took place between 2.00 p.m. and 3.00 p.m. on 31 March, 1994.

Source D

Government of Rwanda, Committee of Experts, 2010. Extract from the Mutzini Report following the investigation of the 6 April 1994 crash of President Habyarimana's Dassault Falcon 50 Aircraft.

The April 6, 1994 assassination of Rwandan President Habyarimana was the work of Hutu extremists who calculated that killing their own leader would torpedo a power-sharing agreement known as the Arusha Accords ... the conspirators tracked the progress of the president's Falcon-50 aircraft from the moment it left Dar es Salaam to return to Kigali. As it

flew west toward the airport, the conspirators fired two SAMs [surface-to-air missiles] from an area just east of the runway and toward the northern part of Kanombe Camp. At least one of the missiles struck the left wing and fuselage, causing the plane to crash into the grounds of the president's Kanombe residence.

Source E

F. Reyntjens. Working paper, "A Fake Inquiry on a Major Event: Analysis of the Mutsinzi Report on the 6th April 1994 attack on the Rwandan President's aeroplane" (2010). University of Antwerp, Institute of Development Policy and Management.

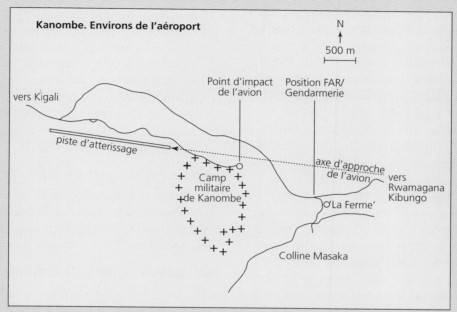

▲ The environs of the airport and Masoke Hill in April, 1994

▲ Google map dated 2008

69

Source F

F. Keane. *Season of Blood: A Rwandan journey,* **pages 27–28 (1996).**

The Arusha Accords were to be his death warrant. The extremists he had cultivated and the men who had grown rich during the days of the one-party state were not about to see their privilege disappear with the stroke of a pen. Now, instead of holding fast, Habyarimana was weakening, threatening to pull the house down around them. It was time to install a more reliable man. On the evening of 6th April as Habyarimana was returning from a session of negotiations at Arusha, two missiles were fired at his jet as it landed in Kigali International Airport. The most likely explanation – one disputed by Hutu extremists and their French supporters – is that soldiers of the presidential guard based next to the airport fired the missiles. There is another theory that members of the French military or security services, or mercenaries in the pay of France, shot down the aircraft. Although no firm proof has been produced, there are senior figures in the Belgian security services who think that the French may have wanted rid of Habyarimana, believing he was about to hand the country over to the RPF. The jet crashed close to the airport. Habyarimana was killed, along with the president of Burundi, Cyprien Ntaryamira, and the chief of staff of Rwanda's army, Deogratias Nsabimana. The MRND government immediately blamed the RPF – and by extension, all Tutsis – for the killing, suggesting somehow that RPF soldiers had managed to locate themselves next to the biggest army base in the country and murder the president. It was possible, of course, but highly improbable... The murder of the president would provide the perfect pretext for implementing the final solution to the Tutsi problem.

Source G

L. Melvern. *Conspiracy to Murder: the Rwandan genocide,* **pages 263–64 (2004).**

There is also another explanation, and this one was first reported in Brussels by the Africa Editor of *Le Sir*, the journalist Colette Braeckman. Some weeks after the crash, in mid-June 1994, Braeckman reported in her newspaper that she had received a letter from someone calling himself "Thadee", who claimed to be a militia leader in Kigali. He told her that two members of the French Detachement d'Assistance Militaire et Instruction (DAMI), had launched the missiles on behalf of the CDR party. Only four members of the CDR were involved. Those who fired the missiles had worn Belgian army uniforms stolen from the hotel Le Meridien. They were spotted leaving Masaka hill by members of the Presidential Guard. The missiles had been portable, probably SAMs, originally from the Soviet Union. Braeckman reported that during the three days after the missile attack some 3,000 people living in the Masaka area were murdered.

First question, part a – 3 marks

What evidence does Source C offer to support the claim that Paul Kagame's rebels were responsible for the shooting down of the presidential aircraft? (See page 68.)

First question, part b – 2 marks

What do the maps in Source E indicate about the likely source of the missiles that shot down the presidential aircraft?

Second question – 4 marks

Compare and contrast the reasons given in Sources D and F for believing that foreign elements were responsible for the assassination of the two heads of state?

Third question – 6 marks

With reference to origin, purpose and content, assess the values and limitations of Source D for historians studying who was responsible for bringing down the president's aircraft.

Fourth question – 9 marks

Using the sources and your own knowledge, how far do you agree that with the claim that those responsible for the deaths of the two presidents came from within Rwanda itself?

1.6 Course and interventions: The genocide begins

The graves are not yet quite full. Who is going to do the good work and help us to fill them completely?

— RTLM radio broadcast, 7 April 1994

▲ Interahamwe and a soldier at a road block in Kigali in the early days of the genocide

Events in Rwanda: From genocide to victory, April–July 1994

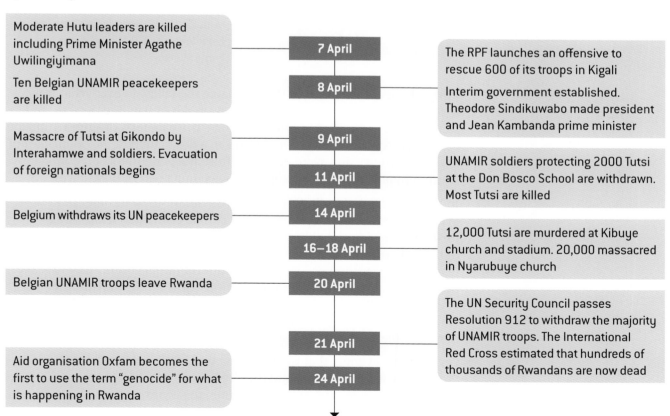

Moderate Hutu leaders are killed including Prime Minister Agathe Uwilingiyimana	7 April	The RPF launches an offensive to rescue 600 of its troops in Kigali
Ten Belgian UNAMIR peacekeepers are killed	8 April	Interim government established. Theodore Sindikuwabo made president and Jean Kambanda prime minister
Massacre of Tutsi at Gikondo by Interahamwe and soldiers. Evacuation of foreign nationals begins	9 April	
	11 April	UNAMIR soldiers protecting 2000 Tutsi at the Don Bosco School are withdrawn. Most Tutsi are killed
Belgium withdraws its UN peacekeepers	14 April	
	16–18 April	12,000 Tutsi are murdered at Kibuye church and stadium. 20,000 massacred in Nyarubuye church
Belgian UNAMIR troops leave Rwanda	20 April	
	21 April	The UN Security Council passes Resolution 912 to withdraw the majority of UNAMIR troops. The International Red Cross estimated that hundreds of thousands of Rwandans are now dead
Aid organisation Oxfam becomes the first to use the term "genocide" for what is happening in Rwanda	24 April	

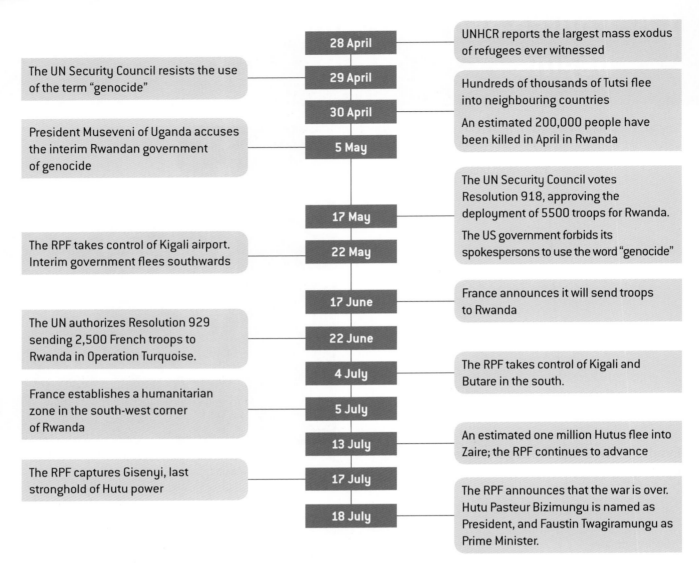

28 April — UNHCR reports the largest mass exodus of refugees ever witnessed

29 April — The UN Security Council resists the use of the term "genocide"

30 April — Hundreds of thousands of Tutsi flee into neighbouring countries

An estimated 200,000 people have been killed in April in Rwanda

5 May — President Museveni of Uganda accuses the interim Rwandan government of genocide

17 May — The UN Security Council votes Resolution 918, approving the deployment of 5500 troops for Rwanda.

The US government forbids its spokespersons to use the word "genocide"

22 May — The RPF takes control of Kigali airport. Interim government flees southwards

17 June — France announces it will send troops to Rwanda

22 June — The UN authorizes Resolution 929 sending 2,500 French troops to Rwanda in Operation Turquoise.

4 July — The RPF takes control of Kigali and Butare in the south.

5 July — France establishes a humanitarian zone in the south-west corner of Rwanda

13 July — An estimated one million Hutus flee into Zaire; the RPF continues to advance

17 July — The RPF captures Gisenyi, last stronghold of Hutu power

18 July — The RPF announces that the war is over. Hutu Pasteur Bizimungu is named as President, and Faustin Twagiramungu as Prime Minister.

Within hours of the death of Habyarimana, the killing began. What was to follow was one of the most efficient examples of slaughter in scale and suffering ever witnessed in human history. The bare facts of almost 1 million dead in 100 days are known to the world, a decimation of the population of a country. The victims were nearly all Tutsi; the perpetrators predominantly Hutu. A family of people attempted to wipe out a part of themselves.

In these first few days following the assassinations, a number of key events were to shape the subsequent course of the genocide. These included the planned killing of opposition or moderate Hutu members of the government and the murder of the UN peacekeepers. The latter was aimed at putting pressure on the international community to leave the country or refrain from taking action – the Somalia syndrome. In addition, these actions included the takeover of power by the Hutu extremists and their plans to carry out a genocide across the country. All of these objectives were achieved in the days that followed.

On the same evening that Habyarimana was killed, soldiers from the Presidential guard went around the city killing opposition figures as well as Tutsi opponents. At the same time, the commander of the

UNAMIR, Lieutenant General Dallaire sent the UN peacekeepers to the Prime Minister's house. With the death of the head of state, the Prime Minister would, according to the constitution, assume temporary power. As the UN peacekeepers entered the premises of Prime Minister Agathe Uwilingiyimana, they found members of the presidential guard surrounding her house. Uwilingiyimana was a moderate Hutu, unpopular with the extremist Hutu Power members and, because of her known sympathies to the moderate cause, was a target for the radicals. In the early hours of 7 April, Madame Agathe, together with her children, climbed into the neighbour's compound where they were found by the members of the Presidential Guard and, according to the account given later at the International Criminal Tribunal for Rwanda the Prime Minister, *"found, killed, and then sexually assaulted."* According to the ICTR:

> ... soldiers discovered Mme Uwilingiyimana in her hiding place. Other soldiers in the area heard the ... shouts of joy and knew that she had been captured. She came out ... without (a) struggle, apparently because she wanted to protect her children who were hiding in the same area. Captain Hategekimana reportedly arrived and gave the order to kill her on the spot. A lieutenant of the National Police shot the prime minister ... Witnesses who came to the house soon after found her nearly naked body on the terrace ...

Uwilingiyimana's husband was also murdered, but the children escaped.

Meanwhile, the UN peacekeepers, 10 Belgian and 5 Ghanaian soldiers, who were outnumbered and under severe pressure, surrendered their weapons to soldiers of the presidential guard. They were taken away to a nearby military camp. The Ghanaian soldiers were allowed to leave. The Belgian soldiers were tortured, castrated and their bodies dismembered by soldiers who had been told that Belgians had been responsible for the shooting

▲ Prime Minister Agathe Uwilingiyimana of Rwanda and her children

down of Habyarimana's aircraft. The informant known as Jean Pierre, a member of the presidential security guard had informed Dallaire of the aim of this plot to remove the UN peacekeepers in January, 1994. Now the plans were being put into action.

The government was in disarray, but the opportunity to rebuild a new Rwanda, and abandon the terms of the Arusha Accords, was already in the minds of those who took control in the days to come. What followed the assassination of the president was not only the murder of moderate Hutu and Tutsi, but a rekindling of the civil war between Rwandan Government Forces (RGF) and the RPF. It is probable that Hutu leaders expected that the killing of the Tutsi would bring about the renewal of conflict, and would give them a chance for victory on the battlefield as well as the possibility to renegotiate better terms than those agreed by Habyarimana. As the presidential guard began the slaughter of their opponents and the Tutsi, the RPF came out of their camps to fight.

In the subsequent days, there was a power struggle in the ranks of the government leadership. In this period the Hutu extremists gained the upper hand, and Colonel Bagosora, chief of staff in the Ministry of Defence, began to play a more prominent role. Dallaire reports him as always being in the midst of key events – or notably absent when he needed to be, commenting that, *"I did not trust him for a minute"* (Dallaire, 2003: 223).

By 9 April the Hutu leadership had come up with an interim government to be led by a figurehead president named Théodore Sindikubwabo and, as prime minister, Jean Kambanda, a younger man and economist who had unsuccessfully challenged Madame Agathe for a position the year before. Bagosora presented these candidates to the crisis committee who accepted their nominations, and they became the new government of Rwanda. Hutu Power extremists were now in control.

In the coming days, the confusion caused by the death of the president and the accusations levelled at the Belgians and the rebel RPF for the assassination of the former leader were served up to the confused and gullible people of Rwanda through the hate radio of the RTLM. The role of the radio station in inciting the conditions for the genocide is now well known. In the days to follow, RTLM urged Hutu to kill, reporting the names of those to be killed, as well as informing the killers where people were to be found.

Jean Kambanda (1955 to the present)

Jean Kambanda was Prime Minister of the interim government of Rwanda during the genocide, April–July 1994.

Kambanda had been appointed by members of the interim government in April and escaped from Rwanda in July 1994. Kambanda was the first person in history to be charged with genocide and crimes against humanity, and the first man to be sentenced by the International Criminal Tribunal for Rwanda (ICTR) when it began its sessions in 1998. He was given a life sentence.

ATL Self management skills

An extract from the RTLM broadcast on 9 April 1994. The speaker was Dr Théodore Sindikubwabo, new President of the Rwandan interim government.

The action we took, … we took this decision in order to pull our country out of the abyss and deadlock, … what they call in English "constitutional vacuum". After the assassination of the Head of State, there was a constitutional vacuum. After the death of the Prime Minister, other ministers and her collaborators, there was a constitutional vacuum. The broad-based transitional government has not yet been put in place. Courageous Rwandans who agree to make sacrifice for their country should make a decision like the one we have made. We therefore ask all Rwandans and those who support us to strive, as usual, to get this decision implemented. The Prime Minister has just briefed us about his Government's program. He has just asked his ministers to go to work immediately and explain to the Rwandans why we made that decision. He further asked them to lead by action and example … As pointed out by the Prime Minister, this body is going to address many sensitive issues, but it is made of men of high calibre, *Interahamwe*, speaking the same language. We think this term should be understood, as it should be. It comprises men who have come together with the one and same goal. We therefore hope that this body will carry out its mandate diligently. We ask everyone to assume his responsibility and support the new Government, to the best of his ability, in achieving its set objectives. Long live all Rwandans. [Applause.]

The actions of the RPF and the interim government

I believe I am in Hell, therefore I am.

— Arthur Rimbaud, 1873

The actions of the rebel RPF were initially based on their reactions to the events which had overtaken them after the first week in April. As the peace accord was shattered, and the international community wrung its hands but did nothing, Kagame and the rebel RPF were forced to look to military options in order to preserve their very existence in the face of the campaign of extermination. That the campaign against the Tutsi and moderate Hutu was pre-planned has since been recognised, but at the time it was unclear – and unbelievable to many that it could be taking place. Members of the Presidential Guard and small bands of extremists committed the first killings but, as the chaos developed, groups of Interahamwe and Impuzamugambi began to coordinate their actions, and together with the solders and police force began killing more systematically.

The military played a decisive role by initiating and directing the slaughter of the Rwandan Tutsi. Witnesses have testified to this and the widespread participation of the military indicating that the highest authorities ordered, or approved of, their actions. Political representatives around the country also supported the genocide, in particular the regional leaders such as the provincial prefects and the burgomasters. Working with local councils, they mobilized the militia, provided weapons and urged the people on. If there were too many Tutsi in an area, the military might be called in, and in some cases even the clergy helped to incite genocide.

In the first few days, Tutsi began to gather at Kabgayi, the seat of the first Catholic Church in Rwanda. When the Hutu militia began to come and take people away, some of the clergy stood aside and let it happen. It was later reported that as many as 60,000 were killed there over the course of the genocide, many of them with the collaboration of the clergy present. Some clergy acted as spokesmen for the interim government and placed the blame on the rebel RPF for attacking Rwanda. At Nyange, on 12 April, the local priest invited the Interahamwe into the building where they killed 1,500 Tutsi with machetes and allowed them to bulldoze the church. Another priest, Athanase Seromba was later convicted with crimes against humanity and is serving a life sentence in prison.

With government officials encouraging people to seek refuge in designated sites such as churches and public buildings, it ultimately made it easier for the killers to accomplish their task. *"It was like sweeping dry banana leaves into a pile to burn them more easily"*, said one. More people were killed in churches than in any other place in Rwanda during the genocide. From 11 April until the beginning of May, the genocidaires carried out the most brutal massacres of the 100 days of terror. Rwanda is littered with massacre sites; in Kigali itself at the ETO school almost 2,000 Tutsi were killed on that first morning, when UNAMIR soldiers were called away leaving the militia and soldiers to begin the killing.

> An eyewitness in Kibuye recalls: Outside, the Interahamwe were joined by police and soldiers. As this mob approached, its members sang:
>
> *Let us hunt them in the forests, lakes and hills*
>
> *Let us find them in the church*
>
> *Let us wipe them from the face of the earth.*

> Early in the morning of April 7, 1994, Tutsi began arriving at the École Technique Officielle (ETO) on the edge of Kigali, seeking the protection of the 90 Belgian UN peacekeepers stationed there. The peacekeepers allowed them to stay in the school but the next day, the Tutsi learned that their protectors were going to leave them to help in the evacuation of foreigners still in Kigali. Many of the Tutsi implored the soldiers not to leave them but almost immediately after the Belgians left, Rwandan soldiers and the militia entered the school grounds. They drove the refugees along a dirt road nearby and, in a clearing, Hutu leaders ordered their men to "begin work". They attacked with machetes and other weapons. By late afternoon most of the people were dead or dying. It is estimated that less than 50 of the more than 2,000 Tutsi were left alive.

The Ntarama massacre, 15–16 April 1994

There were other mass killings in the next three weeks in and around Kigali itself. There were massacres in Musambira and Byimana in Gitarama province. At Ntarama in the prefecture of Kigali, 5,000 Tutsi gathered in the days before 15 April. On 11 April, a Monday morning, the Interahamwe militia attacked townspeople with clubs and machetes. *"They started with prosperous shopkeepers first, because even then they were above all preoccupied with getting rich."* A little later, people heard a lot of gunfire. Soldiers had arrived in town. There was panic, and thousands crowded into the church. Alisa, who had arrived at Ntarama church with her family on 7 April, said, *"We all thought that if we came into the house of God no-one would touch us."*

Class discussion

In your opinion, when a film credits include the phrase, "based on a true story", how much divergence from the facts is permissible? Discuss your explanation with a partner or the class.

Hollywood and history

A film called **"Shooting Dogs"** was released in 2006, telling the story of the massacre at the L'Ecole Technique Officielle during the genocide of April, 1994. The film, starring Hugh Dancy and John Hurt, includes scenes in which machete-wielding Interahamwe militia close in on the building, hacking women and children to death. It was filmed where the atrocity took place, using many local people, including genocide survivors as extras and members of the crew. Linda Melvern, author of *A People Betrayed: The role of the West in Rwanda's genocide*, argued that the film was inaccurate, and criticized the BBC's role in reporting the atrocities, as portrayed in the film.

Source help and hints

Source A

Read this survivor's account of what happened in the Ntarama church on 7 April 1994. It is written by Janvier Munyaneza, a 14-year-old cowherd at the Hill of Kiganna (Kibungo).

Waiting to die

The Interahamwe prowled about the small wood around the church for three or four days. One morning, they all came in a group together, behind soldiers and local policemen. They broke into a run and started hacking people, inside and outside. Those who were massacred died without saying a word. All you could hear was the commotion of the attacks; we were almost paralysed, in the midst of machetes and the assailants' cries. We were almost dead before the fatal blow.

My first sister asked a Hutu of acquaintance to kill her without any suffering. He said yes, and he dragged her by the arm out onto the grass, where he struck her with a single blow of his club. But a next-door neighbour, nicknamed Hakizma yelled that she was pregnant. So he ripped open her belly like a pouch in one slicing movement with his knife. This is what these eyes saw without mistake.

Among the bodies

I crept out amongst the corpses. Unfortunately a boy managed to push me with his metal bar, I dropped onto the bodies, I didn't move anymore, I made dead man's eyes. At one moment, I felt myself being lifted and thrown, and other people fell on top of me. When I hear that the Interahamwe leaders whistle the order to pull out, I was completely covered in dead people.

It was towards evening that some courageous Tutsis from the area, who had scattered into the bush, came back to the church. Papa and my big brother pulled us free from the heap, me and my very bloodied youngest sister, who died a little later in Cyugaro. In the school, people put dressings of medicinal herbs on the wounded. In the morning, the decision was made to take refuge in the marsh. This was to happen again every day, for a month.

http://www.rwandanstories.org/genocide/ntarama_church.html#3

Source B

▲ Hutu killer armed with a machete

Now read these accounts by two of the killers, named Fulgence and Alphonse.

Source C

Fulgence: A very special day

First I cracked an old mama's skull with a club. But she was already lying almost dead on the ground, so I did not feel death at the end of my arm. I went home that evening without even thinking about it. Next day I cut down some alive and on their feet. It was the day of the massacre at the church, so, a very special day. Because of the uproar, I remember I began to strike without seeing who it was, taking pot luck with the crowd, so to speak. Our legs were much hampered by the crush, and our elbows kept bumping.

Source D

Alphonse: Working conscientiously

The Thursday when we went to the church in Ntarama, the people just lay there in the dim light, the wounded visible between the pews, the unhurt hiding beneath the pews, and the dead in the aisles all the way to the foot of the altar. We were the only ones making a commotion. Them, they were waiting for death in the calm of the church. For us, it was no longer important that we found ourselves in a house of God. We yelled, we gave orders, we insulted, we sneered. We verified person by person, inspecting the faces, so as to finish off everyone conscientiously. If we had any doubt about a death agony, we dragged the body outside to examine it in the light of heaven.

http://www.rwandanstories.org/genocide/ntarama_church. html

Source E

▲ Ntarama church altar, the scene of a massacre on 15 April 1994

First question, part a – 3 marks

What evidence is there in Source A that the Interamhamwe militia were aided by government forces?

Examiner's hint: *You need to make two or three clear points in question 1(a). Here are some ideas:*

- The fact that the source indicates that the Interahamwe came in together and "behind soldiers and local policemen". This suggests that there was coordination between the groups.

- The statement that the militia group had been in the vicinity for three or four days before the massacre supports the idea that they had planned the operation but were waiting for the arrival of governments forces, who "came in a group together". This too suggests coordination between the authorities and militia.

First question, part b – 2 marks

What is the message of Source B?

Examiner's hint: *Remember that annotating a visual source can help you to identify key points about its message.*

Here are some ideas for the photograph Source B:

- A message of potential violence; a group of men (from the Hutu militia and probably Interahamwe) stands menacingly with a machete at the ready.

- The collective nature of the group, the brandishing of a weapon and the focused stare of the man in front make this a disturbing photo.

Third question – 6 marks

Compare and contrast the accounts of the two killers in Sources C and D about how and why they joined in the killing.

> **Examiner's comment:** *You should attempt to find at least six points of similarity and difference in your answer. It isn't always possible to achieve a balance but you must have at least two of each in your answer. You can offer the comparisons first and then the contrasts, or try to keep up a clear running commentary between the two sources.*

Second question – 4 marks

With reference to its origin, purpose and content, assess the values and limitations of Source A for historians studying the reasons why some people were able to survive the massacres.

Fourth question – 9 marks

Using the sources and your own knowledge, assess the reasons why so many Hutu took part in the massacres and the role that churches played in the genocide.

Comparisons:

- both sources indicate that the killing took place in a church.

- both mention the noise inside: "an uproar" (Source C) and "making a commotion" (Source D).

Contrasts

- Fulgence in Source C indicates that he went for two days, Alphonse doesn't say if he went on both days.

- Fulgence tells us about the weapon he used – a club; Alphonse doesn't give us this information.

- Alphonse mentions working systematically, "verified person by person, inspecting any faces". Fulgence on the other hand, talks of striking indiscriminately, "taking pot luck".

- Alphonse tells us that they took bodies outside to finish them off; Fulgence doesn't mention doing that.

- Fulgence seems to enjoy the work more; he says that he went home "without even thinking about it". Alphonse doesn't give his personal feelings other than insulting people as they died.

Alphonse describes how many of the people dies, "waiting for death in the calm of the church" whereas Fulgence describes it as "uproar".

The Nyarubuye massacre, 14–15 April 1994

Please don't kill me, I'll never be Tutsi again.

— 3-year-old boy, killed at Nyarubuye on 15 April 1994

In Kibungo province at the Nyarubuye church nine days after the start of the genocide, thousands of Tutsi gathered at the invitation of the local mayor, Sylvestre Gacumbitsi. A member of Habyarimana's MRND party, he was a powerful man in the area. This former church and school buildings were to be the scene of horrific violence, where more than 20,000 people were killed on 14–15 April, 1994.

> Nyarubuye is internationally known because it was the place that Fergal Keane, a BBC correspondent who was in Rwanda in late May and early June 1994, visited and filmed, and left a graphic account of the impact of his visit in his powerful book, "Season of Blood". The chapter on Nyarubuye and Keane's subsequent tracking down and interviewing of Sylvestre Gacumbitsi, and some of the survivors of the massacre are chilling, and excellent reading for anyone interested in the Rwandan genocide.

ATL Communication and thinking skills

Fergal Keane describes his visit to Nyarubuye in May, just a month after the massacre there.

We drove to Nyarubuye with Frank Ndore who was an RPF lieutenant and one they call a Kaadogo, a child soldier. They were our escorts. And I remember driving down through an area that had been liberated a few weeks before by the RPF; the striking thing was you would come across cattle wandering across the roads and, then, dogs. And we were warned to be very careful of the dogs because by this stage, the dogs had gotten very used to eating human flesh. They had lost their fear of human beings, so we were told, you know, whatever you do, avoid these animals … The RPF people were afraid of an Interahamwe coming across at night, so we had to get in and out of there rather quickly. I thought that we would go and we would see a massacre, but I didn't know what a massacre meant.

I had an intellectual understanding of what the word "massacre" meant from reading books. But books don't smell. Books don't rot. Books don't lie in stagnant pools. Books don't leach into the earth the way those bodies did. They can't tell you about it. Nothing can tell you about it except the experience of going there and seeing it.

We got out of the car, and in front of the church there were some bodies on the ground. And then we walked down this path through the church compound, and it was heavily overgrown, heavily overgrown because there had been rains. And then you find yourself walking along and you are stepping around and stepping over bodies. A colleague of mine, you know, almost tripped over the body of a kid. I know he's haunted by it to this day …

And it started to get dark and, then, we would enter the church. And there was no light in the church itself, so we had one little camera light, and we – you are walking around in the dark and suddenly the light points here and you see a kid's body. And you know it's a kid because he's wearing his khaki school uniform, and he's lying there, and his head has been bludgeoned away. And down in another corner, there is a man's body lying there. Up there, there also are bones, probably where dogs have been because there is no body left there, it's just bones.

And then it's really dark, it's really dark by this stage, and we have to go because the escorts are getting uncomfortable, they are starting to get afraid of the area. And as we are coming out, we hear noises, noises from one of the roads. I got very, very scared. And one of the drivers with us, a Ugandan, said, "Don't worry, it's only rats." Rats. And then we left. I just remember looking up at the church itself, and there is this white statue of Christ standing with his arms open. As you look down from him, there is (sic) the remains of a human body underneath, and then – I was raised as a Catholic, and I kind of drifted away big time from religion, but I prayed so hard. I prayed so hard because I was scared, but I prayed so hard, too, because I needed something good to hold onto at that moment. I really did. And I'm not the only one. There were lots of reporters who have had that experience – lots in Rwanda who went to those massacre sites at the time.

Questions

1 In this powerful piece of journalism, Keane comments that, "*I didn't know what a massacre meant*". How does he explain this?

2 Why do you think so many massacres took place in churches?

3 Assess the origin, purpose, value and limitation of this extract as a piece of historical writing. Read the section on the next page, *BBC correspondent Fergal Keane*, to help you with this task.

All Tutsis will perish. They will disappear from the earth. Slowly, slowly, slowly. We will kill them like rats.

— RTLM broadcast

At Nyarubuye the mayor, Sylvestre Gacumbitsi, gave orders for the police and the militia to move in and start the killing. By the time they had finished (two days late) thousands lay dead and dying – the rotting corpses of the dead being the scene Fergal Keane described above. Sylvestre Gacumbitsi was later sentenced to 30 years in prison for organizing and participating in the killing of 20,000 people in Nyarubuye, considered one of the worst acts of genocide in the 100 days. His sentence was later increased to life imprisonment.

This kind of massacre was happening all over the country in the first weeks after the death of the president. As the RPF responded in the only way it could, by taking up arms again, the interim government, well aware of the indecision amongst the international community, grew bolder in its actions and continued with its genocidal policies.

BBC correspondent Fergal Keane (1961 to the present day)

Fergel Keane is a BBC correspondent who, for over a decade, has reported from various international crises. The winner of numerous broadcast awards, including an OBE in 1996 for services to journalism, he was particularly affected by his experiences of genocide in Rwanda which he wrote about in his book *Season of Blood*. In late May and early June of 1994, as the killings in Rwanda were drawing to a close and as pockets of Tutsi were still being hunted down, Keane travelled for several weeks with the advancing Tutsi RPF forces. "*History has always been my great passion,*" comments Keane, who has recently become a professorial fellow at the University of Liverpool in England.

It was history that drew me to conflict, not the other way round. I have long been aware that conflicts have their roots in competing versions of history, and different groups trying to own competing narratives. Wherever I've reported from, I've always tried to ensure that the historical context is well understood.

Season of Blood has been described as essential reading for anyone interested in the madness that engulfed Rwanda in 1994. The opening chapter is as good a summary of the background to the conflict as students will find anywhere. This is a powerful and disturbing book and much more than a description of another terrible episode in human history.

The PBS website – http://www.pbs.org/wgbh/pages/frontline/shows/ghosts/ – is an outstanding resource for students. On this excellent website, which contains some powerful interviews and background material for an undertstanding of the genocide, Keane talks about why, after Rwanda, it was impossible for him to ever feel the same again about societies, humanity and himself.

Nothing prepared me for what I saw in Rwanda. … I will never forget on the way in, being confronted with the image of colleagues of mine whom I knew from the townships of South Africa, and looking at their eyes. They had just come out of Rwanda. And they were shattered. And I said, "What is this?" And one of them pulled me aside and he said, "It's spiritual damage, it's spiritual damage."

This interview was conducted in 2004, 10 years after the genocide. The people of the Nyarubuye massacre are the subject of the dedication in his book.

The nature of the genocide and other crimes against humanity: war rape

Rape was the rule, its absence was the exception.

— UN report

It has probably become more dangerous to be a woman than a soldier in an armed conflict.

— Patrick Cammaert, former commander to the UN Mission in the Congo
(quoted in de Brouwer and Ka Hon Chu, 2009: 9)

The next few weeks saw a wave of anarchy and mass killings in which the army and Hutu militia groups, the Interahamwe and Impuzamugambi played a major role in implementing the genocide. Inflamed by radio broadcasts which encouraged Hutu civilians to kill their Tutsi neighbours, it is obvious from the examples above that many participated in the killing. An estimated 200,000 Hutu participated in the genocide; some joined in gladly and killed for pleasure and gain; some were unwilling, threatened and killed for not complying with what others were doing around them.

When you read the manner of many of the killings, you may ask how and why people were able to do this to each other. The methods of killing were typically brutal, and tools such as wooden, spiked clubs (known as impiri), machetes, spears and crude instruments were often used to wound and incapacitate victims. Sometimes people were disabled and left to be finished off later, or died in slow, deliberately inflicted agony. The sheer number of those killed at Nyarubuye, for example, simply meant they could not all be killed in one day. Some of the killers reported how they cut the tendons of victims, to cause more pain and incapacitate them so they could return and finish them later (see the account by Philip Gourevicth on page 87). Machetes were the most common weapon used in the slaughter. Statistics show that in Butare province nearly 60% were killed with this weapon.

Rape was used as a weapon, including by perpetrators who were infected with HIV. In the genocide, tens of thousands of women and girls were raped and sexually humiliated. The aggressors used rape in a conscious attempt not only to humiliate, but to exterminate the Tutsi. Many had been influenced by the propaganda about Tutsi women promulgated in the period just before the genocide by such magazines as *Kangura* and the RTLM radio station (see the cartoon of Dallaire and the UNAMIR peacekeepers on page 56). Four of the Hutu Ten Commandments published in *Kanguru* (see page 45) portrayed Tutsi women as sexual weapons which could be used to weaken and destroy Hutu men. Tutsi women had traditionally been held in high esteem in Rwanda and depicted as beautiful and treacherous. Hutu rapists were willing to abuse, humiliate and denigrate the women they took. Some women were kept for weeks or months as sex slaves. In one town,

Pauline Nyiramasuhuko

Pauline Nyiramasuhuko, a school friend of Agathe Habyarimana, rose to become the minister for family affairs and women's development in Habyarimana's government. She promoted her son to organize militias to take part in the kidnap and rape of women and girls in Butare where she would also force people to undress before loading them on to trucks taking them to their death. Nyiramasuhuko is the first and only woman to be tried and found guilty by the UN International Criminal Tribunal for Rwanda for inciting rape and genocide. She and her son were both found guilty and sentenced to life imprisonment in 2011.

young women and girls were raped at the communal office, with the full knowledge of the mayor. Sylvestre Gacumbitsi, a friend of the Uwimana family, raped the daughter, Pendo Uwimana at Nyarubuye and then handed her over to other men. "*After that*" she said, "*they raped me with their truncheons.*" Pendo Uwimana survived.

Tutsi men were also sexually assaulted and abused, their genitals mutilated and sometimes displayed in public. Women were subjected to the worst treatment though. Attackers often mutilated women during the course of a rape or before killing them. They disfigured body parts which looked particularly "Tutsi", such as thin noses or slender fingers. They cut off breasts and punctured vaginas with spears or pointed sticks. Humiliation was also a part of the tactics against women. One witness recalls being taken with 200 other women after a massacre in Gitarama province. They were forced to watch as their husbands were killed and then the women were stripped and made to walk, "naked like a group of cattle", to Kabgayi, 10 miles away. When the group stopped at nightfall, some of the women were raped repeatedly.

During almost every conflict in the world, sexual violence has been perpetrated against women. Sexual violation of women erodes the fabric of a community. Violence against women by rapists can be seen as an attack upon the culture and, in many societies, women are viewed as the source of a community's cultural values. In Rwanda, the Minister of Women and the Family, Pauline Nyiramasuhuko, deliberately picked girls to be taken and raped by the militia.

Anne-Marie de Brouwer (2009) wrote:

> In the one hundred days of genocide that ravaged the small Central African nation of Rwanda … an estimated 250,000 to 500,000 women and girls were raped … Sexual violence occurred everywhere, and no one was spared

Many thousands of young women were infected by AIDS at the time and have been dying ever since; the genocide, in that sense, has continued.

In 1998 the ICTR prosecuted Jean-Paul Akayesu for rape and sexual violence against Tutsi women. He was the first man to be convicted by an international court for that crime. In 2004 the UN General Assembly passed a resolution affirming that the survivors of sexual violence faced the hardest task in Rwanda's future. Rape as a weapon in time of war was a notorious feature of the genocide. This was partly because of the organized propaganda which contributed significantly to violence against Tutsi women, and because of the public nature of the rapes.

TOK connections: Language, euphemism and ambiguity

What is the relation between the style of language used and the history written?

Language is a crucial vehicle for the acquisition and dissemination of knowledge. It is also an instrument in facilitating misinformation.

Like many human societies which live with hierarchical structures, whether it be Nazi Germany, Communist China, Stalinist Soviet Union or the government of Hutu Rwanda, euphemism has been used to convey as well as disguise meaning and true intent. Ambiguity in language can be deliberately cultivated in organized societies to have listeners select the meaning they desire, and not always the one intended by the speaker. In Nazi Germany the euphemism "the Final Solution" was used to refer to the plan

to annihilate Jews. The Japanese in China used "Unit 731" as a cover during the second world war for their experiments on Chinese and Russian prisoners, referring to them as "logs" or "Maruta", used in such contexts as "How many logs fell?"

In Rwanda, even prior to the killing in April 1994, genocide was referred to as "akazi gakomeye" in Kinyarwanda, which translates as "big job" or as "umuganda", which means "special work". The term "Inyenzi" has already been discussed. In addition, RTLM radio used the term "simusiga" or "hurricane" for what was happening – hiding the reality of a man-made genocide. Deceptions in language were echoed in deceptions in actions.

Other terms include the following.

Euphemism	Real meaning
"Tree felling"	killing
"Bush clearing"	the slaughter of men
"Pulling out the roots of the bad weeds"	the murder of women and children
"Going to work"	killing the enemy
"Using tools"	machetes, firearms, clubs and spears
"Finishing the work of the revolution"	killing the Tutsi from 1959 onwards
"Interethnic fighting"	genocide
"Accomplices, infiltrators, the minority"	all terms used to refer to the Tutsi
"The great mass, the majority people, and "the innocent"	all terms used to refer to the Hutu

Questions

Consider these points about euphemisms and ambiguity:

1 Examples are often found in campaign promises from politicians.

2 They can also be used for more artistic and pleasant purposes, in songs and poems.

3 Some go so far as to say that vagueness and ambiguity allow creativity.

4 Think of examples of language used in advertising, political speeches or songs to deliberately distort the meaning in a message. Share these will a partner or the group.

The role of the media

The role of the Rwandan media in serving the Habyarimana government and sowing the seeds of genocide has already been partially addressed. The two principal devices used to great effect were the magazine *Kangura* and the **RTLM radio station**. *Kangura* continued to spit forth hatred and propaganda when the genocide began in April, but it was probably the radio which became the most effective. RTLM broadcast in a popular, talk show format; appealing to the young, the unemployed, delinquents and particularly the thugs in the Hutu militia

> **Class discussion**
>
> How can one gauge the extent to which history is told from a particular cultural, national or individual perspective?

groups, the radio station used street language, disc jockeys, pop music and phone-ins. It was immediate, accessible and informative in support of the killers.

Since its introduction early in the 20th century, the radio has proved to be a remarkably powerful tool. It has been used both positively, as a vehicle of liberation and propaganda in the Cold War, and negatively, for example, in Nazi Germany between the two world wars. After the Cold War, nowhere in the world was the radio used as insidiously as in Rwanda, both before and during the genocide.

▼ RTLM – the "hate radio" of the Rwandan genocide

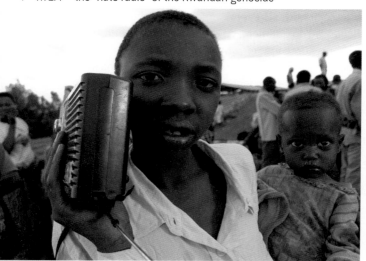

The UN and NGOs had warned of the central role the radio played in inciting ethnic tensions and encouraging murder. When the genocide began, others identified the media, and specifically the radio broadcasts, as an essential component which should be shut down. The UNAMIR commander Romeo Dallaire urged for RTLM to be taken off the air but the UN itself did not have the means to stop the radio station broadcasting – either through jamming, direct air strikes or covert means. The RPF, recognizing the effectiveness of the media in Hutu power, shelled the radio station in the first week of the genocide. However, within hours the station was transferred to a mobile unit from which it broadcast throughout the 100 days, through to the day before the RPF took Kigali on 4 July. Afterwards, it was broadcast from Gisenyi province and then from Zaire, where the Hutu government in exile used it to continue propagating its poisonous message.

It was the consistency of the message that worked so well. Through its informal, spontaneous and lifelike style, its use of eyewitnesses, and walkabout approach, the voices of ordinary people were delivered to the man in the street by political leaders and respected ministers. The impact of the radio made the war immediate for its listeners. Even some of the wounded RPF soldiers listened from their hospital beds. The radio played an active role in the mass killing by reading out lists of "enemies" who should be tracked down and killed. According to the broadcasts, anyone at the road blocks who did not have an identity card, *should be arrested and may lose his head"* (quoted in Metzl, 1997).

Action and inaction

Why didn't the international community attempt to control the media and, in particular, stop the radio broadcasts which they knew were being used to encourage genocide? There are three reasons why the US government did not:

- first, it would have been expensive;

- second, in the aftermath of Somalia, intervention in any African country would have been politically unpopular; and

- third, the issues relating to international law prevented it.

It is highly likely that the second reason was the most significant in determining US actions, although the government explained and justified its inaction by quoting the third reason, regarding international law. In May, the US Department of Defense recognized the role of the radio in the genocide but said that jamming it would be "ineffective and expensive" – it would cost about $8,500 per hour. Others in the administration countered with arguments regarding freedom of speech and the legality of such action. The bottom line was a lack of political will to become involved in Rwanda.

A BBC correspondent, Mark Doyle, said:

> *But why did the outside world allow this to happen in Rwanda, when it knew damn well what was going on? You have to conclude that it's because they're African. I don't see any other conclusion that is possible …*

The international media initially had an impact in Rwanda by its absence. It had been a media image that had contributed to the withdrawal of the USA from Somalia. Dead US servicemen being dragged through the streets of Mogadishu precipitated the US departure; would the same image have made a difference in Rwanda? Ten dead Belgian soldiers made the difference to that country's commitment. The lack of media almost certainly enabled those in the international community to *not* take action; the UNAMIR commander Romeo Dallaire is convinced of this. He commented later that the real crisis of the time was not in a small black African country; the media was more interested in Yugoslavia, the OJ Simpson case and Nelson Mandela's election in South Africa. All of these were, from the evidence, more important to the international media than the situation in Rwanda. The media, Dallaire believes, like so many others in the international community, failed Rwanda.

The importance of the media in the genocide is clearly demonstrated by the fact that afterwards, the UN tribunal for Rwanda established that men armed only with words could commit genocide. The judge stated that, "*Without a firearm, machete or any physical weapon, you caused the death of thousands of innocent civilians.*" It was the first time since the Nuremberg Trials that hate speech and words had been prosecuted as a war crime. Ngeze, the owner and editor of *Kangura*, and Nahimana, the founder of RTLM, were charged with responsibility for the systematic killing of the Tutsi people in Rwanda and each sentenced to 30 years in prison.

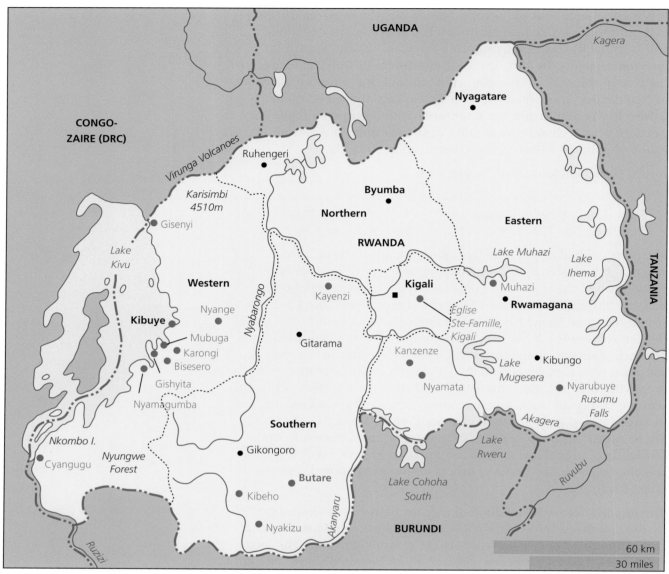

▲ Rwanda showing the sites of massacres in 1994

TOK – What does freedom of speech mean?

Consider the importance of the use of language as well as emotion and the ethics of free speech. The disseminators of ethnic hatred in Rwanda were sentenced to long terms in prison for what they did – or incited others to do. Arthur Koestler wrote in 1978:

Man's deadliest weapon is language. He is susceptible to being hypnotised by slogans as he is by infectious diseases. And where there is an epidemic, the group mind takes over

The "media trials" marked the first time since Nuremburg that hate speech has been prosecuted as a war crime.

You were fully aware of the power of words, and you used the radio – the medium of communication with the widest public reach – to disseminate hatred and violence,

wrote presiding Judge Navanethem Pillay in sentencing to life in prison Ferdinand Nahimana, founder of Radio Television des Mille Collines.

Without a firearm, machete or any physical weapon, you caused the death of thousands of innocent civilians.

Read more at http://www.washingtontimes.com/news/2003/dec/3/20031203-113817-3449r/#ixzz30VFX4wqK

Questions

1 With reference to propaganda and the media, Explain what you think Koestler meant in his quotation above.

2 Find examples of emotive language in a contemporary political speech or statement from the country where you are living, or in the contemporary world.

3 What does "freedom of speech" mean to you? Do you think that anyone ought to be able to express any opinion about anything they like?

4 What about opinions which you may not like or which may even include incitement to hatred, religious bigotry or gender discrimination?

Full document: Genocide in action: The anatomy of a massacre – Nyaraubuye, April 1994

Note: Although these extracts are longer than those which would appear in a Paper 1 exam, they are included to support your learning and understanding of the events in the genocide.

Source A

Note: The title of this publication is a quote from a letter written in an appeal to Pastor Elizaphan Ntakirutimana, who was tried by the ICTR with his son, for their part in killing thousands of Tutsi.

P. Gourevitch. *We Wish to Inform You That Tomorrow We Will Be Killed With Our Families: Stories from Rwanda (1998).*

In the province of Kibungo, in eastern Rwanda, in the swamp and pastureland near the Tanzanian border, there's a rocky hill called Nyarubuye with a church where many Tutsis were slaughtered in mid-April of 1994. A year after the killing I went to Nyarubuye with two Canadian military officers. We flew in a United Nations helicopter, traveling low over the hills in the morning mists, with the banana trees like green starbursts dense over the slopes. The uncut grass blew back as we dropped into the centre of the parish schoolyard. A lone soldier materialized with his Kalashnikov, and shook our hands with stiff, shy formality. The Canadians presented the paperwork for our visit, and I stepped up into the open doorway of a classroom. At least fifty mostly decomposed cadavers covered the floor, wadded in clothing, their belongings strewn about and smashed. Macheted skulls had rolled here and there.

The dead looked like pictures of the dead. They did not smell. They did not buzz with flies. They had been killed thirteen months earlier, and they hadn't been moved. I had never been among the dead before. What to do? Look? Yes. I wanted to see them, I suppose; I had come to see them – the dead had been left unburied at Nyarubuye for memorial purposes – and there they were, so intimately exposed. I didn't need to see them. I already knew, and believed, what

had happened in Rwanda. … at Nyarubuye, and at thousands of other sites in this tiny country, on the same days of a few months in 1994, hundreds of thousands of Hutus had worked as killers in regular shifts. There was always the next victim, and the next. What sustained them, beyond the frenzy of the first attack, through the plain physical exhaustion and mess of it? … The killers killed all day at Nyarubuye. At night they cut the Achilles tendons of survivors and went off to feast behind the church, roasting cattle looted from their victims in big fires, and drinking beer. (Bottled beer, banana beer … Rwandans may not drink more beer than other Africans, but they drink prodigious quantities of it around the clock.) And, in the morning, still drunk after whatever sleep they could find beneath the cries of their prey, the killers at Nyarubuye went back and killed again. Day after day, minute to minute, Tutsi by Tutsi: all across Rwanda, they worked like that.

Source B

"Massacre at Nyarubuye church", by Fergal Keane, 4 April 2004.

Go to http://news.bbc.co.uk/1/hi/programmes/panorama/3582267.stm to read Fergal Keane's report for the BBC.

Source C

Photograph of the corpses of Tutsi that litter the floor of a classroom at Nyarabuyu church, Rwanda, 1994.

Source D

"Heart of Rwanda's Darkness: Slaughter at a rural church", an article by Donatella Lorch, published in *The New York Times* on 3 June 1994.

The banner across the entrance to the red brick church here announces the celebration of a festival. A poster of Pope John Paul II is tacked on the main door and above it is a large white statue of Jesus, his arms beckoning. Inside are the remains of victims of a mass slaughter carried out by Government-trained militiamen in mid-April. In what they had hoped would be a refuge from the deadly irrationality of tribal and political violence, more than 500 members of the Tutsi tribe found their way to the church compound only to be shot or hacked to death by Hutu soldiers in classrooms, bathrooms and courtyards, and then left to rot. It appears that they were methodically hunted down, first in the church, then in the school and finally in the workshops near the soccer field. Residents say that probably 1,000 more were killed and buried in mass graves in the town, which is just inside the border with Tanzania. A frenzy of killing was evident at the rear of the compound. There, eight rooms are filled with hundreds of corpses, shoulder to shoulder, and piled onto one another. One hundred more killed in a courtyard are now half skeletons, their flesh in shreds. There are so many that it is impossible to walk through without treading on them. More corpses are hidden in the tall grass. "It took them two days to kill everyone in the church," said Consolata Mukatwagirimana, 27, a Tutsi whose family was killed at home and who like the rest of the townspeople has fled to a camp 50 miles away. She accompanied reporters to the church. This village, now under control of the Rwandan Patriotic Front, the rebel group led by the minority Tutsi tribe, appears typical of many devastated by regular Army troops or militiamen of the majority Hutu tribe in the early days of the two-month old civil war. The buildings are empty, the livestock is gone. Only corpses and the sound of the wind remain.

The massacre here took place on April 16 and 17. And while it is one of the largest known so far, it is one of more than a dozen uncovered in Rwanda since civil war broke out on April 6 … A dozen bodies lay sprawled in the brick church's main courtyard, some no more than pieces of flesh and skeletons dressed in clothes. One woman was hacked to death as she ran away. She lies face down, one arm outstretched, the other clutching her small child, decapitated. In the church, pieces of human flesh lie in between the low wooden pews. Bones and a skull clutter the altar.

The classrooms still have the chalked lessons on the blackboards. In one, the lesson of the day had been French conjugation. More than a dozen boys were killed there. Almost all the residents have left. But too old to move, Chrisostome Gatunzi, a Hutu who says he is between 80 and 90 years old, stayed behind with his thin, frail wife. They live in a small house several hundred yards off the main road, tended by a nine-year-old grandson who just returned after three weeks hiding in the countryside. Mr. Gatunzi says he heard the screams and watched his neighbours being killed but was too weak to do anything. He talks about how he watched the militias, in groups of 20, round up residents, kill them and then throw their bodies in mass graves a few hundred yards from his house. He cannot hold back his anger and pain. He chokes when he speaks. "I witnessed when they hacked them and put them into a pit," Mr. Gatunzi said. "I knew some of them. I don't know why others want to kill Tutsis. We have lived together for such a long time as neighbours and friends. It's unbelievable seeing your neighbour hacked to death. These people are saying they want to create a new Rwanda. How can you do that by killing neighbours and friends? It has hurt my heart so much."

Source E

Flora Mukampore, a survivor from the massacre at Nyarubuye recalls what happened to her. She knew one of the killers personally.

Gitera was there. Imagine someone leaving their home and knowing their victim, knowing their names and the names of their

children. They all went there and killed their neighbours, their wives and their children. All the people they were cutting fell on me because I was near the door. My hair was all washed with blood. My body was drenched in blood and it was starting to dry on me, so the killers thought I'd been cut all over, they thought I was dead. I lay down on one side with only one eye open. I could hear a man come towards me and I guess he saw me breathe. He hit me on my head saying: "Is this thing still alive?" Immediately I heard my entire body say "whaaagh". Something in my head changed forever. Everything stopped. When the wind blew and the cold passed through my body I woke up and went into the building but I didn't realise that there were bodies around me. I didn't remember what had happened. I just thought they were normal people and so I just slept among them like we had slept together before the killers came. Can you imagine living with the dead. At some point god helped me and made me unconscious because if I hadn't been, I think I would have killed myself. But I was unconscious, and anyway killing yourself needs energy.

Flora was found by some children who'd also survived. 17 of her family members had been killed.

They sat me up and I realised there were maggots and I started taking them off myself.

Can you imagine people died on the 15th of April and I lived among the bodies until the 15th of May?

First question, part a – 3 marks

What evidence does Source D offer as to the numbers of victims involved in the massacre at Nyarubuye? What might account for the discrepancy between these figures and later accounts?

First question, part b – 2 marks

What is the message conveyed through Source C?

Second question – 4 marks

According to Sources A and D, what might have been the motives for which Hutus were prepared to take part in the killing of their neighbours?

Second question – 4 marks

With reference to their origins, purpose and content, assess the value and limitations of Sources C and E, for anyone wishing to understand why a massacre took place at Nyarubuye in April 1994.

Third question – 6 marks

Compare and contrast the motives for killing the Tutsi by the three individuals in Source B.

References and further reading

Dallaire, R. 2003. *Shake Hands with the Devil: The Failure of Humanity in Rwanda*. Random House, Toronto, Canada

Gourevitch, P. 1998. *We Wish to Inform You That Tomorrow We Will Be Killed With Our Families: Stories from Rwanda*. Farrar Straus and Giroux. New York, USA

http://www.pbs.org/wgbh/pages/frontline/shows/ghosts/

http://www.rwandanstories.org/genocide/ntarama_church.html

http://www.washingtontimes.com/news/2003/dec/3/20031203-113817-3449r/#ixzz30VFX4wqK

1.7 The response of the international community

▲ Ambassador Colin Keating of New Zealand, President of the UN Security Council early in 1994. To his right is the Secretary General, Boutros Boutros-Ghali

The United Nations Assistance Mission for Rwanda (UNAMIR)

As the death toll mounted, the calls for international action became louder. Following the deaths of the Belgian peacekeepers, within days, instead of bolstering the mission as requested by Dallaire, the Belgian government turned tail and withdrew its troops. Emboldened by this, the interim government forces stepped up the killing.

Elections are held in the October session of the General Assembly for five non-permanent seats on the UN Security Council. By coincidence, a seat had been handed to the government of Rwanda in January 1994. This meant that as soon as Habyarimana was killed and the interim government took over, Rwanda's representative in New York was privy to all the council's discussions on what was being proposed regarding the situation in Rwanda. So they knew about the Belgians' planned withdrawal and how the United States, France and the UK were unwilling to increase the numbers for UNAMIR, or do anything about what was happening inside the country. On 16 April, civilian and military leaders among the Hutu-dominated government made the decision to extend the genocide; within two weeks, an estimated 100,000 people were killed.

In Kigali, General Dallaire and the UNAMIR appeared to be helpless. Dallaire had requested help, warned the UN Security Council of the prospect of genocide and specifically requested an increase in the numbers of peacekeeping forces. Instead, on 20 April, Belgium's peace keepers withdrew and urged other countries to do the same. The following day the council passed a resolution to reduce the UNAMIR to a token force of 270, and for the remaining peacekeepers to try and arrange a cease-fire between the RPF and the Hutu-dominated interim government. The fact that the UNAMIR continued to save lives is testament to the men who remained behind, and to the will of General Dallaire.

The part played by the UNAMIR

Dallaire sent in daily radio logs describing the situation in Rwanda, which was spiralling out of control. He recognized early on that what was happening was a genocide and later wrote, "*One would have to have been blind or illiterate not to know what was going on in Rwanda*" (Dallaire, 2004: 306). As peacekeepers were pulled out and foreign nationals abandoned Rwanda, the RPF forces and Rwandan government forces were lining up to fight for supremacy. By the end of April, the RPF were beginning to control eastern parts of Rwanda and the pace of killing increased. At that time, the term "genocide" had been used by Oxfam and mentioned in reports made to the UN. On 28 April, a spokesperson for the US State Department was asked whether what was happening in Rwanda constituted genocide. She replied, "*The use of the term 'genocide' has a very precise legal meaning, although it's not strictly a legal determination. There are other factors in there as well*" (Shelley, 1994).

Despite its restricted mandate, the UNAMIR sought to intervene between the Hutu killers and Tutsi civilians and also tried to mediate between the RPF and the Rwandan army. The UNAMIR's inability to play a more effective role in preventing the breakdown of law and order was partially a consequence of the part played by former Cameroonian Foreign Minister Jacques-Roger Booh-Booh. Appointed as Head of Mission by the Secretary General Boutros Boutros-Ghali (a personal friend), in his reports Booh-Booh undoubtedly played down the significance of the Hutu genocide and consistently held a more conservative position in reporting to the Security Council than did the UN commander on the ground, General Dallaire. On 21 April 1994, the Security Council, at the request of the USA (which had no troops in Rwanda), voted to withdraw all but a remnant of the UNAMIR mission. Incredibly, the council took this vote and others in 1994 while the representative of the genocidal regime sat among them. There was no condemnation of the regime until just before the final victory by the RPF. Dallaire was in no doubt who was responsible for the abandonment of Rwanda at this time in the international forum. He blamed the three permanent members of the Security Council: the USA, France and the UK.

Reasons for inaction: the role of France, Belgium and the USA

There is no doubt that the UNAMIR was hampered from the beginning by the lack of support and divisions among some of the leading countries as to what action should be taken. The mandate of the UNAMIR was essentially a watered-down peacekeeping role; it was understaffed, poorly equipped, lacked sufficient funding and was met by stonewalling tactics by the big powers in New York. Days after the genocide began, the UN Security Council had voted to reduce the mission and, as Dallaire and the UNAMIR attempted to sort out what was happening and provide zones of safety for those being killed, the world watched while Rwanda burned.

> *They cannot tell us or tell me that they didn't know. They were told every day what was happening there. So then don't come back to me and tell me sorry, we didn't know. Oh no. Everybody knew, every day, every minute.*

> — Philippe Gaillard, head of the Red Cross in Rwanda throughout the genocide

Some of those on the ground in Rwanda, but not all, saw the war almost immediately as genocide, and not simply as a particularly violent civil war which had re-ignited between the Rwandan government and the rebel RPF. However, the outside world, some of whom did not want to commit troops, money or support, chose not to see it as genocide. Mark Doyle was one of the first BBC reporters in Rwanda, and for a short time the only foreign correspondent there. In an interview in 2003 he commented:

> *The sheer scale of the killing was just unbelievable. Even at the time, I think it would be fair [to say] that we didn't realize the scale of it. It wasn't for several weeks that I realized that this wasn't just a tribal war, one lot of people killing another lot of people and the others fighting back. It was a pretty one-sided operation. It was a very efficient genocide. [But] I didn't use the word "genocide" for several weeks, because I didn't have enough information to be able to say that. It's believed in the first couple of weeks – I remember reporting*

100,000 people had been killed. Well, people don't get killed on that scale in an ordinary war, but there were two wars going on. There was a war between two pretty efficient armies, by African standards – the RPF and the government forces were both serious armies, relatively small, but serious and disciplined in their way. But there was another war going on at the same time, a parallel war, which was the genocide war involving the government army and the government militias, as we now know. But it wasn't clear for several weeks that there were these two parallel wars going on.

This partially explains the inaction of some of the major powers who could have stepped in to prevent such a massacre. In some cases, it was deliberate policy not to become involved. Later, when the UN called for an independent inquiry as to why it had not prevented the genocide, it returned a catalogue of failures. Effective intelligence on the ground was offered as a reason why the UN had failed to take action as well as a shortage of equipment. Overall though, it was a lack of political will among the member states. In this, there are some who surely bear more responsibility than others in the tragedy. Reinforcing his judgement, Dallaire blames the UN as a whole and commented:

Ultimately, led by the United States, France and the United Kingdom, this world body aided and abetted genocide in Rwanda. No amount of cash and aid will ever wash its hands clean of Rwandan blood

— Dallaire, 2003: 323

The role of Belgium

Belgium, as the former colonial ruler of Rwanda, had a close connection with the country. The part Belgium played in its former colony and the impact of its ethnic policies have already been indicated. What is now being discussed is the role Belgium played during the genocide itself. When the UNAMIR was formed in 1993 the Belgians contributed the largest contingent of Western troops to the mission. Belgium presented itself as a specialist on African affairs with considerable connections to the region over many years. However, it was the killing of 10 Belgian peacekeepers, the charges levelled at the Belgians for having been involved in the assassination of Habyramana followed by the rapid decision to withdraw its troops, which set in motion the killing spree. The informer, "Jean-Pierre", had revealed that the people behind the genocide were counting on the fact that Western nations would be unwilling to tolerate casualties and would pull out of the mission if their peacekeepers were killed.

An independent inquiry was set up in 1999 to examine the actions of the UN during the 1994 genocide. It was chaired by Ingvar Carlsson. During the inquiry, in a report to the UN Security Council, Dallaire described Belgium's withdrawal of its remaining troops as a *"terrible blow to the mission."* His assistant, Major Beardsley, stated in an interview:

I think they'd [the Hutu] watched the news media very carefully. They watched Somalia, and they knew that big Western countries did not have the will to go into black Africa and take casualties. They had watched what would happen, that they could get rid of us or thought they could get rid of us any time they wanted, just by inflicting casualties upon our contingent. So

I don't think they were intimidated by us at all. I think they knew us better than we knew ourselves. They definitely knew the strengths of the UN and the weaknesses of the UN better than we did …

Belgium's attitude to the UN proved to be important in supporting the approach of France and the USA to advocate a policy of non-intervention in Rwanda. Following the death of their peacekeepers, Belgium and France sent soldiers to rescue their citizens in the days which followed. This rapid and successful mission demonstrated that they had the capacity to intervene, and possibly to have prevented, or at least mitigated, the genocide had they wished to do so. Essentially, the Belgian government panicked; public opinion at home was evenly split between withdrawal and remaining. Most of the Belgian soldiers wanted to stay in Rwanda to continue the mission and were humiliated by their government's decision to withdraw. In 1999 the Carlsson inquiry, concluded:

The manner in which the troops left, including attempts to pretend to the refugees that they were not in fact leaving, was disgraceful.

Colonel Luc Marchal, the commander of Belgium's UNAMIR contingent, later wrote:

Our political leaders should have known that in leaving UNAMIR, we would condemn thousands of men, women, and children to certain death … It is not surprising that many of them … threw down their blue berets in disgust upon their return to Belgium.

This was a moment of shame for Belgium but more importantly, it was to be a death sentence for untold numbers of Tutsi.

The role that Belgium played in Rwanda had been a highly significant one. Some historians, such as Gérard Prunier, see the country as bearing considerable responsibility as the former colonial power, for the promotion of the Tutsi over the Hutu. This had been done in order to facilitate greater control over Rwanda. Belgium was the best informed and probably the most eligible to speak on Rwanda, and its decision to withdraw from the country was critical.

The role of France

The roles played by both France and the USA have, arguably, aroused the most controversy; the latter for what it could and perhaps should have done, and the former, for the part it played prior to the genocide, during it, and its efforts to bring it to a conclusion. From 1990 to December 1993, France openly supported the regime of Juvénal Habyarimana against the RPF. France encouraged the talks leading to the Arusha Accords while at the same time training the Rwandan army and the Interahamwe militia. Even as French soldiers left Rwanda, there still remained operatives working undercover and helping the Habyarimana regime train members of the presidential guard. Their sending of 600 elite French troops in October 1990 when the RPF invasion began, saved Kigali from possible attack. They were present in Kigali in and near the airport when the president's plane was shot down. Then in the last weeks of the genocide in late June, French soldiers were deployed on the border with Rwanda and Zaire to set up a safe zone

> ### François Mitterrand, 1916–96
>
> President of France throughout the period of the Rwandan civil war and genocide. Mitterrand was a socialist, steeped in the tradition of the left in France. He fought in the Second World War and gained the presidency in 1981. He became the only president to win a second term through popular vote in 1988. His African policies were devised in secret, with virtually no accountability to parliament in France. Many of these policies – including actions in Rwanda – were made in the confines of a special office in the President's Elysée Palace known as the Africa Unit.

under what is known as **Operation Turquoise**. This both offered some protection to the Tutsi from being murdered but also allowed significant numbers of Hutu killers to escape into Zaire.

The policy of the French in supporting the legitimate Hutu-dominated government was to avoid a military victory for the rebel RPF. They were seen as part of an Anglophone plot supported by Uganda to create an English-speaking region in East Africa from which French credibility, prestige and influence in Africa would never recover. Mitterand believed that they needed to stop the francophone country becoming the first domino to fall in the feared anglophone "invasion" (Wallis, 2007: 25).

In recent years, scholars have looked more closely at the French role in Rwanda. Andrew Wallis has written "Silent Accomplice: The Untold Story of France's Role in the Genocide" in 2007 and another scholar, Daniela Kroslak, who has written extensively on the role of France in the genocide, concluded that, while France was not a perpetrator, the country can be held responsible both for what it did, and for what it did not do in Rwanda. Her criteria for judging France's responsibility were knowledge, involvement and capacity. Kroslak argues that France enabled the genocide to take place through its support for the Hutu regime before, during and after the killing in 1994. Supporting the debate regarding France's role in Rwanda has been the work of British journalist Linda Melvern. She is honorary professor at the University of Aberystwyth, a consultant at the International Criminal Tribunal for Rwanda and author of a number of books on the Rwandan genocide. Her analysis suggests that France's position was to avoid a victory by the Tutsi-led RPF. The Mitterrand government was keen to portray the RPF as Ugandan Anglophones, American trained and terrorists. He deliberately discriminated against the RPF, even describing them as "Khmer Noir" (Black Khmers) referring to the genocidal government of Pol Pot and the Khmer Rouge in Cambodia in the late 1970s. Ironically, the French government had supported Pol Pot in their revolution (Wallis p. 26). After the death of Habyarimana, France was the only country to recognize the interim government that committed the genocide. Throughout those fateful months, France continued to send weapons to the genocidiares despite the arms embargo. Recent events too in France have encouraged debate concerning its role in the Rwandan genocide and, far from the whitewash the National Assembly gave itself and the country in 1998, further questions are being asked as more evidence comes to light.

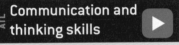

Communication and thinking skills

Go to http://www.france24.com/en/20120112-debate-Rwanda-Genocide/

Watch this clip from a 2011 debate shown on French television, which includes a discussion with Linda Melvern and Gerard Prunier. François Picard's panel argues whether there has been a cover-up in the past.

Operation Amaryllis, April 1994

On 8 April 1994, two days after the president's plane was shot down, France launched **Operation Amaryllis**, dispatching 500 French soldiers to secure the evacuation of foreign residents, nearly all of whom were Westerners. According to the UNAMIR's Colonel Luc Marchal, the French planes brought with them five tons of ammunition. They also evacuated leading members of the Habyarimana regime, including the former president's wife who, it has since been revealed, received $40,000 from the French government when she arrived in France, taken from a sum of money designated for Rwandan refugees.

For some commentators, Operation Amaryllis showed what could have been done immediately to enhance the UNAMIR's chances of preventing violence at the start of the genocide. Operation Amaryllis was terminated on 14 April.

France remained active in discussions at the UN regarding the reinforcement of the UNAMIR and efforts to promote a cease-fire, but the role it played also served to weaken UN efforts to prevent the genocide in April and May. Later commissions of inquiry in France exonerated themselves completely from any responsibility in aiding and abetting the genocidal government. Meanwhile members of the interim government in Rwanda recognized the importance of retaining French support in April 1994 and kept the French ambassador in Kigali informed of what they wanted him to know. Mitterrand's government in Paris welcomed a delegation from Rwanda's interim government and this highly visible contact with the genocidaires was another reason why their role has come under scrutiny. At the time, Bruno Delaye, special adviser to President Mitterrand commented *"You cannot deal with Africa without getting your hands dirty"* (quoted in The Human Rights Report, 1999).

ATL Self-management skills

The role played by France in the Rwandan genocide would make a good Internal Assessment topic. In March 2014 a collection of documents obtained from French archives have been released by the National Security Archive in the USA through George Washington University. This is an extract from the National Security Archive website.

> The documents posted today in English and French are extracted from hundreds of documents released by a French parliamentary commission in 1998 and the so-called "Mitterrand archive", which was leaked to French researchers from 2005 onwards. While the provenance of the Mitterrand archive remains unclear, the authenticity of the documents has been confirmed by former Mitterrand aides, French researchers and lawyers involved in a series of cases related to the genocide. While the documents contained in the Mitterrand archive provide a valuable insight into official French thinking, the unauthorized nature of their release also raises problems for independent researchers. It is impossible to know, for example, how many documents are missing from the archive, and the reasons for their non-disclosure. The motivations of those who leaked the documents also remain unclear.

> http://www2.gwu.edu/~nsarchiv/NSAEBB/NSAEBB461

France continued to maintain links with the Rwandan government throughout April and into May 1994. The UNAMIR and independent bodies also reported seeing French-speaking white men in military uniform in and around Kigali during these months. They may have been mercenaries, but the French government continues to deny any knowledge of them. As more evidence came out of Rwanda regarding the genocide, pressure was put on the French government in France itself. Alain Juppé, French Foreign minister in 1994, announced in mid-June that France would send troops to the country *"to stop the massacres and to protect the populations threatened with extermination"* (quoted in the Human Rights Report, 1999).

Operation Turquoise, June 1994

France called for a cease-fire in late May and into June, even though it was clear that the Hutu government was continuing the genocide. However, the Hutu government was also losing the civil war to the RPF. Kroslak and others believe that there were ulterior motives for the French actions in June. In France, the genocide was certainly now receiving more attention in the media than it had before, and raising questions about the French government's role in support of the previous government. It was an election year and Mitterrand was anxious to show that France still retained a high profile in the region. The RPF was clearly winning and its capture of the important town of Gitarama in mid-June indicated that the rebels might completely sweep aside the Hutu majority. France obtained the backing of the UN to lead Operation Turquoise from 22 June, to protect "threatened populations" on both sides in the conflict. In the National Assembly inquiry in 1998, French Prime Minister Edouard Balladur claimed that France had been *"the only country in the world to have acted"* and rejected all charges of having ulterior motives. (For more details go to http://www.hrw.org/reports/pdfs/r/rwanda/rwanda993.pdf).

The responses to the French decision to send troops from those involved in Rwanda are revealing: the RPF angrily condemned the initiative as a ploy aimed at saving the tottering Hutu government and would not allow French troops into Kigali. RPF leader Paul Kagame said, *"Tell France that Kigali can handle more body bags than Paris"*. The Organisation of African Unity (OAU) let France know that it strongly disapproved of any such move which might bolster the genocidal regime. The UNAMIR commander Romeo Dallaire was suspicious of the sudden nature of the French intervention when he had been petitioning the UN for troops for so long. In France too, there was some cynicism; the newspaper *Le Monde* questioned why it had taken the French government so long to act and why it had chosen to do so just as the RPF was gaining the upper hand in the war.

This intervention would cause problems for the UNAMIR as its role had already been hampered by a severely restricted mandate, whereas it seemed this French humanitarian action was to be granted the wider powers that Dallaire had been asking for, throughout the crisis, and before. In 1999, a UN report for the Security Council agreed with this assessment and noted that the French-led mission Operation Turquoise was conducted with the authorization of the UN Security Council but not under the UN. Having two operations was "problematic" it said, and (as stated in a letter from the Secretary General to the UN Security Council in December 1999) it concluded:

> *The Inquiry finds it unfortunate that the resources committed by France and other countries to Operation Turquoise could not instead have been put at the disposal of UNAMIR.*

On 22 June, 2,300 elite French troops landed at Goma in Zaire and deployed their soldiers in a zone in the south-west of Rwanda. They arrived with heavy equipment and massive firepower, which seemed inconsistent with a humanitarian mission. The Hutu government greeted their arrival gleefully and RTLM even told Hutu girls to look forward to

For more details see http://www.securitycouncilreport.org/

making the French soldiers welcome. In Kigali, General Dallaire noted a hardening of attitudes among the RPF to the UNAMIR.

The deployment of the French intervention force led to a resurgence of killing by the Hutu in some areas. However, once their soldiers were on the ground, the French finally saw the reality of what was happening. In Gikongoro, massacres had taken place in the first weeks of April. One French soldier commented, *"We were manipulated. We thought the Hutu were the good guys and the victims"*.

Despite the belief that the entry of France might help its chances, the Hutu government remained on the point of collapse. The RPF advance across the country, and particularly the siege of the capital Kigali, was to last for less than two weeks after the beginning of Operation Turquoise. In early July, members of the interim government left Kigali for the safe zone, taking with them most of the state funds, the leaders of the Interahamwe and much of the remaining army. Prime Minister Kambanda announced, *"We have lost the military battle but the war is by no means over because we have the people behind us"* (quoted in Melvern, 2004: 248). On 4 July Paul Kagame's rebel RPF took control of Kigali and announced the formation of a new government from ministers previously named in the Arusha Accords. Without this military victory, the genocide would have certainly continued. Two weeks later, a cease-fire was declared in Rwanda.

The French operation certainly saved the lives of many Tutsi as the RPF made its advance. Once the contingent arrived and established a safe zone there were no longer any large-scale killings. However, the French military presence also helped a significant number of Hutu militia and those responsible for the genocide to escape the country. There is some evidence that the French continued to supply some former government soldiers with weaponry, delivered through their ally, President Mobutu of Zaire. In the coming months, the French military flew a number of genocidaires out of Goma to unidentified destinations including Colonel Théoneste Bagosora, the genocide leader, as well as members of the Interahamwe. A number of former members of the interim government were given asylum in France. Until now there has been a complete absence of will within the French government to bring to justice any of the estimated 27 Rwandan genocide fugitives who live on French soil. Only in 2014, 20 years after the genocide, was the first of the genocidaires put on trial: Pascal Simbikangwa, the defendant in Paris,

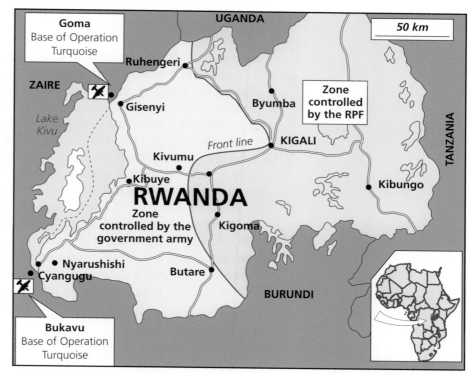

▲ The battlefront in Rwanda, late June, 1994

was a member of the inner circle of power in Rwanda that devised and implemented the genocide.

In August 1994, Operation Turquoise officially ended. By then the RPF had won and the genocide was effectively over, or at least the 100 days of slaughter had ended. The role played by France in Rwanda was a significant one and the consequences of French policy were substantial. Paris continued to formally recognize the genocidal interim government for 10 weeks after it had launched the genocide. Both during and after the genocide, France remained unrepentant of its own role and considered itself to be blameless for any aspect of the Rwandan tragedy. Alain Juppé, French foreign minister in 1994, said later that it was, *"unacceptable to lay the blame on France"*, and Eduard Balladur, the prime minister (quoted in an article published in *The New York Times* on 8 April 2014), commented, *"On the contrary, it [France] of all countries in the world was the only one that took the initiative to organise a humanitarian operation to prevent widespread massacres."* Regarding the part played by Mitterrand himself, some critics of the French president nicknamed him "Mitterehamwe" (Wallis, p.214).

On the 20th anniversary of the genocide in 2014, relations were again strained between Rwanda and France following an accusation by Paul Kagame (quoted in an article published in *The New York Times* on 6 April 2014) that both France and Belgium had a direct role in the *"political preparation of the genocide"*.

The roles played by both European powers still remain controversial.

The role of the USA

The USA is often blamed as the country bearing the most responsibility for the lack of action in Rwanda and, because of the USA's influence and the role it has played in crises around the world in the second half of the 20th century, the record of the US handling of the Rwandan genocide is a poor one. Despite the overwhelming evidence of what was happening (participants such as Gaillard and Dallaire are in no doubt that the US government knew that genocide was happening, and who the perpetrators were), US officials decided against taking a leading role in challenging the situation in Rwanda. What is more damaging to the USA's reputation is that they and other international leaders declined for weeks to use their political and moral authority to challenge the legitimacy of the genocidal government and used their influence to actively discourage a strong UN response.

On 25 March 1998 President Bill Clinton landed at Kigali, stayed for three and a half hours and made a speech to the Rwandan nation delivering what has became known as the **Clinton apology**. He began by saying, *"I have come today to pay the respect of my nation to all who suffered and all who perished in the Rwandan genocide."*

As the genocide was recognized as such in 1994, the USA has come under criticism for its lack of leadership during the crisis. Scholars have examined the role of the US government harshly. Among the figures leading the criticism is Samantha Power.

Indeed, staying out of Rwanda was an explicit US policy objective.

– Samantha Power, US ambassador to the UN

Serving as the US Ambassador to the UN (in 2014), Power is an academic turned diplomat who wrote an excellent critique of US foreign policy in Rwanda entitled "Bystanders to genocide", published in the *Atlantic Monthly* in 2001. You can can read the complete article at

http://www.theatlantic.com/magazine/archive/2001/09/bystanders-to-genocide/304571/

"Bystanders to Genocide" is described as *"a chilling narrative of self-serving caution and flaccid will – and countless missed opportunities to mitigate a colossal crime"*.

In the article, Power questions why the US government played so marginal a role in the Rwandan situation; was it deliberate policy and if so, why was this the case? It is clear that she, along with participants and other historians agree that it was a lack of will by the government. *"Non-intervention was US policy, not an oversight,"* commented John Ryle, in an article published in *The Guardian* on 13 April 1998.

Philip Gourevitch commented that *"the Clinton Administration's policy was, 'Let's withdraw altogether. Let's get out of Rwanda. Leave it to its fate.'"* Alison Forges also believes that the US government knew what was happening and chose to ignore it, *"in part because they saw Rwanda through the prism of Somalia"* (quoted in a Human Rights Watch report, 2004: 946).

So what was the role of the USA in Rwanda? Before the civil war, Rwanda had not been on the radar of the US government to any great degree. After the Cold War there were certainly other issues and interests in areas of the world which, in the eyes of the USA, were more worthy of attention. When Clinton came into office in 1992, the USA's concern in Rwanda was simple – a desire to encourage the peace process and moves towards democracy – however the USA showed little interest in human rights or ethnic issues. The deaths of 18 US soldiers in Somalia in October 1993 shocked the US government and determined official reaction to events elsewhere in the region. In January 1994 a new peacekeeping doctrine established rigorous conditions for any future UN peacekeeping operations involving the USA. This was **Presidential Decree Directive 25 (PDD25)** which was written, in effect, to prevent US forces being used by the UN against US foreign policy interests; in reality it was to make any effort on behalf of the world's remaining superpower negligible in the near future. This determined the role of the USA in Rwanda. Domestic political considerations would take priority over disasters abroad – unless, as cynics pointed out, these involved oil or white people. *"Rwanda was small, poor, remote and African – in their eyes, irrelevant to the national interest"* (Human Rights Watch report).

If Rwanda was not to be a priority for the USA, what made the USA's role much more harmful to the Rwandan people were US actions in the UN Security Council. Not only were the Americans unprepared to do anything themselves in Rwanda during the genocide, they actively dissuaded others from intervening. In 1998, Alan Kuperman (quoted in an article published in *The Washington Post* on 25 December 1998) commented: *"The United States almost single-handedly blocked international action in Rwanda six weeks prior to the genocide, which might have prevented the bloodbath altogether"*. Kuperman later went on to defend US actions in Rwanda arguing that others share the blame and that policy makers did not recognize the

Communication and thinking skills

Read or listen to a speech by Bill Clinton (US president, 1993–2001) using the link given.

PBS "Frontline" – "The triumph of evil": http://www.pbs.org/wgbh/pages/frontline/shows/evil/etc/script.html

Clinton used the term "genocide" 11 times in the speech. After his presidency was over, Clinton often referred to Rwanda as his greatest regret.

Watch or listen to the speech made by Clinton in 1998 by going to:

http://www.history.com/speeches/the-clinton-apology#the-clinton-apology (two-minute extract)
or
https://www.youtube.com/watch?v=R_6CFNwJ9ww

Questions

1 Why did the USA not do more for Rwanda during this period?

2 Debate the role played by the USA in Rwanda?

killings as genocide early enough and lacked the means to prevent it in time. His views on both charges, have been challenged. For more details see http://www.refworld.org/pdfid/4d1da8752.pdf

It has become clear that several factors contributed towards the genocide and that no one nation (outside of Rwanda itself) should bear the blame for the genocide. However, it is also clear that the USA undermined the effectiveness of the UN in Rwanda.

The "dance to avoid the g-word"

As we have seen, the role of the USA in Rwanda was a limited one and the question arises of why this was the case. There are probably two reasons, both based on the lack of political will to be involved – the looming shadow of Somalia was definitely present. The first reason is that the US government resisted the facts of the genocide, and the second was the justification for doing so; the US government's failure to call what was happening genocide. Samantha Power characterized this avoidance as a *"two-month dance to avoid the g-word"* (Power, 2002). It has been confirmed that the major powers knew of the mass killings from the earliest days but refused to recognise them. The US Ambassador in Rwanda, David Rawson, argued that what was happening was part of the civil war and he left Kigali on 10 April. For three weeks at least, the most influential policy makers interpreted the killings as "casualties", ignoring reports from the ground and not engaging in internal debate in Washington on the issue. As we have seen, the word "genocide" was used by NGOs within two weeks, and by the Pope before the end of the month, but avoided by the USA until 10 June, fully two months after the genocide, and when more than 80% of the killings had taken place.

The avoidance of the term "genocide" was a deliberate policy by the USA and supported by the UK in the UN Security Council. Had the events in Rwanda been called correctly earlier, it would have necessitated action by the major powers. Legal advisers informed the US State Department to avoid using the term "genocide" when referring to events in the country. The US representatives at the Security Council were ordered not to use the term. Both the USA and the UK opposed the use of the word "genocide" in the Security Council while, in late April, the President of the Council Colin Keating of New Zealand urged the members to adopt a statement declaring a genocide. The compromise reached meant that, although reference to the 1948 Convention on Genocide was made, the specific use of the term was omitted from the statement. Despite this, on 4 May, Secretary General Boutros Boutros-Ghali acknowledged that there had been a "real genocide" in Rwanda.

Madeleine Albright (1937 – to the present)

Now a US politician and diplomat, Albright was born in the former Czechoslovakia to Jewish ancestry. She emigrated to the USA in 1939 and served as US ambassador to the UN from 1993 to 1997. She is the first woman to become US Secretary of State, serving in this position from 1997 to 2001. In an interview she commented that Rwanda is her greatest regret from her time as UN ambassador and possibly even as Secretary of State.

The Genocide Convention: "Genocide" defined

The Polish scholar Raphael Lemkin first proposed in 1933 that a treaty be created to make attacks on national, religious and ethnic groups an international crime. He did this following the Armenian genocide by the Turks during the Great War in 1915. He developed the term "genocide" from the Greek word "genos", meaning a race or tribe, and the Latin term "cide" meaning to kill.

At the end of the Second World War, the term "genocide" was used in the indictment against Nazi war criminals at Nuremberg who were accused of having

conducted deliberate and systematic genocide, in an attempt to exterminate racial and national groups,

civilian populations in occupied territories and deliberately targeting specific races of people and national, racial or religious groups.

In 1948, the Genocide Convention further clarified the act of genocide making it a crime under international law and incorporating with it both a physical and mental component. Genocidal acts would be those with the specific intent of destroying members of a group or bringing about conditions of life calculated to bring about the physical destruction of that group. This has been incorporated verbatim into the statutes of both the Yugoslavia and Rwanda tribunals, the International Criminal

Court and several other courts established by, or with the support of the UN. The Rwanda tribunal determined that the systematic rape of Tutsi women in Taba Province constituted the genocidal act of *"causing serious bodily or mental harm to members of the [targeted] group"*.

However, it was only in 1988 that the USA ratified the Genocide Convention after 40 years of expressing concerns over its application. Then, as we have seen in Rwanda, the USA was unwilling to apply the clear interpretation of the term to the events that took place.

For more details go to http://www.crimesofwar.org/a-z-guide/genocide/

On 21 May 1994, Secretary of State Warren Christopher authorized department officials to use the formulation, *"acts of genocide have occurred"*. The role of the USA was further exposed to the eyes of the world, most notably in the press conference held on 10 June 1994.

Once nearly all the Americans had been evacuated from Rwanda in mid-April it effectively dropped off the list of major issues which faced the Clinton government. The problems in Haiti and in particular, Bosnia, took precedence. As the RPF advanced and the UNAMIR requested further assistance, US manoeuvres at the Security Council repeatedly undermined all attempts to strengthen the UN military presence in Rwanda; in the end, not a single additional soldier or piece of military hardware reached the country before the genocide ended. National Security Advisor Anthony Lake recalls:

I was obsessed with Haiti and Bosnia during that period, so Rwanda was, in William Shawcross's words, a "sideshow", but not even a sideshow – a no-show

— Power, 2001

Philip Gourevitch wrote:

It wasn't a failure to act. The decision was not to act. And at that, we succeeded greatly

No amount of evidence ever changed the US position. The US role in the Rwandan genocide demonstrates at least three reasons for the USA's lack of action: first, what had happened in Somalia; second, the absence of any real national or economic interest in Rwanda; and, finally, political pressure domestically. The congressional elections coming up in November were more important to some White House aides than what was happening in Rwanda. The American role in the Rwandan genocide was brief, influential and dishonorable. Samantha Power believes that:

the story of US policy during the genocide in Rwanda is not a story of wilful complicity with evil. U.S. officials did not sit around and conspire to allow genocide to happen. But whatever their convictions about "never again", many of them did sit around, and they most certainly did allow genocide to happen.

— Power, 2001

The roles of the major powers involved in Rwanda have thus been examined, but there were other leaders who contributed significantly to what happened. These include those in the UK, whose contribution was negligible. In a more positive light, the part played by other members of the UN Security Council was important. In 1994, five new countries were invited onto the council: the Czech Republic, Argentina, Oman, Nigeria and Rwanda. The Czech Republic was represented by its ambassador, Karel Kovanda, who became the first to use the term "genocide" in an official meeting. Nigeria, supported by Argentina and Djibouti, urged condemnation of the Rwanda genocide in April 1994, and called for reinforcement of the UN mission in the country. However, some of the other veto-wielding permanent members objected. In 1999, the Security Council drew its own conclusions as to why the UN failed:

> *The failure by the UN to prevent and, subsequently, to stop the genocide in Rwanda was a failure by the UN system as a whole. The fundamental failure was the lack of resources and political commitment devoted to developments in Rwanda and to the UN presence there. The UN Report on the Security Council in December 1999 found that there was a persistent lack of political will by member states to act, or to act with enough assertiveness.*

— Independent inquiry, 1999

Full document: The US role in the genocide

Source A

A cartoon by US cartoonist Oliphant, "She's waving goodbye", published in *The Washington Post*, **1994.**

Source B

This is a US State Department press briefing held on 10 June 1994.

At this State Department briefing, spokesperson Christine Shelley responds to the following questions asked by the Reuters correspondent Alan Elsner.

Q: "How many acts of genocide does it take to make genocide?"

A: "That's just not a question that I'm in a position to answer."

Q: "Well, is it true that you have specific guidance not to use the word 'genocide' in isolation, but always to preface it with these words 'acts of'?"

A: "I have guidance which I try to use as best as I can. There are formulations that we are using that we are trying to be consistent in our use of. I don't have an absolute categorical prescription against something, but I have the definitions. I have phraseology which has been carefully examined and arrived at as best as we can apply to exactly the situation and the actions which have taken place … "

Source C

BBC correspondent Mark Doyle, present in Kigali for much of the early conflict, commented on why the USA allowed the genocide to happen.

Because they were Africans, I think. How many peacekeepers were there in Bosnia, Kosovo, [the] former Yugoslavia? There were a lot. In Rwanda, there were a couple of hundred poorly equipped UN [soldiers] without armored personnel carriers, without a proper military field hospital, without a proper logistics supply from Copenhagen and Nairobi, and these places where the UN do their operations. So I don't think there can be any doubt that if hundreds of thousands of Europeans or Americans were being killed in the way that Rwandans were being killed – do you think the world would not have intervened? I think it's because they were Africans"

First question, part a – 3 marks

According to Source C, what were the reasons why the US allowed the genocide to happen?

First question, part b – 2 marks

What is the message of Source A?

Third question – 6 marks

Compare and contrast the reasons offered in Source A and Source B why the great powers did not get involved until it was almost too late.

Fourth question – 9 marks

Using the sources and your own knowledge, to what extent do you agree that a major factor for not intervening in Rwanda was because of the attitude of the major powers in the UN.

References and further reading

Dallaire, R. 2004. Shake Hands with the Devil: The Failure of Humanity in Rwanda. Random House, Toronto, Canada

Melvern, L. 2004. Conspiracy to Murder: The Rwandan Genocide. Verso. London, UK

Power, S. 2001. "Bystanders to genocide", The Atlantic, 1 September, 2001. www.theatlantic.com/magazine/archive2001/09/bystanderstogenicde/304571

Wallis A. 2007. Silent Accomplice: the Untold Story of France's role in Rwandan Genocide. IB Tauris. New York, USA

1.8 The impact of the genocide

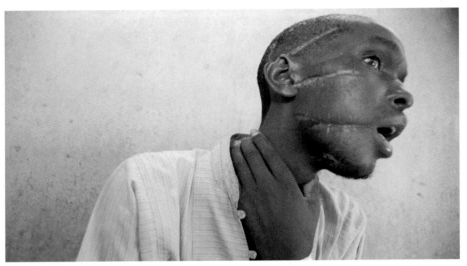

▲ A young Hutu moderate rescued by the Red Cross in Nyanza hospital in June 1994. He bears machete wounds inflicted by the Interahamwe

For the dead and the living, we must bear witness.

— Elie Wiesel (words carved at the entrance of the US Holocaust Memorial Museum in Washington, DC, USA)

Events in Rwanda: Post-genocide Rwanda, 1994–2000

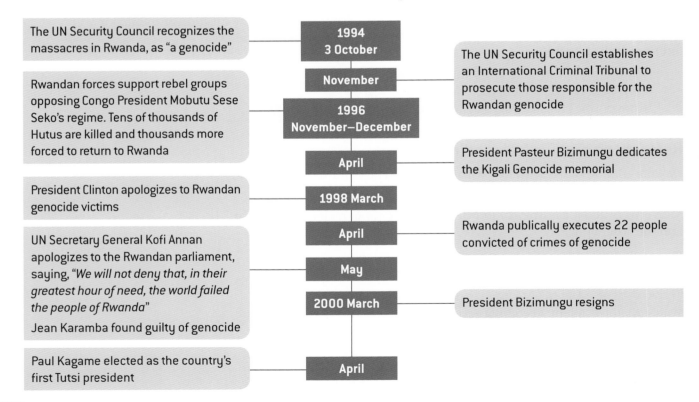

The UN Security Council recognizes the massacres in Rwanda, as "a genocide"	**1994 3 October**
	November → The UN Security Council establishes an International Criminal Tribunal to prosecute those responsible for the Rwandan genocide
Rwandan forces support rebel groups opposing Congo President Mobutu Sese Seko's regime. Tens of thousands of Hutus are killed and thousands more forced to return to Rwanda	**1996 November–December**
	April → President Pasteur Bizimungu dedicates the Kigali Genocide memorial
President Clinton apologizes to Rwandan genocide victims	**1998 March**
	April → Rwanda publically executes 22 people convicted of crimes of genocide
UN Secretary General Kofi Annan apologizes to the Rwandan parliament, saying, *"We will not deny that, in their greatest hour of need, the world failed the people of Rwanda"* Jean Karamba found guilty of genocide	**May**
	2000 March → President Bizimungu resigns
Paul Kagame elected as the country's first Tutsi president	**April**

The social impact of the genocide can still be felt 20 years on; it can be seen in the plethora of memorial sites scattered around the country that testify to the scale and intensity of the genocide. Every country that suffers in war needs to rebuild, and in the case of Rwanda, the very fabric of society, described by one observer as the *"social and moral tissue of the nation"* was torn apart. 10% of the population of the country were dead, 75% of them Tutsi and yet, for the minority Tutsi emerging triumphant in the war, the social and political impact was even greater. Compounding these enormous problems was the predicament of the refugees. Since independence in 1962, Rwanda had experienced an exodus of refugees; but the scale of the crisis following the victory of the RPF in 1994 represented the largest refugee crisis in the UN's history. The task of rebuilding the nation after the trauma it had been through was overwhelming and, given the poverty of Rwanda prior to the genocide, the situation the country faced was grim. It would be a hard challenge for any country to face: a new government to be built, the social fabric of the country to be repaired, the economy restructured and justice to be administered. The escape of many of the perpetrators of the genocide into Zaire led to a new and more complex stage in the Rwandan tragedy, which was to result in another conflict that came to engulf the Great Lakes Region of Africa for the next decade and more.

The social impact of the genocide

At the same time as the people of South Africa were trying to live in harmony through peace and reconciliation, and the inhabitants of the former Yugoslavia were attempting the same following a brutal civil war, the problems of rebuilding the society in Rwanda were even harder. Philip Gourevitch commented, *"Rwanda is the only nation where hundreds of thousands of people who took part in mass murder live intermingled at every level of society with the families of their victims"* (2009). We are comfortable with numbers, but when it applies to the situation in Rwanda, it is almost impossible to comprehend. Imagine a dripping tap: one drop of water every 10 seconds, 6 per minute, about 8,600 drops each day. In Rwanda if one drop represented a life, on average every 10 seconds for those 100 days of genocide, someone was killed. We cannot know the exact numbers of those who died; estimates range from as low as 500,000 to as high as 1 million, with most accounts settling on 800,000 victims. The social impact was devastating.

Studies have been carried out among both Tutsi and Hutu survivors. Most of the victims were men, but males made up the majority of the population; in the following years the resulting social impact meant that 66% of households were headed by women, an increase of 50% over the figures prior to the civil war and genocide. Many of these were widows and, as a consequence, the status of women in Rwandan society had to change. As women constitute the majority of the adult working population, they have become central not only to the restructuring of society but also to the economic development of the country. Prior to the genocide, education for girls traditionally included little formal schooling with illiteracy rates as high as 50% amongst Rwandan females. This had to change, and along with it amendments to the law regarding property rights, land ownership and women's role in state representation. In 2014 almost two-thirds of parliamentarians are women, which represents the highest proportion of any parliament in the world. Gender rights are included in the constitution which imposes a mandate on local and national government to ensure that a minimum of 30% of seats are held by women. Changes in the law have given women the right to inherit land, to own property, to share the assets of a marriage and to obtain credit. There has also been a drive to rid the country of gender-based violence with electronic billboards in Kigali declaring, *"Together we can stop sexual harassment."*

Nowadays, when Rwandans look back on the early years of aftermath, they say "In the beginning"

— Philip Gourevitch, in an article called "The life after", published in *New Yorker* in May 2009.

Today, as many girls as boys receive both primary and secondary education, and the birth rate is falling. Social change is an evolutionary and often prolonged process, but traumatic circumstances such as war do help dictate the pace. Rwanda has recognized the need to rebuild the social structure of the country and with women now comprising the majority of Rwanda's adult working population, they are taking on new roles and responsibilities.

The refugee crisis

The years from independence in 1962 through to the outbreak of civil war in 1990 had been turbulent enough for Rwanda. And then the period from 1993, the year following the signing of the Arusha

▲ Refugee on the road, leaving Rwanda, 1994

accords, up to the victory declared by the new government at the end of July 1994, devastated a country already one of the poorest in the world. It opened a new chapter which, in its own way, was to be as destructive in the area as the genocide before, enveloping the Great Lakes Region in fierce conflict and involving armies and civilians in another conflagration. For this region of Africa, the genocide was only the beginning.

The problems caused by refugees (referred to by the UN as "internally displaced persons" or IDPs) followed a pattern of events that had occurred on a massive scale in the last half of the 20th century. Essentially, the failure to find adequate solutions to certain problems had in turn led to further tragedy. In the case of Rwanda, somewhere between 2 million and 3 million people fled the country in 1994 in what has been termed, *"the messiest and most complex humanitarian operation in modern history"*.

Even before the genocide of 1994 in Rwanda, there were a large number of refugees in the neighbouring countries. Since the exodus of 1959 and the years that followed, Tutsi refugees had sought refuge in Uganda, Tanzania and Burundi. In the 1980s many of these, including Paul Kagame, had joined the forces of Yoweri Museveni in Uganda and helped him come to power in 1986. Tutsi refugees had formed the RPF and launched the civil war in Rwanda in 1990. However, in addition to the Tutsi, there were large numbers of Hutu refugees who had fled Burundi following the assassination of President Melchior Ndadaye, a Hutu, in October 1993. On the eve of the Rwandan genocide it was estimated that there were around 500,000 refugees in Central Africa, the majority of them having come from Rwanda. Each refugee group had their own grievances and objectives, some of them dating back decades. It is easy to see that the failure to deal with these aspirations had created problems not only of a logistical nature, in having to take care of such large numbers by the often reluctant host country, but that many of the refugees had become radicalized by their experiences. As a result, refugees were potential recruits for armed groups such as the RPF and the Interahamwe militia, the latter being responsible for some of the worst massacres in the genocide.

Rwandan refugee population							
Country of asylum	1993	1994	1995	1996	1997	1998	1999
Burundi	245,500	278,100	153,000	720	2,000	2,000	1,300
DR of Congo (ex-Zaire)	53,500	1,252,800	1,100,600	423,600	37,000	35,000	33,000
Tanzania	51,900	626,200	548,000	20,000	410	4,800	20,100
Uganda	97,000	97,000	6,500	11,200	12,200	7,500	8,000
Total	447,900	2,254,100	1,808,100	455,520	51,610	49,300	62,400

▲ Rwandan refugee population, 1933–99

Burundi refugee population							
Country of asylum	1993	1994	1995	1996	1997	1998	1999
DR of Congo (ex-Zaire)	176,400	180,100	117,900	30,200	47,000	20,000	19,200
Rwanda	250,000	6,000	3,200	9,600	6,900	1,400	1,400
Tanzania	444,900	202,700	227,200	385,500	459,400	473,800	499,000
Total	831,300	388,800	348,300	425,300	513,300	495,200	519,600

▲ Burundian refugee populations, 1993–99

Location	Number of Rwandan refugees
Northern Burundi	270,000
Western Tanzania	577,000
South-western Uganda	10,000
Zaire (Goma)	850,000
Zaire (Bukavu)	332,000
Zaire (Uvira)	62,000

▲ Rwandan refugees in the Great Lakes region, end of August 1994

Taken from UNHCR publication "The Rwandan genocide and its aftermath"

The work of the UNHCR in the Great Lakes

The UNHCR is a non-political humanitarian agency without any military or security apparatus of its own. Created in the aftermath of the Second World War, like many agencies of the UN it relies on the good will of its members. The agency seeks ways to help refugees restart their lives, either through local integration, voluntary return to their homeland or, if that is not possible, through resettlement in "third" countries which may offer asylum. The case of the refugees in the Great Lakes region caused a crisis for the UNHCR as well as the countries themselves. The huge number of refugees was not the only problem; difficulties also lay in the manipulation of the refugee populations by the combatants, many of whom were forced to flee and were later held hostage by some of the more radical elements among them. This was also to cause ethical dilemmas for the UNHCR; who had to deal, for example, with Interahamwe killers and genocidaires, who still retained control and influence over large numbers of people in the refugee camps. The High Commissioner for Refugees, Sadako Ogate commented, *"There were innocent refugees, but there were also killers in these groups. The situation was full of contradictions."*

On 28 April 1994, more than 200,000 Rwandans crossed a bridge at Rusumo into Tanzania in 24 hours. It was the start of the largest refugee crisis in history; a human river 25 kilometres in length, fleeing the country. An eyewitness said, *"We looked up at the Rwandan hills. The entire African landscape was awash with people, all headed our way. It was the fastest and largest exodus of refugees in modern times"* (UNHCR *Refugees* magazine, 2004, number 135: 22). More and more people flooded across the borders in the ensuing weeks and in July, following the collapse of the Hutu regime in Rwanda, another new record was set as an estimated 850,000 Hutu crossed into Goma in Zaire, from the north-western province of Rwanda. Located close to the borders of Rwanda, the setting of these camps provided a perfect base to launch raids back into the now RPF-controlled country (see map, page 97). Refugee centres located at Kivu in Zaire provided the world with what was known as the **CNN effect** as hundreds of reporters, by now well aware of the genocide that had taken place in Rwanda, supplied the television audiences of the world with graphic images of the victims and perpetrators of the violence.

According to the UN Refugee Convention of 1951, responsibility for refugees lies in the hands of the host country. The government accommodating the refugees needs to screen and provide security for the people. In practice this can prove extremely difficult, especially given the large numbers of refugees and the speed of their flight. To compound the problem, many of the host governments may themselves be poor and unstable. What happened in the Great Lakes region is that many of the fleeing refugees were armed, desperate and dangerous. As this volatile refugee population mixed with the local population it made the problem even more difficult to handle. The Zairean government's lack of authority in the eastern region of its own country meant that the Rwandan genocidaires were able to establish effective control in the camps, amounting to a government in exile. So not only was the UNHCR faced with the huge problem of trying to support an overwhelming number of refugees, but it had to address a moral issue too. In order to distribute food and aid effectively, the agency had to deal with the military authorities and Interahamwe militia leaders. Critics said that the agency was, in effect, supporting the killers. An exclusion clause in the 1951 Refugee Convention specifically excluded protection and refugee status for those who have committed crimes against humanity; but actually sorting out the killers from innocent civilians was problematic. In the camps in and around Goma, the presence of former soldiers and militia helped to create a state within a state which the international agencies were unable to handle effectively without dealing with the leadership of the genocidaires. These camps close to Lake Kivu thus represented a significant threat to the newly-established RPF government in Rwanda.

In August, the head of the UNHCR suggested four solutions to the problem:

- disarm the ex-Hutu government soldiers

- neutralize the civilian militia leaders

- begin the process of dealing with crimes committed and finally

- ensure that law and order was established inside the camps through the deployment of police forces.

The government in Zaire was unable or unwilling to enforce these recommendations. At the beginning of August, a wave of cholera spread across the camps that killed tens of thousands of refugees. Another catastrophe was set to happen.

Zaire's leader President Mobutu used the refugee crisis as a political ploy to deflect domestic pressure from his beleaguered government, already under severe pressure due to his mismanagement of the economy. Meanwhile, Western countries were wary of providing assistance to the refugees under such circumstances and, despite the UNHCR asking over 50 countries for help, no one stepped forward. The issue of humanitarian needs and military cooperation has remained a controversial matter since this catastrophe in the Great Lakes region, as evident in more recent crises in Iraq, Afghanistan and Syria.

With no help forthcoming from other countries for the refugees in the camps in Zaire, at the beginning of 1995, the UNHCR used soldiers from Mobutu's own guard to establish some sort of order in the camps. This arrangement did not and could not deal with the broader security threats posed by the existence of militarised communities in the camps and these would cause problems later. The repatriation of refugees back

▲ Cramped, crowded conditions in refugee camps in eastern Zaire led to the rapid spread of cholera, causing the death of more than 50,000 within a few weeks

into Rwanda was an ongoing process, and the deteriorating security conditions in camps certainly contributed to the desire of many of the refugees to return to their homes. However, Rwanda had been devastated and the lack of security in the country made many of the Hutu moderates less willing to take their chances back home, despite the pledge for reconciliation from the newly established RPF government.

The Kibeho massacre, April 1995

In April 1995, a massacre allegedly carried out by RPF soldiers took place in a camp in Kibeho, located in south western Rwanda in part of the zone established by the French under Operation Turquoise. The RPF government had ordered these camps to be closed, as they were within the confines of the country itself (and had been the refuge of mainly Hutu when the camps were built in late June 1994). On April 22 1995, when moving in to shut down one of the camps, RPF troops killed over 4,000 civilians in Kibeho. There was disagreement about the number of people killed: the government put the numbers at 300 but eyewitness accounts reported those killed in the thousands; Australian soldiers reported the massacre and initially, put the number of dead as high as 8,000; official UN estimates later reduced the figure to 2,000. Many of the dead were trampled and killed by machetes. The RPF did not carry machetes and this suggests that Hutu militia within the camp were probably responsible.

The frustration of the Zairean government regarding the refugees spilled over again later in 1995 when it tried to close some of the camps and prompt the return of the refugees to Rwanda and Burundi. With ex-Hutu leaders and militia still controlling the camps though, most of the refugees were more like hostages at the mercy of militia who were able to shelter behind their numbers and plan operations inside Rwanda. The situation, barely under control, was likely to spill over into another war in the region. The UN High Commissioner stated:

The link between refugee problems and peace and security is perhaps nowhere more evident than in the Great Lakes region in Africa … Probably never before has my Office found its humanitarian concerns in the midst of such a lethal quagmire of political and security interests. While our humanitarian assistance and protection serve an innocent, silent majority of needy and anxious refugees, they also serve the militants who have an interest in maintaining the status quo. This cannot go on.

Just as the genocide in Rwanda had been unprecedented, the situation in the Great Lakes region became a watershed event that forced both the UN and NGOs to re-evaluate their policies and practices with regards to refugees and donor aid. In 1996 the situation was to slip even further out of control.

▲ Refugees in Rwanda, 1994

UGANDA

Oruchinga
Merama
Nakivale
Murongo
Kyaka
Rutshuru
Nyagatare
Katale
Kahindo
Rugwera
Kagenyi
Karagwe
Sake   Kibumba
Ruhengeri
Byumba
Lake Vert
Umubano
Mugunga
Kyabalisa I & II
Goma   Gisenyi
Omukariro
RWANDA
Chondo
KIGALI
Kabira   Chayo
Gitarama
Bugarula
Kibuye
Kalehe
Maugwere
Kibungo
Bungi
Katana   Karama
Mbuba
Kashusha
Inera   Adi-Kivu
Mudaka/Murhala
Cyangugu
Rukuramigabo
Ngara   Benaco   Mushuhura
Bukavu
Mugano
Lumasi
Chimanga
Nyangezi-Mulwa
Ntamba   Lukole
Karabangira
Butare
Kitali
Izirangabo
Kamanyola
Lubarika
Ruvumu
Keza
UNITED
REPUBLIC
OF
TANZANIA
Kanganiro   Luvungi
Kahanda
Luberizi
Ngozi   Magara
Rwenena
Kajembo
Kibezi
Mwenga
Kibogoye
Biriba   Runingo
Kagunga
Vulne/Uvira
BUJUMBURA
Mtendeli
Uvira
Gitega
Kanembwa
DEMOCRATIC
REPUBLIC
OF
CONGO
Kibondo
BURUNDI
Mkugwa
0   30   60
kilometers
Nyarugusu
Cyangugu
Nyakavogo
Panzi
Mtabila   Moyovosi
Shabarabe
Bukavu
Mushweshwe
Kasulu
Nyamirangwe
Muku   Nyantende
Bideka
Kigoma
Ujiji

Lake Kivu
Lake Tanganyika

Capital
Refugee camp
Main Town
International
Boundary

▲ Refugee camps in the Great Lakes region, 1995

111

Source skills

Source A

Fergal Keane visits a refugee camp at Benaco, Tanzania, in what was then the world's largest refugee camp in September 1994. *Season of Blood: A Rwandan Journey (1996).*

As we came closer and closer, the air thickened and became foggy. Long lines of women and children filed along the roadway. The women carried piles of firewood stacked high on their heads. Beside them children struggled with branches and twigs that scratched along the ground, causing trails of dust to rise up behind them. I rolled down the window and heard a growing murmur of voices. It swelled as we drove to the top of the hill, until the sound resembled a great swarm of bees, into which had been mixed the noise of car horns and growling lorries.

At the top of the hill we pulled in to the side of the road and I found myself looking down on the UN refugee camp at Benaco, the latest receptacle for the displaced of Rwanda. From the hillside the camp spread out before us in the dusk like a ragged flag. There were patches of white where the UN had erected feeding stations, innumerable squares of blue where plastic huts had been erected, and moving between and around them a great mass of brown figures. From my vantage point on the roadway the camp seemed to be a place of incessant movement. In the middle there was a main pathway, along which thousands of people were moving up and down in an orderly line. As we drove down a track towards the UN main compound I noticed that the crowds were moving to and from a lake. They carried water in buckets, pails, plastic bags, anything that could be filled. I had never seen so many people crowded into one place. The air was by now thick with smoke; my lungs began to heave, and I coughed constantly. Down in the heart of the camp, the noise that had seemed a murmur from afar had become a loud, declamatory roll that rose above the refugees and hung in the air with the smoke and the smell of displaced people.

Until a few weeks ago these people had lived and worked in Rwanda. They were farmers, businessmen, teachers – an entire society transplanted on to Tanzanian soil …

The people at Benaco were in a state of wretched poverty dependent on food hand-outs from the international community. They lived in plastic huts without sanitation, having lost their homes and land. Yet, as I moved among them, witnessing the squalor and desolation, I could not shut out the memory of Nyarabuye or the knowledge that among these huge crowds were thousands of people who had taken part in the genocide.

Source B

This source is based on interviews with Hutu killers during the genocide.

This is why, at the end of the Rwandan genocide, when two million Hutus so suddenly rose as one within a few days in the early summer of 1994 to begin their exodus, we understood that they were fleeing from more than the weapons and vengeance of the RPF troops. Without thinking it through clearly, we sensed that a psychological force much greater then the simple survival instinct was at work to impel that immense throng so powerfully towards Congo – abandoning houses, properties, professions, habits, all without hesitation or a backward glance.

Two years later those families returned from the refugee camps to their plots of land still bearing their collective guilt. Their sense of shame is haunted today by the dread of suspicion, punishment, and revenge, and it mingles with the Tutsis' traumatic anguish and infects the atmosphere, aptly described by Sylvie Umubyeyi: "There are those who fear the very hills where they should be working on their lands. There are those who fear encountering Hutus on the road. There are Hutus who saved Tutsis but who no longer dare go home to their villages, for fear that no one will believe them. There are people who fear visitors, or the night. There are innocent faces that frighten others and fear they are frightening others, as if they were criminals. There is the fear of threats, the panic of memories."

After a genocide, the anguish and dread have an agonizing persistence. The silence on the Rwandan hills is indescribable and cannot be compared with the usual mutism [the inability to speak and communicate effectively] in the aftermath of war. Perhaps Cambodia offers a recent parallel. Tutsi survivors manage to surmount this silence only among themselves. But within the community of killers, innocent or guilty, each person plays the role of either a mute or an amnesiac [amnesia: the partial or total loss of memory, usually resulting from shock or psychological disturbance].

Hatzfeld, J. 2008. *A Time for Machetes: The Rwandan genocide – the killers speak*. Profile Books. London, UK.

Source C

Temporary housing of refugees in a camp in Rwanda in late 1994.

Source D

UNHCR Refugees magazine. 1994. "Cooperation crucial in Rwanda crisis". Issue 97, 1 September 1994.

Whether approached from the air or by land, Benaco camp is impressive. Blue UNHCR plastic sheeting, covering tens of thousands of makeshift huts, contrasts with the lush green landscape for as far as the eye can see. On 28 April, some 250,000 Rwandese flooded into Tanzania near the town of Ngara in one single human wave – at the time, it was the biggest and fastest refugee movement UNHCR had ever witnessed.

"On that day, we took the road leading to the border to evaluate the situation," recalled Maureen Connelly, in charge of the UNHCR Emergency Unit in Tanzania. "Suddenly, we were facing a line of refugees 8–12 kilometres long. Nobody expected it. Our car couldn't go on. There were people everywhere."

Jacques Franquin, coordinator of UNHCR activities in Ngara, remembers his initial reaction to the huge influx was to call his NGO colleagues. "The Rusumo road was just one compact mass of people, like a flow of lava descending inexorably toward the Tanzanian border," Franquin said. "I rushed to my radio and called Médecins Sans Frontières to quickly send us reinforcements, supplies and, above all, a water provision specialist. They worked all night to provide a minimum of drinking water to the refugees." Thanks to constant cooperation from non-governmental organizations, UNHCR managed to cope with the arrival of this human tide and saved many lives.

"The cooperation between UNHCR and the NGOs in this emergency situation was almost perfect," said Franquin. "We had an enormous advantage. We were already here and waiting. So were the NGOs. We had been working together on a project for Burundi refugees and knew each other well. So it was very easy to get organized and deal with the exodus of Rwandese. Because of this, we gained a lot of time. In this case, we could respond from the first day on. We gained three precious weeks."

But the choice of Benaco hill as the site of what was then the world's biggest refugee camp had nothing to do with chance. There is an artificial lake at the foot of the site. Every day, a million litres of water are pumped from it and treated before being distributed to the refugees. Each person gets five litres of drinking water per day, which is too little by UNHCR standards but enough, it seems, to fill the needs of the camp. The MSF and Oxfam teams handle the treatment and distribution of water.

Most certainly, the presence at Benaco of UNHCR and the NGOs from the very start of the crisis made it possible to avoid a catastrophe. But chance too played a part. For once, the refugees did not set out in a hurry, and were able to flee with enough supplies to get them through the first few crucial days of the crisis. This was not the first time many of them had fled turmoil in the troubled region, and their past experience taught them to take along some vital supplies; a jerry can of water, a little food – enough to keep going until the arrival of the first convoys of food aid. This gave the international community a few extra hours to mobilize.

Despite the early successes, the battle has not yet been won. Big problems are an everyday fact of life here. Just to avoid starvation, some 200 tons of food must be shipped to Benaco each and every day. "It's a very challenging task," said Marco Onorado, of the International Federation of Red Cross and Red Crescent Societies (IFRC), which is responsible for food distribution. "We can only distribute food to 100,000 people a day. So we give them their rations for three days – corn, beans, and sometimes oil."

But the situation is nonetheless fragile. "With a population at the camp that doesn't stop growing, we are always in a precarious situation," said the IFRC's Onorado. "The provisions depend mainly on the World Food Programme (WFP), which very often can't tell us exactly what's in the pipeline. Our worry is running out of supplies." Supplying the camp with fresh provisions is only the tip of a monstrous iceberg. Add to that the problems of hygiene, the prevention of epidemics, the search for new sources of water, and the security problems inherent in a population of hundreds of thousands of refugees, and you get an idea of the enormity of the task.

The stakes are, in fact, important for the NGOs. Benaco camp, which rapidly became one of the largest "cities" in Tanzania, is a showcase for the organizations working there. "In an emergency situation like this one," Gary McClain of CARE points out, "there is no place for rivalry. Everyone goes ahead and does his job. We don't have time for politics. What is happening here is an excellent example of the response one can make to an emergency situation when everybody works together." With a population of hundreds of thousands, Benaco is on the verge of suffocating. To help ease the congestion, new camps are being created – Lumasi, Msuhura and Kayonza. So the work goes on, day by day, problem by problem. So far, UNHCR and its NGO partners have more than met the challenge.

First question, part a – 3 marks

In Source A the author comments, "I could not shut out the memory of Nyarubuye." What happened there? What connection is he making between the refugees in this extract and the people at Nyarubuye?

First question, part b – 2 marks

What is the message conveyed in Source C?

Second question – 4 marks

Discuss the origins, purpose, value and limitations of Source D and Source A for anyone wishing to understand the problems of refugees.

First question, part b – 2 marks

To what is the author referring to in Source B when he says "perhaps Cambodia offers a recent parallel"?

First question, part a – 3 marks

What do you understand by the author's comment in Source C when he says, "within the community of killers, innocent or guilty, each person plays the role of either mute or an amnesiac."?

First question, part a – 3 marks

In Source D identify the NGOs mentioned in the extract.

Second question – 4 marks

According to Source D, what are the major problems the IFRC spokesman identifies as facing the refugees in Benaco camp?

Justice and reconciliation

If there is to be reconciliation, first there must be truth.

— Timothy B. Tyson, 2004

The aftermath of the Rwandan genocide presented overwhelming problems for the country. Delivering justice in a post-war period has always posed difficulties but, in the case of Rwanda, the scale of the problems was immense. This was due to a number of reasons: firstly, the fact that so many of the judiciary had been killed in the genocide. It is estimated that fewer than 6 judges and only 10 lawyers survived. The second reason was that the scale of the killing and the numbers of those responsible ran into thousands, from all walks of society. Finally, huge difficulties arose from the division of the country into survivors, victims and the temporarily displaced people, subject to the rule of the victorious minority. *"It was,"* said Linda Melvern, *"as though in 1945 the Jews and Germans were to live together in Germany after the Holocaust, under a Jewish-dominated army, with roughly a third of the Germans living outside of the country"*. The desire for justice and need for reconciliation would be paramount in the country in the following years. The pursuit of both would surely be problematic.

As early as May 1994, the RPF had called for an international tribunal to prosecute the guilty. It was finally addressed by the creation of the **International Criminal Tribunal for Rwanda (ICTR)** later that year. There was no more urgent a problem than how to tackle the wide-ranging issue of justice and reconciliation. What punishments were appropriate for those who had instigated the genocide, those who had killed and the others who had either encouraged the killings or stood by and allowed them to happen? The whole issue of justice and punishment, retribution, revenge and accountability need to be examined. Where was the place for mercy, for understanding and compassion if the people of Rwanda were to move forward? Late in 1994 Paul Kagame, leader of the RPF and then vice-president commented: *"There can be no durable reconciliation as long as those who are responsible for the massacres are not properly tried"* (see http://www.refworld.org/pdfid/4d1da8752.pdf, Chapter 18).

There were models that Rwanda could follow in the years to come. After the Second World War, trials of the war criminals had been held at Nuremberg, setting a precedent. In Japan too, a relatively small number of those accused of war crimes and crimes against humanity were tried, imprisoned and some executed. However, these were few in comparison to the number of those involved in the genocide in Rwanda. In South Africa, the government tried a different approach. After the abolition of apartheid in 1991, the release of Nelson Mandela and the election that made him president, the government created the Truth and Reconciliation Commission (TRC). It began its work in 1996 and provided a model that granted individual amnesties in exchange for testimony of crimes committed during the apartheid era. However, to compare what had happened in South Africa and what had occurred in Nazi Germany to the situation in Rwanda is problematic. It was two years after the RPF victory when the legal

TOK connections

In small groups, discuss your beliefs in the principles of punishment and justice: what do you understand by retribution and rehabilitation?

Class discussion

Do you believe that inherently, human beings are essentially good or that some might be evil? What do you understand by this?

framework for prosecuting those involved in the genocide was established in Rwanda and, by 1998, the total prison population had risen to 130,000 whereas only some 1,200 people had been brought before the courts. However, before there could be reconciliation, justice was needed.

To address the problem of dispensing justice in a speedy fashion in the country, at the end of 1998 a tribunal was established at Arusha to help with the public process of post-genocide recovery.

The ideal model would have been for Rwanda to try its own people and in that way determine justice, as well as move on the path towards reconciliation. But the sheer numbers of people involved was overwhelming for one of the poorest and most traumatised countries on earth. The Rwandan genocide had involved a far larger percentage of people, not just those who had been killed, but the number who had participated either willingly or under duress. Each of the judicial initiatives tried in the following years has helped, but not all have met with consensus. In 1999, the Rwandan government established the National Unity and Reconciliation Commission and decided to adapt the traditional Gacaca (pronounced "gacha-cha") community justice system to deal with the crimes of the genocide and promote both justice and reconciliation.

The Gacaca courts consisted of people from the local community who were to elect judges to try cases in front of their peers. A pilot phase was established in 2002, and in 2005 the Gacaca courts began operating across the country. Defendants were given shorter sentences in exchange for confessing and asking for forgiveness from their victims' families. In some cases neighbours had turned on each other, and a number of witnesses who spoke out were murdered. Rwanda's president, Paul Kagame, estimated that these grass roots courts cost the country about $40 million, compared to the $1.7 billion spent on the ICTR. These Gacaca courts tried about two million cases during the 10-year period before they officially closed in 2012.

Through such institutions, and the work of local organizations, Rwandans have moved towards reconciliation, enabling people to live together peacefully, if a little uneasily in some cases. In the same year Rwanda adopted the slogan "Kwibuka", meaning "remember" in Kinyarwanda. Today it describes the annual commemoration of the 1994 Genocide – "Remember, Unite, Renew". The UN has also helped in the process of reconciliation through its publications. One of these ways is through the Outreach programme on the genocide.

(See http://www.un.org/en/preventgenocide/rwanda/education/education.shtml)

TOK connections

Examine the importance of the Milgram Experiment carried out in 1961 in the context of TOK (see www.simplypsychology.org/milgram.html).

Consider the reasons why people follow rules or behave in a conformist manner. What types of institutions help people to behave well?

ATL Self-management skills

Go to http://www.un.org/en/preventgenocide/rwanda/pdf/Tugire_Ubumwe.pdf to view a graphic novel, "Tugire Ubumwe – produced by the Outreach Programme on the Rwanda Genocide and the UN, in collaboration with a Rwandan artist and genocide survivor, Rupert Bazambanza.

This graphic novel has already received very positive feedback. The ICTR Information Office in Kigali described it as

a crucial educative tool in the promotion of unity and reconciliation and the fight against the genocide ideology; [it] will create a big impact among the Rwandan population.

And the Survivors Fund (SURF) International referred to it as

a great piece of work [that] will get young people thinking of managing their troubled history and finding ways of communicating effectively.

Another book is published by the ICTR: "*100 Days – In the land of a thousand hills*" is a cartoon book for children on the subject of the 1994 Rwanda genocide.

The ICTR's goal was to create an illustrated narrative that would convey the events of the genocide at both personal and national levels to children eight years of age and above. The narrative is anchored in the story of Francoise and Kagabo, two young children who are respectively Hutu and Tutsi. They escape the genocide but are both eventually orphaned. Between sections of their story, descriptions of some events around the country are also given.

Source skills

Read the following accounts of survivors living with killers in their community.

Source A

C. Larson. *As We Forgive: Stories of Reconciliation from Rwanda* (2009).

The gash across the face of Emmanuel Mahuro, a seventeen-year-old Rwandan native, is no longer an open wound. Today, like a jagged boundary line on a map, a scar juts down the plateau of his forehead, across the bridge of his nose, and up the slope of his right cheek. It is impossible to look into Emmanuel's eyes without seeing this deep cut, a mark of division etched across his face – and the face of Rwanda – fifteen years after the genocide. My first reaction to such scars is to avert my eyes. But to look away from Emmanuel's scars is to look away from him. Strangely, as my eyes adjust to Emmanuel's face, there is an impulse, not to recoil, but to follow the line of the scar across his skin. Emmanuel's scar testifies to two realities. It is a witness to the human capacity for evil. To look at it is to hear it scream the brutality of an April that aches in the memory of an entire people. Yet his scar testifies to another truth: the stunning capacity of humans to heal from the unthinkable. To trace that scar is to discover the hope of a people who, despite losing everything, are finding a way to forge a common future for Rwanda.

Source B

C. Larson. *As We Forgive: Stories of Reconciliation from Rwanda* (2009).

Rwanda's wounds, like Emmanuel's, are agonizingly deep. Today, they are being opened afresh as tens of thousands of killers are released from prison to return to the hills where they hunted down and killed former neighbors, friends, and classmates. In the everyday business of life … survivors commonly meet the eyes of people who shattered their former lives. How can they live together? This is not a philosophical question, but a practical one that confronts Rwandans daily. In some shape or form, all Rwandans ask this question. Some, like Antoine Rutayisire, himself a survivor, put the question starkly: "If they told you that a murderer was to be released into your neighborhood, how would you feel? But what if this time, they weren't just releasing one, but forty thousand?" For Antoine and his country, which has released some sixty thousand prisoners since 2003, these questions are not hypothetical.

Fatuma Ndangiza, executive secretary of the National Unity and Reconciliation Commission, began wrestling in earnest with the questions on January 10, 2003, when the president first decided to provisionally release forty thousand of the 120,000 Rwandans held in egregiously overcrowded prisons. Even with a fully functional legal system, something which had been wiped out with the slaughter of many Tutsi in 1994, the backlog of cases would have taken over two hundred years. "I was driving in the car around one o'clock, when I heard President Kagame say that these people who are going to be released have to be taken to the Reconciliation Commission for re-education before going back to the community." At first, Fatuma thought the president was crazy. "What sort of education do you give to people who confessed that they killed? What do we tell the victims?" she wondered. Government officials weren't the only ones who worried about the pending release. For Gahigi, a Tutsi who lost 142 family members during the genocide, the question dripped with fear: "This time, will they kill us all?" The survivors could not imagine living side by side with their tormentors. Would Rwandan society, still barely functioning, now collapse entirely?

But even as survivors were tormented with fears and questions, so also were many of the offenders themselves. Saveri, one of the killers, recalls how he felt when he heard he would be released: "I was so overjoyed, but fear lingered also. How was I going to face a survivor and squarely look her in the eyes after I had wiped out her family?" This thought terrorized him. Similarly, John, another man who stained his own hands with blood when he killed his neighbour, remembers, "I had a mixture of fear when I learned I was going to be released from prison. After a long time in prison it was hard for me to come back to the community that I had sinned against. My biggest challenge was how I was going to meet Chantal, whose father I had killed. This was my deepest fear."

Source C

C. Larson. *As We Forgive: Stories of Reconciliation from Rwanda* **(2009).**

There's an ancient craft practised in Rwanda, an age-old art that has been almost lost today. The Umuvumu trees that shade the Gacaca gatherings have another purpose. Once the Umuvumu tree has matured, a small strip of bark is cut away. Like our own bodies, the tree responds to the gash. The Umuvumu produces a fine red matting of slender roots to cover the wound. The ancients then treated that matting to create a cloth, commonly called bark cloth. Historically, the bark cloth was used to make royal clothing. Today, artisans fashion the reddish-brown fabric into traditional African ceremonial dress, wallets, purses, placemats, book covers, and maps of Africa, adding decorative detail through paint, print, or needlework. Strangely, mysteriously, things of beauty and usefulness sometimes come from wounds.

Source D

An extract from an interview with President Paul Kagame in 2004 for PBS called "Ghosts of Rwanda".

Question: Mr. President, you know the village of Nyarabuye – like so many villages across Rwanda, decimated by genocide. Survivors are now having to live in that village alongside people who had killed their families. Is it fair to ask them to do that?

"I don't think it's very fair, but I ask them to do it. So it looks like we are also involved with some unfair things for higher goals in trying to rebuild the country. I think I have asked too much from the survivors of the genocide. They actually bear almost the full burden of reconciliation. The others, the perpetrators, or those associated with them, or those who didn't care what happened – they have less [actually] to do to remedy the situation.

The burden is always put on the shoulders of the survivors. They are the ones we have to ask more than we are asking of others. But that's a very high price to pay. It's understandable, but that's also the cost of the reconciliation and the rebuilding process we have to be involved in for a better future for all of us. So we shall always feel indebted to the survivors, even ourselves, and in that indebtedness we only have to show that it doesn't happen to other people, and [maintain] still [that] it shouldn't happen again to those it has happened to before.

First question, part a – 2 marks

Why, according to Source B, did the government release 40,000–60,000 prisoners back into society?

First question, part b – 3 marks

What do you think the author means in Source A when she states, *"Yet his scar testifies to another truth: the stunning capacity of humans to heal from the unthinkable"*?

Second question – 4 marks

With reference to the origins, purpose and content, analyse the values of Source D for those looking at the role of justice in a post-conflict situation.

Third question – 6 marks

Compare and contrast the attitudes towards the burden of responsibility in Source B and Source C.

Second question – 4 marks

Is the distinction between revenge, retribution and restoration as paradigms of justice a new concept for you? If so, what aspects of each appeal to you and which aspects of each might concern you?

Third question – 6 marks

Read the information about Gacaca in Source C. Then research the approach taken by the TRC in South Africa versus the Nuremberg method of prosecution. What do you think is the purpose of justice? Should it be retribution or rehabilitation?

True peace is not merely the absence of tension: it is the presence of justice.

— Martin Luther King Jr, 1955

The establishment of the International Criminal Tribunal for Rwanda (ICTR)

As the genocide began in April 1994, the UN Security Council, without naming what was happening in Rwanda, called for the creation of a body to investigate violations of human rights, and in November, the ICTR was established through Resolution 995. Modelled on the tribunal already created for the former Yugoslavia, South African judge Richard Goldstone was named as chief prosecutor for the new court. The website for the tribunal (indicated below) states that the purpose of the tribunal was,

> *to contribute to the process of national reconciliation in Rwanda and to the maintenance of peace in the region. The International Criminal Tribunal for Rwanda was established for the prosecution of persons responsible for genocide and other serious violations of international humanitarian law committed in the territory of Rwanda between 1 January 1994 and 31 December 1994.*

In 1995 the seat of the tribunal was located in Arusha, Tanzania where the ill-fated accords had been negotiated two years before. In line with the process of reconciliation the preamble to the statutes of the ICTR states:

> *... the prosecution of persons responsible for serious violations of international humanitarian law would ... contribute to the process of national reconciliation and to the restoration ... of peace.*

http://www.icrc.org/eng/who-we-are/mandate/index.jsp

Problems with the ICTR

As we have already seen, the concept of justice is crucial to understanding how this tribunal and other forms of judicial process such as Gacaca might function in post-genocide Rwanda. The new Rwandan government and the majority of the Rwandan people envisaged that those involved in the genocide would be tried by Rwandan courts, according to the law of the country. However, the practicalities of so doing were extremely difficult. The devastation meant that holding the trials in Tanzania was a practical way of delivering justice as close to the scenes of the crimes as possible and, at the same time, ensuring that those charged with implementing justice would be safe. However, this was not popular with the newly formed government of the country who were still – understandably – deeply suspicious of the international community because of its inaction during the genocide. In addition, there were some outsiders who were concerned that the Rwandans could not be entrusted to administer justice fairly, especially when the maximum sentence the ICTR could hand down was life imprisonment while Rwanda still had the death penalty.

Legally, the findings of the tribunal should take precedence over the national courts of the member states. This potentially could cause problems in challenging the national sovereignty of states. This did occur in the case of one suspect, Pastor Elizaphan Ntakirutimana, a resident in the United States, who was to be extradited to face charges in Arusha. He appealed against his extradition successfully and was released in the USA in 1998. It was only temporarily however, as he and his son Gerard were later sent to the ICTR and received sentences of 10 and 25 years respectively for their part in the deaths of thousands of Tutsi in Mugonero. However, the greatest difficulty the tribunal faced were those regarding administration and mismanagement. The lack of funding and the unavailability of well-trained staff hampered the work of the ICTR in its early years. It wasn't until the end of 1995 that formal proceedings began and the first indictments against eight individuals were processed. The hope had been that those leading the genocide would be tried first, but instead the early prosecutions dealt with local officials who were not the masterminds of the genocide, but people who had come into the hands of the tribunal. In 1998 it was pointed out that the court was functioning with only 50 investigators, while at Nuremberg after the Second World War, there were 2,000 investigators available for handling just 24 Nazi defendants.

Other problems for the ICTR concerned its relationship with the Rwandan government who had been critical of the tribunal. Initially, the RPF government voted against the resolution that created the court over some of the terms of its mandate. This scepticism was reinforced when the tribunal failed to achieve much in its early years up to 1998. Rwandan justice, apart from imposing the death penalty for certain crimes, was also completed quickly, and the slow pace of the ICTR proceedings was incomprehensible to many Rwandans. The ICTR has also been criticized for acting in an uneven manner in not bringing charges against any members of the RPF-led government for human rights abuses and crimes against humanity allegedly committed in the years after the genocide.

The implementation of justice is vital in a society ravaged by the trauma of genocide but was more problematic with the sheer numbers involved in Rwanda as well as the nature of the genocide. Without justice being seen to be done the likelihood of reconciliation is much more challenging to achieve and all of these issues – the lack of a coherent policy, administrative failings, the scarcity of funds and differences in the concept of what constitutes justice – served to hamper the work of the ICTR in its early years. By the end of 1998 only 28 indictments had been issued and 7 of the accused had been convicted. It has since been estimated that there are around 150,000 perpetrators and the vast majority never faced the criminal justice system. In the past 20 years, only 71 people – generally the most severe offenders – have been convicted by the ICTR. The majority (who were mostly living in rural areas, among those whom they killed) confessed and pleaded their case through the Gacaca system. With strong encouragement from the government, most of the survivors have, under the most difficult circumstances, accepted the perpetrators back into their communities.

Achievements of the ICTR

The ICTR did accomplish a number of milestones in its work, which was to be completed by the end of 2015. The first conviction came in 1998 when Jean-Paul Akayesu, a member of the Democratic Republican Movement (MDR) and mayor of Taba commune from April 1993 until June 1994, stood trial on 15 counts of genocide, crimes against humanity and charges of rape during the genocide. He became the first man ever to be convicted for rape as a crime against humanity and was sentenced to life imprisonment.

▲ Jean Kambanda listens to the court before being sentenced to life in prison by the ICTR in 1998

This ... is the first time high-ranking individuals have been called to account before an international court of law for massive violations of human rights in Africa. The tribunal's work sends a strong message to Africa's leaders and warlords.

— Roland Amoussouga from the ICTR

TOK connections

The crimes which were identified by the International Criminal Court (ICC) included genocide, war crimes and crimes against humanity.

1   Why do you think the ICC identified these three crimes?

2   Do you agree with the ICC's decision?

3   What other crimes do you consider could come under the jurisdiction of the ICC?

Later that year former Rwandan Prime Minister **Jean Kambanda** was put on trial. Kambanda, a Hutu, was accused of inciting massacres and ordering roadblocks to help round up Tutsi and in distributing weapons for their slaughter. (For more details see http://www.theguardian.com/world/2014/apr/02/rwanda-genocide-fight-justice).

Kambanda was the first man to plead guilty to the charge of genocide and was sentenced to life imprisonment. Chief Judge Laity Kama said, *"Jean Kambanda abused his authority and the trust of the population. Nor has he expressed contrition, regret, or sympathy for the victims in Rwanda even when given the opportunity."*

Another milestone achieved by the ICTR was in the case of **Pauline Nyiramusuhuko**, the former minister of women's affairs arrested in 1997, who became the first female to be convicted of genocide when the ICTR eventually completed its case against her in 2011.

Other landmark cases include those against the head of the RTLM "hate radio", Ferdinand Nahimana and the editor of Kangura, Hassan Ngeze, in 2003. Both were charged with genocide, incitement to genocide, and crimes against humanity; the court finding both guilty and sentencing them to life imprisonment. These sentences were later reduced to 30 and 35 years respectively. The principle that those responsible for radio broadcasts and newspapers which fomented hatred against in this case, the Tutsi, established the precept that anyone who incites the public to commit genocide can be penalized for crimes against humanity.

Although on paper the ICTR had only brought to justice a relatively small number of those involved in the genocide, the reality of trying to deal with what had happened was an almost impossible task. Challenged by over-burdened prisons and the knowledge that hundreds of thousands of individuals had participated in the genocide, the Rwandan government cautioned that it would take more than 200 years for the ICTR to deal with all outstanding accusations.

TOK: Ethics and Justics

Statement 1: Luis Moreno-Ocampo, the Chief Prosecutor for the International Criminal Court, (ICC) believes that people need judicial institutions to help them behave well. Apart from institutions that may help control behaviour, Moreno-Ocampo states, *"You have to educate people in values"*.

1 What values do you think need to be nurtured in order to sustain peaceful, productive communities?

2 What are effective ways of instilling these values?

Statement 2: Former UNHCR commissioner José Ayala Lasso, has said, *"A person stands a better chance of being tried and judged for killing one human being than for killing 100,000."*

3 What do you think Lasso is trying to express in this comment?

4 How far do you agree with this argument?

5 What are the possible consequences for a community or nation if wrongdoers are *not* brought to justice?

6 From your own experience and knowledge, what evidence suggests that crimes can be prevented if individuals believe they will be punished for committing them?

7 Can you think of any evidence that demonstrates that the fear of being caught and punished does *not* prevent individuals from committing crimes?

8 How does this connect back to your responses to the questions following statements 1 and 2?

9 What do you think can be done to prevent people, especially those in positions of power, from committing crimes?

10 Do you consider that if those in power do commit crimes they should be punished more harshly than others because of their responsibilities?

The political impact

RPF-led governments

With at least 10% of the country's population dead and a further 20% displaced, either internally or in neighbouring countries, the running of the country was bound to be a major problem for some years to follow. Remarkably, 20 years after the genocide, Rwanda has become one of the most stable countries in the African continent. Since 1994, gross domestic product has almost tripled and the population has increased by 25% to more than 10 million. Rwanda can claim to be one of the most well-ordered societies in the region.

For some, the political and economic advances have come at a cost. In July 1994, following the RPF success on the battlefield, the elimination of the Hutu Power Movement and control of the political process was a natural by-product of victory. The RPF took control of the government and attempted to reorganize it along the lines of the agreements reached at Arusha. A new government was created called the Broad Based Government of National Unity and headed by a Hutu, Pasteur Bizimungu. Bizimungu had been a significant figure in the Rwandan government of former President Habyarimana but had fallen out with him in 1990 and joined the RPF that same year, helping to negotiate the Arusha Accords. His appointment as the first president of a post-genocide Rwandan coalition government was in effect a sound decision politically, although many acknowledged that the Vice President, Paul Kagame, retained real political power behind the presidency.

The political process was heavily controlled with the radical Hutu party, the MRND, banned and the formation of new political parties prohibited until 2003. Meanwhile, the new government controlled the political debate through the repression of dissent. As ethnicity had been used to cause the genocide, the government abolished any discrimination based on ethnicity, race or religion. Unity, reconciliation and a collective national "Rwandaness" has been stressed. This has been at the heart of the political process. In addition one of the new government's first actions was to reopen schools and undertake a revision of school curricula. The importance of teaching history has long been recognized by all national governments and formal teaching of Rwandan history was not carried out in primary and secondary schools until at least 10 years after the genocide. Rwanda's entire school curriculum is undergoing a comprehensive overhaul and is due to be relaunched in 2016.

The RPF dominated the government after 1994, and Bizimingu soon came into conflict with Kagame over a number of issues including the suppression of Hutus, political dissent in general and the corruption charges which were levelled against him. The RPF claimed to have introduced stability and a multi-party democracy, but its critics claim it has centralized power within a Tutsi elite and crushed potential opponents. In March 2000, Bizimingu was forced to resign in a dispute over a new government cabinet and was replaced as president by Paul Kagame. In 2003, the first elections were held following the genocide and Kagame swept to power through a landslide victory, winning 95% of the vote. In the following year Bizimungu was put on trial, found guilty of embezzlement and inciting violence and sentenced to 15 years in jail. He served his sentence until 2007 when Kagame released him under a presidential pardon.

The RPF have dominated Rwandan politics since the genocide. This is understandable given the horrors which preceded their takeover, and the priority of the RPF has been survival. The methods they have chosen to retain power have been considered by critics and liberals in the West to be harsh. Rwanda has a history of authoritarian rule and in this sense the domination of the political scene by one party is hardly an exception. The RPF has dominated the mechanisms to retain power in the country including the media, the state bureaucracy, the banks, many state-owned companies, the judiciary and the security services. However, under the RPF, the people of Rwanda are better off than before the genocide.

The economic impact

Rwanda prior to 1994 was already one of the poorest countries in the world and the state of the economy was a contributing factor to the onset of genocide. The events of that year decimated the population as well as destroying Rwanda's fragile economic base. To rebuild the economy was another major challenge facing the new government. However, Rwanda has made significant progress in attracting foreign investment and in stabilizing and restoring its economy so that since 1995, the Rwandan economy has been one of the fastest growing in Africa and the world. Real annual GDP growth averaged 8.2% from 1995–2001, more than double the sub-Saharan African average. The main reason for this impressive growth rate is that the country has been steadily recovering from the economic decline of the years prior to 1994 and, importantly, has received considerable assistance from foreign donors.

Rwanda has been a major recipient of international development assistance since the genocide. Some have argued that this has been partially to compensate for ignoring the genocide but, for whatever reason, between 1995 and 2000 almost US $4 billion was pledged to support the rebuilding of Rwanda's economy. Assistance levels remain among the highest in Africa with the EU, World Bank, IMF, and bilaterally, the USA and the UK as the largest donors. Rwanda's rebuilding of its economy since the genocide has been driven by three main sources: the export of tea and coffee; foreign aid and, more recently, tourism. Economic growth has averaged an 8% growth since 2001. The government has restored security throughout the country, rebuilt rural and urban infrastructure and controlled price inflation. All these factors have contributed to Rwanda's economic recovery. Rwanda's economic growth has also been dependent upon a well-educated middle class, but it is still one of the most densely populated countries in the world with 75% of the population tied to agriculture, and coffee and tea providing almost 80% of Rwanda's export revenues.

Poverty nonetheless remains severe among some of the population; recent figures estimate that 45% of the population live in poverty with an income of less than $1.50 per day. With very few natural resources, the government's main economic challenge is to cultivate new areas such as information and communication technology and to diversify agricultural production. Foreign donors supply Rwanda with a significant percentage of their aid budget and largely turn a blind eye

to the regime's deficiencies. This is partly out of consideration for its security concerns, and partially because the RPF-controlled government has done such a good job of rebuilding the nation.

Continued warfare in the Democratic Republic of Congo (Zaire)

In 2014, on the 20th anniversary of the Rwandan genocide, the former president of the Security Council in 1994, Colin Keating, made a speech in which he said:

> Twenty years later, you are still dealing with the consequences in the Democratic Republic of the Congo (DRC). The failure in Rwanda in 1994 caused not only genocide, but it also led to an appalling humanitarian catastrophe in eastern DRC in 1995. This led directly to the civil wars in the DRC and to human tragedy on an even larger scale. Some estimates suggest that up to 5 million died. Major instability afflicted the region.

What had started in Rwanda spiralled beyond the borders of the country to have an impact on others, but most emphatically the DRC, formerly the country of Zaire.

The existence of a large number of Hutu soldiers, militia and hard line genocidaires so close to Rwanda's border was a thorn in the side of the new RPF government and one they could not tolerate for long. The UN refugee agencies and NGOs were incapable of preventing incursions back into Rwanda, and Zairian President Mobutu was unwilling to curb the actions of the Hutu refugee forces. The existence of the latter was both a political and a military problem and not simply a humanitarian one for all concerned. The RPF itself had begun as a refugee army and had now taken power in Rwanda.

In 1996, a human rights report confirmed the complicity of Mobutu and the Zairean army in the arming of Hutu soldiers. This problem was compounded by the situation in North and South Kivu, two provinces located in eastern Zaire which had been centres of opposition to the regime of President Mobutu and which also contained a mixed ethnic population of Tutsi and Hutu. These ethnic groups are known as the **Banyarwanda**, located primarily in North Kivu, and the Banyamulenge who lived in the south. Many of them were Tutsi, (sometimes known as Congolese Tutsi) and had also been persecuted by the Zairean government. It was fertile ground for conflict. There is evidence that the RPF government supported the Tutsi in Zaire to frustrate the Hutu as well as to signal their discontent with the attitude of the Mobutu government.

Opponents to the Mobutu regime also included the Alliance of Democratic Forces for the Liberation of Congo (ADFL) under Laurent-Désiré Kabila. Kabila had been a Marxist, and had been assisted by Che Guevara when the famous revolutionary was in the Congo in the mid-1960s. Kabila was a self professed Marxist and an admirer of Mao Zedong who had waged rebellion in the east of Zaire for the last thirty years. According to Che Guevara, he was not a committed nor an effective leader. Naturally, Kabila was seen as a committed communist by the USA who later backed the Mobutu regime. The ADFL came together in October 1996 with the backing of Rwanda and three more of

Class discussion

What might be the impact of the considerably larger numbers of Hutu refugees who were displaced in the surrounding countries of Tanzania, Burundi and now Zaire?

Banyarwanda

Meaning "those who come from Rwanda".

▲ Refugees fleeing during the Congo war

Zaire's African neighbours, Uganda, Burundi and Angola, each of which had grievances against the Mobutu regime. The catalyst for the outbreak of the movement against Mobutu were the conditions in the camps and the presence of Hutu opponents to the government in Kigali. Kagame had stated that if no one was prepared to do anything about the camps, the RPF would have to deal with the problem themselves.

What began in October 1996 is known as the **First Congo War**, called by some, Africa's first world war. By mid-November it was certain that thousands had been killed – many innocent refugees as well as Hutu soldiers – and the world watched again as the camps were broken up and over 600,000 refugees made their way back across the border into Rwanda from where so many had fled less than two years before.

Other refugees, including many génocidaires, escaped into the forested interior of Zaire where appalling human rights abuses were committed by troops pursuing the extremists. By May 1997, the rebels were advancing on Kinshasa and the corrupt and unpopular regime of President Mobutu was toppled. Kabila became the new head of state, renaming the country the Democratic Republic of the Congo (DRC). The old dictator fled into exile and died in Morocco four months later.

The war had taken the lives of hundreds of thousands of people – the majority of them innocent civilians caught up in the maelstrom. A year later conflict broke out again as the former friends became enemies and the **Second Congo War** began. The crisis which had begun in Rwanda now spiralled out of control, once more engulfing the Great Lakes region with its epicentre in the DRC. This new war involved armed forces from more than seven nations in addition to numerous rebel groups and militias. Rwanda and Uganda withdrew their support from Kabila and found themselves in opposition to Angola and Zimbabwe. What was to transpire became one of the deadliest conflicts since the Second World War, causing the deaths of at least 5 million people and was only brought to a temporary conclusion by a peace agreement in 2003. Meanwhile, Laurent Kabila was assassinated by one of his bodyguards in 2001 and was replaced by his own son, Joseph Kabila, present head of state of the DRC.

The genocide of 1994 had lit the fuse of death and destruction in Congo and the Great Lakes region. The inability of the international community to prevent the genocide in Rwanda or to halt the militarisation of the refugee camps and control the bloodthirsty Hutu militia, demonstrated that the consequences of civil conflict and massive human displacement helped cause an even greater human catastrophe in the region. Splinter conflicts drew in armies from nine African nations fighting a series of complicated wars over an area the size of western Europe. Once again the international community was reluctant to intervene. The UN chose to commit more peacekeepers to the DRC than they had to Rwanda, but their actions were in sharp contrast to their commitment to the former Yugoslavia and Kosovo.

Individuals who fought the genocide

In all conflicts there are people who go along with what the majority are doing and those who follow orders. A crucial question in today's world is: what enables people to oppose a greater power or to resist? This could be to defy orders you know to be wrong, illegal, immoral or against your own or others' interests. It can take the form of racist ideology such as those preached in Rwanda, Nazi Germany

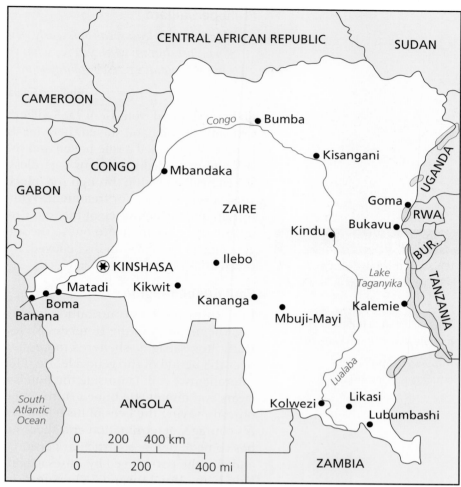

▲ Zaire (Democratic Republic of the Congo)

or elsewhere, and also the active participation in mass atrocities. The consequence can often be to place yourself in considerable danger and, in the case of Rwanda, we will now look at a number of individuals who did just that.

What is heroism?

How we look at heroes gives us an insight into how we look at ourselves and our role in the world today.

If dehumanising the victims, as happened through media such as RTLM and Kangura as well as group conformity, led to so many deaths, we can ask, what encourages resistance? The individuals below each saved countless lives and put themselves in considerable danger through most of the period of the genocide. One of them, a UN peacekeeper, lost his life, and has been recognised for his huge contribution to saving the lives of hundreds of potential victims by the United Nations in May 2014 through the "Captain Mbaye Diagne Medal for Exceptional Courage". This United Nations peacekeeper is credited with saving hundreds of, perhaps even a thousand Rwandans from death during the 1994 genocide.

Here is a brief summary of each of the individuals.

Class discussion

Who do we hold up as heroes and why?

What do they represent?

ATL Research skills

Research Philippe Gaillard and each of the individuals on the following page.

Philippe Gaillard

*If you don't at least speak out clearly, you are participating in the genocide …
If you just shut up when you see what you see, morally and ethically you
can't shut up. It's a responsibility to talk.*

— Philippe Gaillard, director of the Red Cross in Rwanda

Philippe Gaillard from Geneva, Switzerland was the head of the Red
Cross in Rwanda and stayed there for the entirety of the genocide. The
Red Cross provided a safe haven and medical support for thousands of
sick and wounded Rwandans regardless of their ethnicity. Gaillard often
risked his life passing through roadblocks bringing wounded Hutu and
Tutsi survivors back for treatment. With the constant support of the
International Committee of the Red Cross in Geneva, Gaillard worked
untiringly to get the word out to the international media about the
genocide in Rwanda, and is believed, through the Red Cross, to have
saved an estimated 65,000 lives.

Paul Rusesabagina

Paul Rusesabagina's contribution is not so clear as that of the others. He
was the manager of the Hotel des Milles Collines in Kigali, Rwanda. A
Hutu, Rusesabagina sheltered more than 1,200 people inside his hotel
over the period of the genocide. He offered them protection from the
Interahamwe militia outside the hotel, whom he bribed with alcohol,
cigars and money. He bribed Hutu soldiers and petitioned influential
officials, saving the lives of his fellow Rwandans in this period through
his courage, determination and sheer luck. The 2004 Hollywood film
has come to define a particular version of what happened in Rwanda
and also the part played by Rusesabagina. A more recent book called
"Inside the Hotel Rwanda: The Surprising True Story" written by
Edouard Kayihura, a Rwandan, shows a different version of events
inside the hotel during the genocide. The book exposes Rusesabagina
as a manipulating, self-seeking individual at odds with the Hollywood
image. It demonstrates just how slippery historical truth can be when
the mass media is involved. Students can learn a lot about the dangers of
media-generated versions of history as they attempt to interpret the facts
of history and perceptions of the genocide.

General Roméo Dallaire

Canadian General Roméo Dallaire was the Commander of the UNAMIR
in Rwanda from 1993 and through the genocide in 1994. During the
conflict, General Dallaire maintained safe areas for thousands of terrified
Rwandans, threatened by Hutu killers and government soldiers. He did
this with fewer than 1,000 troops, few resources, and very little support
from the UN or the international community. His role has been explored
in some detail earlier in this chapter.

Carl Wilkens

*And when Christ said that he would come and die just for one person, how can
we think of anything less … Because … I'm not alone as I am working here.
There are many, many other people (gunfire) … who are doing their best.*

— Extract from Carl Wilkens' home video taken in Kigali in April 1994

ATL Thinking skills

Why was the Red Cross more
effective than the UN in Rwanda?

You can listen to Rusesabagina's
interview with Oprah Winfrey at:

http://www.oprah.com/
omagazine/Oprah-Talks-To-
Paul-Rusesabagina

Carl Wilkens was the head of the Adventist Development and Relief Agency (ADRA), an independent NGO working in Rwanda supporting orphans and other children in the community. Wilkens and his family had been in Rwanda since 1990. He was the only American to remain in the capital Kigali throughout the entire genocide. He protected his Tutsi servants in their house where they stayed hidden for three weeks. Afterwards, Wilkens ventured out each day into Kigali, working his way through roadblocks, dealing with the Interahamwe killers and soldiers in order to bring food, water and medicine to groups of orphans and children trapped in the city. On one occasion he went to an orphanage in Gisimba where armed militiamen were waiting for an occasion to kill those inside. Apparently the presence of Wilkens stopped them. Recognising that as soon as he left the militia would probably enter the buildings and kill them all, he gambled by driving to find the governor, who might help him to save the orphans. When he was in his office, the interim Prime Minister, Jean Kambanda, appeared and Wilkens confronted him and asked for help. Surprisingly, Kambanda spoke to aides and had the militia removed from Gisimba thus saving the lives of the orphans. Wilkens appealed to the genocidal leaders to relocate the orphans which they did by loading them into vehicles and escorting them through some of the most dangerous roadblocks in Kigali to Saint Michel church where they remained unharmed.

Wilkens negotiated with known genocidaires to save the lives of people; this was a dilemma that confronted a number of those who resisted the genocide, risking their own lives to save others. General Romeo Dallaire, Diagne, Gaillard and each of those mentioned in this section faced the same dilemma: was it morally acceptable to "shake hands with the devil" in order to save someone's life? Carl Wilkens wrote a book called *I'm Not Leaving* and, with his wife, founded the educational non-profit organization "World Outside My Shoes" in 2008 to facilitate education to share stories and teach about genocide and human rights.

> *People need to understand the genocide didn't come from the grassroots. The genocide was a top-down catastrophe organized by extremist elements within the government, using the government's infrastructure.*
>
> — Carl Wilkens in an interview by Jeff Boyd

Rwanda through the eyes of the only American to remain in the country through the 1994 genocide.

I'm not leaving.

Carl Wilkens

The PBS programme "Ghosts of Rwanda" made in 2004 is an excellent source of information containing a large number of interviews with key personalities including a number of those featured in this section. Another radio broadcast is called "The few who stayed – defying genocide in Rwanda." From an American RadioWorks documentary produced in cooperation with the PBS programme "Frontline":

http://americanradioworks.publicradio.org/features/rwanda/transcript.html

You can listen to interviews with Carl Wilkens at:

http://www.atoday.org/article/1193/features/interviews/2012/carl-wilkens-interview-by-jeff-boyd

Captain Mbaye Diagne

Captain Mbaye Diagne of Senegal served with the UN mission in Rwanda. Unarmed and in the face of extreme danger he saved hundreds, perhaps a thousand Rwandans from death during the genocide. He is the only one of the select group of individuals described here to lose his life during the genocide. In May 2014, the Security Council created the "Captain Mbaye Diagne Medal for Exceptional Courage" in honour of this peacekeeper.

As a member of the UNAMIR from Senegal, Mbaye Diagne serving in Rwanda during the genocide ignored the UN's orders not to intervene and saved the lives of potential victims by persuasive means, bribing, buying and charming his way through checkpoints of killers and conducting independent and unauthorized rescue missions. He saved lives armed only with courage and his sense that what he was doing was right.

Diagne rescued the children of the Prime Minster Agathe Uwilingiyimana and conducted several missions through dozens of checkpoints to save up to 1,000 people during the genocide. In the days of the genocide, he became a legend among UN forces in Kigali. On another occasion he found a group of 25 Tutsis hiding in a house in a Kigali neighbourhood that was particularly dangerous; Diagne transported the Tutsis to the UN headquarters in groups of five, on each trip passing through 23 militia checkpoints with a UN vehicle full of Tutsi. Somehow, he convinced the killers to let them pass. Those who met Diagne in Rwanda remember him as a hero who had refused to be a bystander in the face of evil and the UN's medal is a recognition of his courage and also a reminder of what a UN peacekeeper should be; someone guided by moral rules and principles dedicated to preserving peace, saving lives and protecting the defenceless. The medal will be awarded to UN personnel *who demonstrate exceptional courage, in the face of extreme danger, while fulfilling the mandate of their missions in the service of humanity and the United Nations*", according to a resolution unanimously adopted by the Security Council.

A real-life Cool Hand Luke …

The bravest of the brave …

… the greatest man I have ever known …

… the kind of guy you meet once in a lifetime.

— Some words from those who knew Captain Mbaye Diagne

Diagne was killed instantly, on 31 May 1994, when a mortar shell hit his jeep as he drove back to the UN headquarters in Kigali. He was buried in Senegal with full military honours. Those who met him however, knew that they were in the company of the "sort of man" that you met "only once in a lifetime." BBC reporter Mark Doyle reflects on the impact of meeting Mbaye Diagne and has an excellent podcast called "A good man in Rwanda" and a BBC documentary of the same name.

Look at the UN press release for the Captain Mbaye Diagne Medal for Exceptional Courage at:

http://www.bbc.co.uk/news/special/2014/newsspec_6954/index.html

http://www.un.org/News/Press/docs/2014/sc11385.doc.htm

ATL Thinking and communication skills

Some of these individuals claim that what they did was "normal" and that they were only doing the right thing. How difficult is it sometimes to take what you consider to be the right course of action when others are doing something different?

There are excerpts from the video Diagne recorded from mid-May until his death on 31 May which he filmed in the time between his UN peacekeeping duties and his rescue missions to save hundreds of lives. These excerpts offer a glimpse of how his charm and personality won over so many, even the genocidaires. (See http://www.pbs.org/wgbh/pages/frontline/shows/ghosts/video/mbaye_hi.html)

Conclusion

My soul is overwhelmed with sorrow to the point of death.

— Matthew 26:38

The genocide in Rwanda was one of the defining moments in the last years of the 20th century. For 100 days in the spring and early summer of 1994 at least 800,000 people were put to death by their neighbours, and their own government in an unmistakable case of state-sponsored genocide. Linda Melvern said it would *"surely be one of the defining scandals of the twentieth century"* (2004: xiv).

For many of those who played a part in the events it represents a fundamental moment in their lives. For the people of Rwanda and for all humanity, it was a tragedy; for some of the key figures involved in decision-making it was a cause of bitter regret. Boutros Boutros-Ghali said, *"It was one of my greatest failures. I failed in Rwanda."* Madeleine Albright commented, *"It sits as the greatest regret that I have from the time I was UN ambassador."* It has scarred Romeo Dallaire forever: *"Rwanda will never leave me. It is in the pores of my body. My soul is in those hills, my spirit is with the spirits of all those people who were slaughtered … ".*

Overwhelming guilt at the failure to stop the genocide has been a crucial factor in some government's and individual's responses to what happened in Rwanda. It had a profound impact on the country, the region and the world. In terms of justice, the Rwandan genocide and the wars in the Balkans indicated a landmark in the international community's commitment to accountability for crimes under international law. Nevertheless, cynics can be critical of the phrase "never again" which was heard from the mouths of many as events after Rwanda continue to demonstrate man's callous indifference to the suffering of others and the furtherance of their own ambition. The "typhoon of madness" (Rucyahana, 2007) which swept through Rwanda in 1994 will forever remain as a scar on the landscape of humanity.

Class discussion

Why did so few people, in and out of Rwanda, speak out? What happened when people did speak out?

Thinking and communication skills

Former US Presiodent Roosevelt, speaking about the century's first genocide (against the Armenians), said:

Unless we put honour and duty first, and are willing to risk something in order to achieve righteousness both for ourselves and others, we shall accomplish nothing.

What do you think he meant by this statement in the context of the behaviour of those in this section.

TOK connections

How can studying history, and events such as the genocide in Rwanda where individuals and nations act honourably but some in the opposite manner, help us to understand the present?

Thinking skills

George Santayana said, *"Those who do not remember the past are condemned to repeat it."*

What is he suggesting by this and how far do you agree with what he is saying?

References and further reading

Berry, J and Pott Berry, C. 1999. *Genocide in Rwanda: A Collective Memory*. Howard University Press. Washington, DC, USA

Cahiers Lumière et Société Dialogue IV. 1999. December issue, number 16

Dallaire, R. 2003. *Shake Hands with the Devil: The Failure of Humanity in Rwanda*. Random House, Toronto, Canada

de Brouwer and Ka Hon Chu. 2009. *The Men Who Killed Me: Rwandan Survivors of Sexual Violence*. Douglas & McIntyre. Vancouver, Canada

Hatzfeld, J. 2008. *A Time for Machetes: The Rwandan Genocide – the killers speak*. Profile Books. London, UK

Hochschild, A. 1999. *King Leopold's Ghost: A story of greed, terror, and heroism in colonial Africa*. Houghton Mifflin. New York, USA

Human Rights Watch report. 2004. "Leave none to tell the story", page 946. New York, USA

Kangura magazine: A complete list of *Kangura* articles is available online at http://www.rwandafile.com/Kangura/

Keane, F. 1996. *Season of Blood: A Rwandan Journey*. Penguin. London, UK

King, E. 2013. *From Classrooms to Conflict in Rwanda*. Cambridge University Press. Cambridge, UK

Larson, C. 2009. *As We Forgive: Stories of Reconciliation from Rwanda*. Zonderva. Grand Rapids, Michigan, USA

Melvern, L. 2000. *A People Betrayed: The Role of the West in Rwanda's Genocide*. Zed Books. London, UK

Melvern, L. 2004. *Conspiracy to Murder: The Rwandan Genocide*. Verso. London, UK

Metzl, J. 1997. "Rwandan genocide and the international law of radio jamming". *American Journal of International Law*, volume 91, number 4, pages 628–51.

Power, S. 2002. *A Problem from Hell: America and the Age of Genocide*, page 359. Basic Books. New York, USA

Prunier, G. 1995. *The Rwanda Crisis: History of a Genocide*, page 4. Columbia University Press, New York, USA

Rucyahana, J. 2007. *The Bishop of Rwanda: Finding forgiveness amidst a pile of bones*. Thomas Nelson, Nashville, TN, USA

Somerville, K. 2012. *Radio Propaganda and the Broadcasting of Hatred: Historical Development and Definitions*. Palgrave Macmillan. Basingstoke, UK

Tyson, T. 2004. *Blood Done Sign My Name: A True Story*. Three Rivers Press. New York, USA

UNHCR *Refugees* magazine. 2004.

Wallis A. 2007. *Silent Accomplice: the Untold Story of France's role in Rwandan Genocide*. IB Tauris. New York, USA

2 KOSOVO, 1989-2002

Introduction

One day the great European War will come out of some damned foolish thing in the Balkans.

— Otto von Bismarck, 1888

A chronology of key events up to 1989

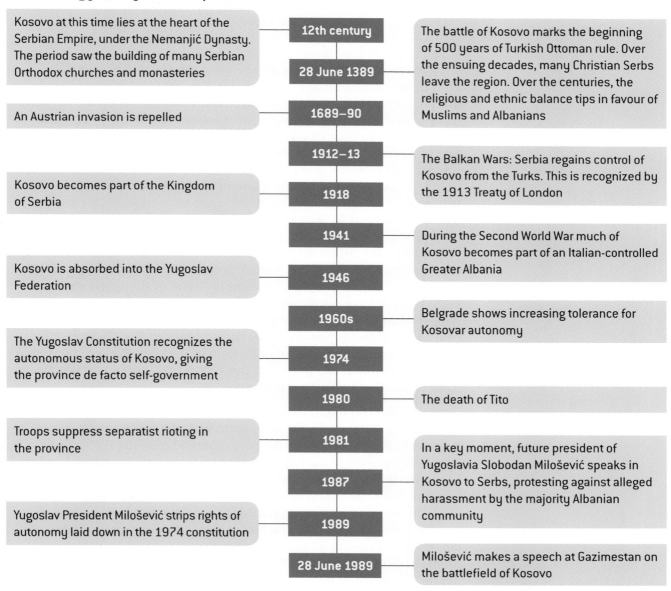

12th century — Kosovo at this time lies at the heart of the Serbian Empire, under the Nemanjić Dynasty. The period saw the building of many Serbian Orthodox churches and monasteries

28 June 1389 — The battle of Kosovo marks the beginning of 500 years of Turkish Ottoman rule. Over the ensuing decades, many Christian Serbs leave the region. Over the centuries, the religious and ethnic balance tips in favour of Muslims and Albanians

1689–90 — An Austrian invasion is repelled

1912–13 — The Balkan Wars: Serbia regains control of Kosovo from the Turks. This is recognized by the 1913 Treaty of London

1918 — Kosovo becomes part of the Kingdom of Serbia

1941 — During the Second World War much of Kosovo becomes part of an Italian-controlled Greater Albania

1946 — Kosovo is absorbed into the Yugoslav Federation

1960s — Belgrade shows increasing tolerance for Kosovar autonomy

1974 — The Yugoslav Constitution recognizes the autonomous status of Kosovo, giving the province de facto self-government

1980 — The death of Tito

1981 — Troops suppress separatist rioting in the province

1987 — In a key moment, future president of Yugoslavia Slobodan Milošević speaks in Kosovo to Serbs, protesting against alleged harassment by the majority Albanian community

1989 — Yugoslav President Milošević strips rights of autonomy laid down in the 1974 constitution

28 June 1989 — Milošević makes a speech at Gazimestan on the battlefield of Kosovo

Kosovo, a tiny province in the Balkans, was the location of the last great European war of the 20th century. From the assassination that triggered the First World War to the ethnic warfare of the last decade of the century in Serbia, Croatia and Bosnia, the Balkans have been the crucible of Europe in the 20th century; the place where terrorism and genocide became tools of policy, spilling over to engulf the region and beyond. It was by no means the only country where blood was spilt in the last decade of the century but it was probably the most visible. Few countries received anything like the intense scrutiny and media coverage that was devoted to the Balkans. As we have seen in the case study of Rwanda, much of the world largely ignored what happened there. However, the Balkans and Kosovo are part of Europe and therefore more accessible to examination by the international media than conflicts waged in other parts of the world. In contrast to what happened in Rwanda, developments in the Balkans were shaped much more by the actions of major powers.

Kosovo is on the doorstep of Europe.

— Tony Blair, 1999

The root cause of the crisis in Kosovo was the collapse of Yugoslavia and the nationalism that engendered it; Kosovo was both a victim and a catalyst of this nationalism and, like Rwanda, suffered from the drive to defend an ethnic group. Kosovo has only recently become a new country. In February 2008, it declared independence, becoming one of the world's smallest countries in the middle of one of the most prosperous economic and political regions on earth. Kosovo's pathway to independence caused conflict among some European powers and throws light on another of the major issues causing problems for the contemporary world, namely the exercise of self-determination, which may conflict with the right of the territorial integrity of nation states. In recent times the problems of separatism, whether it be evidenced among the Russians in the Ukraine, Islamic groups within the Philippines, the Basque or Catalans in Spain, Tibetans in China or the Québécois in Canada, each have ramifications for other political entities. So what happened in Kosovo is important: the conflict prompted an intervention by a group of major powers under the umbrella of NATO, ostensibly to prevent ethnic cleansing of one group by another. These actions by the international community – in this case NATO – present a significant contrast to what took place in Rwanda.

Consider why this might have been the case. Ethnicity was certainly a contributing factor. As in Rwanda, there were demographic issues in Kosovo, in this case between majority Serb and minority Albanians. However, the scale of the killing in Kosovo was small compared to what happened in Rwanda. A major reason for this was the geographical locations of the two areas of conflict. As we have seen, Rwanda was, to put it simply, of lesser importance to the major powers than Kosovo and the Balkan region. The inaction of some of those powers in Rwanda did, however, contribute towards different policies being pursued and ultimately towards a more active intervention in Kosovo. How and why did NATO launch its first-ever war – a three-month campaign of advanced air strikes against Serbia, followed by an on-the-ground intervention that resulted in the creation of a newly independent state?

It is necessary to set the story of Kosovo, both in the recent past and the present, within the context of the Balkans and Europe. After this, we need to consider why conflict in this region promoted intervention and what the consequences of this conflict and intervention have been for the modern world.

The Balkan peninsula, showing the states of the former Yugoslavia after 1919

Place names
Most towns have both an Albanian name and a Serbian one; for example, Prishtina in Albanian and Priština in Serb. This text will use the name most familiar to people in the West.

THE BOILING POINT.

▲ A cartoon entitled "The boiling point", published in the British satirical magazine *Punch* in October 1912. It shows the major European powers attempting to keep the Balkans under control as war threatens

The development of Albanian nationalism in the 20th century

In order to understand what took place in the last decade of the 20th century in the Balkans, it is necessary to go back to the beginning of the century. In 1900, neither Kosovo nor Yugoslavia existed independently. The Balkan peninsular was considered a poor, backward part of Europe that had been ruled by the Ottoman Empire for almost 500 years. Bordered in the north by the old Austro–Hungarian Empire, itself a ramshackle collection of nationalities and the Tsarist empire of Russia, the Balkans constituted a mass of ethnic groups consisting of Christian, Orthodox, Muslim and Jew, all nominally under the control of foreign rulers.

Albanian nationalists had begun to flex their muscles following the Congress of Berlin in 1878, when some of them met in the small town of Prizen in Kosovo and created the League of Prizren. This was formed to defend their language and culture, which were threatened by the imminent collapse of the Ottoman Empire. Around 750,000 Albanians lived within the Ottoman Empire, concentrated mainly in present-day Albania, Kosovo, Macedonia and Greece, and had served the Ottomans in many ways disproportionate to their small numbers. They had been valued mercenaries in the army, had led commercial enterprises and had been advisers to the Sultans. About 70% of Albanians adopted Islam; some were Catholic and others Orthodox Christian, like the majority of people in the Balkan states. Albanian

▲ The Balkans around 1910, showing the Austro–Hungarian, Russian and Ottoman Empires

nationalists had gained little out of the Congress of Berlin though. When others, such as Serbia and Romania, had their independence confirmed, Albania remained subject to Ottoman rule. The growth of Albanian nationalism in Kosovo challenged Serbian aspirations there. It was to be another 30 years before the First Balkan War concluded that Albania was to gain its statehood, and then only as a result of a compromise deal.

The Balkan Wars, 1912–13

Due to political upheavals and power politics, the region of the Balkans and beyond was caught up in "great power" rivalry that was to eventually result in the inferno of the First World War. This was, up until then, the largest and most destructive conflict in world history. Immediately prior to this, the Balkans had experienced two wars that had deprived the Ottoman Empire of almost all its remaining European territory. These wars also confirmed Serbia as the aggressive new power in the Balkans and saw the emergence of the new state of Albania. The First Balkan War in 1912 was a loose alliance of Balkan states, consisting of Serbia, Bulgaria, Greece and Montenegro, up against the ailing "sick man of Europe", the Ottoman Empire. These states formed the Balkan League with Russian support early in 1912 – originally to break Macedonia away from Turkey's control. At the time, Turkey was already engaged in a war with Italy; when Montenegro began the First Balkan War by attacking the Turks in October 1912, the other Balkan states soon followed.

The Balkan allies were quickly victorious, and the Turkish collapse was followed by an armistice in December 1912 and a peace conference in London. The Treaty of London, signed in May 1913, removed almost all of the Ottoman Empire's remaining European territory, including the whole of Macedonia and Albania. Serbia had wanted to gain control of Albania to give them access to the sea and was opposed in this ambition by Austria-Hungary who, having already annexed the province of Bosnia in 1908, wanted Albania too. As rivals in the area, the Russians opposed this and, as a concession, Macedonia was divided among the Balkan allies, with Albanian independence insisted upon by the European powers. In 1913, Albania gained its sovereignty just a year before war broke out in Europe.

The Second Balkan War began almost immediately, when Serbia, Greece and Romania quarrelled with Bulgaria over the division of Macedonia. In June 1913, Serbia and Greece made an alliance against Bulgaria and defeated their former ally. Under the terms of the treaty signed in August, Bulgaria was left with a tiny portion of Macedonia while the remainder was given to Serbia and Greece.

The Balkan Wars were the first all-European conflicts of the 20th century; the NATO intervention in Kosovo 90 years later was to be the last of that turbulent century. These early Balkan Wars have been submerged under the much greater conflict that followed less than a year later, but have been called *"the first phase of the First World War"* (Hall, 2000). However, these bloody wars were significant in that they introduced an age of modern warfare that saw mass armies, industrial warfare and civilian displacement on a large scale. Conflict that began in the Balkan Peninsula in 1912 would continue in Europe, with short interruptions, up to 1945, and then emerge again in the last decade of the century when the Balkans again became an arena for nationalist conflict following the collapse of Yugoslavia in 1991.

▲ The Balkan Peninsula after the First and Second Balkan Wars in 1912–13

The Balkans and the First World War

For many Serbs and other Slavs living in the Balkans under foreign rule at the time, Serbia was seen as their champion. Unfortunately, it was one of these young radicals, a Bosnian Serb named Gavrilo Princip, whose shots killed the heir to the Austro–Hungarian throne, Franz Ferdinand, and his wife Duchess Sophie, on their visit to Sarajevo on 28 June 1914. Six weeks later, most of Europe was at war. The Balkan Wars and the First World War were devastating for the people of the Balkans as well as for both Kosovo and Albania. Even though Albania managed to maintain a precarious neutrality during the First World War, all its neighbours were involved in the conflict and the effects were felt throughout the region. Balkan nationalism was challenged by Austria-Hungary but, as its military threat diminished, some feared that Italy would exercise its claims to the Dalmatian coast. Another threat to Balkan and Albanian nationalism was that, with victory, Serbia and Italy might carve up what had been the former Ottoman and Austro–Hungarian Empires in the Balkans.

Meanwhile, in October of 1918, Serbia managed to occupy Kosovo, which many Serbs regarded as their own heartland, reclaiming the battlefield of Kosovo where their ancestors had died in 1389. The majority Albanian population of Kosovo was uneasy; Albanians were not Slavs and were unhappy that Kosovo had not been incorporated into Albania. For much of the world, though, Serbia had been little David standing up to mighty Goliath, and the spoils of war were going to the victors.

The Balkan Peninsula between the wars: the creation of Yugoslavia

A number of new states in central, eastern and south-eastern Europe emerged out of the First World War, many of them created from the defeat and partial destruction of the four major empires. These empires were those of Imperial Germany, Russia, Austria-Hungary and Ottoman Turkey. The allies (France, Britain, the USA and Italy) felt that compensation of some kind should be offered to Serbia and so a new union was proclaimed, which was officially named the Kingdom of Serbs, Croats and Slovenes. In 1929, it was renamed Yugoslavia (literally, "land of the South Slavs"). Yugoslavia was therefore a nation born out of the ashes of the First World War and consisted of a fusion of the provinces of Slovenia and Croatia, together with Serbia and Montenegro. Also included in the new state was Bosnia, a province that was an ethnic and religious mixture of Orthodox Serbs, Catholic Croats and Muslim Slavs. In the south of Yugoslavia lay the small province of Kosovo, made up of a majority of Albanians, which had not been given to Albania but rather to Serbia.

For over 20 years, the federation, dominated by Serbia, held together fairly well. As the largest ethnic group in the Balkans, Serbia maintained that it should take the lead and, due to the price it had paid in gaining independence for the region, should dominate the federation. Others, such as the Croats and Slovenes, argued for a federation to balance the economic and political dominance of Serbia. Ultimately, it was the failure of politicians to secure such an agreement that eventually resulted in the break-up of Yugoslavia at the end of the century.

The Balkan states that emerged out of the First World War still remained highly unstable: each of the states, old and new, faced the challenges of economic underdevelopment, ethnic tensions and weak institutions. Every country was to experience stresses that would eventually be resolved by the establishment of some form of military or monarchical dictatorship.

THE POWER BEHIND.

AUSTRIA (*at the ultimatum stage*). "I DON'T QUITE LIKE HIS ATTITUDE. SOMEBODY MUST BE BACKING HIM."

▲ A cartoon from the UK magazine *Punch*, published in 1914, showing Austria-Hungary, Serbia and Russia (behind the rock)

Yugoslavia, as a federation, had to struggle with each of its neighbours (with the exception of Greece) in the decades between the wars, but it was the Italians who probably caused the most problems. The killing of the Croatian leader Stjepan Radić in 1928 prompted the Serbian monarch King Aleksandar to declare a dictatorship the following year. The king himself was assassinated in Marseilles in 1934 by Croatian extremists, during an official visit to France.

▲ The Yugoslav state and the federated states in the 1930s

Bulgaria and Romania both became more authoritarian as economic and political problems developed in the 1930s; the Greeks had their parliament dissolved and a dictatorship developed under Ioannis Metaxas. Turkey, too, became a one-party state under Kemal Atatürk until his death in 1938.

The people of Kosovo, now nominally under Serb rule, found themselves caught up in the internal politics of Albania when Albania's interior minister, Ahmed Zogu, seized power in 1922. Later, in 1928, he declared himself the self-styled King Zog of the Albanians. Despite its nominal independence, Albania was effectively a puppet state under Italian influence for the remainder of the time prior to its annexation, six months before the Second World War broke out in 1939.

King Zog of the Albanians

Born Ahmet Muhtar Bej Zogolli in 1895, he took the surname Zogu after 1922, when he gained power in Albania. He led the country from 1925 to 1939, and declared himself king in 1928. He is the only Muslim king ever to have ruled in Europe. Zog tried to modernize his country by building roads, schools and promoting public health and education. His supporters (or Zogists) claimed that he had inherited a throne with an Albanian line going back 2,500 years. He adopted the symbol of the double-headed black eagle on a crimson background, which he took from the great Skanderbeg, who had led a rebellion against the Turks in the 15th century.

Zog wanted to be treated as an equal to the monarchies of Yugoslavia, Romania and Bulgaria, yet the established monarchies shunned him. He married a 22-year-old Hungarian countess in 1938 and they had a son the following year. In 1939 , he fled Albania after Mussolini's troops invaded and never returned. Zog died in France in 1961.

Albania was swallowed up by Mussolini's Italy in April 1939. Then, in April 1941, the Axis Powers (consisting of Germany, Italy, Japan and Hungary) invaded Yugoslavia and occupied the whole of the Balkan Peninsula.

▲ A Soviet cartoon showing Italian designs on little Albania

⌖ Thinking and communication skills

Read the source below and answer questions 1 and 2 that follow. Then discuss question 3 with a partner.

In 1937, Vaso Cubrilović, a historian at Belgrade University, wrote the following. (Note: Cubrilović had taken part in the Black Hand plot to kill Archduke Franz Ferdinand in Sarajevo in 1914.)

Judah, T. 2008. *Kosovo: What everyone needs to know*. Oxford, UK. Oxford University Press.

The only way and the only means to cope with them is the brute force of an organised state ... if we do not settle accounts with them at the proper time, within 20–30 years we shall have to cope with a terrible irredentism [a national policy which supports the acquisition of some region in another country for reasons of sharing a common linguistic, cultural, historical, ethnic or racial ties], the signs of which are already apparent and which will inevitably put all our southern territories in danger. Who would object to such a policy ... when Germany can expel tens of thousands of Jews and Russia can shift millions of people from one part of the continent to another?

Questions

1 How does the source demonstrate a racist attitude?

2 How does the writer attempt to justify his position?

3 With a partner, discuss the difference between nationalism and racism.

Yugoslavia in the Second World War

This country can only be a Croatian country, and there is no method we would hesitate to use in order to make it truly Croatian and cleanse it of Serbs, who have for centuries endangered us and who will endanger us again if they are given the opportunity.

— Miroslav Žanić, 1941

It took less than two weeks for the Germans to force the surrender of Yugoslavia, following which, German, Italian and Hungarian troops occupied the divided country. Old ethnic divisions surfaced into what was to become a very bitter civil war. This conflict primarily pitted the Croats (who allied themselves with the Axis Powers) against the Serbs. The leader in Croatia, Ante Pavelić, took the opportunity to begin a campaign against the non-Croatian minorities, Serbs, Roma gypsies and Jews, which was effectively a genocide. He carried this out through the Ustaša, the fascist movement that ruled Croatia during the war. The word *ustaša* means "rise up" or "insurgence" in Croat; the organization's aim was to achieve Croatian independence from Yugoslavia, and its members modelled themselves on the Italian fascist movement. The impact of this campaign, brutal even by German standards, had an important impact on future relations within the Balkans and particularly for Serbo–Croat interactions. The Croatian state set up concentration camps in the country. The largest was at Jasenovac, near Zagreb, where tens of thousands were killed, the majority of them Serbs. In total, an estimated 500,000 people were killed during these years and more expelled to become refugees in the Balkans. The US Holocaust Memorial Museum estimates that the Croatian Ustaša regime murdered between 80,000 and 100,000 people in Jasenovac between 1941 and 1945.

▲ *Chetnik* group photographed in 1944

Yugoslav resistance to the Axis occupation came from two major factions: the royalists and heavily pro-Serbian *Chetniks*, led by Draža Mihailović, and the partisans led by Josip Broz Tito. The word *Chetnik* comes from the Serbo-Croatian *Četnik*, or *čete*, meaning "armed band". *Chetniks* were formed to resist the Axis invaders and Croatian collaborators. Tito's movement consisted largely of communists, but both factions resisted the occupying German forces. However, political differences soon led to armed conflict between the *Chetniks* and the partisans. In later years, partially due to brutal reprisal killings by the Germans against Yugoslav insurgents, Mihailović came to favour a more restrained policy of resistance. However, Tito's partisans remained much more aggressive and, in 1944, the Allies switched their support from Mihailović to Tito.

After the war, Mihailović was captured by the partisans and charged with treason and collaboration with the Germans by the Yugoslav government. He was executed in Belgrade in 1946.

The Yugoslav partisans were probably the most effective resistance movement against the Axis Powers during the war, and largely succeeded in driving the German forces out and taking over much of the former Yugoslavia by early 1945. One of the reasons for their success was their inclusion of all ethnic groups within Yugoslavia, but the price the people paid was high: estimates of those killed during the war run from 1 million upwards. This meant Yugoslavia was one of the countries that suffered most, per capita, of all the nations who fought the Nazis. The country paid a terrible price under occupation and liberation, particularly when internal tensions surfaced to cause so many of the deaths and suffering. What is worth noting, in view of what happened later, is that the first Yugoslav state was certainly undermined by its own internal squabbles. These were a result of ethnic tensions, but the principal cause of its suffering was foreign invasion and occupation.

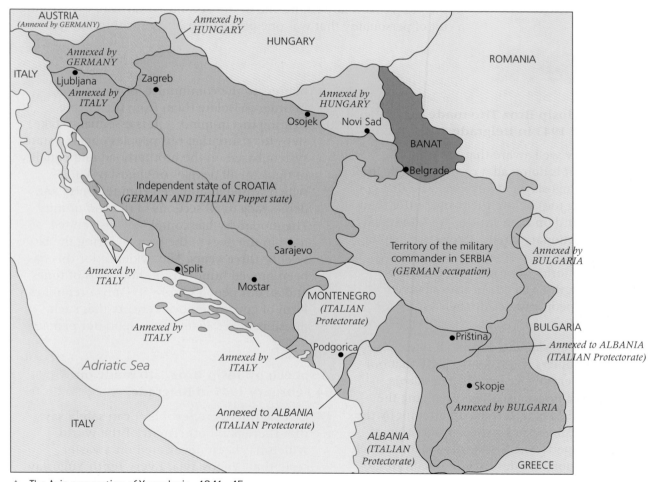

▲ The Axis occupation of Yugoslavia., 1941–45

▲ Josip Tito and General Popovitch, who became foreign minister in Yugoslavia after the war, in 1943

The idea of a Balkan federation began to take root once more but the defeat of the Axis Powers was to leave a political vacuum, which both the Soviets and pro-Western democracies sought to fill. The surrender of Italy, and thus of Albania, in 1943 meant that Kosovo became a pawn once more of larger interests. Kosovo was liberated in 1944 with the help of Albanian partisans together with the communists and, in February 1945, the province was formally annexed to Serbia, becoming an "autonomous region". Inside Albania, the resistance leader, Enver Hoxha became first secretary of the Communist Party and he was to rule the country as its dictator until his death in 1985. Hoxha, was one of the toughest and most uncompromising of the communist strongmen in the 20th century. He followed the precept that "the religion of Albania is Albanianism" and was, in essence, to isolate his country and its regime from the eyes of the world in the years that followed the end of the Second World War, establishing a cult of personality that was one of the most bizarre within Europe.

Source skills

Source A

A speech by Josip Broz Tito made on 29 November 1943 in Belgrade.

We are very well aware that the traitor-government is doing all it can to smuggle itself back into Yugoslavia at any cost (and that goes for the king too) before the people utter their decisive word on their future. We know that certain reactionary circles abroad are helping that government. But we also know that the vast majority of progressive democratic elements in the Allied countries sincerely desire our people to decide their future for themselves …

We have been slandered from all sides … All the occupiers and traitors … say that our people's liberation struggle in Yugoslavia is purely a communist affair, involving the bolshevisation of a country, an attempt by the communists to seize power, the abolition of private property, the destruction of the church and of religion, the destruction of culture and so on … Very few people believe these lies any longer, and least of all the people of Yugoslavia … The times are past when a handful of reactionaries could ascribe such matters to the communists of Yugoslavia, in order to isolate them from the people. Bearing this in mind … It is essential to take steps to ensure that our peoples obtain a state system based on the brotherhood and equality of rights of all peoples of Yugoslavia and which would guarantee genuine liberty and democracy to all sections of the community. The monarchy has completely discredited itself in the eyes of the people during the last twenty-three years. The evidence for this has been proved hundreds of thousands of times and all our peoples know it. Only a republican form of government can ensure that such disasters never again come upon our people.

Source B

A speech by Josip Broz Tito made on 14 February 1945 in Belgrade.

Our sacrifices are terrible. I can safely say that there is no other part of the world which has been devastated on a vaster scale than Yugoslavia. Every tenth Yugoslav has perished in this struggle in which we were forced to wrest armaments from our enemies, to freeze without clothing, and to die without medication.

Nevertheless our optimism and faith have proved justified. The greatest gain of this conflict between democracy and fascism lies in the fact that it has drawn together everything that was good in humanity. The unity of the United States, the Soviet Union and Great Britain is the best guarantee to the peoples of the world that Nazi horrors will never again be repeated. In organizing our country on the sacred principles of democracy and of concern for the common man, we Yugoslavs believe that we are making our best contribution to this harmonious community.

Source C

A speech by Josip Broz Tito made on 9 May 1945 in Belgrade.

Peoples of Yugoslavia! Serbs, Croats, Slovenes, Macedonians, Montenegrins, Moslems! The long-desired day has dawned which you have been waiting for with such yearning. The day of rejoicing has come to us here, too. Finally the greatest fascist power in Europe is vanquished, Germany, which inflicted so much suffering upon our people and took so many victims. The powers that tried to enslave you have been vanquished. You were offered enticements by the German and Italian fascists in order to lead you to exterminate each other. But your best sons and daughters, inspired with love for their homeland and for you, her peoples, thwarted this diabolical enemy plan. Instead of mutual dissension and hostility, you are today united in a new and happier Yugoslavia. Instead of the old Yugoslavia, rotten with corruption and injustice, today we have the Democratic Federal Yugoslavia of equal peoples. This is the result of the victory of our glorious Yugoslav Army, it is the result of your endurance, your self-sacrifice and faith in your just cause … We must make our brotherhood and unity even stronger, so that never again can any force destroy it.

First question, part a – 3 marks

What is Tito referring to in Source A when he speaks of the "traitor-government"?

First question, part b – 2 marks

What does Tito mean by "reactionary circles" and "reactionaries" in Source A?

Second question – 4 marks

With reference to its origin, purpose and content, assess the values and limitations of Source C.

Third question – 6 marks

How does Tito mix elements of both socialism and nationalism in Sources B and C, and why do you think he does this?

Fourth question – 9 marks

Using the sources and your own knowledge, what evidence is there to support Tito's statement in Source B that there is "*no other part of the world which has been devastated on a vaster scale than Yugoslavia*"?

ATL Thinking and social skills

With a partner, share your responses to the questions above. Peer edit each other's work and suggest how you can each improve your answers.

References and further reading

Hall, R. 2000. *The Balkan Wars, 1912–1913: Prelude to the First World War*. Routledge.

Judah, T. 2008. *Kosovo: What everyone needs to know*. Oxford, UK. Oxford University Press.

A RIFT IN RED LANE
"Traitor!"
"Liar!"

▲ A cartoon published in the UK magazine *Punch* on 7 July 1948. The title is "A rift in Red Lane – Traitor, liar!"

Conceptual understanding

Key concepts

→ Change

→ Consequence

→ Continuity

Key questions

→ How did the forces in place shape the future society in Yugoslavia?

→ To what extent did Tito have an impact on the development of the federation?

The Balkans produce more history than they can consume.

— Attributed to Churchill by Margaret Thatcher, Fulton, 1996

When Yugoslavia and the Balkans states emerged from the Second World War they, like the rest of Europe, faced immense difficulties in reconstructing their severely damaged countries. What kind of new country was going to come out of the chaos in Yugoslavia? To an extent the answer to this question was dictated by Tito himself. It was based on the internal dynamics of the former states that had made up the country, and by the pressures of what was happening around them. Tito was to reunite Yugoslavia under his firm hand, and it was he who was to shape Yugoslavia more than any other leader in the 20th century. For the next 40 years, the country was to change beyond all recognition. To begin with, Tito tried to model the state on the Soviet Union but after 1948 the relationship between Yugoslavia and the Soviet Union broke apart and Yugoslavia began to find a "third way", a position that tried to reconcile elements of both the right and left in politics and economics.

Following Tito's death in 1980, the system he held together slowly began to unravel. The country he had ruled for so long descended into chaos.

Yugoslavia in the Cold War: The break with Stalin

We study and take as an example the Soviet system, but we are developing socialism in our country in somewhat different forms ... No matter how much each of us loves the land of socialism, the USSR, he can in no case love his own country less.

— Josip Broz Tito, 1948

In 1945, the Soviet Army liberated nearly all of the Eastern Europe countries that had been under German occupation, and began to install communist-led governments. Yugoslavia was the only country which effectively liberated itself and, due to its geographical situation not bordering Soviet frontiers, it was able to exercise a much more independent line. The rest of the world saw the Soviets and Yugoslavs as natural allies but within three years a split came about which was due to a number of factors. These factors included Tito's tentative plans to absorb Albania, to support the communists in Greece, and to enter an economic cooperation and possible federation with Bulgaria. This potentially powerful Eastern European bloc, which might lie outside of Moscow's direct control, was of concern to Stalin, who was unaccustomed to this kind of individuality and independence from such states. Representatives were summoned to Moscow and warned of their mistakes. Relations broke down further and Bulgaria caved in to follow Stalin's line. The Cominform, which the Soviet Union had established in 1947 to coordinate the new communist parties in other European states and which had its headquarters in Belgrade, moved out of Yugoslavia. The representatives of what were becoming satellite states of the Soviet Union voted to expel Yugoslavia from their organization at the end of 1947. In January 1948, Yugoslavia and its communist-led government under Tito found itself alone in a potentially hostile world.

Your trouble is not errors, but that you are taking a line different from ours.

— Joseph Stalin, Feb. 1948

After the split with Moscow, Tito and Yugoslavia steered a course between the Eastern bloc, which became known as the Iron Curtain satellite states, and the West. The British and Americans held Tito up as a maverick who challenged Stalin's power and influence, and they offered Tito various enticements, usually of a financial nature, to move towards the Western bloc. Tito was astute enough to recognize the advantages, and the dangers, of Yugoslavia's position, and by the mid-1950s emerged as one of the leaders of the so-called Non-Aligned Movement. Evidence has come to light of Stalin's attempts to eliminate Tito through assassination, just as he had done to his great rival Trotsky in Mexico in 1940. One of these schemes to kill Tito involved the use of a plague bacterium, which would be placed in a jewellery box presented to the Yugoslav leader by an agent called Max. After Stalin's death in 1953, the operation was terminated.

▲ Tito (seated) with Stalin behind him and Molotov, the Soviet foreign minister to the right. Taken in 1945

ATL Communication skills

The plan to kill Tito using a plague bacterium was revealed by the Russian military historian Dmitri Volkogonov. To find out more, see *The Cold War International History Project Bulletin*, Issue 10: http://www.wilsoncenter.org/sites/default/files/CWIHP_Bulletin_10.pdf.

2

▲ Yugoslavia between 1945 and 1991

Albania during the Cold War

Immediately following the Second World War, Albania effectively became a Yugoslav satellite until the break with Moscow in 1948. Albania gave up its demands for Kosovo, and Yugoslavia became the first country to recognise Albania's provisional government. Economic cooperation followed and Stalin was reported to have recommended that Yugoslavia take over Albania. This was according to Milovan Djilas, an important communist who was Tito's close friend at the time (although he later became a critic of Tito and was imprisoned). In January 1948, Djilas was sent to Moscow to negotiate with Stalin and reported that the Soviet leader said:

> "We have no special interest in Albania. We agree to Yugoslavia swallowing Albania! ..." At this he gathered together the fingers of his right hand and, bringing them to his mouth, he made a motion as if to swallow them.

— Milovan Djilas, 1962

Albania's relationship with Yugoslavia was never going to be an easy one, especially regarding Kosovo. As the communist Enver Hoxha took control, the West sponsored support for the former King Zog, who was busy recruiting Albanian refugees abroad. However, the movement never came to anything and Hoxha, particularly after Tito's split with Stalin, became more authoritarian and aligned his country with Moscow. Hoxha closed the country's borders with Yugoslavia and began a programme of social engineering that went some way towards transforming Albania. Hoxha's regime improved health care, education and illiteracy, the latter declining to only 10% in the following two decades. Freedom of thought was never high on Hoxha's agenda, though, and when Stalin died in 1953 and was replaced by Khrushchev, relations with the Soviets worsened. Bizarre policies such as the compulsory shaving of beards and the banning of all private car ownership, combined with a strict xenophobia, meant that Albania became more and more isolated. Suspicious of Khrushchev's "different roads to socialism" programme, Hoxha's regime broke with the Soviet Union early in the 1960s and aligned itself with the Chinese.

ATL Thinking skills

1. What do you think Stalin meant by the gesture Djilas described in the quote on the left?

2. What might the gesture show about Stalin's attitude to the Balkans?

"PERSONALITY CULT" SITUATION

▲ A cartoon by David Low, published in the UK newspaper *The Guardian* in January 1962

For Albania, the economic and technological assistance the Chinese provided for the regime was limited, and stagnation of Albania's economy followed. Hoxha even tried his own cultural revolution to mirror that of

Mao's China in the late 1960s, sending the few intellectuals in Albania back to the countryside to learn from the masses and closing all religious institutions. Within a decade, relations with the Chinese broke down too. Hoxha had made Albania independent but the price the people paid was very high. When Hoxha died in April 1985, he left behind a legacy of repression and a country that was isolated, backward and intensely suspicious of the outside world.

Tito's rule in Yugoslavia

Meanwhile, by contrast, Yugoslavia became one of the most "open" socialist countries in Europe. Tito was half Slovene and half Croatian, and he worked hard to prevent the Yugoslav state from falling under the control of the biggest nation in the federation, Serbia. The Serb population was twice the size of the next minority, the Croats, and in order to achieve some kind of equilibrium between the ethnic groups, Tito tried to balance power between the constituent republics as well as ruthlessly to suppress any signs of resurgent nationalism. No other European communist leader was as respected as he was. Managing a course between both East and West, particularly after the split with Stalin in 1948, required political cunning as well as a little luck. When he re-established relations with Khrushchev a decade later, Tito still retained the independence he had developed during the war and afterwards.

Although Tito broke with Stalin, he did not break with the principles or the methods of communist rule. He never held real democratic elections in Yugoslavia, although it is probable that he would have won a legitimate vote. Tito ruled in Yugoslavia through a policy referred to as "self-management". Part of this meant that decision-making could be taken away from the political centre and devolved to the workers' councils, the original *soviets*. The basic structure of the Yugoslav state was a federation of six republics – Serbia, Croatia, Slovenia, Bosnia and Herzegovina, Montenegro, and Macedonia – and Tito's approach to decision-making meant that "self-management" could be applied to these republics in their relationship with the central government in Belgrade. The position of Kosovo in this structure remained, as it had for some time been, unclear and in 1945 Kosovo and Vojvodina were made autonomous units within the Serbian state.

▲ A British cartoon showing Tito seated between two chairs representing the West and the East, published in *The New Statesman* in April 1958

Tito dealt with issues of ethnicity and nationalism with an iron fist: nothing could break the federation he had helped to establish and rule after the war, and he exercised absolute power until his death in 1980. Politically astute, Tito was able to react to popular expressions of discontent in the 1960s and 1970s by granting a measure of autonomy where he felt it was needed, but without surrendering any of the central power of the federation.

In comparison with the other communist regimes of the time, Yugoslavia was remarkably liberal and open. "Brotherhood and unity" (*bratstvo i jedinstvo*) was a shared theme, aimed at creating a common identity for all Yugoslavs. It was said that *"a weak Serbia means a strong Yugoslavia"* and this is a tenet Tito followed. One of the ways he managed this was to dilute the Serb population through the establishment of the autonomous regions of Vojvodina in the north and Kosovo in the south. In addition, he separated Montenegro and made it an independent republic in the south of Yugoslavia. Kosovo's situation was difficult in the first two decades of communist rule, but conditions began to improve as the Yugoslav government implemented policies which favoured the Albanian minority. This, in turn, encouraged the increasing migration of Serbs out of Kosovo who, due to lower birth rates, saw their percentage of population in Kosovo fall from 50% after the war to about 25% by the time Tito died in 1980. In 1966, the dismissal of prominent Serbian communist official Aleksandar Ranković was seen as an indication that Croats, Slovenes and the people of Kosovo were being rewarded with more autonomy against potential Serb domination within the federation. Tito visited Kosovo in 1967 and is reported to have said, *"One cannot talk about equal rights when Serbs are given preference ... and Albanians are rejected although they have the same or better qualifications"* (Malcolm, 1998).

Tito was a friend to the people of Kosovo in that he saw support of them and other minorities within the federation as a way to offset possible Serb domination.

Yugoslavia was not immune to the student protests that took place in a number of European countries in 1968 and in this year Albanian students rioted in Priština, the provincial capital of Kosovo. For the first time, they carried banners declaring "Republic for Kosovo". They were rewarded by the establishment of the University of Priština in 1969–70, with the languages of instruction in Albanian and Serbo-Croat, and were allowed to display the Albanian flag, featuring the double-headed black eagle on a red background. It was the beginning of a decade that many would look back on as the zenith of their achievement during the Tito years.

Yugoslavia's economy had boomed in the 1960s but a decade later growth began to stagnate. In 1974, a new constitution was passed that attempted to address some of the problems between the federal republics and the centralized government. This legislation was to give both Kosovo and Vojvodina an equivalent status to that of the six republics. While he ruled, Tito could control any separatist or ethnic conflicts but, following his death in 1980, the removal of his strong presence was to put immense strains on the federation.

The state consisted of six republics and two provincial parliamentary bodies under a federal governing body. With Tito as head of state, he neither permitted nor nominated an heir apparent to succeed him. The Yugoslav state under Tito was essentially a personal dictatorship; he was the epitome of a one-man, single-party state. When he died in May 1980, one comment was, *"We all cried but we did not know we were also burying Yugoslavia."* (Silber and Little, 1995: 29).

▲ The flag of Albania, which was flown in Kosovo in the 1970s by nationalists

Research skills

Turn back to the comments on page 149 about Milovan Djilas, then carry out your own research to find out more about him.

151

Source skills

Source A

An extract from an interview between Milovan Djilas and Robert Kaplan in 1981.

Our system was built only for Tito to manage. Now that Tito is gone and our economic situation becomes critical, there will be a natural tendency for greater centralization of power. But this centralization will not succeed because it will run up against the ethnic-political power bases in the republics. This is not classical nationalism but a more dangerous, bureaucratic nationalism built on economic self-interest. This is how the Yugoslav system will begin to collapse.

Source B

A political cartoon by "Vicky" (Victor Weisz) published in the UK newspaper, the *Evening Standard*, in December 1962.

▲ The cartoon shows Soviet leader Khrushchev (on the left) pulling Tito, and Chinese leader Mao (centre right) with Albania.

First question, part b – 2 marks

What is the message of the cartoon in Source B?

Second question – 4 marks

With reference to its origin, purpose and content, assess the values and limitations of using Source A as a reflection of Tito's rule in Yugoslavia.

References and further reading

Malcolm, N. 1998. *Kosovo: A Short History*. London, UK. Macmillan.

Silber, L and Little, A. 1995. *Yugoslavia: The Death of a Nation*. Harmondsworth, UK. Penguin.

2.3 The decade of change: Yugoslavia, 1980–89

▲ Milošević speaks at the "Field of Blackbirds", 28 June 1989

There is no doubt Kosovo is a problem of the whole country, a powder keg on which we all sit.

— Milan Kučan, 1987

After Tito died, the system began to fall apart. For Kosovo and the rest of Yugoslavia, this rupture was to show itself almost immediately. *"The Yugoslav crisis began in Kosovo, and it will end in Kosovo"* is a well-known maxim. In the remaining two decades of the century, the federation fell apart, bringing with it more death and destruction than any had thought imaginable. The break-up of Yugoslavia and the wars that ensued formed the most important conflict for Europe and the West in the period immediately following the Cold War. It was the largest, most destructive conflict Europe had seen since the end of the Second World War, and it brought about the demise of the Yugoslav state and with it the deaths of thousands of people.

Ethnic tensions between Serbs and Kosovar Albanians

The rise of nationalism

The origin of the Yugoslav war and the Kosovo conflict can be traced to the rise of Serb nationalism in the mid-1980s. It began innocuously enough, in retrospect, with a protest over the quality of food in the university canteen in Priština, the capital of Kosovo, in March 1981. Student protests turned into something more widespread, and people began to criticize the authorities. The consequences were to be fundamental in changing the future history of Kosovo and, ultimately, Yugoslavia and the Balkans. The political dispute in Kosovo stemmed from a number of serious social and economic problems that plagued not just the province but the whole of the Yugoslav state. Kosovo's unemployment levels were the highest in the country. As protests in Kosovo spread over the next month, tanks rolled onto the streets and the federal government rushed troops to the province, declaring a state of emergency. Official figures initially reported a dozen killed but the true figure could be in the hundreds. The most damaging effect of this political reaction was that it unleashed the latent nationalism among both Kosovar Albanians and Serbs that had been present but suppressed by Tito. Many members of what was to become the Kosovo Liberation Army (KLA) were put on trial or imprisoned after 1981 and a series of purges of party officials took place in the province. The reaction to the initial protests did much to harm relations between Kosovo and the central government and, in turn, increased the lack of trust and hostility between the two.

By the mid-1980s, a steady stream of propaganda was emerging from the printing presses of Belgrade. Most of it, like all propaganda, was false and loosely based on myth and perceptions. Unfortunately, it had a heavy impact on Serbian public opinion and fanned the flames of nationalist sentiment. Particularly against the Kosovars themselves by the Serbs who lived in that province. Stories of rape, assault and intimidation were fuelled by the reality that, although Serbs still held most of the positions of power in Kosovo, many had chosen to emigrate to other parts of the country. The vast majority of those who left Kosovo were economic migrants; Kosovo was still the poorest of the Yugoslav regions. The political problems in Kosovo were part of a deepening problem of the federal organization as a whole. Slovenia and Croatia, too, were complaining about the weaknesses of the Yugoslav system, but the resentment felt by Serbs who had left Kosovo was used by the nationalists to fuel the fires of discontent against the Kosovars. The special status that Kosovo held in the mythology of the origins of the Serbian state meant that any problems there would resonate loudly among the ultra-nationalists.

Demographics also played a part in the Kosovo situation. Even if census statistics are not very reliable, there were visible trends indicating potential trouble brewing and this, too, played into the hands of the extremists. Just after the Second World War more than 25% of the population of Kosovo had been Serbs and almost 70% Albanians. By the mid-1960s, the percentage of Serbs had dropped to a little over 20% (although both ethnic groups had grown in real terms). By 1981, however, the number of Serbs had dropped in real terms and they constituted only 15% of the total population of Kosovo. Albanians now represented over 77% of the total population and this trend was increasing. Why was this? One of the reasons was the emigration of Serbs from this relatively poor province, but the disparity was also fuelled by the simple fact that Muslim Albanians were having more children than the Christian Orthodox Serbs. The greater degree of urbanization had led to a steep decline in the birth rate of Serbs everywhere, not just in Kosovo. By the early-1990s, Serbs had the highest rate of abortions in the whole of Europe. There was no conspiracy involved, just basic demographics.

The rise of Slobodan Milošević

It was into such a volatile atmosphere that Slobodan Milošević, an ambitious member of the Serbian Central Committee, emerged. In 1986, he was a determined young communist who had gained a degree in law in Belgrade and then moved into banking. He was a protégé and close friend of Serbian President Ivan

Stambolić, who saw promise in him. In April 1987, Stambolić sent Milošević to Kosovo to deal with some of the problems there. This simple political act was to mark the rise to power of a man who would emerge as the embodiment of the dark side of European rule and become the most dangerous figure in Europe after the Cold War. Milošević rode the wave of Serbian nationalism that had manifested itself through a significant document leaked by a Serbian newspaper the previous year (see below). He was destined to rise to the heights of power in Serbia and ultimately to become the first European head of state to be prosecuted for genocide and war crimes. However, this lay in the future.

In a memorandum of 1984, the Serbian Academy of Sciences and Arts (SANU) had begun to examine the claim that Serbs living outside of Serbia were being subjected to "genocide". The deliberate use of this term raised issues that unleashed the tiger of Serb nationalism and was to prove a key moment in the ultimate destruction of Yugoslavia. The SANU Memorandum, as it became known, claimed that Serbs outside of Serbia and particularly in Kosovo, representing a total of 25% of the Serbian people, were facing extermination at the hands of aggressors. The communist authorities, including Stambolić, condemned the document, warning that its publication and dissemination could bring about the destruction of Yugoslavia.

Milošević declined to condemn the memorandum in public and, a year later, adopted its tone and substance to further his own purpose and to destroy the political career of his mentor, Ivan Stambolić. In April 1987, Milošević was sent to Kosovo on a visit that would change the course of history.

> **Thinking skills**
>
> You can read the memorandum (and its justification and apologists) at chnm.gmu.edu/1989/items/show/674.
>
> How does the SANU Memorandum link to the statement made in 1937 by Čubrilović (see page 142)?

Serbian Academy of Sciences and Arts (SANU) memorandum, September 1986

SANU was the most prominent academic body in Yugoslavia at the time in question. Dobrica Ćosić, called by some the spiritual father of the Serb nation, is considered by many to have been SANU's most influential member.

The president of Serbia, Ivan Stambolić, asked the academy to investigate the process of reform in Serbia and to come up with some recommendations. He later claims that what the academy produced was completely unexpected, and that he knew nothing about who had written it.

The SANU Memorandum argued that Serbs had been oppressed in Yugoslavia for many years and that in Kosovo they faced genocide. It blamed this on the dysfunctional Yugoslav government. The weakened state of the Serbian economy was also blamed on the 1974 constitution that threatened the very existence of the Serb nation. The memorandum highlighted the fears and tensions that had grown within Yugoslavia as the state began to fragment in the mid-1980s following the death of Tito. The memorandum, its tone clearly shrill and hysterical, was a call to arms by radical Serbs who, it said, were facing their greatest threat since the war against the Turks at the beginning of the 19th century. It stated that *"Serbia must not be passive and wait and see what others will say, as it has done in the past"*. It concluded with the warning that if the Serbs did nothing, their very existence as a nation was under threat.

All Serbs everywhere saw it (Kosovo) as a battle cry.

— Ivan Stambolić, 1995

A meeting took place at Kosovo Polje, the field where the Battle of Kosovo took place in 1389. Its name means "Field of Blackbirds" in the Serbian language and it is located just outside the capital of Kosovo, Priština. The meeting saw the presence of Milošević ostensibly to quell any trouble, and to reassure the Serbs living

Slobodan Milošević (1941–2006)

Milošević was Serbia's party leader and president (1989–97), and pursued Serbian nationalist policies that contributed to the break-up of the Yugoslav Federation. He, more than any other, brought Serbia into a series of conflicts with the other Balkan states. A Serbian politician, known by the nickname of "Sloba", he dominated events in Yugoslavia in the last decade of the 20th century.

He gained a degree in law from the University of Belgrade in 1964 and entered the business world, eventually becoming head of the state-owned gas company and president of a bank. Both his parents committed suicide, his father in 1962 and his mother in 1974. His wife, Mirjana Marković, who later became known as the Lady Macbeth of Serbia, was a devoted communist and became her husband's main political adviser. Milošević entered the political scene in 1984 as a protégé of the communist leader in Serbia, Ivan Stambolić. Milošević used Serbian nationalist sentiment to become popular with rank and file Serbs and to overthrow Stambolić in December 1987. As Serbia's party leader, Milošević demanded that Yugoslavia's federal government restore full control of the autonomous provinces of Vojvodina and Kosovo to Serbia. In 1989, he replaced Stambolić as president of Yugoslavia and was re-elected again in 1992. He took his country to war with the other provinces in the same year. Milošević became the most dangerous figure in Europe after the Cold War.

Later sections cover the following events in more detail. To summarize here, after the NATO bombing campaign against Serbia in 1999 due to the situation in Kosovo, Milošević lost the presidential election in 2000 and was arrested by the Yugoslav government. In 2001, he was handed over to the International Criminal Tribunal for the former Yugoslavia (ICTY) on charges of genocide and crimes against humanity. His trial began in February 2002 but, due to his ill health, it was delayed several times. In March 2006, he was found dead in his prison cell.

there of the government's concern. From the vantage point of history, we now know that Milošević, the arch-manipulator of the media, had planned for the Belgrade media and television to be there to broadcast events he had orchestrated. Having listened to the Serbian protestors screaming at the police and chanting "murderers", Milošević delivered the line which would propel him into history and become a rallying call for Serb nationalists in the years to come: *"No one should dare to beat you,"* he said, staring straight at the cameras. It was theatre in the making.

> *No one should dare to beat you.*

— Slobodan Milošević, 1987

The speech transformed the relationship between Milošević and Stambolić and, three months later, Milošević was ready to make his move against his mentor in another contrived televised episode. In September 1987, in the Central Committee meeting of the Serbian communists, Milošević turned on the Serbian leader with the words, *"The fatherland is under threat"*. Within days, this appeal to nationalist sentiment in Serbia, latent but always present in the century, was exploited by Milošević to win popularity and to change the landscape of Yugoslavia's political scene. Stambolić resigned in December 1987 and was replaced by his protégé and his eventual executioner, Milošević. Stambolić later commented, *"When somebody looks at your back for twenty-five years, it is understandable that he gets the desire to put a knife in it at some point. Many people warned me but I didn't acknowledge it"* (Silber and Little, 1995: 45).

Constitutional reform in Yugoslavia, 1989–91

The coming to power of Milošević was to change the pace of events in Yugoslavia. Over the next two years, he moved to consolidate his position and foster the flourishing nationalist sentiment that had brought him to power. Never since Tito and the communists took power in 1945 had anyone played the nationalist card so openly, and the media played a powerful role in Milošević's campaign (as it did in Rwanda). Now that Milošević had emerged as the leader of Serbia, he continued to orchestrate large demonstrations in other areas of Yugoslavia and made Kosovo a leading issue. The 1974 constitutional reforms had given each republic one vote in the federal presidency; the votes of the six republics, plus the votes (since 1974) of Vojvodina and Kosovo, gave a total of eight. In order to gain control of the Yugoslav state, Milošević was to turn firstly on the two autonomous provinces of Vojvodina and Kosovo, and then on Montenegro. He would replace their leaders with his allies to create a major voting block in the Yugoslav presidency in order to gain control of Yugoslavia itself. In the summers of 1988 and 1989, the Serbs organized what were called "meetings of truth", which many compared to religious revival meetings. Milošević was the evangelist, the man with the message that he would bring salvation to the Serbs.

In October 1988, the leadership of Vojvodina was ousted by a stage-managed campaign organized by a follower of Milošević named Miloslav Šolević, who had arranged the pivotal meeting in Kosovo Polje the year before. Rallies were arranged to demonstrate against the Vojvodina leaders, who responded to the demonstrators by giving them bread and yogurt. In return, yoghurt containers were thrown at the parliament building by the angry protesters, lending the name "yogurt revolution" to the event. Simple slogans such as *"Kosovo is Serbia; Vojvodina is Serbia; Together we are stronger"* were cleverly used by supporters of Milošević. Next, the Serbian nationalists turned on Montenegro and, in January 1989, Yugoslavia's smallest republic, ripe for unrest, succumbed to the same fate as Vojvodina. The old leaders, who were disorganized and incompetent, resigned and were replaced by men loyal to Milošević. Kosovo was to be the next target.

In November 1988, the leaders of Kosovo's Communist Party had been dismissed and Belgrade announced that it was going to strip Kosovo of the autonomy it had gained under the 1974 constitution. Two Albanian Kosovar leaders, Jashari and Vllasi, were removed from the party committee by Belgrade, and this provoked demonstrations by the miners of Trepča. One of the richest mining companies in Yugoslavia, Trepča, yielded 70% of the country's wealth. The Romans mined there and it was the most important source of lead for the Germans in the Second World War. The miners marched to Priština. The Serb media dismissed these actions as counter-revolutionary moves and Serb nationalists organised a massive rally to be held in Belgrade. In the "meeting of all meetings", Milošević spoke to an estimated 1 million people, telling them, *"Kosovo is the pure centre of its history, culture and memory. Every nation has one love that eternally warms its heart. For Serbia it is Kosovo. That is why Kosovo will remain in Serbia"* (Silber and Little, 1995: 63).

The people have happened!

— Slobodan Milošević, slogan

Thousands of workers had been brought in from nearby companies and state workers in Belgrade had been given the day off. The Serbian people loved Milošević. A national awakening was propelling him to the height of his power at the expense, ultimately, of the Yugoslav state. A week later, the federal parliament adopted the constitutional changes and Kosovo effectively voted for its own dissolution as an autonomous unit.

The impact on the other republics was significant; the bullying tactics of Serbia frightened the others, particularly Slovenia, which was the most developed of the Yugoslav states. In the capital Ljubljana, people protested in support of the Trepča miners in Kosovo, incensing many Serbs. Meanwhile, Milošević pushed ahead with his proposals to strip Kosovo of its

▲ Protesters in Priština, Kosovo in 1989

autonomy and, with the help of Yugoslav army tanks and police deployed across Kosovo, a new constitution was declared. On 28 March 1989, as people continued to protest in Kosovo, Serbs turned out to celebrate the creation of a whole Serbian state.

By abolishing the autonomy of both Vojvodina and Kosovo, and replacing the leaders in Montenegro with its own followers, Serbia now controlled four out of the eight votes in the federal presidency. Milan Kučan, party head in Slovenia, said this was *"turning Yugoslavia into Serbo-slavia"* (Davis, 2013: 31). Milošević seemed unstoppable.

The Gazimestan speech

The anniversary of the Battle of Kosovo, 28 June 1989

On 28 June 1989, the Serbs celebrated the 600th anniversary of the battle fought in Kosovo in 1389 between the Turks and the Serbs. The date of 28 June reverberates throughout the history of Serbia and the Balkans: it is also the date upon which the Bosnian Serb assassin, Gavrilo Princip, shot dead Archduke Franz Ferdinand of Austria in 1914, bringing about the First World War six weeks later. However, for the Serbian nationalists, there can be no more significant date than 28 June 1389 when, on Kosovo Polje (the "Field of Blackbirds"), the smaller army of Christian Serbs fought a much larger force of Ottoman Turks and were beaten. The importance of the battle in Serbian consciousness is impossible to overestimate. One historian has noted, *"The story of the battle of Kosovo has become a totem or talisman of Serbian identity … this event has a status unlike anything else in the history of the Serbs"* (Malcolm, 2002: 58).

When Milošević stepped onto that field, to which he was flown by helicopter, he was well aware of the significance of the event. He had an audience of up to 1 million Serbs. Important figures there to witness his speech included the hierarchy of the Orthodox Church and, uncomfortably for many, the leaders of the other Yugoslav states. It was high drama.

ATL Communication and thinking skills

Read Milošević's Gazimestan speech and watch versions of it recorded by Serbian state television. You will find one version at: www.youtube.com/watch?v=p8QwHrRzpeo.

Also, read some of the commentaries about the speech and the day itself to learn about its powerful impact, and the importance of bias and interpretation in studying history.

Based on the television broadcasts or images of the Gazimestan speech, what can you observe about media coverage and politics?

TOK connections

The spreading of the Battle of Kosovo myth is as important as the event itself. Historians still debate whether the battle was a victory for the Turks or for the Serbs and Christian Europe. How the facts and the myths have been intertwined and manipulated is significant for an understanding of how history "works", and what it means in the context of the time and for awakening national consciousness.

The Battle of Kosovo, June 1389

The facts as they are known to us tell that a smaller Serbian army led by Stefan Lazar faced the might of a large Turkish army under the command of Sultan Murad I. Both leaders were killed and there were heavy losses on both sides, with the Turks holding the battlefield afterwards.

The Serbs were to acknowledge they were vassals of the Turks and the descendants of both leaders went on to govern their respective countries. Murad I is the only sultan known to have been killed in battle. Other than that, the battle of Kosovo has become embellished in myth, particularly for the Serbs.

ATL Research and thinking skills

Read other accounts of the 1389 Battle of Kosovo and answer the following questions.

1 Who killed the sultan and how did he die?

2 Was it a crushing victory for the Turks or did the Serbs, in their stubborn resistance, hold up the advance of Islam into Europe for almost a century?

3 Was Stefan Lazar offered a choice of an earthly kingdom or a heavenly covenant?

Imagine a part of the USA, from which the USA started – where is the cradle of your history? This is Kosovo for Serbia.

— Novak Djokovic, 2011

What Milošević said on Kosovo Polje in 1989 was not in itself inflammatory, and defendants of the Serbian leader have claimed that, although it was a speech ringing with nationalism, the occasion demanded it. Milošević began by referring to the historical uncertainty about the battle 600 years earlier:

Today, it is difficult to say what is the historical truth about the Battle of Kosovo and what is legend … It is difficult to say today whether the Battle of Kosovo was a defeat or a victory for the Serbian people, whether thanks to it we fell into slavery or we survived in this slavery.

— Milošević, 1989

However, critics of the Serbian president have pointed to allusions he made in the speech to his willingness to fight for Serbia's position.

Six centuries later, now, we are being again engaged in battles and are facing battles. They are not armed battles, although such things cannot be excluded yet.

— Milošević, 1989

Class discussion

What is a fact in history?

History can be told and viewed from different cultural perspectives. How does this affect our understanding?

1989: The the year of change

The reaction of the other republics to this manifestation of Serb nationalism and the bullying tactics of Milošević were of great concern. In Kosovo itself, in 1989, the protests continued but were dealt with by the forces of law and order. Later in the year, Slovenia made a determined effort to secure its own position as Yugoslavia's richest republic by changing its constitution, arguing that if the Serbs could amend theirs, the Slovenes could do the same. The divisions in the Yugoslav Federation were beginning to widen.

The events in Yugoslavia were mirrored in an even more impressive way in much of Eastern Europe towards the end of this momentous year. The flow of asylum seekers out of the Soviet bloc countries and into Austria and West Germany signalled the break-up of the Soviet Union; and, in November, the Berlin Wall, the greatest symbol of communist oppression, came tumbling down as thousands of people crossed from East to West. In that sense, what was happening in Yugoslavia was a sideshow. Nevertheless, as Slovenia stood up to what it saw as Serbian domination, Croatia, too, began to take sides, while in Kosovo the Albanians watched and waited. The growing conflict broke to the surface ostensibly as a trade war and the Croatian leaders, their old rivals, came to the fore in the meeting of what was to be the last Party Congress of Yugoslavia in January 1990 in Belgrade. As communism in the rest of Europe seemed to be dying, in Yugoslavia the gulf between the sides had become irreparable. The three most powerful republics – Serbia on one side, and Slovenia and Croatia on the other – confronted one another. The delegates from Slovenia and Croatia walked out of the Party Congress and Tito's Yugoslavia, which had held together for almost 40 years, appeared to be breaking apart.

▲ The breakdown of communism in Europe in 1989

159

▲ Milan Kučan, Slovenia's first president, 1991–2002

Conceptual understanding

Key concepts

→ Change

→ Causation

→ Consequence

Key questions

→ What were the consequences of the break-up of Yugoslavia?

→ Why did Yugoslavia fall apart?

A chronology of key events in Kosovo and the Balkans, 1989–98

Democratic League of Kosovo (LDK) formed with Ibrahim Rugova elected as its head

1989 December

1990 July — Albanian leaders declare their independence from Serbia

The Belgrade government dissolves the Kosovo Assembly

The sacking of more than 100,000 ethnic Albanian workers prompts a general strike

September

1991 June — Slovenia and Croatia both declare their independence from Yugoslavia; there is war between Serbia and Slovenia (lasting ten days)

Bosnia breaks away from Yugoslavia and declares independence

October

1992 April — War breaks out in Bosnia

Ibrahim Rugova is elected president of the self-proclaimed republic

July

December — US President George Bush warns Milošević that Serb aggression in Kosovo could bring a military response. This is referred to as the "Christmas warning"

Stari Most, the old bridge in Mostar, Bosnia, is destroyed by Croats

1993 November

1993–97 — Ethnic tension and armed unrest escalate in Kosovo

The Srebrenica massacre takes place in Bosnia

1995 July

August–September — NATO air strikes against Serb positions in Bosnia

The Dayton Accords are signed, in Dayton, Ohio, USA, ending the Bosnian war

November

1996 February — The Kosovo Liberation Army (KLA) is formed and carries out attacks against Serbs in Kosovo

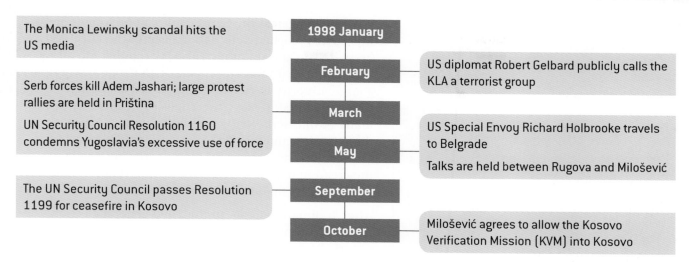

The Monica Lewinsky scandal hits the US media — **1998 January**

February — US diplomat Robert Gelbard publicly calls the KLA a terrorist group

Serb forces kill Adem Jashari; large protest rallies are held in Priština — **March**

UN Security Council Resolution 1160 condemns Yugoslavia's excessive use of force — **May** — US Special Envoy Richard Holbrooke travels to Belgrade / Talks are held between Rugova and Milošević

The UN Security Council passes Resolution 1199 for ceasefire in Kosovo — **September**

October — Milošević agrees to allow the Kosovo Verification Mission (KVM) into Kosovo

---

Franjo Tudjman (1922–99)

Tudjman was the first president of the state of Croatia after it broke away from the former Yugoslavia in 1991. He remained its president until his death in 1999. A fervent nationalist, he fought with the partisans during the Second World War and later joined the military to become the youngest general in the Yugoslav army. He later gained a university degree in history and his outspoken manner led him to be expelled from the Communist Party in 1967.

He continued to be a defender of Croatia's record and became even more nationalistic. He was imprisoned for political activities against the government, although it is said that Tito, who was himself half Slovene and half Croat, was sympathetic to him and so his prison sentence was a soft one. Tudjman revered and greatly admired Tito.

He said in 1990:

> If Yugoslavia is to exist, it can exist only as an alliance, a confederation of independent states.

In the 1980s, Tudjman formulated the Croatian Nationalist Programme. In 1989, he founded the Croatian Democratic Union (HDZ), which won Croatia's first free parliamentary elections the following year.

Tudjman's autocratic style and hardline approach made him unpopular with many outside his country, but he led the country at a crucial time in its history. He has been accused of human rights violations during the early 1990s and in 2008 was indicted for war crimes, even though he had died almost a decade before. Tudjman is credited with creating an independent Croatia, and with helping the country move away from communism and towards greater democracy.

In the next year, both Slovenia and Croatia broke away from the Yugoslav Federation and held their own multi-party elections. In April, Slovenia elected Milan Kučan as its new president and Franjo Tudjman became head of state in Croatia. There is little doubt that the inflammatory nationalist rhetoric and actions of Serbia contributed to the decisions that brought about the breakdown in relations between the Yugoslav states.

Although Slovenia was the state that led the way, it was in Croatia that most of the problems developed. This was partially due to the fact that, ethnically, Slovenia had hardly any Serbs living in its territory. In contrast, in Croatia there existed a significant number who had been living there for generations. The percentage of those who declared themselves Serbs living in Croatia was, according to the census of 1991, almost 12% of the total population, living among an 80% Croat majority.

Apart from the desire to ensure the well-being of Serbs in the whole of Yugoslavia, the relationship that had existed before 1990 between Serbs and Croats was a rocky one. The actions committed by the collaborationist Croatian state and the Ustaša during the Second

The Republic of Serbian Krajina inside Croatia (shaded in red-pink), which proclaimed its independence in 1991 up to 1995

World War against the Serbs could not be forgotten. As Milošević preached Serb nationalism in the late 1980s, pressure was put on other Yugoslav republics to allow Serb nationalist rallies, particularly in Croatia, where a large minority lived. Now it appeared as though Croatia wanted to leave the Yugoslav Federation, while many ethnic Serbs living within its borders opposed the secession and wished Croatia to remain a part of Yugoslavia. The answer for many Serbs in Croatia was the creation of a new Serb state within that republic, or to be allowed to join a Greater Serbian state.

After Tudjman's victory in the 1990 general election, the Croatian parliament changed the status of Serbs in Croatia from residents of a constitutional nation to that of a national minority. Croatian Serbs in the southern town of Knin (a *Chetnik* heartland in 1941–45), under the leadership of local Knin police inspector Milan Martić, formed a separatist body called the SAO Krajina. This organization's demand was to remain in union with other Serb populations in the Krajina region (see the map) if Croatia decided to secede. In the summer of 1990, SAO Krajina organized resistance to the Croatian authorities with the support of Milošević, who was wary of Tudjman's nationalistic and separatist stance. The Yugoslav army, dominated by Serbs, was urged by Milošević to defend the rights of Serbs in Croatia. In December 1991, the Croatian Serbs created the Republic of Serbian Krajina. Yugoslavia was in imminent danger of imploding.

Bombardment of Dubrovnik in 1991

The independence of Slovenia and Croatia: War in 1991

Croatia's War of Independence

As a result both of the victory in the 1990 multi-party parliamentary elections of nationalist groups in Slovenia, Croatia, Macedonia, and Bosnia and Herzegovina, and also of the failure of the politicians to agree to remain in a federated Yugoslavia, Slovenia and Croatia declared their independence in June 1991. Both Tudjman and Milošević had decided that force was going to solve their problems. Meanwhile, in April, fighting had already broken out between the Croatian government and the rebel ethnic Serbs in Krajina, supported by the Serb-controlled Yugoslav People's Army or JNA. The Croatian War of Independence set the scene for greater conflicts in the coming years in Bosnia and later, at the end of the decade, in Kosovo. It soon became clear that this first war in Croatia was going to be a bloody one, with ethnic hatreds quickly coming to the surface. Civilians were caught up in the conflicts and brutality was common on both sides. In the early months of the war, the Yugoslav People's Army deliberately targeted civilian areas in the coastal treasures of Split and Dubrovnik, both UNESCO World Heritage sites.

What happened in episodes such as the siege and bombardment of cultural sites like Dubrovnik and Split appalled many but it was a taste of things to come. After the war, an ex-minister commented:

All armies in the past did their best and refused to wage war or to target and to bomb the city of Dubrovnik. It was simply impossible for anyone to attack and demolish Dubrovnik. In the 1800s, Dubrovnik was captured by Napoleon, but without a fight. The Russian fleet of Admiral Senyavin came to attack Dubrovnik but they lowered their guns … there was not a single shell or bullet fired at Dubrovnik. That's Dubrovnik's history, and that indicates the level of the human civilisation, the level of respect afforded to Dubrovnik. What we did is the greatest shame that was done in 1991.

— Nikola Samardžić, 2004

▲ Shelling of the old town in Dubrovnik in 1991

Slovenia's War of Independence: The Ten-Day War

Slovenia had long regarded itself as Yugoslavia's most developed state. Slovenia's borders with Italy, Austria and Hungary; its attractions, which included some of the largest sources of tourist revenue in Yugoslavia, and its open attitude went a long way to accounting for this outlook among the Slovenes. The fighting was a short affair, lasting only ten days before peace was declared. In June 1991, the Slovenian government took control of the republic's border posts and the international airport in the capital, Ljubljana. After three days and a handful of casualties on both sides, the European community took action and met to propose a ceasefire. Eventually, both sides agreed to this and the conflict was concluded on 7 July. It had cost less than 100 dead on both sides, but the consequences were significant for Yugoslavia. The Slovenes had counted on the international community stepping in to prevent fighting and, in this, they were correct. They also knew that the Milošević's government was not as concerned about Slovenia's independence, given the small number of ethnic Serbs in the country; besides, the issue of Croatia was more important to the Serbs.

For Slovenia, the Ten-Day War marked its independence from Yugoslavia, which was officially recognized by the European community in the following year. For the international community, there were more pressing issues. In 1990, Saddam Hussein's Iraq had invaded Kuwait, bringing about UN intervention in March 1991. The attention of the United States and the world was on Iraq and the gulf war in 1991, along with a sharp rise in oil prices and a slowdown in the world economy. In addition, there had been a coup in the former Soviet Union and Boris Yeltsin had replaced Mikhail Gorbachev. With both Slovenia and Croatia now independent, the stage was set for a much more violent conflict in Bosnia in 1992, the bloodiest of all the battles waged in the break-up of the Yugoslav state. Meanwhile, in Kosovo, the majority Kosovars watched and waited.

Source A

A cartoon by De Angelis showing the break-up of Yugoslavia, published in the Italian newspaper *Il Popolo*.

Source B

A cartoon, "Welcome to Yugoslavia", also by De Angelis, published in the Italian newspaper *Il Popolo*.

First question, part b – 2 marks for each source

What is the message of each of the cartoons?

First question, part a – 3 marks

In Source A, what is the significance of the two oars Montenegro and Serbia having broken off?

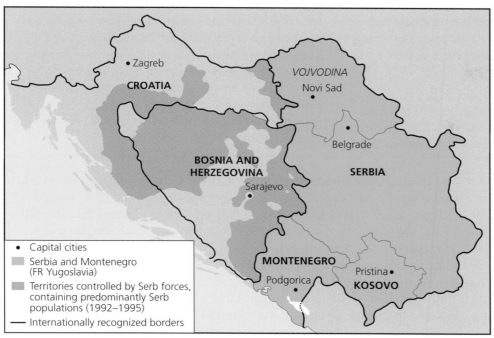

▲ Serb populations in the Republics of Croatia and Bosnia

Thinking skills

How accurate was the message of Source A in 1992?

The repression of the Albanian independence campaign, 1991–95

The secession of both Slovenia and Croatia in 1991 meant the end of Tito's federation, and worse was still to come in Bosnia. However, for the remaining republics, particularly for the formerly autonomous region of Kosovo, the choice was unpalatable: should they remain with the remnants of the Yugoslav state and strive to make it work or should they go it alone?

Ethnicity in Kosovo and the wars in Yugoslavia

The issue of ethnicity in the conflict in Yugoslavia and Kosovo has been overplayed. In Rwanda, the divide between the Hutu and the Tutsi was accentuated by other factors as well as by recent developments under colonial rule. In the case of Yugoslavia, one of the accusations levelled at Milošević by the War Crimes Tribunal was his overt nationalism and that he tried to create a "Greater Serbia". This was to comprise a Serb-dominated state, which included the Serb-populated areas of Croatia, Bosnia, and Kosovo.

However, it is reasonable to say that it is a common misconception about the Yugoslav wars in the 1990s that they were the result of centuries of ethnic conflict. There is little evidence to support such a contention. Ethnic groups had existed side by side for centuries and, with the coming of Ottoman rule in the 14th century, the influence of Islam added a religious element to this ethnic mix. In the late 19th and early 20th centuries, Serbs and Croats lived together harmoniously in the ethnically mixed region of Dalmatia and many early advocates of a united Yugoslavia came from this region. Among them was the Croat Ante Trumbić. Nevertheless, by the time of the outbreak of the Yugoslav wars in the 1990s, the hospitable relations between Serbs and Croats in Dalmatia had broken down. This saw Dalmatian Serbs fighting on the side of the Republic of Serbian Krajina. This supports the claim that ethnic conflict between the different groups in Yugoslavia became conspicuous in the 20th century, starting with the tensions over the establishment of the Kingdom of Serbs, Croats and Slovenes after the First World War escalating in the late 1920s following the assassination of the popular Croatian politician Stjepan Radić. It is without doubt that severe ethnic conflict took place during the Second World War when the Croatian Ustaša movement committed genocide against Serbs. In return, the Serbian *Chetnik* movement responded with violence against Croats and Bosniaks. Only Tito, when he came to power, was able to promote a Yugoslav nationalism that held the state together.

When Tito died in 1980, the federation he had helped create fell apart and for this Milošević must bear a significant share of the blame, although he is not alone. Tudjman was certainly a key partner in this but it was the promotion of a Serb nationalism that did much to bring

about the ethnic hatreds that ensued from the bitter wars that broke up Yugoslavia in the 1990s. Finally, when the Kosovar Albanians began to demand their own state, Serb nationalists were unwilling to grant this ethnic minority any of the freedoms they wanted for themselves. The consequence was bloodshed, the break-up of the federation and a Europe thrown into turmoil because of the exploitation of ethnic divisions.

The events happening in Yugoslavia, the rest of the communist world and in the Middle East overshadowed Kosovo and its campaign for possible independence. The removal of the Albanian Kosovar leaders Jashari and Vllasi, and Kosovo's autonomous status in 1989, was followed by the adoption of special measures to control any dissent in the province to separate from Serbia. In the summer of 1990, as Slovenia and Croatia began to hold multi-party elections, there were further protests in Kosovo. In July, a number of Albanian delegates met in the street outside the assembly building to declare Kosovo an independent republic as *an equal and independent entity within the framework of the Yugoslav federation* (Elsie, 2011: 66). A week later, the Serbian parliament dissolved the Kosovo Assembly and took measures to ban Albanian language media and broadcasts.

In September of the same year, many of the same delegates who had gathered in July to declare Kosovo an independent republic met again, in secret, in the small town of Kaçanik in the south of the province to draw up a constitution for the Republic of Kosovo. The most important impact of the Yugoslav wars on the thinking of the Albanian nationalists in Kosovo was that, instead of striving towards remaining part of the Yugoslav Federation, they would seek full independence. A year later, in September 1991, the Albanians held a referendum and declared Kosovo an independent state, claiming a 99% vote in favour. Despite the repression of Albanian nationalist sentiment in Kosovo, the people of the province were determined to resist. A key part of this political movement was centred on the Democratic League of Kosovo, known by the initials LDK, from its Albanian name *Lidhja Demokratike e Kosovës*. This was originally founded in 1989 and led by Ibrahim Rugova.

Ibrahim Rugova (1944–2006)

Ibrahim Rugova was born at the end of 1944. His father and grandfather were killed by communists only six weeks after his birth. Rugova was brought up in Kosovo, where he attended Priština University before going to Paris for a year to study literature.

In 1988, he was elected the president of the Kosovo Writers Association, which became the focus of the growing Albanian opposition to Serb rule in Kosovo. In 1989, Rugova became the president of the Democratic League of Kosovo (LDK).

Rugova was president of Kosovo between 1992 and 2006. He did not look like a man who might change

history. His office was a bungalow behind the football stadium in Priština, where he spent much of his adult life until he died in 2006. He was hailed by some as the "Gandhi of the Balkans"; with his trademark silk scarf, and a cigarette in his hand, he cultivated a bohemian air. A journalist once described him disparagingly as *a kind of loser who sat in a corner drinking too much coffee* (http://www.economist.com/node/5436910). However, this man held the aspirations of almost 2 million Kosovo Albanians and led his tiny country on the road to independence.

The role and significance of Ibrahim Rugova

Rugova was essentially a pacifist as well as an academic, and spent the last 18 years of his life at the centre of Kosovan politics, where he advocated that the province should be a democratic sovereign state, independent of Serbia. Initially, when Rugova became head of the LDK, he believed he could win independence without the use of force. He worked towards developing a parallel system of education, health services and local government for the ethnic Albanian majority in Kosovo when they were denied many of these by the Serbian government in the 1990s. Events overtook both him and his methods, however. Before the Bosnian war broke out in 1992, Rugova had resisted pressure by the Croats to open up a campaign against Serb rule the year before, fearing the possible consequences for his people. Instead, as Bosnia was carved up and thousands died, his low-key, peaceful approach led to Kosovo being totally ignored in the Dayton Accords signed in Ohio in 1995 to bring an end to the Bosnian conflict.

▲ Ibrahim Rugova

After 1995, Rugova's role changed, as Milošević and the Serbs turned their focus back towards Kosovo. Rugova had been elected president of the self-proclaimed Republic of Kosovo in 1992 but he was not granted international recognition and, following the signing of the Dayton Accords, for some Albanians at least, more radical measures were needed. They formed the Kosovo Liberation Army (KLA) in 1996. Rugova's policy of passive resistance had managed to maintain peace in Kosovo during the wars with Slovenia, Croatia and Bosnia during the early 1990s but this came at the cost of increasing frustration among Kosovo's Albanian population, hence the emergence of the KLA. Despite this more radical stance by some, Rugova was re-elected president in another unofficial vote in 1998. In 1999, Kosovo was attacked by Serbia and defended by NATO. Rugova went on to be elected as president again in 2002 and 2004, a position he held until his death in January 2006. His significance for the people of Kosovo is huge. Throughout the 1990s, he was seen as the moderate, intellectual face of Albanian opposition that stood against Milošević's Belgrade regime and is, by some, regarded as the "father of the nation".

The Bosnian war, 1992–95

The face of passive resistance which Rugova presented to the world was at odds with what happened in neighbouring Bosnia in the early years of the decade. The attention of the world was to be drawn to Bosnia and the full horrors of the conflict examined. In Rwanda, the genocide developed and the international community did little of practical use to stop the killing. Lessons learned in Rwanda were to have an impact in Bosnia and for Kosovo, finally leading to intervention in 1999. In Bosnia, the United States, Britain, France, Germany, Russia and countries of the Middle East followed widely differing policies.

Why might this have been the case? According to a census taken in 1991, Bosnia and Herzegovina's population consisted of 44% Muslims, 31% Serbs, 17% Croats and 5% "other". The birth rate of the Muslim community was higher than that of the others, so the probability was that Muslims would dominate the state within one or two generations.

As happened in Croatia, the Serb minority objected to any situation that might leave them as a minority in an independent state. When the Bosnian leader Alija Izetbegović declared Bosnia's independence in April 1992, the leader of the Bosnian Serbs, Radovan Karadžić, challenged this declaration as representing the "road to Hell" and threatened that, as a result, *"the Muslim nation may disappear altogether"* (Nation, 2003: 151). The stage was set for the bloodiest conflict of the Yugoslav wars.

The Bosnian war was fought because Serbs and Croats living in Bosnia wanted to annex Bosnian territory for their own states. Milošević and Tudjman met in March 1991 at Tito's old hunting lodge at Karadjordjevo, in Vojvodina, to work out a deal over the division of Bosnia should war break out. Prior to the outbreak of war in the summer of 1992, Karadžić, with the support of Milošević in Serbia, created a Serb army in Bosnia; when fighting did break out, Bosnian Serbs began a policy of "cleansing" large areas of Bosnia of non-Serbs. The term "ethnic cleansing" came to the fore, a literal translation of the Serbo-Croatian phrase *etnicko ciscenje,* and was widely employed in the 1990s to describe the brutal treatment of civilians in the Yugoslav conflicts.

There were horrific scenes that had not been witnessed in Europe since the Second World War. After the war, the International Court equated these actions with genocide, and some of the perpetrators were charged with crimes against humanity.

Ethnic cleansing

The use of the term "ethnic cleansing" became common in the 1990s after its use in the media as a result of the images of the Yugoslavian conflicts. As a concept, it has generated some controversy. Some critics see little difference between ethnic cleansing and genocide; however, defenders of the term argue that the two can be distinguished by the intent of the perpetrator. One such defender is Raphael Lemkin, who introduced the term "genocide" during the Second World War to describe Nazi policies of systematic murder in reference to the destruction of the Jews in Europe. (For more on this, see the references to genocide in the Rwanda case study.) Lemkin created the word "genocide" by combining the Greek word for race ("geno") and the Latin word for killing ("cide").

The principal goal of genocide is the destruction of an ethnic, racial, or religious group; whereas, argue its proponents, the main purpose of ethnic cleansing is to create areas in which the inhabitants are ethnically homogeneous, that is, of the same race. Ethnic cleansing also includes the elimination of all vestiges of those being "cleansed", including their culture, buildings, places of worship and monuments.

Some people argue that ethnic cleansing has taken place earlier in human history in various parts of the world. These include North America, following the arrival of European settlers, and even as far back as the destruction of Jewish monuments by the Egyptians and Assyrians a thousand years or more before Christ.

The war in Bosnia was the bloodiest conflict in Europe since the Second World War. It is estimated that over 100,000 people were killed and over 2 million people displaced. Similar to the events in Rwanda, probably as many as 50,000 women were raped during the war. When examining the crimes committed during the conflict, the International Criminal Tribunal for the former Yugoslavia (ICTY) attributed 90% to the Serbs and around 6% to the Croats. The war lasted for over three and a half years, from April 1992 until the ceasefire in December 1995, when peace agreements were negotiated and signed in Dayton, Ohio. These partitioned the former province of Bosnia and Herzegovina. Events that characterized the fighting and brought the struggle to the world's attention included:

- the massacres which took place in Prijedor in 1992 and Srebrenica in 1995

- the scenes at Omarska detention camp in Northern Bosnia in 1992

- the siege of Sarajevo in 1992, in which over 11,500 people died

- the destruction of the bridge in Mostar by Croatian forces in 1993

- the declaration, in 1995, of UN safe zones for Muslims in Sarajevo, Tuzla, Bihac, Srebrenica, Zepa and Gorazde

- NATO air strikes in 1994 and 1995, and the use of air power in Bosnia in 1995; this was the first time since its creation in 1949 that NATO had used its military strike force against an opponent.

▲ The signing of the Dayton Accords in 1995. In the centre (with eyes closed) is Milošević, next to him, Izetbegović, and to his left, Franjo Tudjman, leader of Croatia

TOK guiding questions

1 How can one gauge the extent to which history is told from a particular cultural or national perspective?

2 Is it possible for historical writing to be free from perspective?

3 What distinguishes a better historical account from a worse one?

4 How can historians assess the reliability of sources?

The events of the conflict in Bosnia are probably the most graphic and best known of the Yugoslav wars.

Thinking, communication, research and social skills

Research the events of the conflict in Bosnia. Consider the importance of the media and the role it played in bringing the events to the world's attention. Then work in pairs or small groups and examine Sources A–F below.

For each source, prepare a presentation lasting 3–5 minutes. Include visuals, maps, political cartoons and other source materials in your presentation. Be sure to address at least **one** of the TOK guiding questions given above.

Source A

Omarska Camp: The power of images

Look at this famous cover of *Time* magazine from 1992: http://content.time.com/time/covers/0,16641,19920817,00.html or search "Time magazine: Must it go on?"

What is your immediate reaction to the scene featured on the cover? What happened there? Consider how emotion

plays a part in the selection of images on such a well-known publication in the world's media.

Source B

The Siege of Sarajevo, 1992–96

The siege of the Bosnian capital Sarajevo took place from April 1992 until February 1996. Lasting over 1,200 days, it is the longest siege in modern European warfare. People grew accustomed to hearing about "Sniper Alley" during the siege. There were bloody scenes as civilians tried to go about their business and were picked off by snipers or killed by artillery and mortar rounds. In the Markale market, the largest single attack in 1994 caused the deaths of 68 civilians. The images are powerful ones. Research what happened there and why. Consider the following images in your research and presentation.

Source C

The Srebrenica massacre, 1995

▲ Markale market deaths, Sarajevo, February 1994

▲ The Bosnian parliament building after being hit by tank fire in Sarajevo

The events which took place in Srebrenica shocked the world. The massacre was the worst episode of mass murder in Europe since the Second World War and has been called *"the single biggest crime of the Bosnian war"* (Glenny, 1999: 650). Over 8,000 mostly Muslim men and boys were massacred and it was this single event that did the most to arouse the international community to urge a ceasefire and end the conflict.

Research how the Srebrenica massacre came about and what happened there.

Source D

UN safe zones for Muslims

Investigate one or two of the six so-called safe zones in Sarajevo, Tuzla, Bihac, Srebrenica, Zepa and Gorazde. These represented the only international attempts to protect civilians in these areas. Established as the United Nations Protection Force in Yugoslavia (UNPROFOR), the mission lasted for three years from early 1992 until 1995. Look at how and why these zones were established, the problems they experienced and why they did not provide either a solution to the situation or protection to their inhabitants.

Source E

The destruction of the Mostar bridge

This was considered one of the worst acts of deliberate cultural destruction in the entire war. The old bridge in Mostar, the capital of Herzegovina, was one of the best examples of Islamic architecture in the Balkans. Designed by the renowned architect Sinan, it joined the two sides of the town. In 1993, the Croatians destroyed the bridge.

Go to www.youtube.com/watch?v=CM3B-6CFo9k to watch this act of destruction.

Source F

The NATO air strikes over Bosnia, 1994–95

After the Serbs shelled Sarajevo with mortars, killing dozens of civilians in the marketplace, NATO aircraft attacked Serb positions. Operation Deny Flight spanned more than two years of the Bosnian war; Operation Deliberate Force followed this in 1995. Examine what happened in the air strikes, the targets identified and the significance of this campaign for NATO itself. How did it bring about a resolution to the war?

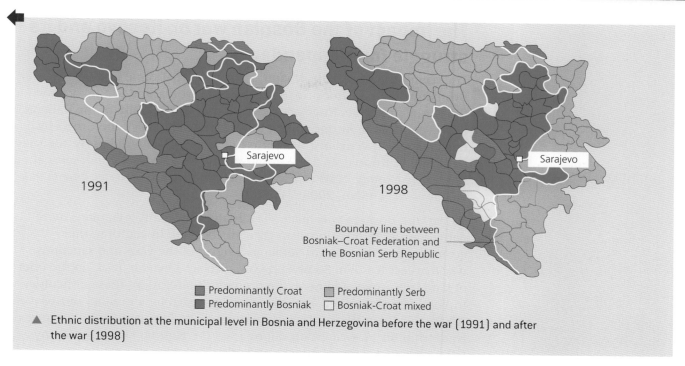

Boundary line between
Bosniak–Croat Federation and
the Bosnian Serb Republic

■ Predominantly Croat   ▣ Predominantly Serb
■ Predominantly Bosniak   ☐ Bosniak-Croat mixed

▲ Ethnic distribution at the municipal level in Bosnia and Herzegovina before the war (1991) and after the war (1998)

Source skills

First question, part b – 2 marks

What is the message of this cartoon?

First question, part b – 2 marks

How accurate do you think this source is regarding Western inaction?

The impact of the Bosnian war on Kosovo and its struggle for independence

The scenes of carnage, death and destruction that came out of the Bosnian war were shocking to much of the world, and to Rugova and the Kosovan people. Rugova's reputation as the "Gandhi of the Balkans", however accurate or not, meant that his refusal to back the Croats by raising a rebellion against the Serbs in the early 1990s did prevent ethnic cleansing in Kosovo. In 1992, Rugova said, "*We would have no chance of successfully resisting … We believe it is better to do nothing and stay alive than to be massacred*" (Judah, 2008: 71).

In fact, the Bosnian war made the situation for many Albanians more dangerous as Serb nationalism grew unchecked. In addition, the economic deterioration in Serbia as a result of the wars and sanctions was to affect Kosovo. Some Serbians, displaced by war, took up the offer of land in Kosovo, adding to the problems there. All of these difficulties in Yugoslavia provoked a more radical approach by a number of Kosovar Albanians, frustrated at the lack of progress and unhappy with Rugova's leadership. In 1996, a group calling itself the Kosovo Liberation Army (KLA) began a series of attacks on Serbs. The stage was set for an escalation of the situation in Kosovo.

Source skills

Source A
Milošević speaking in Kosovo in 1989.

Source B

Preface to the website "Dedicated to giving people the chance to read some of the speeches and interviews with Milošević" (translated into English).

No man on Earth has been lied about more than Slobodan Milošević. One of the most popular lies is that he whipped up nationalism among the Serbian people, and through that nationalism he incited the wars that destroyed the Socialist Federative Republic of Yugoslavia. Milošević's speeches were never nationalistic, nor did they contain any racism. We have posted the complete and unedited transcripts of Milošević's speeches and interviews spanning his entire political career. Read his words and judge for yourself whether he was trying to whip up nationalism and incite wars.

http://www.slobodan-.org/speeches.html

Source C

Speech Milošević gave at Kosovo Polje (the "Field of Blackbirds") to a crowd of largely Serb Kosovars on 24–25 April 1987.

Nationalism always means isolation from others, being locked in a closed circle, and that also means stopping growth, because without cooperation and connection with Yugoslavia, and then widening vistas, there is no progress. Every nation and nationality which shuts itself off and isolates itself behaves irresponsibly toward their constituents' growth. That is why, before anything else, we communists must do all that is required to eliminate the consequences of nationalist and separatist behaviour …

But our goal is to emerge from a state of hatred, intolerance and mistrust. That all people in Kosovo live well. And that is why, in relation to that goal, I want to tell you colleagues, yes, you need to stay here. This is your land. Your homes are here, your memories … You need to stay here because of your forefathers and because of your descendants. You would shame your forefathers and disappoint your descendants … We'll change it together, we, Serbia and all of Yugoslavia! … we can at least stop the exodus, we can assure the condition that all people that live on Kosovo be in their homes, live under equal rights and equal allotment of Kosovo economic opportunity before anything else, and then all other opportunities … All of Yugoslavia is with you. The issue isn't that it's a problem for Yugoslavia, but Yugoslavia and Kosovo. Yugoslavia doesn't exist without Kosovo! Yugoslavia would disintegrate without Kosovo!

Yugoslavia and Serbia will never give up Kosovo!

Source D

Excerpts from the speech by Milošević at a rally in Belgrade, 19 November 1988.

Comrades, no meeting as big as this has been held in Belgrade since its liberation. The last time such a great number of people, united by a great idea, gathered in the streets of Belgrade was on 20th October 1944. At that time the people in the streets of Belgrade were celebrating victory in the war. At that time, just as today, members of all Yugoslav peoples and nationalities assembled here in togetherness.

The most important thing that we must resolve at this time is to establish peace and order in Kosovo. There is no more urgent task for Serbia, nor should there be any other more pressing task for all of Yugoslavia, because the solidarity of the Yugoslav peoples and especially of Yugoslav workers have always been their greatest and strongest characteristic … For this reason, it is difficult to explain why this solidarity has been late in manifesting itself to a greater extent, more quickly, and with a greater love when citizens of our own country have been concerned. The long absence of this solidarity with the boundless suffering of the Serbs and Montenegrins in Kosovo constitutes an incurable wound to their hearts and to the heart of all of Serbia.

We shall win the battle for Kosovo regardless of the obstacles facing us inside and outside the country … Nobody should be surprised that all Serbia rose up last summer because of Kosovo. Kosovo is the very centre of its history, its culture, and its memory. All people have a love which burns in their hearts forever. For a Serb that love is Kosovo. That is why Kosovo will remain in Serbia. That will not be at the expense of Albanians. I can tell the Albanians in Kosovo that nobody has ever found it difficult to live in Serbia because he is not Serbian. Serbia has always been open to everybody to the homeless, to the poor and the rich alike, to the happy and the desperate, to those who were only passing through and to those who wanted to stay.

All Albanians in Kosovo who trust other people and who respect the other people living in Kosovo and Serbia are in their own country. I ask them now to rally against the evil and hatred of their own chauvinists, because they bring evil not only to Serbs and Montenegrins, but also to their own Albanian people. They embarrass their people in front of the entire world, shame it before its children, and offend its dignity. For the sake of all this, I call on the Albanians throughout Kosovo and say to them that Albanian mothers and fathers should tend to peaceful dreams, calm schooling, and carefree games of Serb and Montenegrin girls and boys instead of militia and army units. Terror and hatred run riot in Kosovo today, and Kosovo is in our country of Yugoslavia.

Comrades, the day after tomorrow, a conference of the Serbian LC will open here. This conference is devoted to reforms. The reform which we need to carry out concerns great social changes which should take place as soon as possible. The most important changes should take place in the field of economy. These changes should raise the standard of living of all of society and every individual. As far as the political system is concerned, the changes should establish unity in Serbia as a republic, and its equality with other republics in Yugoslavia. The reforms should improve and remedy everything that is of importance to people's lives: prices, medical care, education, and the information system. … This is a great programme and we shall achieve it if we remain resolute and united as we have been in the last few months and here today. Today, when Yugoslavia is experiencing difficulties, we should all raise our voice together, rouse our hearts, use our brains and unite our forces in order to preserve our country.

Yugoslavia was created through a great struggle and will defend itself through a great struggle. Long live all comrades gathered here at the meeting for brotherhood and unity, for Yugoslavia, and for better days!

Source E

Excerpts from the speech by Milošević at Gazimestan, Kosovo, 28 June 1989 (the 600th anniversary of the Battle of the Blackbirds between Serbian and Ottoman forces).

At the time when this famous historical battle was fought in Kosovo, the people were looking at the stars, expecting aid from them. Now, six centuries later, they are looking at the stars again, waiting to conquer them. On the first occasion, they could allow themselves to be disunited and to have hatred and treason because they lived in smaller, weakly interlinked worlds. Now, as people on this planet, they cannot conquer even their own planet if they are not united, let alone other planets, unless they live in mutual harmony and solidarity.

Therefore, words devoted to unity, solidarity, and cooperation among people have no greater significance anywhere on the soil of our motherland than they have here in the field of Kosovo, which is a symbol of disunity and treason. In the memory of the Serbian people, this disunity was decisive in causing the loss of the battle and in bringing about the fate which Serbia suffered for a full six centuries. Even if it were not so, from a historical point of view, it remains certain that the people regarded disunity as its greatest disaster. Therefore it is the obligation of the people to remove disunity, so that they may protect themselves from defeats, failures, and stagnation in the future.

Six centuries later, now, we are being again engaged in battles and are facing battles. They are not armed battles, although such things cannot be excluded yet … Our chief battle now concerns implementing the

economic, political, cultural, and general social prosperity, finding a quicker and more successful approach to a civilization in which people will live in the 21st century.

Six centuries ago, Serbia heroically defended itself in the field of Kosovo, but it also defended Europe. Serbia was at that time the bastion that defended the European culture, religion, and European society in general. Therefore today it appears not only unjust but even unhistorical and completely absurd to talk about Serbia's belonging to Europe. Serbia has been a part of Europe incessantly, now just as much as it was in the past … In this spirit we now endeavour to build a society, rich and democratic, and thus to contribute to the prosperity of this beautiful country, this unjustly suffering country, but also to contribute to the efforts of all the progressive people of our age that they make for a better and happier world.

Let the memory of Kosovo heroism live forever! Long live Serbia! Long live Yugoslavia!

Long live peace and brotherhood among peoples!

First question, part a – 3 marks

According to Milošević in Source D, what were the main reasons why "*Terror and hatred run riot in Kosovo today*", and to what does he attribute these problems in Kosovo?

First question, part b – 2 marks

What is the message of Source A?

First question, part c – 3 marks

Source B states that "*Milošević's speeches were never nationalistic, nor did they contain any racism*". Through an examination of Source C, how far is this claim accurate regarding both nationalism and racism?

Second question – 4 marks

With reference to its origin, purpose and content, assess the values and limitations of Source C for someone looking at ethnic issues in the former Yugoslavia.

Third question – 6 marks

Compare and contrast Sources C, D and E with regard to what support each has for the proposal that keeping the Yugoslav Federation together was a key aim of Milošević in these speeches.

Fourth question – 9 marks

Using the sources and your own knowledge, how far can it be said that Kosovo lies at the heart of an understanding of its importance to Serbia as a nation?

References and further reading

Elsie, R. 2011. *Historical Dictionary of Kosovo*. 2nd edition. *(Historical Dictionaries of Europe No. 79)*. Plymouth, UK. The Scarecrow Press.

Glenny, M. 1999. *The Balkans*. Harmondsworth, UK. Penguin.

Nation, C. 2003. War in the Balkans 1991–2002. Carlisle, PA, USA. Strategic Studies Institute.

2.5 Course and interventions: The actions of the KLA, the Serbian government, the police and the military

The badge of the KLA (*UCK* in Albanian)

A chronology of key events in Kosovo and the Balkans, 1999

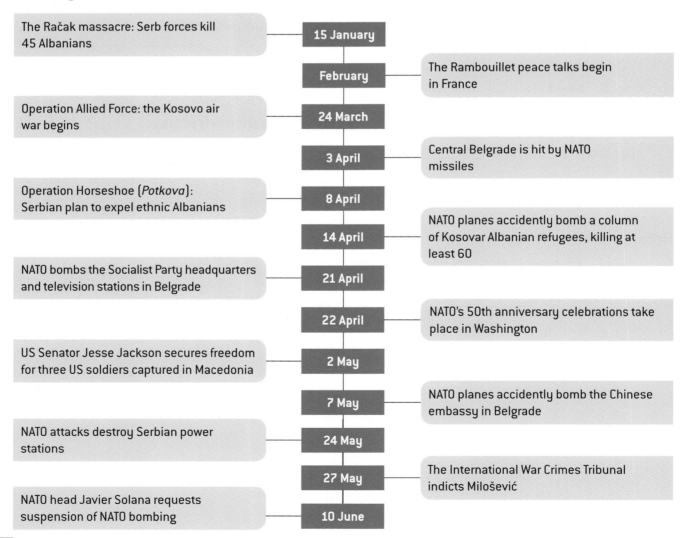

15 January	The Račak massacre: Serb forces kill 45 Albanians
February	The Rambouillet peace talks begin in France
24 March	Operation Allied Force: the Kosovo air war begins
3 April	Central Belgrade is hit by NATO missiles
8 April	Operation Horseshoe (*Potkova*): Serbian plan to expel ethnic Albanians
14 April	NATO planes accidently bomb a column of Kosovar Albanian refugees, killing at least 60
21 April	NATO bombs the Socialist Party headquarters and television stations in Belgrade
22 April	NATO's 50th anniversary celebrations take place in Washington
2 May	US Senator Jesse Jackson secures freedom for three US soldiers captured in Macedonia
7 May	NATO planes accidently bomb the Chinese embassy in Belgrade
24 May	NATO attacks destroy Serbian power stations
27 May	The International War Crimes Tribunal indicts Milošević
10 June	NATO head Javier Solana requests suspension of NATO bombing

The war started in Kosovo and it will end in Kosovo.

— Shkelzen Maliqi, 1998

The Dayton Accords of 1995 temporarily resolved the Bosnian conflict, but failed to address the issue of Kosovo's status, and many Kosovar Albanians began to look for other solutions. This was a crucial shift for Kosovo, and allowed the development of a more radical approach. Members of the Democratic League of Kosovo (LDK) represented some moderate opinion but their desire for a peaceful solution lost support among much of the population and was replaced by the greater militancy of the Kosovo Liberation Army (KLA).

The slide into war, 1996–98

The KLA (or, in Albanian, the *UCK*) emerged in the difficult period of the bloody events in Bosnia and the breakdown of law and order in the former Yugoslavia. It was easy to predict that, sooner or later, Kosovo would again become the focus of attention. The KLA, founded in the early 1990s, was a disorganised collection of disaffected Kosovar Albanians, including intellectuals and those fired by nationalist ardour. Following the conclusion of the peace agreement at Dayton, some members of the KLA began actively to engage in coordinated attacks targeting Serbian individuals, including attacks on a number of Serbian police stations and on public places where Serbians were known to gather. In 1996, three Serbs were killed in a cafe in Priština, and attacks against Serb targets and politicians steadily escalated over the next two years.

For some, enough was enough; it seemed to many that Rugova's pacifist stance had got them nowhere. One of the leaders of the KLA was Adem Demaçi, a Kosovar Albanian writer, intellectual and activist who had been striving for Kosovar independence for many years. The issue of free speech echoed as a cause throughout the 20th century. Adem Demaçi, who won the European Parliament's Andrei Sakharov Prize for his human rights work, was once an admirer of the hardline Stalinist Enver Hoxha but had since moderated his views. Nevertheless, as a prominent Albanian activist, he was imprisoned for 28 years in a communist jail for his promotion of Albanian rights. Many Kosovars see him as the Balkan Nelson Mandela. In 1993, he went on hunger strike, protesting against the closure of the only remaining Albanian language press in Kosovo. Pjeter Arbnori, the speaker of parliament in neighbouring Albania commented,

> *When dictatorships want to oppress a people, they first try to close their mouth. Writers, journalists, the press, radio and television are the mouth of a people. Now they have closed this mouth*

— Arbnori, June 1993, quoted in
http://www.independent.co.uk/news/world/europe/

TOK connections

In pairs or small groups, discuss the quotation on the right by Pjeter Arbnori. It suggests that it is wrong to "close the mouth" of a people. Consider the following questions.

1 What do you think about freedom of speech? Should it be allowed in principal, even if you do not approve of what someone is saying?

2 Give examples of where you might allow complete freedom of speech. Would this include religious opinions, statements about class, sexuality, gender and race?

3 Does your opinion mean that you have to listen to what you may not agree with, or that you consider biased? For example, in Rwanda, does that give RTLM "hate radio" the right to preach hatred and racism? Considering what happened in Rwanda with RTLM, should that "mouth" have been closed too?

4 The radical Serbian militia leader known as "Arkan" had a sign in his office in Priština saying, "*Croats, dogs and Albanians not welcome*". What is your opinion of this?

▲ KLA soldiers carrying the Kosovo flag

In 1996–97, the KLA was a disorganized group of nationalists who took up terrorist methods. Armed confrontation would, in the short term, bring them into conflict with the Serbian authorities and that is precisely what they wanted: to force the hands of Rugova, Serbia and even the international community to deal with the situation of Kosovo. Milošević still continued to be seen as a necessary partner by the West because of the Dayton Accords. However, five years of conflict in the Balkans and elsewhere had exhausted many; it was events in neighbouring Albania that acted as a catalyst for developments in Kosovo in 1998.

In the summer of 1997, Albania descended into chaos. Following a financial collapse, the government of Albania's President Berisha lost control and weapons became easily available, many of which found their way across the border into the hands of the KLA. Priština saw clashes between students and the authorities, and again on Albania's national day in November. Reasonably, the Serbian authorities regarded the KLA as a terrorist organization. The US State Department had listed the KLA on its list of terrorist groups in 1998. As in the case of Rwanda, the use by US spokespeople of the term "genocide" prompted a word game of some significance.

Early in 1998, Robert Gelbard, the US special envoy sent by President Clinton to the region, referred to members of the KLA as terrorists; a month later, he back-pedalled slightly, saying that the group had "committed terrorist acts". In June, the US government initiated talks with members of the KLA. Meanwhile, in March, the Serbian police had tried to arrest Adem Jashari, one of the leaders of the KLA in Prekaz. Jashari was one of the founders of the movement and was called, by some, the "father of the KLA". He was killed in the attempt, along with about 50 of his followers and members of his family, including many women and children. It made a martyr of him and elevated his status to that of a saint in Albanian Kosovo. The National Theatre and Priština International Airport have been named after him.

Ethnic cleansing and crimes against humanity

By 1998, the Serbian government's response confirmed that it considered the KLA's actions to be an armed insurrection. The government's heavy-handed reaction only served to increase support for the KLA and, as violations of human rights and massacres became more frequent, the situation began to spin out of control. Rugova's leadership, still advocating a more moderate position, was out of step with a growing number of Kosovar Albanians who, although they re-elected him as president in 1998, urged him to demand full independence. Violence continued to escalate as Serbian forces attempted to regain control of Kosovo and destroy the KLA. Milošević had always referred to members of the KLA as terrorists, and there was unease among leaders in the West over what was happening in Kosovo. In Kosovo, it was not as clear-cut as simple Serbian brutality against helpless Kosovo civilians. One of the leading spokesmen for the KLA, Hashim Thaçi said:

> It was simply a necessity to free and democratize Kosovo. And nothing happened accidentally, neither the organization nor the beginning of the armed struggle.

— Hashim Thaçi, 2001

The KLA was directing its own form of diplomacy using the limited weapons it had at its disposal. After the signing of the Dayton Accords, in which Kosovo was ignored, the lesson learned by the KLA was that violence was the way to get the attention of the West. Ethnic cleansing was taking place, and not just by the Serbs against ethnic Albanians. In parts of Kosovo, a number of Serb and non-Albanians were also being driven out. Some Serb Orthodox monasteries and churches were attacked and looted, and monks deported.

> I think Kosovo was maybe the first casualty of the Lewinsky affair.

— Bob Dole, 1998

In the summer of 1998, President Clinton was fighting for his political life. While the attention of the world's media was glued to his supposed affair with White House intern Monica Lewinsky, his administration was desperately trying to get a handle on developments in Serbia and Kosovo. In June, Richard Holbrooke – the US government's chief negotiator, who had been involved in the peace agreement at Dayton and in an earlier Yugoslav crisis – was sent to Belgrade for talks with Milošević. He also met representatives of the KLA, which seemed to endorse the group's legitimacy in the process, much to the annoyance of Serbia. With neither side willing to back down, the KLA demanding independence and the Serbian authorities retaliating against attacks on their people, something had to give way.

▲ US Ambassador Richard Holbrooke meeting KLA representatives in 1998

Once again it was media images, including those of streams of displaced civilians and a bloody doll among the 35 dead in the village of Gornje Obrinje in September, which prompted the UN Security Council to adopt Resolution 1199 in the same month. However, the UN actually did little more than urge those involved to come to a solution.

The UN had passed four resolutions in 1998 concerning Kosovo. In March, as a result of the meeting of the contact group of foreign ministers from leading Western states and Russia, the UN recommended that a comprehensive arms embargo be imposed to include Yugoslavia

ATL **Communication skills**

There are a number of good documentaries on Kosovo and the NATO intervention that can be found on the internet.

- One of these is an award-winning documentary made in 1999, prior to NATO's intervention. Called *The Valley*, it runs for about 70 minutes and focuses specifically on the conflict in the Drenica Valley of Kosovo. Filmed during the bloodiest summer of the war, 1998, it is a powerful documentary containing graphic images. In it, you meet the inhabitants of a Muslim village which was attacked and destroyed by Serbs. You also see a unit of the KLA known as the Black Tigers. Some of the scenes are harrowing and graphic.

- The second documentary is from the *Frontline* series by PBS and is called *War in Europe*. Go to www.pbs.org/wgbh/pages/frontline/shows/kosovo/. This is an excellent website containing many very useful resources such as interviews, maps, and timelines, and also access to a two-part documentary on the war and NATO intervention.

and Kosovo. This was Resolution 1160, which encouraged dialogue, and continued to recognize Kosovo as a part of the Federal Republic of Yugoslavia (FRY). In September, the second resolution stated clearly that the situation in Kosovo had deteriorated, and that it constituted "*a threat to the peace and security of the region*" (see unscr.com/en/resolutions/doc/1199).

This was followed by Resolution 1199, which called for international monitors to be placed in Kosovo to help facilitate the return of refugees, and to allow humanitarian aid to reach those who needed it. Diplomatic initiatives continued and, in October 1998, an agreement was reached between President Milošević and Richard Holbrooke, paving the way for the verification missions that followed. Two further resolutions were adopted in 1998; the second of these, in November, condemned the Yugoslav government for failing to hand into custody individuals wanted by the International Criminal Tribunal for Yugoslavia (ICTY). UN Secretary General Kofi Annan warned of the deteriorating situation in the region.

Meanwhile, the US government was determined to get the European countries involved in any action to be taken and through NATO, threatened air strikes against Serbia. They prevaricated about the use of force though (as illustrated in Source C, the cartoon "To bomb or not to bomb", on page 182). In October, the Kosovo Verification Mission (KVM) agreement for a ceasefire was established. Among other things, it provided for unarmed observers to monitor the peace in Kosovo, for aerial surveillance to ensure compliance and for elections in Kosovo within nine months, to offer more representation for Kosovar Albanians. This KVM initiative was to be headed by the US diplomat William Walker.

The Kosovo Pact, October 1998

- *A 2,000-member international inspection force will be deployed in Kosovo under the auspices of the Organization for Security and Cooperation in Europe (OSCE). The force will be unarmed and will verify compliance with demands of a UN Security Council resolution, which include the withdrawal of Yugoslav special forces from Kosovo.*

- *NATO reconnaissance planes, not combat planes, will make flights over Kosovo to verify government compliance. Details of these missions remain to be worked out.*

- *Yugoslavia also agreed to 11 unilateral steps, including:*

  - *Partial self-government will be established in Kosovo, and the police force there will be made up of personnel proportionate to the ethnic makeup of the province.*

  - *A general amnesty will be issued for people accused of criminal acts related to the seven-month conflict, but war crimes can still be prosecuted.*

  - *The following timetable has been agreed upon:*

    By Oct. 19: Details on the OSCE inspection force to be completed.

    By Nov. 2: Agreement on procedures to reach a political solution to be completed.

    By Nov. 9: Agreement on procedures for elections in Kosovo to be completed. Elections to be held within nine months.

http://www.washingtonpost.com/wp-srv/inatl/longterm/balkans/documents/kosovoaccord.htm

Source skills

Source A

A cartoon by Chris Priestley, "Bill and Slobo", published in the UK newspaper, *The Independent*, 14 October 1998.

Source B

A cartoon by Dave Brown showing Milošević and an observer from the KVM, published in the UK newspaper *The Independent* on 28 October 1998.

Source C

A cartoon, "To bomb or not to bomb?", published in the UK newspaper, the *Daily Express*, 13 October 1998.

First question, part b – 2 marks

Explain the significance of the comment in Source A by Milošević regarding having "an inappropriate relationship". Which relationship is "Bill" referring to in the first frame of the cartoon?

First question, part b – 3 marks

In Source B, why is Milošević depicted holding back the tanks? Is the cartoon in any way sympathetic to the Serbian situation? What is the message of the cartoon?

First question, part a – 3 marks

In Source C, what do the words of the NATO soldier allude to? In what ways do you think it may be appropriate?

Despite the agreements made in the Kosovo Pact of October 1998, the KVM mission achieved little, and the violence continued to intensify. Before the end of the year, the decision was made to withdraw the KVM from Kosovo, as military activity was continuing on both sides. In mid-January 1999, international observers reported that Serbian security forces had killed a number of Albanian civilians in a village called Račak. This proved to be a turning point in the whole conflict.

The significance of the Račak massacre, January 1999

What happened at Račak in January 1999 has been disputed. Referred to by some as *"the massacre that forced the West to act"*. In an interview for *Frontline*, US Secretary of State Madeleine Albright commented, *"it was a galvanizing event"*.

> *The massacre at Račak? I think it was pivotal, yes.*
>
> — Tony Blair, 1999

The bare bones of the story are that about 45 Kosovar Albanians were killed in a small village in central Kosovo. Over the previous months, the village had been in the centre of actions by the KLA and, a week earlier, four Serbian policemen had been killed nearby. The Serbs prepared an offensive against KLA members and occupied the village, herding a number of civilians to its outskirts, where they were shot by Serbian security forces. The Serbs have hotly contested this version of events in Račak. Considering that they were legitimately pursuing rebel KLA fighters in the area, some of whom put on civilian clothing after they had been in a firefight, the Serbian government had legitimate claims. The US diplomat William Walker, head of the KVM, was taken to the village. He describes what he saw in an interview.

ATL **Self-management skills**

William Walker in an interview for *Frontline*.

www.pbs.org/wgbh/pages/frontline/shows/kosovo/interviews/walker.html

Late in the afternoon, January 15, my British deputy told me that he had just been informed that a military clash had taken place out by a village called Ra čak. Neither he nor I had ever heard of Ra čak. The Serbs reported encountering a column of the KLA. They engaged them in fighting, and had killed 15 of them … Next morning, on January 16, I went into the office fairly early. I asked my British deputy if we'd followed up, and he said we had sent another patrol into the village. He said, "I'm telling you, Mr. Ambassador, there's something fishy here. Something doesn't smell right." And he suggested that I should maybe go out to the village and take a look. So I said, "Sure, let's do it." …

There were a lot of women around in tears and crying. We came out of the village. The village is down at the bottom of a couple of hills. There's a ravine, a sort of empty riverbed going up the hill from the village. It was covered with rocks, debris, and ice and snow. We started up this ravine. After about 500 yards, we came across the first body. A couple of journalists were there, and a cameraman was taking some pictures. It was a man's body. There was a small blanket over where his head

should be. They lifted the blanket to show me that his head was gone. You could tell just by looking at the body that his clothes were the clothes of a peasant. He was obviously an old man. There were bullets all through the body, and blood all on the ground. I was a little shaken by this thing with the head gone.

We started up the hill again and, every 15 or 20 yards, there was another body, all in sorts of grotesque postures. All the ones that I saw were older men, and they were obviously peasants. There was no sign of uniforms or weapons. They were killed where they lay, the way the bullets were in their bodies, in their eyes, and in their tops of their heads, they had been killed where they lay. There was no way this could have been faked. We saw about 10 bodies while going up the hill. We finally reached a pile of bodies, maybe 17, 18, 19 bodies just helter-skelter in a big pile, all with horrible wounds in the head. All of them were in these clothes that peasants in that part of the world wear when they're out in the fields doing their jobs. A good number of them had lost control of their bodily functions, and so their clothes were stained, and that sort of thing. This had not been concocted by anyone, even though this was later the claim of the government.

I talked to some of my people who'd been there, and to some of the journalists. Then I talked to some of the villagers … The men had gotten out of the village before the troops moved in. All the stories were very consistent. The day before, either in late morning or early afternoon, the village was surrounded by the army, and they had lobbed shells in — a sort of artillery barrage. That was followed by the special police coming in, including some masked paramilitary guys with these hoods on.

They herded the women and the small children into the mosque, and rounded up the men and boys they could find. In mid-afternoon, they marched the men and boys off. The villagers did not assume they were being taken off to be killed. They assumed they were being taken off for interrogation, which quite often happened … It got dark, and the villagers that were still there went to sleep. When they woke up the next morning and went out of the village, the bodies were discovered.

▲ William Walker at Račak in January 1999

When Walker was questioned by journalists there in the ravine, he was angry and accused the Serbians of perpetrating a massacre. His frank and heated statements about the events at Račak helped to incite international opinion in favour of the Kosovar Albanians. This led the USA to adopt a more forceful policy against the Serbs, to the NATO bombing campaign and ultimately, to the defeat of Serbia and the withdrawal of Serbian forces from the province of Kosovo.

What has become controversial is what actually happened at Račak. Was it a "massacre" or was it a lawful reaction by Serb forces against attacks carried out against their men in a time of undeclared war by rebellious, armed terrorists fighting the legitimate government? Remember that, at the time, Kosovo was recognized by the international community as a part of the Federal Republic of Yugoslavia and operated under Serbian law.

William Walker in an interview for *Frontline*.

www.pbs.org/wgbh/pages/frontline/shows/kosovo/interviews/walker.html

TOK connections

Consider the difficulty in establishing the truth of what happened, even when investigating such a recent event with a relatively large number of witnesses still alive.

Class discussion

1 How can a historian assess the reliability of sources?

2 How can historical accounts be assessed?

Oh, I was angry, yes, absolutely. I think the anger came through. My statement wasn't exactly balanced, but I said, "Here's what I saw. It was obviously a crime against humanity." I called it a massacre, and I said, "My opinion is that those responsible are in the security services. We have to get to the bottom of this. The international criminal tribunal in The Hague should be invited to come in here with its investigators to do a real criminal investigation. I would hope that the government would pursue those responsible, and punish them."

When asked why he wanted to have a press conference he continued:

I thought the world should know that this sort of a thing was occurring. To this day, I'm very glad I did it. It was a turning point. The world, certainly Europe and North America, could no longer buy whatever excuse the Belgrade government came up with for some of the things they were doing there. I have yet to encounter a single person who actually was up on that hill in that ravine who came to any other conclusion. And there were an awful lot of cynical journalists there who would have poked holes in it, if that were possible.

ATL Communication and thinking skills

Go to: balkanwitness.glypx.com/racak.htm.

This website, Balkan Witness, publishes controversial articles, some apologetic to the Serb position.

Examine a selection of the articles that appear.

In addition, go to www.youtube.com/watch?v=3ehf4n5UIdo.

This YouTube video, *Serbian War Crimes in Kosovo – The Račak Massacre* (9 minutes), was ostensibly taken the day after the massacre. It contains eyewitness accounts and footage that is graphic and disturbing. William Walker's interview with journalists is also part of this video, as is a Serbian

justification for taking actions in Kosovo, "defending their past and their future".

Another YouTube video (3 minutes) is taken from the BBC documentary made in 2000 called *Moral Combat*. The video clip includes comments by the KLA leader Hashim Thaçi. He admits that Račak was a KLA stronghold and therefore a legitimate target of the Serb military at this time.

Go to www.youtube.com/watch?v=1DchHIrgATo to watch the clip, and assess the information included there.

Viewing and assessing these sources may help you to address what happened at Račak and to answer the two TOK guiding questions for class discussion above.

Walker called for an independent enquiry by the international community to investigate what had happened at Račak. Two days later, the Serbs shelled Račak and took away the bodies. They had the evidence, and took the corpses to Priština where they performed autopsies. On the same day, the chief prosecutor for the ICTY, Louise Arbour, was refused entry into Kosovo by Milošević's government. The Yugoslav authorities conducted the autopsies together with a Belarusian team. Two weeks later, a Finnish team of forensic pathologists conducted a second post-mortem; the bodies were finally released early in February. Subsequent investigations have failed to clearly establish what took place in Račak, other than to conclude that 45 people were killed. Was it, as the Serbs claimed, that some of the bodies had been KLA fighters from around the area but had been dressed in civilian clothing after they had been killed? Were the dead civilians those caught in the crossfire of battle, their bodies brought to the ravine under KLA orders to influence international sentiment against the Serbs?

Remarkably, considering what the events in Račak led to and how they stirred emotions in the media at the time, only one man faced charges for crimes committed there. In 2001, a Serb police officer called Zoran Stojanović was sentenced to 15 years for attempted murder by a joint UN–Kosovo panel of judges. His trial was controversial, partially because the testimony of witnesses whose

Source skills

A cartoon from the UK newspaper, *The Times*, published on 20 January 1999.

First question, part b – 2 marks

What is the message of the cartoon regarding NATO and Western governments, and what message might the Serbian leadership gain from this?

accounts were inconsistent and altered. In 2007, Stojanović was granted a pardon and freed. The Račak massacre was added to the charge sheet for the trial of Milošević by the ICTY, but was dropped later due to the lack of clear evidence of war crimes having been committed.

ATL Communication and research skills

Debate assignment

Who was responsible for the Račak massacre, which helped to engender the international community into action against Serbia in 1999?

Specific debate question

What actually happened at Račak and who was responsible?

Examine Sources A–F on pages 187–190 and use them to structure your arguments in the debate. Before you start, here is some guidance.

1   Before we collect evidence or attempt to answer a question, we need to decide on some **criteria for making a judgment**. Critical thinkers base their decisions, and make **knowledge claims and reason**, on criteria rather than emotion or other **ways of knowing**.

2   Read the required sources carefully. and answer the questions that accompany them. These are designed to guide you to important arguments and considerations of the values and limitations of the documents.

3   Consider the debate assignment above as you read the sources, and record evidence in an evidence collection chart (see below) in support of a position you think is best demonstrated by the evidence. **Use different coloured highlighter pens to identify relevant evidence in the sources**.

4   Come prepared to debate and discuss the question in class and share your evidence-based analysis of the sources.

5   After participating in the debate, and after considering the different perspectives and counterpoints of other participants, write your final conclusion on this issue. You may be asked to do this as a summary speech for the prosecution, or the defence, depending on whether or not you propose to find someone or some group guilty of the massacre.

TOK connections: Judgment criteria

Before making judgments about the guilt of one party or another, we need to establish some criteria under which a decision might be valid or justifiable.

Criteria for finding one party guilty: When is it valid or justifiable to bring charges against one group?	
Criteria	Explanation

Use the criteria above to evaluate your position on this question and to collect your evidence.

Source skills

Source A

A photograph, taken in January 1999, of some of the dead at Račak.

Source B

An article by Bill Neely, ITN's Europe correspondent in Priština, entitled "Serbs rewrite history of Račak massacre" from the UK newspaper, *The Independent*, published on 23 January 1999.

Exactly one week ago yesterday, history kicked down the door of the tiny village of Račak. Just before dawn several hundred Serbian police attacked with mortars and machine-guns. By nightfall more than 40 villagers were dead. The following day I saw their bodies scattered all over Račak – 17 of them in a heap on the stony hill above the village.

The Serbs now claim there was no massacre. Their pathologist says there is no sign that the victims were executed. A government minister suggests that the dead were rebels whose uniforms were stripped off and replaced with civilian clothes. Serbian television news gives extensive coverage to two French newspaper articles that cast doubt on the villagers' account of the killings. No massacre. To assist in the struggle of memory against forgetting, walk with me through the village and up the hill above Račak on a frosty Saturday morning. The first six bodies are of men in their sixties: not the typical recruits of the rebel Kosovo Liberation Army. They have all been shot more than once, most in the head, although one has no head. They have been killed near their homes; three brothers together on a path leading away from the Serb attack. A Swedish monitor notes that the dead are all in civilian clothes and unarmed, and that there are no signs of a battle.

A few hundred yards away are three more bodies on the hillside. Each has been shot. Then in a gully, strung out like a hideous necklace, are six old men fatally and terribly injured, the line of their bodies ending in the heap of corpses. Many in this pile are teenagers and young men. Many have been shot in the head, several directly between the eyes. Moving around them, taking photographs and notes, and speaking into small cassette recorders, are half a dozen international monitors. After working for two hours one monitor, a London police officer, tells me he believes many of the victims have been shot at close range.

After viewing the scene, the chief monitor, William Walker, says: "As a layman, it looks to me like executions." Mr. Walker is no mere layman. He was an American diplomat and ambassador in Central America during the murderous Eighties and is no stranger to state-sponsored killing. His feisty British right-hand man, John Drewienkiewicz, says of the dead: "These were old men, most of them, in their work clothes." …

We must not forget Račak. I never will.

Source C

An article entitled, "The truth behind the killings of 45 ethnic Albanians in Kosovo must be found", Amnesty International, 18 January 1999.

Those responsible for killing some 45 ethnic Albanians in Račak village on 15 January 1999 may never be brought to justice unless independent investigators are immediately allowed to do their work, Amnesty International said today. The organization also expressed fears for the safety of the villagers still in Račak and in at least two surrounding villages to which the recent violence seems to have spread. The victims' bodies – including three women, a 12-year-old child and several elderly men – were found on 16 January 1999 by members of the Organization for Security and Co-operation in Europe (OSCE) Verification Mission, in and around Račak, less than 30 kilometres south of the capital, Pristina.

"This brutal crime is chillingly similar to the first reports of large-scale killings of ethnic Albanian civilians, less than one year ago," Amnesty International said. "The truth about what happened then was never established, and those responsible are therefore still free. .... If history is not to repeat itself it is essential to find out what happened in Račak on 15 January and bring those responsible to justice …Given the present situation in Kosovo, domestic investigations cannot be regarded as impartial. The authorities should therefore do everything in their power to protect the site of the killings, and to preserve the victims' bodies to allow for thorough independent and impartial autopsies to be performed," Amnesty International said.

Attempts by the Pristina district investigating magistrate, Danica Marinkovic, to investigate the scene of the killings on 17 January failed, apparently because the area was still too dangerous. On 18 January, Serbian police forces, stationed on hillsides overlooking the village, reportedly resumed firing at Račak village. On 18 January, the chief prosecutor of the International Criminal Tribunal for former Yugoslavia, Louise Arbour, was stopped at the border between the Former Yugoslav Republic of Macedonia and the Federal Republic of Yugoslavia, and banned from entering the country. The Federal Republic of Yugoslavia has denied Tribunal investigators access for the past 10 months, claiming that the Tribunal has no jurisdiction over its territory. "The authorities should cooperate fully with the independent investigators, and provide them with all information concerning the police and security forces' operations," Amnesty International said.

Source D

"Pretext for war in Kosovo was a hoax", from the issue of *Workers World* newspaper, published on 8 June 2000.

"Report finds no evidence of Račak massacre" by John Catalinotto

A team of Finnish pathologists sent to Kosovo in January 1999 to investigate the so-called Račak massacre has at last publicized its findings. The result is further proof that the U.S. government manipulated both events in Kosovo and media coverage of them as part of its effort to justify U.S./NATO aggression against Yugoslavia.

The NATO powers prevented the truth from being publicized before or during the war. The reason is obvious. U.S. manipulation of the Račak incident was an essential step in initiating the war.

On Jan. 15, 1999, Serbian police – accompanied by observers from the OSCE Kosovo Verification Mission and an Associated Press video team who were French citizens – had entered the village of Račak, a stronghold of the so-called Kosovo Liberation Army. A firefight ensued, in which the Serb police bested their attackers. The next day, KLA members led William Walker, the head of the OSCE mission, and journalists of the international media to a gully at the edge of the village. Walker was also serving as U.S. ambassador to Yugoslavia at the time, and had a record of not exposing but covering up heinous crimes earlier when he was U.S. ambassador to El Salvador and Nicaragua. The KLA took them to the bodies of some 20 people lying there, and another 20 throughout the village. Before the international media, Walker immediately accused Serbian security forces of having committed a massacre of ethnic Albanian "unarmed civilians". He declared, "I don't hesitate to accuse the Yugoslav security forces of this crime."

The story was spread worldwide. U.S. President Bill Clinton condemned the "massacre" in the most absolute terms. He spoke of "a deliberate and arbitrary act of murder". The German foreign ministry

proclaimed, "Those responsible have to know that the international community is not prepared to accept the brutal persecution and murder of civilians in Kosovo."

The Yugoslav government categorically denied the allegations and called the incident a manipulation. It accused the KLA of gathering the corpses of its fighters, killed in the preceding day's battle, and arranging them so as to resemble a mass execution of civilians.

The "Račak massacre" was without doubt the trigger event that made NATO's war against Yugoslavia a certainty. The Washington Post of April 18, 1999, described Račak as having "transformed the West's Balkan policy as singular events seldom do". NATO immediately convoked an emergency meeting. On Jan. 19, U.S. Secretary of State Madeleine Albright called for bombing Yugoslavia as "punishment". The punishment was delayed, however, as Washington went through the charade of talks in Rambouillet, France – at which it imposed demands that it knew the Yugoslav government could not accept.

In the meantime, teams of forensic experts arrived in Račak from Belarus, from Yugoslavia and – sent by the United Nations – from Finland. In February 1999, the Belarus and Yugoslav experts both said there had been no massacre. But the Finnish spokesperson gave a vague report that allowed Walker's unsupported charges to stand. Now, after the most brutal war in Europe since World War II, the same team of Finnish pathologists isn't sure there was a massacre after all.

CBC Radio News learned and reported on May 22 that the Finnish pathologists' autopsy report reveals no evidence that the 40 bodies were intentionally mutilated. Only one of them showed any sign of being killed at close range. The doctor in charge of the autopsies is expected to release a full report within a few weeks. But the most reasonable conclusion is that there was a firefight, that KLA fighters were killed, and that the United States and NATO kept the report suppressed to help confuse public opinion. There was no massacre – other than NATO's massacre of the Yugoslav people.

Source E

An article by Christophe Chatelot, entitled "Were the Račak dead really coldly massacred?", published in the French newspaper, *Le Monde*, on 21 January 1999.

The version of the facts spread by the Kosovars leaves several questions unanswered. Belgrade says that the forty-five victims were UCK "terrorists, fallen during combat", but rejects any international investigation. Isn't the Račak massacre just too perfect? New eye witness accounts gathered on Monday, January 18, by Le Monde, throw doubt on the reality of the horrible spectacle of dozens of piled up bodies of Albanians supposedly summarily executed by Serb security forces last Friday. Were the victims executed in cold blood, as UCK says, or killed in combat, as the Serbs say?

According to the version gathered and broadcast by the press and the Kosovo verification mission (KVM) observers from the Organization for Security and Cooperation in Europe (OSCE), the massacre took place on January 15 in the early after-noon. "Masked" Serbian police entered the village of Račak which had been shelled all morning by Yugoslav army tanks. The broke down the doors and entered people's homes, ordering the women to stay there while they pushed the men to the edge of the village to calmly execute them with a bullet through the head, not without first having tortured and mutilated several. Some witnesses even said that the Serbs sang as they did their dirty work, before leaving the village around 3:30 p.m.

The account by two journalists of Associated Press TV television (AP TV) who filmed the police operation in Račak contradicts this tale. When at 10 a.m. they entered the village in the wake of a police armored vehicle, the village was nearly deserted. They advanced through the streets under the fire of the Kosovo Liberation Army (UCK) fighters lying in ambush in the woods above the village. The exchange of fire continued throughout the operation, with more or less intensity. The main fighting took place in the woods. The Albanians who had fled the village when the first Serb shells were fired at dawn tried to escape. There they ran into Serbian police who had surrounded the village. The UCK was trapped in between. The object of the violent police attack on Friday was a stronghold of UCK Albanian independence fighters. Virtually all the inhabitants had fled Račak during the frightful Serb offensive of the summer of 1998. With few exceptions, they had not come back. "Smoke came from only two chimneys", noted one of the two AP TV reporters. The Serb operation was thus no surprise, nor was it a secret. On the morning of the attack, a police source tipped off AP TV: "Come to Račak something is happening." At 10 a.m., the team was on the spot alongside the police; it filmed from a peak overlooking the village and then through the streets in the wake of an armored vehicle. The OSCE was also warned of the action. …

The next morning, the press and the KVM came to see the damage caused by the fighting. It was at this moment that, guided by the armed UCK fighters who had recaptured the village, they discovered the ditch where a score of bodies were piled up, almost exclusively men. At midday, the chief of the KVM in person, the American diplomat William Walker, arrived on the spot and declared his indignation at the atrocities committed by "the Serb police forces and the Yugoslav army". The condemnation was total, irrevocable. And yet questions remain. How could the Serb police have gathered a group of men and led them calmly toward the execution site while they were constantly under fire from UCK fighters? How could the ditch located on the edge of Račak have escaped notice by local inhabitants familiar with the surroundings who were present before nightfall? Or by the observers who were present for over two hours in this tiny village? Why so few cartridges around the corpses, so little blood in the hollow road where twenty three people are supposed to have been shot at close range with several bullets in the head? Rather, weren't the bodies of the Albanians killed in combat by the Serb police gathered into the ditch to create a horror scene which was sure to have an appalling effect on public opinion? … Whatever the conclusions of the investigators, the Račak massacre shows that the hope of soon reaching a settlement of the Kosovo crisis seems quite illusory.

Source F

Extract from an interview that took place in 2001 with William Walker, Head of the KVM.

It was not my judgment alone. It was the judgment of everyone who was up there. The government story was ridiculous. The village story was dead-set consistent with everything that was on the ground. It was a scene we saw within hours of it taking place. It makes no sense to think that people up on that hill in the middle of the night on that icy slope were changing clothes, and painting people with blood, and shooting them. I can't imagine it.

We then get to the question of the government refusing to allow the investigators to come in. If they really thought that I was blowing smoke, all they had to do was let some serious investigators come in to look at the situation, and determine that their story could've been accurate and truthful. They refused. The chief prosecutor, Judge Arbour, went down. I sent one of my deputies to meet her at the border, to try and bring her across. She was denied entry. It all fit in with a very consistent picture that what happened was the result of the security forces going into that village, taking the men out, executing them, and thumbing their noses at the world … If Račak had just slipped by the way, there would have been another Račak, and eventually, we would've had to tell the world what was happening. Račak just happened to present what I consider to this day to be overwhelming evidence of the truth that I declared at the press conference.

First question, part a – 3 marks

What evidence does Source D offer to suggest that *"there was no massacre – other than NATO's massacre of the Yugoslav people"*?

Second question – 4 marks

With reference to origin, purpose and content, assess the values and limitations of Sources C and F for anyone wishing to allocate responsibility for what happened at Račak in January 1999.

Third question – 6 marks

What support do Sources D and E have for the proposal that what happened at Račak was "just too perfect" and that there was some manipulation of events by both sides in the conflict?

The response of the UN and the international community

Despite the outrage caused by news of the massacre, the events at Račak were, by the standards of recent conflicts, relatively insignificant. Compared to the massacre at My Lai in Vietnam in 1968, where more than 500 Vietnamese were killed, and what happened at Babi Yar in 1941, where nearly 34,000 died in a day, the killings at Račak were minor. Judged against what happened in Rwanda, it would hardly be noted. However, the Račak massacre began a process that led to Europe's biggest air campaign since the Second World War. It would also lead to threats of invasion that, in the end, brought about the downfall of Milošević and the end of Serbian rule in Kosovo.

The Rambouillet peace talks, February 1998

Pressure from many sources was brought to bear on the two sides to meet and talk in the days following Račak. In the same week, US Secretary of State Madeleine Albright expressed her frustration with the lack of control the international community had over events in the Balkans.

We're just gerbils running on a wheel.

— Madeleine Albright, 1999

Meanwhile, the USA itself was gripped by the ongoing Lewinsky scandal in the White House, and articles of impeachment were served against President Clinton. In the Balkans, the State Department saw the need to promote regional stability and to preserve their own, and NATO's, credibility. Someone had to act.

Before the end of the month, Western leaders assembling in London demanded that representatives from Serbia and the Kosovar Albanians meet to discuss their issues. At the beginning of February,

▲ The Château de Rambouillet

leaders from the two sides, together with representatives from the USA, France, Britain, Germany, Italy and Russia, met in the French château of Rambouillet on the edge of Paris. Outside the château, supporters of the Kosovar Albanians chanted slogans in support of the KLA and independence, which was not even on the table for discussion.

The reason they refused to agree to the peace package was that they were not willing to agree to the autonomy for Kosovo, or for that autonomy to be guaranteed by an international military presence.

— British Foreign Secretary, Robin Cook.

Milan Milutinović, whose hardline approach alienated some of the Western leaders, represented the Serbs. The real decision-maker remained in Belgrade. The delegation of the Kosovar Albanians included Ibrahim Rugova and the elected head of the delegation, the 30-year-old Hashim Thaçi. A young radical, Thaçi was one of the founding fathers of the KLA, who himself had been declared a terrorist by the US government the year before. It was not going to be easy to persuade the two sides to agree or even to compromise.

Some critics of the whole process saw the West as looking for an excuse to deal with Serbia once and for all, and that the talks were nothing but a sham. Both sides at the meeting had concerns about the contents of the final draft of the Rambouillet Accords that was drawn up over the next three weeks. Initially, both sides refused to sign the document.

For the Serbs, this was still a domestic issue concerning a province within their own internationally recognized boundaries. What they were being asked to do through the Rambouillet Accords was to allow an international body, in this case NATO, almost complete access not only to Kosovo but to the rest of Yugoslavia, in order to see that the terms of the agreement were being met. It was tantamount to a surrender of sovereignty and the Serbs refused to sign. As well as this requirement, another key paragraph in the agreement stated that, after three years, an international conference would be convened to come up with a final settlement to the future of Kosovo.

The Kosovar representatives also had a number of issues with the final document, which did not promise a referendum on eventual independence, and would require the KLA to disarm before proceeding any further. Nevertheless, the Kosovars did not reject the document outright, and pressure was brought to bear on them to consult further with other representatives. Whereas Serbia was essentially being controlled by one man's policies, the Kosovar Albanian delegation was a much less cohesive group of people, made up of intellectuals, would-be politicians and radicals.

The representatives broke at the end of February and agreed to meet again on 15 March, following consultations with the other parties. When they returned, pressure had been put on both sides to sign the accords and, finally, the Albanians did so. The US government stated clearly that the Albanians had to sign. Behind the scenes, critics of the US government said that this pressure was brought to bear so that the Serbs could be blamed for the breakdown and moves towards military action could be undertaken. Richard Becker, head of an international action group based in New York, believed that the Rambouillet Accords were presented to Yugoslavia as an ultimatum, that there were, in fact, no negotiations at all and that it was a "take it or leave it" proposition: *"The Rambouillet Accord [document] was, in truth, a declaration of war disguised as a peace agreement"* (Becker). (For more on this, see www.globalresearch.ca/the-u-s-nato-military-intervention-in-kosovo/1666.)

▲ The Kosovar Albanians, President Elect Rugova (left) and KLA representative Hashim Thaçi sign the Rambouillet Accords, March 1999

US spokesman Richard Holbrooke visited Belgrade again early in March to warn Milošević that failure to sign the agreement would mean military action. Behind these events lay a definite burden of guilt, which was carried by a number of Western leaders, regarding what had happened in Rwanda in 1994 and in Srebrenica in 1995. On 18 March 1999, the Albanian, US and British delegations signed the Rambouillet Accords; the Serbian and Russian delegations refused to do so.

On 20 March the international monitors were pulled out of Kosovo in preparation for action. William Walker reported that as soon as they began to pull out, Yugoslav forces were waiting, ready to move into Kosovo. "*They wanted us out of the way as soon as possible*", he commented, "*so they could start doing what they were going to do, and then did it*".

On 21 March, Holbrooke once again visited Belgrade to warn of impending action. He recorded what he said to Milošević:

> "*If I leave here without an agreement today, bombing will start almost immediately … and it will be swift, severe and sustained.*" And I used those three words very carefully after consultations with the Pentagon. Milošević replied, "Yes, you'll bomb us."

> — Richard Holbrooke, 1999

The talks had failed to produce a settlement of the disputes but they did provide the pretext for the next stage in the conflict. What happened next at Rambouillet was not, in the end, a peace conference with much margin for real diplomacy aimed at solving problems. Serbia would not accept a NATO force on its territory. The NATO organization, on its 50th anniversary, wanted to show that it was still relevant as an organization and could act. By acting through NATE, the Europeans and Americans bypassed the UN, and were thus also able to bypass the opposition from Russia and China. On 24 March 1999, Operation Allied Force was launched against Serbia.

Source skills

Source A

The text of the appendix for the Rambouillet Agreement.

Appendix B: "Status of Multi-National Military Implementation Force be granted freedom of movement throughout all Yugoslavia … Article 8 of this Appendix reads: "NATO personnel shall enjoy, together with their vehicles, vessels, aircraft, and equipment, free and unrestricted passage and unimpeded access throughout the FRY [Federal Republic of Yugoslavia] including associated airspace and territorial waters. This shall include, but not be limited to, the right of bivouac, maneuver, billet, and utilization of any areas or facilities as required for support, training, and operations."

Source B

Response from the National Assembly of the Republic of Serbia, at its session on 23 March 1999.

The Serbian state delegation cannot be blamed for the failure of the talks in Rambouillet and Paris, as it had constantly been insisting on direct talks and consultations. The fault lies solely with the delegation of the separatist and terrorist movement and with all who had allowed them to behave in such a manner and sign a text which they had not wanted to discuss with the Serbian state delegation at all, but which they proclaimed as a complete agreement … this document was imposed by force in Paris by the US, which thus openly sided with one party diplomatically, politically and militarily, placing NATO in an alliance with separatists and terrorists.

Source C

Former US Secretary of State Henry Kissinger's comments on the Rambouillet Agreement, published in the UK newspaper, *The Daily Telegraph,* on 28 June 1999.

The Rambouillet text, which called on Serbia to admit NATO troops throughout Yugoslavia, was a provocation, an excuse to start bombing. Rambouillet is not a document that an angelic Serb could have accepted. It was a terrible diplomatic document that should never have been presented in that form.

Source D

A cartoon entitled "Balkan diplomacy", published in the UK newspaper, *The Herald* (Glasgow), on 16 March 1999.

First question, part a – 3 marks

In what ways do the contents of Source A support the contention in Source B that *"this document was imposed by force in Paris by the US, which thus openly sided with one party diplomatically, politically and militarily"*?

First question, part a – 3 marks

What is the message of the cartoon in Source D and how does its title relate to the message?

Third question – 6 marks

Using Sources A and B, compare and contrast how they promote understanding of the point of view of the side they represent.

Third question – 6 marks

Compare and contrast the message of Source D with what is said in Sources B and C.

▲ The man shown is Robin Cook, the British Labour government's foreign minister.

2.6 The NATO bombing campaign: Operation Allied Force

Conceptual understanding

Key concepts

→ Change

→ Significance

→ Perspective

Key question

→ How did the international community respond to the crisis in Kosovo?

▲ General headquarters of the Yugoslav army in Belgrade, damaged during NATO bombing

The Kosovo campaign was a just and necessary war. And I believe that Blair, of whom I have many criticisms, in this case showed real determination in conducting it.

— Margaret Thatcher, 2002

If we lose this war, NATO is ended.

— Ivo Daalder, 1999

The NATO bombing campaign against Serbia lasted for 77 days and was finally brought to a conclusion on 10 June 1999. The decision to use force was controversial: NATO launched an attack against a sovereign state attempting to quell a domestic insurgency. The legitimacy of NATO's action had been questioned from the start. Bear in mind that NATO was an organization founded after the Second World War to defend Europe against aggression that was thought might come from the Soviet Union. By taking sides in a domestic dispute, NATO was acting beyond its own supposedly neutral position. It had existed for years and had never, up until the short campaigns against Bosnian Serbs in 1994–95, used its military power. There had even been a joke circulating that suggested the acronym "NATO" stood for "No Action, Talk Only". Now NATO's actions proved this wrong.

NATO was going to use its considerable firepower against a sovereign state in defence of an ethnic group, and without the approval of the UN Security Council. In the years prior to the bombing campaign, a relatively small number of around 2,000 people had been killed in the violence in Kosovo. This was hardly genocide. Nor could the number of refugees driven from their homes by the conflict be called an overwhelming human tragedy, as we had seen in Rwanda, the Congo and other parts of the world. Fewer than 250,000 people had been displaced by the conflict in Kosovo up until that time. However, when all was said and done, NATO and the international community had tried to solve the problems emerging in the Balkans. There was a firm belief, even if to some it may have been unjustified, that the actions of Milošević over the last decade had shown him to be unscrupulous in his exercise of power. Diplomatic means had been tried, coercive pressure had been applied, and none of it seemed to work. Now it was the turn of force, plain and simple.

In the air campaign, which lasted 77 days, approximately 38,000 missions were flown over "enemy" territory. Of these, one third were strike missions, where specific targets were hit. Extraordinarily, by the end, only two allied aircraft failed to return and there were no combat fatalities. It was a remarkable example of a precision campaign against an enemy that had used all means at its disposal, including hiding military hardware in hospital areas and schools, and moving troops under the cover of Red Cross convoys. Operation Allied Force was easily the largest combat operation in the history of NATO and the most sustained military operation in Europe since the Second World War. It was also probably the most successful example of strategic bombing in the history of warfare. In total, 14 allied nations contributed aircraft: the USA provided the lion's share of over 700 aircraft, while the rest of the allies supplied just over 300. Of the latter, the French and Italians provided the most, while Britain was the fourth largest contributor.

I do not intend to put our troops in Kosovo to fight a war.

— Bill Clinton, 1999

Source skills

Source A

A British cartoon published in the UK newspaper, *The Times*, in 1998.

Source B
A Dutch political cartoon from 1999.

First question, part b – 2 marks

What is the message of the cartoon in Source A?

Now answer the same question with reference to Source B.

First question, part a – 3 marks

Why might the cartoon in Source A be seen as ironic? Explain your reasoning.

Now answer the same question with reference to Source B and explain your reasoning.

Initially, the Western allies thought it would be a short campaign lasting only a few days, and after which Milošević would agree to terms. In Bosnia, that is what had happened, but it soon became clear that both sides had miscalculated. In a television address to the American people, President Clinton announced that the USA would not be putting troops on the ground. Some in the military thought this was a mistake as it showed the Serbs that, if they could survive the bombing, perhaps they could exploit the potential divisions within the Western alliance. Clinton's public statement indicated that the Western allies might face domestic pressure from those opposed to the use of force. It is also possible that the Serbs thought that the Russians, led by Boris Yeltsin, would come to their aid in some form or another.

Targeting the Serbs

You go after the head of the snake, put a dagger in the heart of the adversary, and you bring to bear all the force that you have at your command.

— US General Michael C Short, 2000

The air campaign had been devised by NATO commanders to hit Serbian targets hard and fast in a devastating display of firepower; it was designed to bring about a change of heart from the Serbian leadership. Over 1,000 targets had been identified throughout Yugoslavia, which included military installations and the security forces themselves, as well as facilities, factories and state infrastructure.

There were political constraints in fighting this campaign: dealing with an opponent militarily had to be balanced with the political ramifications of winning the war. Essentially, this meant it was a "consensus war" that had to be fought by a large number of countries, all of which had to agree to hit specific targets. Politicians demanded the power to approve or veto the potential strike targets of the allied aircraft. General Michael C Short, who directed NATO's air operations against Serbia in 1999, said:

> There were numerous occasions where airplanes were airborne, and the senior national representative would run in to me and say, "Our parliament won't allow us to strike that target," or, "Our authorities will not allow your airplanes, which took off from our soil, to strike that target."

— Michael C Short, 2000

These considerations could and did lead to some frustration and probably prolonged the campaign.

After the war, General Short became a critic of NATO's conduct with regard to how political requirements influenced target selection and other issues.

Why did NATO have to fight in this manner?

NATO needed to:

- be able take advantage of its massive air superiority
- avoid, at least if possible, putting ground troops into the area
- be seen to be minimizing the casualties in the combat zone
- avoid direct conflict between the Yugoslav military and NATO combatants.

> Belgrade is a city of Europe, and you cannot launch a military campaign without the support and the understanding of the people that support the governments who take that decision.

— NATO Secretary General Javier Solana, 1999

How the war was fought

The superior weaponry of the NATO allies could immediately be seen in the first three days following the expiry of the 24 March deadline when hundreds of targets were hit. In total, 1,000 aircraft were involved. In addition, Tomahawk cruise missiles fired from aircraft, ships and submarines played a crucial role in the air campaign. An estimated 450 missiles were launched, destroying over 50% of key headquarters and power stations. Mostly launched from the sea, these missiles achieved a 90% success rate in hitting vital targets. Each missile cost approximately US$1 million.

The opening days of the campaign saw the destruction of Serbia's air defences and key military targets. After that, operations focused mainly on smaller targets on the ground and in Kosovo and Montenegro. As in most military campaigns, the opinions of the military commanders fighting the war were sometimes at odds not only with the politicians and diplomats conducting the war on another level but also, to lesser but important extent, with the civilian populations involved. We have seen how the role of the media played an increasingly important part in the conduct of war in Rwanda and in recent conflicts. In Yugoslavia,

ATL Thinking skills

Should all means necessary be employed to win a war? For the combat troops or pilots involved, and for the enemy targeted, what might be the impact of having restrictions on the selection of targets or the use of firepower? Explain your reasoning.

the government in Belgrade was especially concerned that the public saw the war only through the lens of the government, and Serbia quickly portrayed itself as the innocent victim of NATO aggression, trying to maintain its own territorial integrity.

The position of the UN was difficult. UN Secretary-General Kofi Annan supported the intervention in principle, even though the Western powers had not used the Security Council. However, the UN had identified the Kosovo crisis as a threat to international peace and security through its resolutions in 1998. NATO did not ask the UN for authorization to use force because of the opposition it would have received from the Russians and the Chinese, as well as their probable use of their respective vetoes. Annan agreed that there are times when the use of force may be legitimate in the pursuit of peace, but was critical of NATO taking unilateral action, arguing that the Security Council should have been involved in any decision to resort to the use of force.

The day that Operation Allied Force began, Annan issued this statement:

▲ A Tomahawk cruise missile launched on 24 March 1999 from the USS Philippine Sea in the Adriatic Sea, in support of NATO Operation Allied Force

> *I speak to you at a grave moment for the international community. Throughout the last year, I have appealed on many occasions to the Yugoslav authorities and the Kosovo Albanians to seek peace over war, compromise over conflict. I deeply regret that, in spite of all the efforts made by the international community, the Yugoslav authorities have persisted in their rejection of a political settlement, which would have halted the bloodshed in Kosovo and secured an equitable peace for the population there. It is indeed tragic that diplomacy has failed, but there are times when the use of force may be legitimate in the pursuit of peace. In helping maintain international peace and security, Chapter VIII of the United Nations Charter assigns an important role to regional organizations. But as Secretary-General, I have many times pointed out, not just in relation to Kosovo, that under the Charter the Security Council has primary responsibility for maintaining international peace and security – and this is explicitly acknowledged in the North Atlantic Treaty. Therefore, the Council should be involved in any decision to resort to the use of force.*

— Kofi Annan, 1999

The air campaign continues

In the West, the images of refugees fleeing the fighting as Serbian troops moved in and began to "cleanse" areas of KLA resistance did not help the cause of the Serbian government. However, those images were rarely, if ever, seen within Serbia and Montenegro. The high percentage of support sorties (where targets are identified by accompanying aircraft, as opposed to strike sorties where aircraft use their weaponry) was a result of the special circumstances of the war and the aims established by NATO. These aims were first published in a 17-point statement, almost a month after the bombing campaign was underway. It is worth examining some of these points, which are given on the following page..

Javier Solana (1942 – present)

Javier Solana served as Secretary General of NATO from 1995 until the end of 1999. Born in Spain in 1942, he was a professor of Physics before entering politics and becoming a member of parliament, where he served for almost 20 years. He took the post in NATO and immediately had to confront the problems caused by the Bosnian war and NATO's intervention there. Solana is widely seen as being an effective leader of NATO during his period in office and after he stepped down he took up a role in the EU. He was knighted for his work in diplomacy by the King of Spain in 2010.

Source skills

Extract from NATO's Statement of Aims.

- Agree to the unconditional and safe return of all refugees and displaced persons, and unhindered access to them by humanitarian aid organizations; and

- Provide credible assurance of his [Milošević's] willingness to work for the establishment of a political framework agreement based on the Rambouillet Accords.

6 NATO is prepared to suspend its airstrikes once Belgrade has unequivocally accepted the above-mentioned conditions and demonstrably begun to withdraw its forces from Kosovo according to a precise and rapid timetable.

14 We reaffirm our support for the territorial integrity and sovereignty of all countries in the region.

17 It is our aim to make stability in Southeast Europe a priority of our trans-Atlantic agenda. Our governments will cooperate … in forging a better future for the region, one based upon democracy, justice, economic integration and security cooperation.

http://www.washingtonpost.com/wp-srv/inatl/longterm/
balkans/stories/natopoints.htm

It is clear, at least in some of the statements, that NATO had clarified its war aims and was determined to deal with the problems of the refugees as well as attempting to solve the wider regional issues.

Operation Allied Force was a remarkably successful air campaign and marked a turning point in aerial warfare for the 21st century. At the beginning of the 20th century, the primitive aircraft then in existence were used primarily for reconnaissance, to provide information for the artillery to range their guns and hit their targets. Once aircraft began to be armed with weapons that grew more sophisticated as technology developed, they were used in conjunction with other branches of the military in a more strategic manner. The most notable example of this is probably the use by the Nazi war machine in carrying out *blitzkrieg* ("lightning war") during the Second World War. The weapons used in Operation Allied Force were guided by sophisticated global positioning satellite technology and so-called "smart" bombs, which could hit precise targets in a manner that avoided casualties. Long-range missions with the sophisticated B-2 stealth bomber were carried out from bases as far away as the USA. Flying halfway around the world to drop their 2,000-pound bombs and returning safely demonstrated the intensive use of modern precision-strike systems. Amazingly, only two aircraft were lost and no servicemen were killed on active service.

Pilots carrying out NATO operations reported some of the difficulties in fighting a consensus war where individual targets had to be identified. It was determined that flying and bombing would be from 15,000 feet, to avoid planes being put at excessive risk from surface-to-air missiles such as Stingers. Without troops on the ground to find the Serbs, support air spotters had to direct bombers to their targets. One pilot, Squadron Leader Christopher Huckstep of the Royal Air Force remembers one example:

▲ Kosovo

Found the target, (he said) happy with that. I can see the little tiny vehicles that we're talking about. And then just as I round out to set up for the attack, the American calls…. "Hold it!" or words to that effect. "There's a civilian bus has pulled up next to them."

— Christopher Huckstep, 2000

Communication skills

The CNN webpage has details of each day of the bombing, gathered from press conferences. These feature a number of NATO's military personnel, including NATO Supreme Allied Commander Europe Wesley Clark, speaking about the day's missions and targets.

Go to edition.cnn.com/WORLD/europe/9904/01/nato. attack.03/nato.maps/days.1.18

You can learn a lot from listening to some of the content, such as the following:

- NATO military spokesman Colonel Konrad Freytag uses maps to explain days 17 and 18 of NATO air attacks on Yugoslavia

- British Air Commodore David Wilby describes days 9–16.

- US General and NATO Supreme Allied Commander Europe Wesley Clark describes days 1–8.

The air strike was postponed

In fighting this war, NATO was spending a lot of its assets to get relatively little in return, but that was the nature of the air campaign in Kosovo. Accidents inevitably happened. Some of the more publicized news stories in the air campaign were just those: the few mistakes that were made and which resulted in casualties and headline news.

▲ Bridges and communications were struck from the earliest days of the air campaign. This shows the Ostruznica Highway Bridge after NATO attack

▲ Pre-strike and post-strike bomb damage assessment photograph of the Novi Sad Radio Relay and TV-FM Station in Serbia, 1 June 1999

Mistakes made: Collateral damage in the air war

The term "collateral damage" refers to damage inflicted on people or structures other than the intended target. Collateral damage happens in any war and may include civilian casualties or damage to structures such as schools, hospitals or other public buildings.

In the middle of April, NATO targeted what it thought was a military convoy. However, the strike hit a column of Kosovar Albanian refugees, killing more than 80 civilians. It was a mistake, but one which highlighted the risks of the campaign; it was used by the Serbs, who showed these pictures of dead civilians on Belgrade television stations, as propaganda. A week later, when NATO leaders gathered for the 50th anniversary celebrations for the founding of the organization, there was some disquiet about how the air war was progressing.

The accidental attack on a convoy, 14 April 1999

In a strike against a convoy believed to consist of Yugoslav army troops, NATO planes struck a column containing a number of Albanian refugees. They were located over a 12-mile stretch of road near the village of Đjakovica in Western Kosovo, close to the border with Albania. A total of 82 were killed and 50 injured in the attack. The event was the biggest military blunder of the campaign. It is useful to examine this tragedy as a means of ascertaining how mistakes are made in war and also how events such as these can be used as propaganda in the media.

> *NATO does not strike anything which is not directly connected with fuelling the Yugoslav war machine.*

> — NATO spokesman Jamie Shea, 1999

Initially, the German defence minister accused the Serbs of the bombing, but the next day NATO acknowledged that it was responsible and that about a dozen planes had been involved in attacks on more than one convoy, dropping a total of nine bombs. The organization said in a press release that the attack was carried out because military vehicles were presumed to be in the area: *"Serbian police or army vehicles might have been in or near the convoy"*. The spokesman clarified that the mistake had been made because the lead vehicles of the convoy had *"several characteristics of military movement – uniform size, shape and colour as seen from the air, as well as consistent spacing between vehicles and a relatively high speed"* (see http://www.au.af.mil/au/awc/awcgate/un/nato061300.htm#IVB2).

Later that day, Serbian authorities took foreign journalists to the scene to show them the site of the attack. They found scenes of disaster, with *"bodies charred or blown to pieces, tractors reduced to twisted wreckage and houses in ruins"* (http://www.hrw.org/reports/2000/nato/Natbm200-02.htm).

It was useful for the Serb authorities to highlight such mistakes. NATO on the other hand, while acknowledging its "mistakes", blamed the government of Slobodan Milošević for the incidents. Days later, NATO spokesman Jamie Shea referred to the lack of constraints on Milošević's government regarding press freedom:

> *Night and day, I am under pressure from journalists to justify NATO's actions, but I am struck that Slobodan Milosevic is not asked to justify anything ... Milosevic is unaware of the constraints connected with the media.*

> — Jamie Shea, 1999

The UN investigation that took place after the war blamed the mistake on the height the aircraft were flying over the supposed target:

> *It is the opinion of the committee that civilians were not deliberately attacked in this incident ... it is difficult for any aircrew operating an aircraft flying at several hundred miles an hour and at a substantial height to distinguish between military and civilian vehicles in a convoy. As soon as the crews of the attacking aircraft became aware of the presence of civilians, the attack ceased.*

> — ICTY report

▲ A cartoon published in the UK newspaper, *The Times*, on 16 April 1999

▲ Tractors burn after the bombing of the village of Korisa, Yugoslavia, 14 May 1999

The pressure on NATO to accomplish the task was greater after this example of collateral damage. However, pressure is always felt more keenly in a democracy where the different constituents have the freedoms often curtailed under more authoritarian governments. In spite of NATO protestations that it was not targeting civilians, the attack increased international pressure to halt the whole campaign.

The man in charge of the war

US General Wesley Clark commanded NATO forces during Operation Allied Force in the Kosovo war and served as the Supreme Allied Commander Europe of NATO from 1997 to 2000. Born in 1944, he graduated as valedictorian of his West Point class in 1966 and gained a degree from the University of Oxford in Philosophy, Politics and Economics. Clark served in the US army for over 30 years, including in Vietnam, where he was wounded and received commendations.

Clark was an academic as well as a military man, and was appointed to US European Command in the summer of 1997, during the Clinton administration. He had served in the Bosnian war, meeting a number of the Serb leaders including Milošević. His approach was sometimes criticized by politicians back home when he pushed for the deployment of ground troops. Clark was, though, a popular and successful commander in winning the war against Serbia. He was frequently seen in media broadcasts, and came across to the public as a straight-talking, effective military commander. Clark led NATO to victory and, as there were no combat deaths during the campaign, he became the first US general to win a war without losing any soldiers in combat.

At the end of the war in July, it was reported that Clark would be relinquishing his position as NATO commander and returning to the USA. This tarnished his reputation, and evidence suggests that it was due to issues such as his strong advocacy of the use of ground troops and his high public profile. These views alienated some of Clinton's top advisers in the Pentagon and members of the National Security Council (NSC). Clark did have his strong supporters, however, among them Swanee Hunt, former ambassador to Austria.

Hunt wrote directly to the White House on 30 July 1999, asking the president to consider the consequences of removing General Clark. Extracts from the letter are given below. This source is an unusual example of an appeal sent by a private individual to the White House, indicating support for one of the key players in the Kosovo war.

Source skills

Letter from Swanee Hunt to the White House on 30 July 1999, asking President Clinton to allow General Clark to continue as NATO commander.

Dear Mr. President,

The International Herald Tribune and Boston Globe have, very sadly, carried several stories of your administration publicly slapping General Wes Clark following his successful leadership of the Kosovo campaign. I believe you can turn this around, and I respectfully ask that you make amends for this public disgracing of one of your most courageous advocates. Wes Clark should serve out his full term as NATO commander. He has been a robust champion for you in winning the war in Kosovo, and he has earned the respect of our NATO allies … From what I read, he now appears to retain his command without the support of key players in the Pentagon, and, most important(ly), without your backing. As a direct result, he will be unable to speak convincingly for us or for NATO.

How on earth can a military leader face a Milošević with that sort of apprehension about his career? Should he look at the enemy in front of him, or over his shoulder? Wes leaned forward, and thank God he did. He should not be punished now by those who disagreed. History will show he was one of the only right-thinking military leaders in this whole Balkan mess. If he is now disgraced, that lesson will become precedent in future military situations … You have displayed exceptional leadership in this recent conflict. Please don't let a passionate advocate for your values and vision of a multi-cultural world, in which tyrants are courageously confronted, be publicly demeaned because of internal disagreements within your administration. Your leadership is needed now.

Sincerely, Swanee.

Second question – 4 marks

With reference to its origin, purpose and content, assess the values and limitations of this source.

Communication and thinking skills

There are a number of sources — written, audio, visual or audio visual — that you can use to learn about the events of the attack on 14 April 1999. Examine some of these and come to your own conclusions. Here are some suggestions:

- You can listen to a BBC report on the attack (1 minute 34 seconds) at: news.bbc.co.uk/olmedia/315000/video/_319760_kay7am_vi.ram.

- Go to www.youtube.com/watch?v=6zfFkS4hh58 and watch the YouTube news broadcast (9 minutes 30 seconds) *Refugee Convoy Bombing Near Đjakovica April 14, 1999.*

- Go to edition.cnn.com/WORLD/europe/9904/14/refugees.02/ to read the CNN news report "Convoys of Kosovo Albanians bombed; 85 dead". This report also contains audio broadcasts.

Swanee Grace Hunt (1950–present)

Swanee Hunt, a democrat from Texas, served as US ambassador to Austria from 1993–97. She became an advocate of the Bosnian cause and supported women's rights there. Later, she lectured in Public Policy at Harvard University. She has also organized women's conferences in Bosnia and worked to secure peace in the former Yugoslavia.

General Wesley Clark was not reappointed to command NATO. He retired from the army in 2000 and later entered the political arena, running for the presidency in 2004 as a democrat. He lost the nomination to John Kerry.

Waging war

Despite the gap between the two sides in air power, the Yugoslav army was in fact one of the best-equipped military forces in Eastern Europe. In size, the army was approximately the sixth largest in the world and possessed a considerable amount of ex-Soviet weaponry. For most of the time though, it had to hide from air attacks carried out by NATO forces and it turned out to be remarkably successful in doing so. In part, the Serbs were able to do this due to the rugged terrain of Kosovo

▲ F-117A stealth fighter, part of Operation Allied Force

and Southern Serbia, as well as the very poor weather experienced during the campaign, which lasted two and a half months before it finally came to a close in June 1999. In addition, the Serbs put their troops under bridges, in villages and towns, and anywhere near to civilians to make it more difficult for the allied forces to attack. Locals even reported seeing Serb soldiers walking in civilian convoys to avoid being targeted and using Red Cross vehicles to transport military equipment, an act specifically banned by the Geneva Convention.

In April, to put further pressure on the Serbian government, NATO took the bombing campaign into Belgrade itself. NATO Commander Wesley Clark recognized that *"it was time to ratchet up the intensity of the air campaign. We had to take the targets in downtown Belgrade under attack. We had to go to the headquarters of the organization that were doing the ethnic cleansing"* (http://www.pbs.org/wgbh/pages/frontline/shows/kosovo/interviews/clark.html).

Missiles took out the Ministry of Interior in downtown Belgrade and then concentrated on electrical grids, refineries and bridges. On 23 April, NATO aircraft attacked media outlets, bombing the Serbian state television in Belgrade, one of the companies run by Milošević's wife, Mirjana Marković. Eleven civilian employees were killed in the strike, which became one of the more controversial of the campaign. The facility was undoubtedly being used to disseminate war propaganda, and so was considered a legitimate target.

There is a link here to the case study on the Rwandan genocide. Recall the debates over the Hutu use of RTLM radio and *Kangura* newspaper to broadcast the killings and identify targets during 1994.

US pilots were interviewed later on their experiences. These interviews demonstrate the concern as well as the level of training and skill required to fight in a way that minimizes collateral damage. Captain Thad Darger, who flew one of the A117 stealth fighters recalls, *"The plane is flying itself. The auto pilot on the stealth fighter was made to take us to the target, to get us there on time"*. On his last mission, he *"was given a target, specific to the 117 community, we call it a 'non-collateral damage target' where we couldn't accept anything besides the target itself being destroyed ... I was probably as nervous as I've ever been in my life for the last 60 seconds. It was exciting"* (http://www.pbs.org/wgbh/pages/frontline/shows/kosovo/interviews/darger.html).

One of only two allied aircraft shot down in the air war, an F-117A stealth fighter was brought down over Serbia in the first week of the bombing campaign. It is now on display at the Museum of Aviation in Belgrade. The aircraft, called "Something Wicked", was shot down by an anti-aircraft missile battery at 8.15am on 27 March 1999. The Serbian crew reportedly saw the aircraft on their radar when its bomb bay doors were opened. The crew fired a surface-to-air missile, striking the aircraft and bringing it down. The NATO pilot ejected and was rescued.

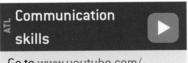

ATL Communication skills

Go to www.youtube.com/watch?v=2ciqsq-H-zk.

Watch the video clip about the bombing of the Chinese embassy.

The bombing of the Chinese embassy, 7 May 1999

In one of the most infamous mistakes of the campaign, on 7 May 1999, NATO aircraft bombed downtown Belgrade, accidently hitting the Chinese embassy and killing three journalists. The embassy building was hit by five bombs from aircraft that had taken off from bases in the USA. The real target, the government supply and procurement building, was over 400 metres away, and the embassy was struck as a result of a technological error made by the CIA intelligence operatives guiding the NATO planes to targets in the city that evening. The US government later said that the mistake had been made due to "outdated maps".

▲ Protesters carry portraits of journalists killed in NATO's bombing of the Chinese embassy, May 1999

The Chinese reaction was swift and severe. Li Peng, chairman of the Standing Committee of the National People's Congress, called it a *"gross violation of China's sovereignty"* (http://english.peopledaily.com.cn/english/200006/13/eng20000613_42856.html). US embassies and businesses in China were attacked and protests took place in Chinese cities. These continued for four days until Chinese state television allowed a broadcast by President Clinton, in which he publicly apologized for the error. Subsequent investigations supported the accidental nature of the bombing, but the incident worsened relations between NATO and the Chinese and Russians, both of whom were against the use of force. Later in 1999, the US government agreed to pay $28 million in compensation for damage caused to the Chinese embassy.

Working together: NATO allies and public opinion

At the same time as force was being used, diplomatic efforts were being employed in an effort to get Milošević to agree terms. At the start of the air campaign, Clinton had denied that the USA would be putting ground troops into Kosovo: *"I do not intend to put our troops in Kosovo to fight a war"*, he stated in his 24 March address to the American people. This angered some in the military who saw the similarities to the USA's role in Vietnam: the USA's ability to win a war being held back by political necessities. In a sense, NATO was fighting with one arm tied behind its back. General Short commented:

> *If you take the country to war … then you get it done as quickly as you can … We use force as a last resort, in the NATO alliance and in my country, so when the decision is made to use force, then we need to go in with overwhelming force, quite frankly, extraordinary violence that the speed of it, the lethality of it … the weight of it has to make an incredible impression on the adversary, to such a degree that he is stunned and shocked.*

— Michael C Short, 2000

However, all governments in the West were concerned about public opinion. They had to be. Some believe that the pressure from a critical public certainly encouraged Milošević to take his chances and stand firm. He had seen the NATO alliance in action in the four days of bombing raids conducted by Britain and the USA in December 1998 against Saddam Hussein in Iraq. These had precipitated protests in Western capitals and Milošević thought that, if Serbia could be resolved to resist, then pressure might also be brought on allied governments at home to halt the bombing. This, with the support he believed Serbia would get from Russia, might help Serbia's position in a negotiated settlement.

The impact of a sustained and bloody bombing campaign on civilian centres such as Belgrade could backfire on the allies. In an interview after the Kosovo campaign NATO Commander Wesley Clark reminded people that:

> In Europe, quite understandably, there's a terrible aftermath of World War Two. There are memories of the terror of bombing, and what it does to civilian populations. Many NATO leaders, as children, experienced the aftermath of World War Two or lived through bombing raids. There was a particularly vicious German raid against Belgrade on April 6, 1941 where 17,000 people reportedly were killed in Belgrade in a single night – a real blot in German memories, and in the memories of many others. European leaders were acutely aware of the sensitivity of their publics to the dangers of unrestricted aerial warfare. So we had to explain that we weren't into unrestricted aerial warfare. We had to convince them of the validity of the targets, the accuracy of the delivery systems, the skill and courage of the airmen, and their ability to deliver weapons with pinpoint accuracy. Over a period of time, we did that … our plan was to escalate as rapidly as possible, to do as much as we could. But we also recognized that no single target, no set of targets, and no bombing series was more important than maintaining the consensus of NATO.

— Wesley Clark

In the end, public opinion in the West was critical at times but the media campaign and the conduct of the war were sufficiently balanced to achieve consensus and support from the vast majority in the NATO countries.

> Right now, in the middle of Europe, at the doorstep of NATO, an entire people are being made to abandon their homeland or die – not because of anything they've done, but simply because of who they are.

— Bill Clinton, 1999

▲ NATO air bases and targets used during Operation Allied Force

Ethnic cleansing and the refugee crisis

What the Serbs were doing to the civilian population in Kosovo certainly encouraged public opinion in the West to support the NATO campaign. One of the principal aims of Operation Allied Force had been to respond to the campaign of ethnic cleansing being carried out by the Serbs against the Kosovar Albanians. If the aim of the air campaign was to quickly persuade Milošević to change his mind and abandon Kosovo, and to stop his campaign of ethnic cleansing, then the allies were diasppointed. By day 4 of the bombing campaign, there was a mass exodus of people from Kosovo. It was, of course, entirely predictable that the Serbian government would have used the NATO attack as a cover to continue its campaign against the Kosovars, and some Western analysts were critical of the NATO campaign because it added to the misery of many refugees. The scenes of civilians streaming out of the province were alarming for many.

The allies coordinated humanitarian assistance operations under the umbrella of what was known as Operation Allied Harbour, which continued both during and after the conflict. Soon, statements were being made by NATO leaders to justify the continued bombing campaign and to clarify the aims of NATO. In a speech given in Norfolk, Virginia, USA in April 1999, Clinton said:

▲ Smoke rises from burning houses in the village of Glavotina, 15 kilometres north of Priština, during the Kosovo war

Our objective is to restore the Kosovars to their homes with security and self-government. Our bombing campaign is designed to exact an unacceptably high price for Mr. Milosevic's present policy of repression and ethnic cleansing and to seriously diminish his military capacity to maintain that policy.

— Bill Clinton, 1999

The bombing of Belgrade in April certainly accelerated the process of ethnic cleansing in Kosovo. There was now evidence of large-scale operations going on throughout the province, with the police, local forces and the Yugoslav military involved. Few really predicted the scale and the speed of expulsions from Kosovo. Within three weeks of the start of the bombing, over half a million refugees had left Kosovo and fled to neighbouring countries. The UN High Commissioner for Refugees (UNHCR) has estimated that a total of 850,000 ethnic Albanians were forced out. This represented more than 80% of the population of the province, and in all, a total of 90% of all the Albanians were forced to move (see http://www.hrw.org/reports/2001/10/26/under-orders-war-crimes-kosovo).

One Serb soldier described how they went about the process.

There was a system that was applied throughout all the Yugoslavian wars. You would surround the village on three sides, and the fourth would be left for the civilians to run out of, so they had the opportunity of leaving the village. When a young Albanian was caught, it was assumed he was KLA. He'd be taken away and questioned, and afterwards he'd be shot. The questioning was a formality.

— Anonymous Serb soldier, PBS "Frontline", 2000

The NATO bombing campaign had not caused the campaign of ethnic cleansing but it certainly provided the impetus and the cover for the Serbian authorities to carry out their plans, thus accelerating the movement of people out of the province. It probably also contributed to some of the atrocities that were committed by the Serbs. The frustration and resentment many Serbs felt might be blamed on the Kosovar Albanians, and revenge killings certainly happened as a result. One of Milošević's aims appears to have been to take advantage of the bombing to get rid of as many Albanians as possible in Kosovo. At the borders, many refugees were stripped of their valuables and belongings, as well as their personal identification documents, even their car license plates, in a strategy known as "identity cleansing". This illegal practice supports the argument that what was happening was a deliberate policy carried out by the Serbian authorities, which would have made it much more difficult for refugees to return to their homes.

If the first few days of the Operation Allied Force had not been good publicity for NATO, the images coming out of Kosovo of the lines of refugees tarnished the image of the Serbian government in the eyes of the world. By the end of March, tens of thousands of Albanian refugees had been lined up at gunpoint and deported from the country, many of them into Montenegro. One of the more controversial questions is whether this was a planned campaign by the Serbian government. According to Human Rights Watch, the forced expulsions were well-organized, suggesting that they had been planned in advance. Many towns and villages were cleared and people were escorted towards the border on buses, trains and convoys of tractors.

Communication skills

A number of short video clips showing refugees are available, many of them on YouTube. For example, go to www.youtube.com/watch?v=zcWYY9Zfh08 and watch the clip *(14 minutes 30 seconds) Kosovo Refugee Crisis - US Soldiers on Trial - NATO bombs Belgrade (1999).*

This video is particularly worth seeing for its coverage of the refugees on the Macedonian and Albanian borders. In addition, it has interviews with relief agencies, material on the captured US airmen when their plane was shot down over Serbia, as well as material on the bombing campaign against Belgrade. Finally, there is an interesting interview with a Serbian government spokesman, who argues that the NATO bombing has caused the refugee crisis.

Why were Kosovar Albanians forced to leave?

The forced mass exodus of Kosovar Albanians served the Serb purpose in a number of ways.

- It may have been intended rapidly to change Kosovo's demographic make-up.

- It may also have been done with a view to forcing a split into separate Serbian and Albanian provinces.

- Finally, the very nature, speed and ruthlessness of the forced expulsions may have been designed to tie down NATO's efforts, weaken their resolve to fight and to terrify people into submission.

Thinking and communication skills

A cartoon by Dave Brown, showing Slobodon Milošević in Kosovo, published in the UK newspaper, *The Independent*, on 11 March 1999.

With a partner, discuss and make notes on what you think the cartoon is trying to portray.

Ultimately, the forced exodus achieved none of these things. The sight of helpless refugees provoked sympathy for the Kosovars and outrage against the Serbs for their actions. Whether these expulsions were a planned campaign coordinated by the Belgrade government has been called into question. Information came out very soon after the start of NATO's bombing campaign suggesting that the expulsions were part of long-term Serbian planning.

Operation Horseshoe

The name given by the Serbian government to the plan of ethnic cleansing in Kosovo was Operation Horseshoe (or *Potkova*). In April 1999, the German foreign ministry said it had received information about the operation from the former Bulgarian Foreign Minister Nadezhda Neynski, during a television documentary. Although she claimed it could "not be verified", the plan showed a concerted campaign to rid Kosovo of as many Albanians as possible. This would be done in two phases: first, destroy the Kosovo Liberation Army (KLA); and second, "cleanse" Kosovo of ethnic Albanians. The latter phase would be accomplished by squeezing the Albanian population from three sides, and driving the population out through the south-western corner of the province and into Albania and Macedonia: a horseshoe strategy.

In April 1999, Germany's Defence Minister Rudolf Scharping said:

> *The clear objective (of Operation Horseshoe) was to ethnically cleanse Kosovo and remove the whole civilian population. The operation was prepared by President Milosevic and his regime. It was organised at November 1998, started during the Rambouillet negotiations and intensified after the talks ended.*

— Rudolf Scharping, 1999

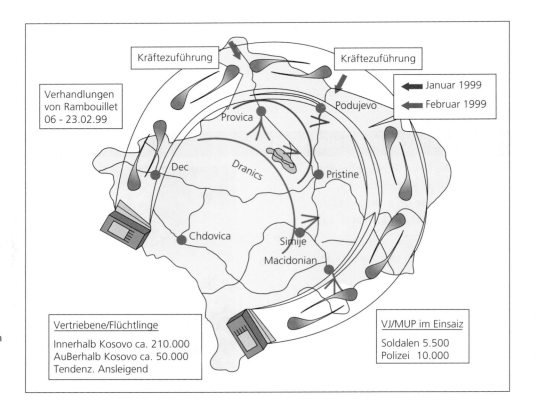

▶ Diagram showing Operation Horseshoe, from German security files

The Serbs denied there was a systematic plan to rid Kosovo of the Albanians, but that they were entitled to move elements of the population "for their own safety". They claimed it was NATO bombing that was driving refugees out of the province. Amnesty International stated there was clear evidence that Yugoslav security forces were expelling ethnic Albanians en masse from their homes, and committing war crimes, including rape. After the war, the ICTY brought charges against Milošević and other Yugoslav officials for this forcible population displacement. However, the existence of a formal government plan (Operation Horseshoe) has never been clearly proven. Critics of the NATO policy called the revelation of Operation Horseshoe "Western disinformation" designed to justify the continued bombing. At his trial in The Hague, Milošević denied the existence of the plan and, in the end, documents regarding Operation Horseshoe were withdrawn from the trial proceedings, as they could not be independently verified. In 2001, a German documentary called *It Began With a Lie* claimed there was no clear evidence of the planned campaign to rid Kosovo of ethnic Albanians. To date, the Serb government continues to deny there ever was a plan, and Serbian security files remain closed to the public.

▲ Hundreds of ethnic Albanian refugees from Kosovo arrive in trucks at the Albanian town of Kukes in March 1999, bringing with them tales of psychological terror and brutal killings by the Serbs

ATL Communication skills

Go to: www.youtube.com/watch?v=xYW_oui7LvI.

Watch footage from the German documentary *It Began with a Lie*, presented on YouTube in two parts, with German commentary and English subtitles.

Source skills

Source A

An 11-year-old girl who survived the massacre at Prekaz in February 1998 recalls what happened.

We heard gun shot noise, we heard the tanks. ... We went in the basement, covered ourselves with the blankets and laid down. [My uncle] and his wife were upstairs.

How long did the fight last?

Three days and three nights. ... The third day they shot at us and killed my uncle. He was in the other room. [My cousin] saw him and said "They killed our father," and started crying and he shot three times in the air. [Then the Serbs] threw a grenade in the room. [My cousin] got wounded and almost everyone else. [His sister] was trapped because something from the sofa was on her leg. My mother said we should help her but they threw another grenade in another room. All were killed almost. Me with my sister were alive, and [two of my cousins] ... I asked [my cousin] where [her brother was]. She said he went out. Two policemen came near the door and they threw another grenade in. They killed [her]. I was left alive with my other sister only. They called me. They were speaking Serbian, I didn't know what they were saying so I thought I'd run away. My sister was screaming. I realized they had taken her. They were looking if anyone was left alive and he noticed that I was breathing. They captured me and they took me out and I saw my sister dead outside. They put me in a truck. ... One policeman asked me where was [my uncle and my father]. I told him they were in Germany. One policeman was fooling around with me, he touched my hair. I took his hand away and said, "Don't touch me." They put me in a van and took me to the factory. They left me there and covered me with a sack. ... Then they took me with the other people and left me with them. Then they let us go ... Some friends of my sister took me with them. I stayed with them three days and then my uncle came and took me to K.

Source B

A 45-year-old female survivor of the January 1999 massacre at Račak recalls what happened.

At six in the morning we were asleep. We heard shootings. My daughter said we should take some things, but I said we should just run away. My brother came [and] called us to go to him; as we were going they shot him first in the leg. We lay down. ... One of my cousins wanted to help my brother but he was killed. Also my brother was killed at that time. ... We tried to run away. We knew that the [OSCE] observers were in Shtimje, and we tried to go there. I crawled to the house. I left the dead there. I tried to save the others of my family. But here they fired again and more civilians tried to run away. They fired with all the weapons they had ...

There were some other people killed and injured. The police came later and found us there, around 50 people, men, women and children. They took us men out. When I went out I saw the policemen putting their masks on. Some of them were local Serbs who worked in the police force. Three of them I knew very well and I recognized them. ... We were 22 men. They put us in line. They told to one of them, "You are in the KLA." They tied our hands, and told us to leave. We ran, and fell in a hole. They fired at us, and we didn't move so that they would think that we were dead. We were like that for some time. Afterwards I came to take the bodies of my brother and my nephew. ... I learned later that the others in that place were massacred very bad. They cut the head from one of them, took out a heart from the other. The world must know that Serbs left women without husbands, mothers without children. ... Yes, I think it is worth it. I am 45 years old, and all these years, no Albanian did anything to any Serb. But they did terrible things to us.

Source C

Another female survivor of the January 1999 massacre at Račak recalls what happened.

We were sleeping around six o'clock. My husband heard the noise and we ran. ... All our family ran for their lives. They started shooting at us. My husband was shot ... My husband was shot for the second time and died. My second son was shot also, my husband's brother as well. ... We ran then, when I came back I saw my son dead. ... We were afraid to stay in our houses so we just left the bodies there and we went in the bushes hiding. We were without water, without food. It was very cold. ... Serbs did terrible things to our people. I have lot of pain. I have five others [remaining in my family] but my pain for the two [I lost] is so big. The international community helped us but I don't know what is going to be in the future. One thing we know. We don't want to see any Serb here. Our heart is burned. They killed, massacred, raped our children. I can't imagine living with them anymore. ... They (the Serbs) drove us out of the mountains and beat us, separated the men and finally we arrived in Albania. They took money from us, they took women, they killed a child in the main street. ... I thank them [NATO] they did what they could. Thank God they came with the land forces, because from air they were doing nothing. ... I am still afraid. I don't know why NATO still takes care of Serbs. I am a woman but if I can I would do something to them. Personally I can't see a Serb living here.

Source D

An account from a Serbian soldier who served in a tank unit in Kosovo.

There was a village around B. Early in the morning, we were given an order to take the village in front of us ... that's how it was said ...we have to take this village ... we were told to take our places and wait for the support which was the police. ...They arrived, we had to take our positions and fire a few projectiles, after which the [police] would go into the village. This particular one was

Albanian civilians, there were no terrorists, and because there was no planning, there was this big incident where one of the men, because one of his friends was killed in the previous night, took around 30 women and children, put them against the wall, and shot them. ... When he heard the news that his first neighbour was killed in the bombing, he wasn't the same person any more, he went berserk. I was just passing when I saw a lot of civilians, mainly women and children. They were crouching. He was in front of them with a machine gun. From the noise of the motor I couldn't make out what he was saying to them, I just saw that he was shouting at them, he was probably saying that they were guilty for his neighbour's death. He lifted his gun and started firing at them. The women and children were just falling. When he finished his business, his crime, he turned around and went away. They were left there lying in the grass. I felt crazy, heavy. My colleague was trying to calm me down saying, "You didn't do this, you are not to blame for this, we had to come here, we were mobilised. You have your family at home. Think of them. You have to make it back." He managed to calm me down a little, but that picture will be in front of my eyes for the rest of my life.

First question, part a – 3 marks

In what ways does Source C suggest that it would be very hard for the two ethnic groups to live side by side again in the future?

Second question – 4 marks

With reference to their origin, purpose and content, assess the values and limitations of Source A and D for anyone wanting to understand the role of ethnicity in the war.

Third question – 6 marks

What evidence is there in Sources A–D that the police were involved in the process of ethnic cleansing?

Third question – 6 marks

What evidence is there in Sources A–D that individuals acted out of their own volition?

The end of the bombing campaign

In April, pressure began to grow among the allies for ground forces to be used in Kosovo. The biggest proponent was the British Prime Minister Tony Blair. Statements made by President Clinton in March regarding the use of US soldiers on the ground had been questioned by both the military hierarchy and other allied governments. Nevertheless, as we have seen, maintaining the integrity and unity of the coalition forces under NATO command had been achieved, and the bombing campaign had undoubtedly brought about severe strains on the Yugoslav government, destroying much of its ability to resist. On 24 May, NATO attacks destroyed Serbia's power grids in and around Belgrade, and news was leaked of the possible use of ground troops. That week, Clinton made the following comment to King Abdullah of Jordan:

I don't think that we or our allies should take any options off the table, and that has been my position from the very beginning.

— Bill Clinton, 1999

It can be argued that this had not been Clinton's position from the beginning. This comment represented a change of tone that opened the possibility that troops might be deployed; this, together with the success of the air strikes, almost certainly convinced Milošević that a new phase was coming. It was time to make some kind of peace.

At the same time, behind the scenes, diplomats were trying to find a resolution to the conflict without rewarding Milošević with a division of the spoils or seeing Kosovo still occupied by Serbian forces. The impetus for negotiation came, not surprisingly, from Serbia's old ally, Russia. The leader of the Russian Federation, Boris Yeltsin, had sanctioned Security Council resolutions, but would not have approved any military action through the UN. Both Russia and China opposed the use of force and, of course, both wielded veto power in the Security Council.

It was time for Russia once again to play its role as supporter of the Serbs. Yeltsin sent his representative Viktor Chernomyrdin, former Russian prime minister, to Belgrade for talks with Milošević. Chernomyrdin was to meet with Milošević on a total of five occasions. Below is an extract from an interview in which he describes his impression of meeting the Yugoslav president and outlines Russia's concerns at NATO actions.

I met Milosevic five times. Five times I flew out to Belgrade. But only last time, fifth time, I've been there with [Finnish President] Ahtisaari. I was always on my own before. Milosevic made great impression on me in the beginning of my first meeting, which was a bit unusual. He was calm and purposeful. He was confident in that he was right, he would win, NATO would lose and his nation was supporting him, which was true at that time. There was no opposition. Everybody was in harmony. We had long nonstop dialogue for 8 or 9 hours. I was convincing him: why he was not right, what could happen, what will happen and how will be all end up. The fact is when someone talks about those events or regulation of the process or stopping war; then, everybody emphasizes that it was Milosevic who gave up. It wasn't like that. ... Both sides settled by compromise: both Milosevic

and NATO. The compromise was from both sides. When I was convincing Milosevic, I convinced USA and the other countries' leaders the same time. So they came to decision and we could stop this war all together as a result.

Russia was acted towards in not polite way. First time since the Second World War, the Alliance invaded the independent country. Russia was against. China was against. If you remember, Security Council didn't approve. Two countries out of five were against. It happened first time in postwar history. We know it was a humiliation of my country. It was sacred to me to stand up for my country, first. Second, I knew that there were many people who wanted Russia to join this conflict. Who wanted? Well, first of all Milosevic. He tried very hard to join us [sic] this conflict, to defend Serbs.

— Viktor Chernomyrdin, 2000

ATL Communication and thinking skills

1   In the interview above, Chernomyrdin comments, "*Both sides settled by compromise: both Milosevic and NATO*". From your own knowledge, what do you think were the "compromises" each side had to make in order to come to an agreement for a ceasefire?

2   What do you think Chernomyrdin means by "*Russia was acted towards in not polite way*"? How far might those who sympathize with Russia's position agree and why?

3   What impression do you get from this extract of how diplomacy was able to bring about a ceasefire?

4   The value of a primary eyewitness in situations like this is extremely high, but it can also be problematic in trying to determine what actually happened. Why might this be so? Is there any bias evident in this extract? Although Chernomyrdin spoke some English, what might be lost in translation given the language he is being interviewed in is not his primary language? When addressing each of these issues, try to explain your reasoning.

▲ Finnish President Martti Ahtisaari, the EU's envoy (centre-right with glasses), and Russian envoy Viktor Chernomyrdin (on Ahtisaari's left) meet with Yugoslav President Milošević (centre-left) in Belgrade on 3 June 1999 to secure his acceptance of the international community's peace plan for Kosovo

Meanwhile, the EU asked Ahtisaari to support the Russian efforts for a negotiated settlement. Together, Ahtisaari and Chernomyrdin went to Belgrade to meet Milošević in May. A week later, Yeltsin invited Milošević to Moscow and informed the Serbian leader that Russia would support an international proposal for a 10-point programme calling for a ceasefire, international monitoring and a settlement of the Kosovo issue. Russia's own economy was hurting badly, and Yeltsin needed backing from the West. Supporting Milošević was looking like a poor option to the Russian leadership. On 10 June 1999, the ceasefire agreement was incorporated into UN Security Council Resolution 1244, bringing about a formal end to the war in Kosovo. The air strikes stopped. NATO had won the war.

In Belgrade, Milošević tried to put on a brave face. On 10 June, he spoke in a televised address to the nation following the suspension of the bombing and the beginning of the Serb withdrawal from Kosovo. It is worth examining elements of this speech to ascertain how political leaders can choose to interpret victory from defeat and to retain their own political position in the face of what had been, for Milošević, the fourth loss in a war since he came to power in 1989.

Work with a partner to examine the two sources below. Source A is a speech made to the Yugoslav people by President Milošević in Belgrade on 10 June 1999. Source B is a speech made on 11 June 1999 in Washington by President Clinton, who is flushed with victory as he addresses the American people.

With your partner, choose one of the speeches each and, as you read yours, note:

- how the president makes use of language and imagery
- how the president makes use of nationalism
- where there are appeals to emotion
- which segments of society are appealed to in particular
- how the president begins and ends his speech
- how "misdirection" is used to get a point across
- how the president is using the media.

Consider drawing a chart or a table with columns such as "Language and imagery", "Nationalism", "Appeals to emotion", and so on, to help you record all the relevant points. Take turns with your partner to present and explain the notes you have made about the speech you analysed.

Source skills

Source A

Serbian President Milošević addresses Yugoslavia. This speech was made on 10 June 1999 in Belgrade, Yugoslavia. The remarks were delivered in Serbian and translated by the Associated Press.

Dear citizens. Happy peace to us all!

At this moment, our thoughts go out to the heroes who have given their lives for the defense of the fatherland in the struggle for freedom and dignity of our nation. ... 462 Yugoslav army soldiers and 114 police were killed. We shall never be able to repay them. The entire nation participated in this war – from babies in hospitals to intensive care unit patients, to soldiers in air defense trenches and soldiers on the borders. The people are the heroes and should feel like heroes and behave as such: with dignity, nobility and responsibility. Throughout the rallies in this past year in our country, one motto was often heard: We will not give up Kosovo.

We never gave up Kosovo.

Today, the territorial integrity and sovereignty is guaranteed by the G-8 nations, the U.N. This guarantee is in the draft resolution. Open questions regarding the possible independence of Kosovo in the time before the aggression have been sealed with the Belgrade agreement.

[A] political process will take place. ... This political process can only involve the autonomy of Kosovo and nothing else.

We have shown that our army is invincible – I am sure the best army in the world. Because the people were the army and the army was the people.

We face the reconstruction of the country. We shall begin rebuilding our bridges immediately, our factories, our roads. ... We have defended the only multiethnic society left over as a remnant of the former Yugoslavia – this is another great achievement of our defence.

I wish all citizens of Yugoslavia much joy and success in reconstruction of our country!

Source B

US President Clinton addresses the USA: "We did the right thing". This speech, made on 11 June 1999, is President Clinton's address to the nation on the conflict in Kosovo.

My fellow Americans, tonight, for the first time in 79 days, the skies over Yugoslavia are silent. The Serb army and police are withdrawing from Kosovo. The 1 million men, women and children driven from their land are preparing to return home. The demands of an outraged and united international

community have been met. I can report to the American people that we have achieved a victory for a safer world, for our democratic values, and for a stronger America.

The result will be security and dignity for the people of Kosovo, achieved by an alliance that stood together in purpose and resolve, assisted by the diplomatic efforts of Russia. This victory brings a new hope that when a people are singled out for destruction because of their heritage and religious faith and we can do something about it, the world will not look the other way.

I want to speak with you for a few moments tonight about why we fought, what we achieved and what we have to do now to advance the peace. … We should remember that the violence we responded to in Kosovo was the culmination of a 10-year campaign by Slobodan Milosevic, the leader of Serbia, to exploit ethnic and religious difference in order to impose his will on the lands of the former Yugoslavia. That's what he tried to do in Croatia and Bosnia and now in Kosovo. The world saw the terrifying consequences. … For these atrocities, Mr. Milosevic and his top aides have been indicted by the International War Crimes Tribunal for war crimes and crimes against humanity.

For these things to happen, security must be established. To that end, some 50,000 troops from almost 30 countries will deploy to Kosovo. Our European allies will provide the vast majority of them. America will contribute about 7,000. We are grateful that during NATO's air campaign we did not lose a single serviceman in combat.

I want to say a few words to the Serbian people tonight. I know that you too have suffered in Mr. Milosevic's war. You should know that your leaders could have kept Kosovo as a part of your country without driving a single Kosovar family from its home, without killing a single adult or child, without inviting a single NATO bomb to fall on your country.

You endured 79 days of bombing, not to keep Kosovo a province of Serbia, but simply because Mr. Milosevic was determined to eliminate Kosovar Albanians from Kosovo, dead or alive. … Because of our resolve, the 20th century is ending, not with helpless indignation, but with a hopeful affirmation of human dignity and human rights for the 21st century. … So tonight I ask you to be proud of your country and very proud of the men and women who serve it in uniform. For in Kosovo we did the right thing. We did it the right way. And we will finish the job.

Good night and may God bless our wonderful United States of America.

The consequences of the conflict

The establishment of Kosovo Force (KFOR)

When the fighting had stopped, the peacekeepers could move in. Ironically, in the years to follow, considerably more soldiers died in that role than during the war itself. The mandate to maintain peace is often costly. A task force of peacekeepers, Kosovo Force (KFOR), was created through the UN Security Council Resolution 1244 of June 10th, and its principal objectives were to bring about the return of a safe and secure environment for the people of Kosovo. These would be achieved through:

- the immediate and verifiable end of violence and repression in Kosovo

- withdrawal from Kosovo of military, police and paramilitary forces

- establishment of an interim administration for Kosovo, to be decided by the UN Security Council

- the safe and free return of all refugees and displaced persons, and unimpeded access to Kosovo by humanitarian aid organizations

- a political process towards the establishment of an interim political framework agreement providing for a substantial self-government for Kosovo, taking full account of the Rambouillet Agreement and the Federal Republic of Yugoslavia (FRY)

- the demilitarization of the Kosovo Liberation Army (KLA)

- the stabilization and economic development of the crisis region.

KFOR was to operate under the auspices of the UN but to remain under NATO's military command. In total, 30 countries – the 19 members of NATO and 11 "partners for peace" – pledged 48,000 troops to serve as the peacekeeping force in the area. They were to be sent there under the name "Operation Joint Guardian" and would ensure the immediate withdrawal of Serbian forces within 11 days of the signing of the agreement. The largest contingent of forces came from the UK, which contributed 13,000 soldiers. Germany sent 8,000 troops; the USA and France each contributed 7,000; and the Italians sent 5,000. Those countries willing to send soldiers to join the peacekeepers and to make a political statement of support included Switzerland, Morocco, Finland and the Ukraine. KFOR's first commander was to be Lieutenant-General Michael Jackson from the UK.

▲ KFOR soldiers wave at returning Kosovo refugees

KFOR is a force designed to promote democratic values and human rights, not to destroy them.

— Jamie Shea, 1999

The task facing the soldiers of KFOR was not a combat operation but a role supporting the development of a stable and peaceful Kosovo, and to ensure that the terms of the agreement through Resolution 1244 were met. Thus, ensuring security and maintaining public order, facilitating the return of displaced persons, confiscating illegal weapons, providing medical assistance and expediting the return to a functioning political, social and economic life were all included in the mandate. Special attention had to be paid to the protection of minorities. On June 12 1999, the work began.

The five leading NATO members – the USA, the UK, France, Germany and Italy – were each given a zone or sector of Kosovo to administer, following a similar arrangement used in the Bosnian war. The British were to control the capital, Priština, and the airport. An incident happened right at the beginning of the KFOR mission that illustrated the fragility and complexities of such peacekeeping operations.

KOSOVO FORCE SECTORS (KFOR)
SERBIA
Kosovo Autonomous Province
May 2002
KFOR Sector Boundary

▲ The KFOR sectors

The incident at Priština, June 1999

There was a confrontation between the incoming troops of KFOR and Russian forces over control of Priština International Airport on 12 June 1999, just as the ceasefire had been agreed. The Russians were eager to secure a foothold in Kosovo, having helped to negotiate the ceasefire agreement and having been frustrated throughout the NATO campaign by their inability to influence events. Without prior warning, Russian military high command dispatched about 250 elite Russian soldiers to take control of the airfield. Upon hearing the news, General Wesley Clark, NATO Supreme Allied Commander Europe, asked NATO Secretary General Javier Solano if he had complete control over the mission and whether he was authorized to put soldiers on the ground. Receiving an affirmative answer, General Clark ordered the NATO troops closest to the airport to take control by force if necessary. These happened to be British soldiers under the command of Lieutenant-General Michael Jackson. Jackson wrote later in his autobiography:

> I've thought about this quite a bit since, and my view is that the Russians were making a point by sending a column into Kosovo. They had been worsted in the Cold War, and there was considerable upset, even indignation, on the Russian side about NATO's expansion and the fact that the alliance had undertaken military action against Serbia without a UN Security Council resolution. The intervention was a reminder that the Russians were still players on the world stage, that they still needed to be treated with respect.

— Michael Jackson, 2007

Clark's contentious decision to challenge the Russians when they were landing soldiers at the airport in Priština was a risky manoeuvre. At the time, Clark's order was to disarm the Russian soldiers, which would have been highly confrontational. The leaders on the ground refused to do this. Instead, Jackson met the commander of the Russian force, shared a whisky with him and sorted out the potential problems. Jackson refused to enforce Clark's orders, which were to block the runway and prevent more Russian soldiers landing. Jackson reportedly told Clark, "I'm not going to start the Third World War for you" (in an interview on news.bbc.co.uk/2/hi/europe/671495.stm).

▲ Lieutenant-General Michael Jackson (right) with NATO Supreme Allied Commander Europe Wesley Clark (centre) and Charles, Prince of Wales, in Kosovo

▲ American KFOR soldiers at a checkpoint near Vitina, Kosovo, in July 1999

Referring to General Clark, Jackson commented:

Wes Clark was something of a loner, a driven, intensely ambitious man with a piercing stare. Often described as "tightly wound", he seemed to bring a disturbing zeal to his work. He had a reputation as a very political sort of general, antagonising his military superiors by going over their heads when they did not give him what he wanted. He was not popular among many of his colleagues, who knew him as the "Perfumed Prince". Like Bill Clinton, he had adopted his stepfather's name, and, like Bill Clinton, he came from Little Rock, Arkansas. A Vietnam veteran, Wes Clark was a highly educated man – and, again like Bill Clinton, a former Rhodes scholar.

— Michael Jackson, 2007

Clark's order to block the runway probably also served to alienate some diplomats back in the USA and contributed to the decision to bring him home early from his NATO command. The episode illustrated not only the fragility of relations between the major powers, but the strength and determination of NATO to follow through with its mission.

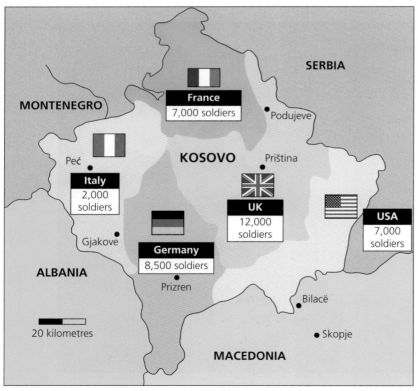

▲ KFOR deployments in 2000

At first, the KFOR soldiers who served in Kosovo faced all kinds of humanitarian problems in trying to establish a safe and secure environment. Technically, this meant treating everyone as fairly as possible: the Serbian soldiers in the province, the KLA guerrilla fighters, and civilians of all ethnic groups. In order to establish a safe and secure environment, we need to examine the social and economic consequences of the campaign, the damage to infrastructure in the region, as well as the refugee crisis. After the immense dislocations and deaths as a result of the Bosnian war and the break-up of the Yugoslav Federation, the allies had now committed themselves once more to administer another part of the former Yugoslav state, at great expense and for the unforeseeable future.

The bombing of the Chinese embassy in Belgrade

Source skills

Source A

A cartoon by Steve Fricker on the Chinese embassy bombing, published in the UK newspaper, *The Daily Telegraph*, on 10 May 1999.

▲ The man in the cartoon is President Milošević

Source B

An article entitled "Li Peng delivers speech in Belgrade", published in the Chinese newspaper, *The People's Daily*, on 13 June 2000.

Li Peng, chairman of the Standing Committee of the National People's Congress, said in Belgrade Monday that peace cannot be forged out of bombings. Referring to air strikes against Yugoslavia by a US-led NATO force last year, Li said the assault was a violation of the intent of the United Nations Charter and universally recognized norms governing international relations. The air strikes seriously threatened stability in Europe.

"Today, the gun smoke has dissipated. But, regrettably, the Kosovo issue is unresolved," Li told a joint session of the Federal Assembly of Yugoslavia. "Regional conflicts and disputes can only be resolved through peaceful consultations by parties concerned."

Li said the US missile attack on the Chinese Embassy in Belgrade 13 months ago that killed three Chinese journalists and rendered the embassy building unusable is "a case of grave international wrongdoing seldom seen in the history of diplomacy and a gross violation of China's sovereignty." "The attack outraged the Chinese people," said Li, who arrived in Belgrade on Sunday for a three-day official visit. The embassy bombing and the deaths of the Chinese journalists sparked anti-American protests in China.

Li expressed his gratitude for the help provided by Yugoslavia. China is in favour of multi-polarity because it is better than having the world dominated by one country. "Given the complexity of international affairs, it is harmful and also impossible for any one country or a handful of countries to dominate international affairs," Li asserted.

Source C

An article entitled "NATO missiles hit Chinese embassy" by Daniel Williams published in the US newspaper, *The Washington Post,* on 8 May 1999.

http://www.washingtonpost.com/wp-srv/inatl/longterm/china/stories/embassy050899.htm

BELGRADE, May 8 (Saturday) – NATO missiles plowed into the Chinese Embassy in Belgrade during a ferocious allied bombardment Friday that also struck the Interior Ministry and army headquarters and again plunged the capital city into darkness.

The official New China News Agency reported that two staff members were killed, two were missing and more than 20 injured. The strike on the embassy, which NATO acknowledged and said it regretted early today, seemed likely to complicate Western efforts to secure a diplomatic settlement to the Kosovo conflict and to raise new strains in U.S.-Chinese relations.

The government in Beijing, which has opposed the NATO bombing of Yugoslavia since it began 46 days ago, is a permanent member of the U.N. Security Council, which means it could veto the peace framework the United States, its leading allies and Russia agreed to Thursday and want the council to approve. China called the council members into session today to consider the embassy bombing but the United States said the airstrikes would not stop, Reuter's news agency reported.

Earlier Friday, NATO cluster bombs struck a residential neighborhood and hospital grounds in Nis, Yugoslavia's third-largest city, killing at least 14 civilians and wounding 30 others. NATO said later that it was "highly probable that a weapon went astray and hit civilian buildings" during an attack on a nearby airfield. Chinese television carried an extensive report on the bombing during its noon newscast. A somber announcer read an official statement condemning the "gross violation of China's sovereignty." The statement said, "the U.S.-led NATO attack used three missiles from different directions to attack China's embassy in Yugoslavia."

"We are greatly shocked by reports of NATO's bombing of the Chinese Embassy. We strongly condemn NATO's act and express our indignity," Qin said. "NATO should be held responsible for all consequences," he added, and repeated China's call for an immediate halt to the bombing.

At NATO headquarters in Brussels, alliance officials said that while each target was "meticulously planned" to minimize civilian loss of life, they acknowledged the strike on the embassy. "NATO regrets any damage to the embassy or injuries to Chinese diplomatic personnel," a statement said.

Pentagon spokesman Kenneth Bacon said NATO authorities were investigating the Chinese Embassy bombing but could provide no details. "It is a heavy night [of bombing] in Belgrade," Bacon said, with the attacks focusing on "power facilities and command and control targets." Friday's attacks on Belgrade broke a four-day period of relative calm in the capital and concluded a day of relentless allied bombing across the country. At about 9:25 p.m. (3:25 p.m. EDT), power went out all over Belgrade, the result of an apparent hit on the city's electric power grid. Anti-aircraft fire lit up the clear night sky.

Source D

Anti-USA protestors in Beijing in May 1999.

First question, part a – 3 marks

In what ways does Source D confirm the information given by Li Peng in Source B?

First question, part b – 2 marks

In Source A, why is the NATO bomb pointing to the pile of bodies in the top right corner of the cartoon?

First question, part b – 2 marks

What is the message of the cartoon in Source A?

Second question – 4 marks

With reference to their origin, purpose and content, assess the values and limitations of Source B and D for anyone wanting to study what happened as a result of the bombing of the Chinese embassy in Belgrade.

Fourth question – 9 marks

Using the sources and your own knowledge, assess the importance of the NATO strike against the Chinese embassy in the Kosovo campaign between March 1999 and June 1999.

2.7 The impact of the war: Social and economic consequences

▲ A US cartoon entitled "The dilemma"

Conceptual understanding

Key concepts

→ Change

→ Consequence

→ Significance

Key question

→ How did forces for change shape a new society in Kosovo?

A chronology of key events in Kosovo, 1999–2008

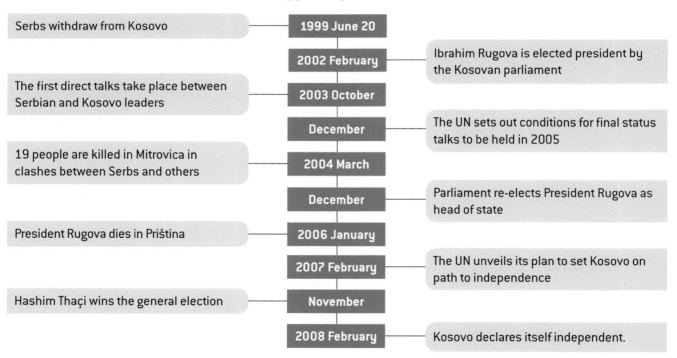

Serbs withdraw from Kosovo	**1999 June 20**
	2002 February — Ibrahim Rugova is elected president by the Kosovan parliament
The first direct talks take place between Serbian and Kosovo leaders	**2003 October**
	December — The UN sets out conditions for final status talks to be held in 2005
19 people are killed in Mitrovica in clashes between Serbs and others	**2004 March**
	December — Parliament re-elects President Rugova as head of state
President Rugova dies in Priština	**2006 January**
	2007 February — The UN unveils its plan to set Kosovo on path to independence
Hashim Thaçi wins the general election	**November**
	2008 February — Kosovo declares itself independent.

Kosovo is a small country but it also has a lot of riches that were granted to us by God.

— Ibrahim Rugova

In June, the peace agreement between NATO and Yugoslavia ended a period of conflict that had been going on for years. The impact had been felt by almost everyone within Kosovo and, following NATO's bombing campaign, by many of the people inside Yugoslavia too. It was time to rebuild. The scale of the damage to society was nothing like what had happened in Rwanda; nevertheless, it would take considerable investment of time, money and resources to try and rebuild the shattered economy and society of Kosovo. There were almost 1 million ethnic Albanians as well as another 500,000 displaced within the province. Given the choice, most Serbs left the region, and there were reprisals against those who remained. The KFOR mission had to address all of these problems.

Kosovo, already poor, had suffered from NATO bombing during the war and much of the infrastructure of the state, including houses, roads and bridges, had been bombed or damaged. Law and order had collapsed and, as the Serbs retreated, the KLA attempted to gain control. Under the terms of UN Security Council Resolution 1244, jurisdiction in Kosovo was handed to the UN, which then created the United Nations Interim Administration Mission in Kosovo (UNMIK). This was headed by a Special Representative of the Secretary-General (SRSG). The civil administration, police and justice were run directly by UNMIK, and economic reconstruction was under the jurisdiction of the EU. The arm of that mission in Kosovo was KFOR. Institutions were in place to help Kosovo get back on its feet.

It is always difficult to rebuild both an economy and a society after a period of civil strife, but these can really only come about with a stable political situation and an improvement in the quality of life for the people. The bedrock of a stable society is the ability of a government to offer the possibility of prosperity for people through employment and the opportunity to develop and make progress. The future of Kosovo and the region therefore hinged on its ability to advance economically and socially in the face of the challenges posed by nationalist sentiment.

Source skills

Look at the cartoon on the previous page and answer the following questions.

First question, part b – 2 marks
Explain the object on the ground and the labels on the road sign.

First question, part b – 2 marks
What is the message of the cartoon?

Evidence suggests that the major consequences for Kosovo in the years immediately after the NATO intervention were scarcity of economic opportunities, unemployment and lack of security. Recalling that Kosovo was the poorest province of the Yugoslav Federation, even prior to the break-up of the state, it is hardly a surprise that poverty continued to plague the development of Kosovo in the years after 1999. However, the tensions between Albanians and Serbs that had caused the war in the first place continued into the 21st century. Sporadic violence occurred between the two ethnic groups, for example in 2004, when anti-Serb riots broke out in numerous towns and cities in Kosovo. The unrest claimed 30 lives and caused the displacement of more than 4,000 Serbs and other minorities, a feature of what had been happening since the ceasefire in the summer of 1999. It is worth noting that, according to *The World Factbook*, in 2008 92% of Kosovo's population were Albanians, with the other 8% made up of several groups, including Serbs, Gorani, Bosniaks, Roma, Turks, Ashkali and Egyptians (see https://www.cia.gov/library/publications/the-world-factbook/geos/kv.html). As an example, by 2014, one of these groups, the Ashkali community, probably comprised fewer than 50,000 people.

The Ashkali traces to Persia (Iran). In Kosovo, the Ashkali speak mainly Albanian as their mother tongue, and most follow Islam.

Rebuilding Kosovo's society and economy

Kosovo's population had been predominantly Albanian for a long time and the region is one of great ethnic, cultural and religious diversity. However, Kosovo is also a region of great divisions, and we have seen how the Serb government attempted to expel the Albanians and tilt the demographic balance more in the favour of the Serb minority. Rebuilding a nation out of a civil society already economically poor and divided would prove even more of a challenge.

Put simply, the mission facing UNMIK and the international community in Kosovo was nothing short of a relaunching of the economy and a simultaneous rebuilding of the society. These tasks went hand in hand. Considering the poverty that existed in Kosovo and the fractures in society, the achievements of the international community are impressive.

Kosovo's economy

It is useful to look at the economic situation in Kosovo prior to the conflict and also in the decade that followed. As Rugova stated, Kosovo is a land with a number of natural resources, particularly mineral deposits. These include significant reserves of silver, zinc, nickel, chromium magnesite, bauxite, lead and, most importantly, lignite. Lignite is a fossil fuel, sometimes known as "brown coal". Most of it is burned to generate electricity and to generate natural gas, but it also yields fertilizers for use in agriculture.

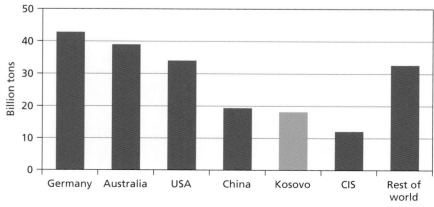

Lignite is the greatest natural resource that Kosovo possesses, and its deposits there are ranked fifth in the world in quantity. The Romans mined lignite in the Balkans 2,000 years ago, and the high quality of the lignite in Kosovo makes it invaluable to its economy, providing over 90% of the country's electricity from its deposits. The problem lies in extracting the deposits, which requires investment capital.

▲ Kosovo's lignite reserves compared to lignite reserves elsewhere

The mining of minerals and metals formed the backbone of the economy in the Yugoslav Federation, especially at the Trepča mines, where British investment in the previous century had helped to modernize the process of extraction. The whole economy needed modernization though, as much of the infrastructure was outdated. Kosovo's industrial drive required more direct investment and inclusion into the wider European market.

After the war, the economy of Kosovo was still based heavily upon agriculture, with over 80% of the output in this sector a product of subsistence farming. Products included wheat, potatoes, corn, dairy products

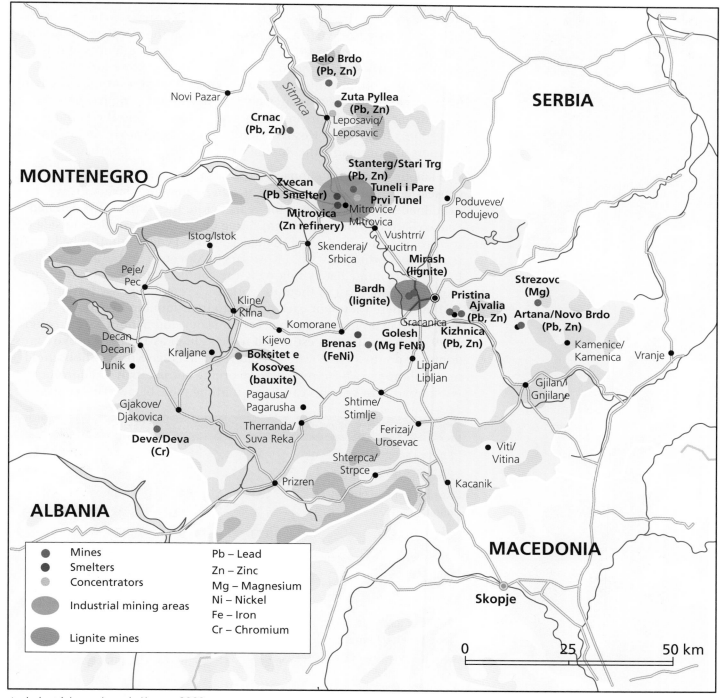

▲ Industrial complexes in Kosovo 2002

and fruit, contributing about 13% of the gross national product (GNP). The majority of these agricultural products were used by the Kosovars themselves and so generated very little income for the country's economy.

Overall, the economy of Kosovo in the post-war period became heavily dependent on foreign aid and the international community. Post-war reconstruction played a large part in helping the regrowth of the market, generating a temporary boom that disguised the deep-rooted problems within the Kosovo economy. Hundreds of thousands of houses were destroyed in the war and these needed to be rebuilt. Housing and basic infrastructure reconstruction was tackled in the three years after the war. Remembering that Kosovo was never a self-sustaining province, Yugoslavia benefited from the resources of Kosovo, but gave little in return. After the conflict, the consequences of this could be clearly seen. Kosovo's economy is geared more for demand than production, meaning that it uses most of what it produces, leaving little for export to make money abroad. Its main trading partners are its immediate neighbours in Europe; Italy, Albania and the Republic of Macedonia buy half of Kosovo's limited exports. Kosovo's main import partners are Germany, the Republic of Macedonia and Serbia.

The labour market also impacts Kosovo's economic situation. The consequences of the war, as well as other demographic factors, will be examined shortly. However, for years before the conflict, Kosovo had been reliant on remittances sent home by Kosovars working outside of the province. In the days of the old Yugoslav Federation, this had meant remittances principally from Kosovars in Slovenia, Serbia and Croatia. In the years immediately following the conflict, a number of Kosovars moved abroad, most of them to work in Germany and Switzerland, and from here they sent back money to their families in Kosovo. This diaspora had an impact on the economic development of Kosovo after 1999, with remittances estimated to be as high as 14% of Kosovo's gross domestic product (GDP). Remarkably, the average Kosovar household received more cash from relatives working abroad than it did from working in Kosovo. This can be seen in the table below. This shows

Source	2000	2001	2002	2003
Kosovo general budget – domestic revenues	43	167	337	413
Kosovo general budget – donor grants	161	84	39	25
UNMIK budget	413	449	388	368
Reconstruction assistance by NGOs	635	541	292	270
KFOR	5,000	4,000	3,000	2,000
Public enterprises (fixed capital formation)	10	10	10	10
TOTAL	6,262	5,251	4,066	3,086

▲ Public expenditure in euros (millions)

Kosovo Ministry of Finance and Economy, 2004, quoted in *Roukanis* (2007)

public expenditure four years after the end of the Kosovo war, and indicates some of the deep-rooted problems within Kosovo's economy.

When the war ended in 1999, Kosovo adopted the German mark, which replaced the Serbian dinar. However, within two years, it adopted the euro, which remains the official currency of the country (although the Serbian dinar is also still used illegally in Serb enclaves). Kosovo's tie to the euro has helped keep the country's inflation low. Although Kosovo's economy has shown some progress in the transition from a small, state-controlled system to a market-based system, it is still very reliant on the international community and on Kosovars living abroad. The bottom line is that Kosovo's citizens remain the poorest in Europe: they had a per capita GDP of US$7,600 in 2013.

Unemployment is very high in the country; for example, in 2013, it was estimated at 45%. Over one third of the population lives on less than 2 euros (about US$4) a day. This encourages people to emigrate and fuels a substantial black market economy. The website of the government of Kosovo indicates that 34.5% of the population live in poverty and a further 12% are classified as living in extreme poverty. With a population of less than 2 million (the 2012 census gave the country a population of 1.8 million), Kosovo remains one of the poorest countries in the world, ranked 132nd in a 2012 survey (see https://www.cia.gov/library/publications/the-world-factbook/geos/kv.html).

Finally, this can clearly be seen through the statistics for average incomes for private households in Kosovo, which reflect the poor economic situation for the majority of people. A report by the Kosovar Stability Initiative, a think tank, in 2008 stated that *"Kosovo is an island of poverty in Europe. Kosovo looks, feels like, and is, a poor part of Europe"* (Judah, 2008: 106).

Type of income	Type of residence		Kosovo	% of income
	Urban	Rural		
Cash wages and salaries, net of tax	201,23	175,13	192,68	60%
Pensions	13,51	23,56	19,82	6%
Social welfare benefits	6,50	5,16	5,38	2%
Wages in kind	2,35	13,68	9,85	3%
Rent, dividends, interests	5,64	0,00	2,50	1%
Cash remittances from Kosovo	9,26	5,12	6,44	2%
Cash remittances from abroad	34,43	58,83	48,91	15%
Other income	29,48	42,64	36,27	11%
TOTAL	302,40	324,12	321,85	100%

▲ Average monthly income of private households in euros, June 2002–May 2003

Household budget survey 2002–03, quoted in *Roukanis* (2007)

The social consequences and the refugee problem

The social impact of the conflict in Kosovo cannot be measured solely in the statistics of those who were killed. The number of deaths was, relative to what had taken place in Rwanda, small. Indeed, compared to those who had been killed in the other Yugoslav wars, the numbers were small too. Social consequences can be measured in ways other than by statistics. The dislocation of a society and the suffering seen through the media had a major impact on the decision to go to war in the first place in the context of the break-up of the Yugoslav Federation. Ethnic cleansing appeared once again on the doorstep of Europe and could not be tolerated.

The death toll in the Kosovo war is not accurately known and has become the focus of some debate. During the war, NATO officials suggested that as many as 100,000 people had been killed. The numbers were certainly nothing like as high as that. US Secretary of Defense William Cohen referred to 100,000 missing, possibly killed, as a justification for NATO's need to intervene. He was supported in this by NATO spokesman Jamie Shea, who described Milošević as *"the organiser of the greatest human catastrophe since 1945"* (quoted at http://archiv.medienhilfe.ch/News/Archiv/1999/KosoWar/r-s-f1.htm) and compared what was happening in Kosovo to the genocide carried out by Pol Pot and the Khmer Rouge in Cambodia (Kampuchea) in the 1970s. This was a huge exaggeration.

In 2001, the ICTY surveyed a number of mass graves and exhumed approximately 4,300 bodies of people killed by Yugoslav troops and paramilitaries in Kosovo. Human Rights Watch and other organizations, including the Red Cross, added another 3,500 casualties, including ethnic Serbs who were missing in the conflict. More recent estimates from 2008 raised the final figure to approximately 10,000 deaths in Kosovo between 1998 and 1999. Add to that an estimated 800,000 Kosovar Albanians who fled to neighbouring countries (most of whom have returned) and we have a figure of between 10,000 and 11,000 dead. You may want to consider the scale of suffering in the light of what you know about other conflicts, particularly in the 20th century. The raw numbers are certainly lower than those in several other wars, notably in the case study of Rwanda where the scale of death and suffering, as well as the social consequences, are staggering. However, does an assertion of the numbers of dead – be it 10,000, 800,000 or 6 million – really diminish the scale of the crimes committed?

We have seen that the generally accepted figure for the death toll in Kosovo is approximately 10,000 people. In Serbia, the government claimed that NATO was responsible for the deaths of around 500 people. The largest single incident was the death of 87 Albanian refugees killed on 14 May 1999 at Korisa, the victims not Serb soldiers,

▲ Kosovar refugees on the move

but innocent civilians caught up in the war and killed as a result of collateral damage. Considering the extent of bombing by NATO forces, the figures are remarkably low. However, the signing of the ceasefire agreement on 12 June 1999 did not bring an end to the killing, or the suffering, felt by many in Kosovo and the region. The Serb and Roma minority groups in the province felt the social consequences immediately. What was to happen in the months immediately following the conclusion of the NATO intervention was another bout of ethnic cleansing, albeit on a smaller scale, that transformed the society of the new state emerging from the Kosovo conflict.

Acts of revenge

In the aftermath of any war there are often acts of reprisal taken by the victors against the defeated and those caught up in the conflict. In Kosovo, the Serb minorities and the Roma were immediately targeted for revenge by many ethnic Albanians who regarded them as complicit in, if not actively supportive of, the ethnic cleansing that had gone on in the previous decade. The KLA was principally responsible for many of these reprisals in the weeks of the summer that followed the arrival of the small KFOR contingent. Burning and looting of homes and the destruction of a number of Orthodox churches and monasteries took place, as well as the displacement of Serb and Roma minorities. The social consequences were profound and led to a restructuring of Kosovo society. By the end of the first decade after the war, when Kosovo declared its independence in 2008, the society in the new country was significantly different from that which had existed in the early 1990s, when the conflict began.

During the war, the Serbs had driven the Kosovar Albanians (an estimated 90% of the Albanian population) from their homes and at least 1,200 cities, towns and villages had been damaged or destroyed. It is clear that, during the conflict, Serbian forces and paramilitaries had instigated a systematic campaign of ethnic cleansing in Kosovo. Then, in 1999, after the Serb defeat, came the removal from Kosovo of non-ethnic Albanians in order to justify the move towards the creation of an independent state. However, there is no clear indication that there was a coordinated policy on behalf of the KLA or Kosovo's political leadership. This means that there is a moral difference between what the Serbs were trying to do and what occurred afterwards. That is certainly not to excuse what did happen; there is rarely an excuse for violence, certainly where unarmed civilians are concerned. The social consequences have become apparent. According to surveys carried out by the UN High Commissioner for Refugees (UNHCR), more than 150,000 displaced people fled to Macedonia and Serbia after 12 June 1999. The majority were Serbs, but the number also includes 25,000 Roma. Other minority groups were displaced, too, including Gorani, Croats and Bosniaks (a South Slavic ethnic group, many of whom are Islamic and living in Bosnia and Herzegovina, as well as in the region). Albanians accused of collaborating with the Serbs also suffered. An estimated 1,000 Serbs and Roma disappeared after the Kosovo ceasefire, missing and unaccounted for.

Prior to the war, the Serbs and Serb institutions were predominant in Kosovo, even if the majority of the population were ethnic Albanians. After the war, society changed rapidly: the use of the Cyrillic alphabet, and nearly all the Serb media institutions, including television and newspapers,

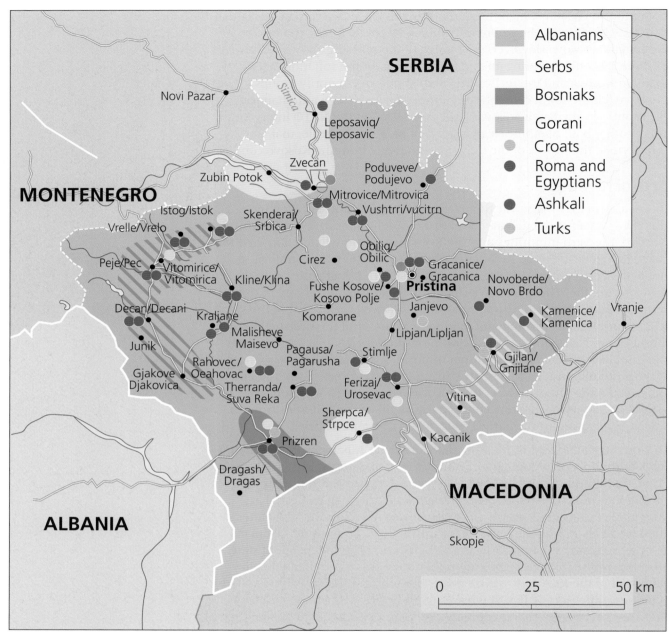

▲ Ethnic diversity in Kosovo, 2002

disappeared. As Serb rule ended in Kosovo, so too did Serb domination of society. The demographic consequences for the society of Kosovo are highly significant. The few remaining minorities are concentrated into enclaves inside Kosovo, which can be seen from the map above. There are still an estimated 130,000 Serbs living in Kosovo, representing almost two thirds of the pre-war population. Those who left were predominantly urban Serbs; the majority of those who remained were rural Serbs who make a living from farming. Many Serbs stayed in Kosovo simply because they had always lived there and there was nowhere else to go.

The majority of Serbs who left went because they did not want to live in an Albanian-dominated state any more than the Albanians had wanted to live under Serb rule. In this lies the fundamental problem facing Kosovo: that of social inclusion. Social inclusion means a more active form of citizenship and the refusal to accept any type of discrimination. Society in Kosovo is fragmented along social lines and it is this, combined with economic problems and poverty, this prevents the building of a stable and functioning society. The social consequences of the war were bitter lessons and the task of rebuilding a new state was daunting.

The state-organized campaign against ethnic Albanians and their institutions that took place in 1998-99 in Kosovo included targeting houses and places of worship. In the years following the NATO victory, acts of random violence peppered areas where Serbs, or reminders of Serb culture remained. There was more violence in 2003 and 2004, most of it directed toward the remaining minorities.

Large-scale violence broke out in March 2004 due to an incident in which three Albanian boys drowned, allegedly, being chased into the water by Serbs. The reports were false, but indicative of social instability. Widespread anti-Serb riots and attacks by Kosovar Albanians led to the death of 28 people and the destruction of over 500 houses. In 2004, UN personnel and vehicles were also targeted. The socio-economic problems are the most striking consequences of post-conflict Kosovo.

▲ The Church of St Basil of Ostrog at Ljubovo, November 2002

Source skills

Source A

A Serbian newspaper account from *Gracanica*, published on 17 November 2002, entitled "Albanian extremists attack two Serbian Orthodox churches in Kosovo".

Early this morning Albanian extremists attacked two Serbian Orthodox churches in the Pec area and caused great material damage. Attacks on two churches in a single night demonstrates once again that the intentions of the Albanian extremists remain to erase the last traces of the existence of the Serb people, their culture and history in this region. It represents a serious challenge to UNMIK and KFOR, especially after last week's statement by Michael Steiner in Berlin that security in Kosovo and Metohija has improved significantly and that the UNMIK mission has achieved a great success. The recent attack on Serb pensioners in Pec, frequent desecrations of cemeteries, and these most recent attacks on churches speak eloquently in the language of fact that not even minimal security exists for Serbs in this area and that security cannot be improved by propaganda but only by decisive action against extremists and their political mentors. It is tragic that so far not one perpetrator in the destruction and desecration of more than 100 Orthodox churches since the war in Kosovo and Metohija has been found nor brought to trial. No one has been held accountable even though these crimes were committed in the presence of more than 30,000 KFOR troops before the eyes of the entire world.

Furthermore, it is a disheartening fact that not one Serbian church destroyed since 1999 has yet been restored. This response clearly demonstrates the acceptance of the rule of terror and ethnic violence as accomplished facts which the international community apparently does not intend to change.

Source B

A newspaper account entitled "Two Serb Orthodox churches destroyed in Kosovo" published by the Western news agency, Associated Press, on 17 November 2002.

Sun Nov 17, 5:27 AM ET

"PRISTINA, Yugoslavia – Two Serb Orthodox churches were destroyed in western Kosovo in separate explosions, a U.N. spokesman said Sunday. The first church, in the village of Djurakovac, 50 kilometers (30 miles) west of Pristina, was damaged inside when targeted with explosives late Saturday, U.N. spokesman Andrea Angeli said. The second church, in the village of Ljubovo in the same area, was almost completely destroyed in an explosion early Sunday, he said. No one was injured in the explosions, Angeli said. An investigation was under way.

Kosovo has been run by the United Nations and NATO since 1999, when the alliance bombed Serb troops to stop former Yugoslav President Slobodan Milosevic's crackdown on ethnic Albanian separatists. Some 200,000 Serbs and other minorities since have left the province in fear of revenge attacks by majority ethnic Albanians avenging the crackdown by Serb forces, which killed thousands of ethnic Albanians. Although ethnically motivated incidents have since decreased, tensions between the rival ethnic groups remain high.

Source C

A political cartoon from a US source, published in 2000 and entitled "Serbian real estate weekly".

Second question – 4 marks

With reference to origin, purpose and content, assess the values and limitations of Source C for anyone looking at the aftermath of the conflict in Kosovo.

Third question – 6 marks

Compare and contrast the information in Source A with the cartoon in Source C. How might you account for the differences?

The political impact of the war in Kosovo

Ibrahim Rugova did not have a good war. His appearance on television with Serbian President Milošević in April 1999 tarnished his reputation badly. Just two weeks into the NATO bombing campaign, the de facto political leader of the Kosovar Albanians was seen, once again, bowing to the will of the powerful Serbs. Rugova claimed that he was taken to Belgrade against his will. On the drive from Priština to Belgrade, Rugova saw the exodus of ethnic Albanians from Kosovo and the destruction inflicted upon his country. He is reported to have said:

> I am a president without a people … what is the point of holding out as the last hero of Priština?

The situation in Kosovo at the end of NATO's bombing campaign had opened the door for the removal of Serb political control over Kosovo, but the new political framework to be established in the province was still undecided. UN Security Council Resolution 1244 stipulated that there would be no change in Kosovo's constitutional status. Ibrahim Rugova, the de facto head of state elected back in 1992, assumed with reason that he would take political power. However, Rugova and the Democratic League of Kosovo (LDK) had lost ground in the late 1990s to the more aggressive KLA. Rugova's strategy of passive resistance had been popular among many Albanians until the meeting at Dayton. However, it did not gain him supporters inside Kosovo when it became apparent that non-violence would not achieve independence for Kosovo.

During the bombing campaign, Rugova was summoned to Belgrade to appear with Milošević and both men condemned the bombing. Rugova remained under house arrest in Priština until, in May 1999, he was allowed to leave for Italy in temporary exile. He did not return until a month after the cease-fire, and was criticized by some for this delay. His arrival in Priština after the war ended was greeted by Kosovo's main newspaper with the headline: "The loser is back" (*The Economist*, 2000: http://www.economist.com/node/413320).

▲ Rugova and Milošević meet in Belgrade, April 1999

The divisions within Kosovo's new political scene were largely shaped by their experience under Serb rule. The emergence of the LDK and the KLA had an enormous impact on deciding the political future of Kosovo. Initially, though, it was to be run by UNMIK as a UN protectorate until a decision was made about its future status. Certainly the Serbs wouldn't let Kosovo go easily, and there was nothing in the ceasefire agreements to indicate that Kosovo would gain its independence. UNMIK worked on the basis that Kosovo would become a multi-ethnic state, but this was unlikely given what had happened before the war, and became even less likely after Milošević's campaign of ethnic cleansing during the bombing operation. Kosovo wanted independence; it was a matter of how and when it would get it.

The disbanding of the KLA

The international community continued to insist that a future Kosovo be multicultural. This meant that, after years of ill treatment, the Kosovo lambs had to lie down with the Serbian lions. The KLA, having taken a hard line since 1997, now found itself less popular; its extremist position was needed less in a period that focused on rebuilding. In the first weeks after the cease-fire, the KLA attempted to gain power locally and to fill the vacuum left by the Serb administration. Under the terms of Security Council Resolution 1244, political jurisdiction was passed to the UN which governed via UNMIK.

The UN body was faced with challenge of building a transitional administration and establishing self-governing institutions to attempt a return to normality for the population, an objective which was successfully achieved. Resolution 1244 had called for the disarming of the KLA and this was primarily achieved by absorbing most of its members into the Kosovo Protection Force (KPC), a civilian defence force which, effectively, became an army in waiting. As well as disestablishing the KLA, the interim administration of the UN set up a police force, the Kosovo Police Service, that attempted to maintain law and order. KFOR Commander General Jackson and Hashim Thaci, the young radical who commanded the KLA, signed the agreement for the transformation of the KLA. Thaçi was a 31-year-old former political science student and military man who had had represented the Kosovars at Rambouillet before the air campaign started and had also been elected as prime minister of the provisional government in Kosovo. The KLA now overshadowed other political parties in Kosovo. It emerged not only as the strongest military force, but it enjoyed widespread popularity and support among a significant number of the Kosovar Albanians. Kosovo was to experience its first political tug-of-war between the KLA and the LDK, with the international community sitting more easily with the moderate position of Rugova's party.

In January 2000, UNMIK set up a constitutional framework that would lead to general elections. The head of UNMIK, and a special representative of the UN Secretary-General, was a French former politician and a founder of Médecins Sans Frontières (Doctors without Borders), Bernard Kouchner. He played a very important role in the early years of Kosovo's new situation, holding his position until January 2001. In the summer of 1999 he announced optimistically, "*I intend to build a multi-ethnic Kosovo which will not ignore history*" (Cohen, 2000: 43).

It soon became clear that the expulsion and flight of a number of remaining Serbs meant that Kosovo was on its way to becoming a nearly ethnically homogeneous state, almost entirely Kosovar Albanian.

The elections of October 2000

The first ever local elections held for the newly constituted Kosovo state were due to take place in October 2000, and campaigning for these began in the New Year. The parts played by UNMIK and KFOR were vital in helping the transition, but neither was able to fully prevent the violence that took place during the political campaigning. Some observers felt that, with the rifts that already existed within Kosovo and the bitter divisions exacerbated by the decade preceding the NATO war, Kosovo could have fallen into a state of civil war at this time. It was significant that the UN bodies and Bernard Kouchner were able to prevent this happening.

The reformation of the KLA into a political party

In the early weeks of the post-war period, the KLA made considerable effort to assume control of a number of areas, collecting taxes and beginning to control sources of revenue from the illicit activities that emerged when law and order were absent. With the cease-fire agreement (including the disbandment of the KLA), many former KLA members transferred into the Kosovo Protection Force (TMK). Others, including Hashim Thaçi and some of the KLA hardliners who wanted more power (and felt they deserved it after their resistance to the Serbs), formed a new political party, the Democratic Party of Kosovo (PDK). Meanwhile the more moderate supporters of the KLA established the Party of Democratic Progress (PPDK) in July 1999.

The LDK under Ibrahim Rugova had dominated Albanian political life in the 1990s and the unofficial elections in 1992 had made Rugova the head of the Kosovo Albanians in the eyes of the world. The LDK perpetuated the myth of Rugova as the "father of the nation" and their spiritual leader. However, the KLA and its splinter political groups were credited with the victorious war of liberation against the Serbs, so there was no obvious winner in the October 2000 elections. The USA and other Western governments preferred the pacifism of Rugova over the radicalism of Thaçi. Nevertheless, Ibrahim Rugova's position was essentially as uncompromising as that of the hardliners in Thaçi's party, in that he was adamant that Kosovo's independence was necessary.

> We will not live under the UN guardianship forever. We make no secret that we wish for a separate and independent Kosovo.

— Hashim Thaçi, January 2000

Early in 2000, Thaçi made clear what he hoped to achieve:

> We are still a part of Yugoslavia during the three year transition period [stipulated in the Rambouillet Accords]. But afterwards, staying in Yugoslavia or Serbia after everything that has happened is incomprehensible for the Kosovars, and I think for the entire world as well.

— Cohen, 2000: 46

Hashim Thaçi (1968 to present)

Hashim Thaçi served as the prime minister of the Republic of Kosovo from 2008 until 2014. He was a former leader of the KLA (the paramilitary organization active during the Kosovo war in opposing the Serbs). Thaçi's nickname was "the Snake". His critics have accused him of being involved in organized crime, smuggling and prostitution within the province to finance KLA training and acquire weapons. He became known to the West through the talks at Rambouillet in 1999, and some diplomats, including US Secretary of State Madeleine Albright saw him as a "voice of reason".

Following Rugova's death in 2006, Thaçi's power in Kosovo was unchallenged and he was elected prime minister in 2008. The following month, in February, Kosovo declared its independence.

Both political leaders had the same vision. While Rugova's style of leadership was regarded as soft and liberal, the chain-smoking, scarf-wearing bohemian concealed a will of steel when it came to Kosovo's independence. When interviewed about a possible future tie with Serbia he commented, *"No, not with Serbia, never again with Serbia"* (Cohen, 2000: 47).

In October 2000 the people of Kosovo voted. Some, fearful of the violence of the political scene, saw the corruption and lack of law enforcement as a consequence of the militarism of the PDK. The local elections gave Rugova's LDK party almost 60% of the votes with Thaçi's PDK party polling less than 30%.

> *My vision is to have an independent Kosovo, democratic, with a politically tolerant society and with a solid economy, integrated into the EU, the NATO and to continue with our good relations with the USA.*

— Ibrahim Rugova

The election of Ibrahim Rugova as president

The problems facing Rugova and his LDK party were severe. Over the next two years, UNMIK and KFOR played a role in guiding the newly fledged province. Western leaders recognized that Rugova's popularity in Kosovo was indispensable to dealing with the future status of Kosovo.

Violence against members of political parties continued after the elections in October, although this was not always politically motivated. This violence revealed the deep-rooted problems facing the province. Economic issues as well as huge social difficulties were compounded by the lack of effective action taken by the UN and the peacekeeping forces. As in Rwanda, the problems were compounded by the absence of law enforcement and an effective judiciary.

ATL Communication and thinking skills

When Bernard Kouchner marked the end of his tenure as special representative of the UN early in 2001, Russian newspaper *Pravda* reported an interview with him in its English edition. Read this report and answer the questions that follow.

> Bernard Kouchner, the high-profile doctor, one of founders of Médecins Sans Frontières organisation, who was was the head of UN administration in Kosovo for 18 months, has admitted that the United Nations has failed to protect the province's Serbian minority. In a flamboyant ceremony to mark the end of his 18 months in the post, he warned the province's Kosovo-Albanians that, in the eyes of the international community, they had turned from victims to oppressors, BBC reports. *"My final message to you is*

very simple," the Frenchman told hundreds of people, overwhelmingly Kosovo-Albanians, at a sports hall in the Kosovo capital Pristina. *"Please, my dear friends, stop the killings. Please, my dear friends, stop the violence."* Dr Kouchner leaves his post of the head of UN administration in Kosovo on Saturday. Danish former Defence Minister Hans Haekkerup arrives to take over from him.

1 How accurate is the observation in the source that the UN *"failed to protect the province's Serbian minority"*?

2 Why do you think *Pravda* reported this section of his farewell speech?

3 Do you think this report shows any bias? Explain your reasoning.

In March 2002 the Kosovo Assembly appointed Ibrahim Rugova as president of Kosovo – the "comeback kid" had made it to the pinnacle of political power. As the new president, Rugova never shied from his stated aim, which was to achieve independence for his country. The question at this stage was how and when this goal would be realized. Rugova had begun his political career as a pacifist and he maintained that pacifism was the means to achieve independence. He was also astute enough to recognize that having strong relations with the USA was in the best interests of his country and the most effective way to achieve his aim.

His methods as a politician were always slightly unorthodox. As president he received visiting diplomats in his private home and gave gifts of crystals from his rock collection. Most of these came from the Trepča mines, and demonstrated the potential wealth of Kosovo. Some critics pointed this out as indicating his lack of touch with reality; but for his supporters it showed his essential humanity. The silk scarf and cigarettes may have been an anachronism but they distinguished Rugova for most Kosovar Albanians who remained loyal to him. He was widely regarded as a fervent nationalist who rose above party politics to lead his country to independence.

Unfortunately, Rugova was not to see that achievement himself. Rugova's critics in Kosovo continued to condemn him for being too passive when it came to pursuing the standards of democracy and protecting the minorities in Kosovo. He survived a botched assassination attempt by radicals in 2005 and in the same year had to receive medical treatment for illness. Kosovo's Albanians wanted the talks on Kosovo's future to get underway, and his support rallied when it was announced that he would be leading the Kosovar delegation at the forthcoming talks on Kosovo's status. In the end, Rugova did not quite live to see the fulfilment of his dream of independence for Kosovo. He died in January 2006 and is buried in a place of honour in Priština, the capital of his beloved Kosovo.

Parliamentary elections were held in 2007 when the PDK, under Hashim Thaçi, formed a coalition and took power. On 17 February 2008 Kosovo declared its independence. In the days that followed, a number of states recognized the status of Kosovo with the majority of the world following in the ensuing years. Kosovo's independence has never been recognized by Serbia or Russia, and Kosovo has been unable to apply for recognition as a member state of the UN.

▲ A cartoon depicting Rugova's victory over the KLA

The International Criminal Tribunal for the former Yugoslavia (ICTY)

Bringing war criminals to justice: Bringing justice to victims.

— Slogan on the website of the ICTY

The International Criminal Tribunal for the former Yugoslavia (ICTY) was set up in May 1993 at the beginning of the excesses of the Bosnian war and before the genocide in Rwanda. In February of that year, Resolution 808 called for the creation of "*an international tribunal … for the prosecution or persons responsible for the serious violations of international humanitarian law … in Yugoslavia since 1991"* (http:// daccess-dds-ny.un.org/doc/UNDOC/GEN/N93/098/21/IMG/N9309821. pdf?OpenElement).

Established under Resolution 827, the tribunal had jurisdiction over a series of crimes alleged to have occurred in Yugoslavia since the outbreak of hostilities. These included violations of the Geneva Convention, methods of waging war, crimes against humanity, and genocide. The tribunal was established for a set period with the aim of bringing all trials and appeals to a conclusion by the end of 2015. The establishment of the UN court of law represented the first tribunal since the Nuremburg and Tokyo trials, which tried German and Japanese war criminals. The court was established initially to try cases of humanitarian law in a time of war, but has since been modified to enable it to address cases in post-conflict situations, such as in Kosovo in 1999–2001. The ICTY is made up of three main branches: the chambers, containing the judges and support staff; the registry, responsible for administrative duties; and the office of the prosecutor to investigate crimes and present cases at trial.

▲ The International Criminal Tribunal for the former Yugoslavia (ICTY) in The Hague

The first reference in the tribunal to occurrences in Kosovo was in 1998, after the Serbian attack in Drenica. Within months, investigations began into war crimes in the province. The Yugoslav government refused to cooperate with the work of the tribunal, arguing that it was interfering with terrorist actions in Kosovo, an internal dispute which did not concern the international body. Later that year Serbian police prevented a Finnish forensics team from investigating a reported massacre at Gornje Obrinje. In January 1999, Chief Prosecutor Louise Arbour was refused entry into the country to investigate the Račak massacre (although a Finnish team was permitted to examine the bodies in March).

As soon as the NATO bombing campaign began in March, the ICTY set up an office in Albania to begin investigations into serious humanitarian law violations. In April the US State Department issued a statement declaring that any army commander issuing an order which allowed or encouraged a war crime would be individually responsible for charges, and there would be no statute of limitations on war crimes. On 27 May 1999 the tribunal announced that the president of Yugoslavia, Slobodan Milošević, was to be indicted for war crimes and crimes against humanity. He was the most significant individual to be charged to date, a serving head of state of a European nation. At the same time, four other leading Serbian officials were to be arraigned on charges that included "murder, persecution, and deportation in Kosovo" between January and May 1999. The four indictees were:

- Milan Milutinović, then president of Serbia

- Dragoljub Ojdanić, chief-of-staff of the Yugoslav army

- Nikola Sainović, deputy prime minister of the FRY

- Vlajko Stojiljković, minister of internal affairs of Serbia.

Significantly, these charges did not relate to crimes committed in other wars in Yugoslavia but specifically to crimes in the Kosovo conflict. The tribunal had already tried cases against those involved in crimes against humanity in the Croatian and Bosnian wars, and these involved military men of various ranks as well as members of the police forces. High-ranking diplomats included Milan Babić, head of the Republic of Krajina in Croatia, and a summons had also been issued to apprehend the two most notorious Bosnian Serb leaders: Radovan Karadžić, former president of the independent Serbian Republic of Bosnia (renamed Republika Srpska) and Ratko Mladić, the commander of the Bosnian-Serb army.

The chief prosecutor of the ICTY from 1999 to 2007 was Carla Del Ponte, who also served as the prosecutor for the tribunal established at Arusha to try those accused of involvement in the Rwandan genocide. She presented her findings to the UN Security Council in the summer of 1999, reporting on the tribunal's work. This included the exhumation of bodies at grave sites in Kosovo to establish an accurate figure of those killed as well as to identify who was implicated in crimes of war and humanity. A year later, in an address to the Security Council at The Hague on 24 November, she commented, *"it will never be possible to provide an accurate figure for the number of people killed, because of deliberate attempts to burn the bodies or to conceal them in other ways"* (http://www.icty.org/sid/7803).

In the same speech, she appealed to the Council to extend the tribunal's jurisdiction to allow it to investigate crimes committed after the conflict had ended. This was to address allegations of ethnic cleansing against Serb and Roma populations. She stated, *"We must ensure that the Tribunal's unique chance to bring justice to the populations of the former Yugoslavia does not pass into history as having been flawed and biased in favour of one ethnic group against another"* (http://www.icty.org/sid/7803).

The dispensing of justice in Kosovo

In Rwanda, the sheer number of trials was overwhelming; this was not the case in Kosovo. It was reasonable to assume that local courts could handle some of the crimes brought before them in the aftermath of the conflict. However, as was the situation in Rwanda, the lack of appropriate machinery and expertise meant that, in reality, much of the justice dispensed had to be through the UN and initially through UNMIK. The lack of expertise inside Kosovo led to criticism over its handling of one or two cases where local Serb Kosovars were found guilty on spurious evidence. The Serbian government argued, reasonably, that there were others besides the Serbs who should face charges. It had always held that the KLA was a terrorist group responsible for war crimes.

Carla Del Ponte (1947 to present)

Carla Del Ponte is a Swiss citizen and international prosecutor and diplomat. Within the UN system, she is a former chief prosecutor of two UN international criminal tribunals and is probably the most recognized person to serve in those offices. Del Ponte was born in Switzerland, and speaks Italian, German, French and English. Her work as a public prosecutor in Switzerland includes investigating and prosecuting cases of terrorism, weapons smuggling, money laundering, and transnational crimes.

In August 1999, Del Ponte was appointed prosecutor for the ICTY and the International Criminal Tribunal for Rwanda (ICTR). She remained prosecutor at the ICTR until 2003, when she stepped down in an effort to expedite the backlog of work that had built up there. Del Ponte replaced Louise Arbour as head of the ICTY in 1999, and remained in that position until 2008.

A total of 91 indictments were filed during Del Ponte's term, including those brought against Slobodan Milošević while he was an acting head of state. Her achievements include proving beyond reasonable doubt that genocide was committed at Srebrenica in Bosnia, and that rape constituted a crime against humanity. In a 2001 interview, Del Ponte emphasized: "*Justice for the victims and the survivors requires a comprehensive effort at international and national level.*" After retiring from the position on the ICTY, Del Ponte served as Swiss ambassador to Argentina from 2008 to February 2011. In 2008 she published a book called *The Hunt* in which she claimed that Kosovar Albanian had taken organs from Serb prisoners. The Kosovo government refuted these charges. Since 2012, Del Ponte has served as a commissioner of the Independent International Commission of Inquiry for Syria.

Individuals were brought before courts in Kosovo, including members of the KLA, some of whom were tried and convicted of war crimes. Once its mandate was extended, the ICTY also indicted some former KLA members in 2003 but found that, although some KLA members did commit atrocities, prosecutors were unable to prove that the KLA itself had a policy of targeting civilians or engaging in war crimes. Some of those tried included high-ranking KLA leaders, however most were acquitted. These included Fatmir Limaj, a KLA commander, who was to serve as Minister of Transportation and Telecommunications in Kosovo from 2008 until 2010, as well as Ramush Haradinaj, one of the KLA commanders who became Kosovo's prime minister in 2004, but stepped down the next year to stand trial.

Rape as a weapon of ethnic cleansing in Kosovo

As happened in Rwanda, rape and other forms of sexual violence were perpetrated against women in Kosovo. Human Rights Watch began investigating the use of rape and sexual violence by all sides in the conflict in 1998, and continued to document rape accounts throughout the refugee crisis in 1999. As in Rwanda, evidence clearly established that rape was used in Kosovo in 1999 as a weapon of war and an instrument of ethnic cleansing. As with the Hutu in Rwanda, the widespread use of rape was not a rare and isolated act committed by individuals but was used deliberately by Serbian and Yugoslavian forces as an instrument to terrorize the civilian population and force people to flee their homes.

ATL Thinking skills box

Carla del Ponte's address to the Security Council (an excerpt of which is given as the source below) covers many issues and concerns regarding justice. Read this source and answer the questions that follow.

The address to the Security Council given by Carla Del Ponte, prosecutor of the ICTY and ICTR, The Hague, 24 November 2000.

In completing my report on my activities, Mr. President, I must, of course, make reference to the recent developments in Belgrade, which have led to the removal of President Milosevic from office, the lifting of sanctions, and the return of the Federal Republic of Yugoslavia into the international community.

The world has embraced President Kostunica despite the fact that he has repeatedly said that co-operation with the ICTY "is not a priority" for him. If he chose that phrase himself, I admire him – it is a clever line, one capable of different interpretations – a true politician's phrase.

But it is not a solution either, and the Milosevic question cannot so easily be brushed aside. Milosevic must be brought to trial before the International Tribunal. There simply is no alternative. After all the effort the international community has invested in the Balkans to restore peace to the region, after the weeks of NATO bombing to prevent massive human rights abuses against the citizens of Kosovo, and given the enormous residual power and continuing influence of the hard liners in Belgrade, it would be inconceivable to allow Milosevic to walk away from the consequences of his actions. It is not enough to say that the loss of office is punishment enough, nor is it satisfactory to call him to account for election offences or some such national proceeding. We have already seen that there can be no "deals" with figures like Milosevic. It is to the great credit of the international community that the temptation to offer him an easy escape route was resisted. The consequences for international criminal justice would have been devastating, if that had happened. I urge the Security Council not to allow the same result to be achieved in slow motion by lingering inactivity. It is of crucial importance that double standards be avoided in dealing with the FRY, Croatia, and Bosnia and Herzegovina. Any softening in the position adopted by the international community towards Yugoslavia will encourage other states to discontinue their co-operation with ICTY. And we should not forget that other fugitives, such as Ratko Mladic, are in FRY. The authorities must also co-operate with the Tribunal in the arrest of these persons.

1   What do you think Del Ponte means when she quotes President Kostunica's statement that co-operation with the ICTY "*is not a priority*" and when she says, "*If he chose that phrase himself, I admire him – it is a clever line, one capable of different interpretations – a true politician's phrase.*" What is a politician's phrase? Can you give examples of any which have been used in recent elections in your country or elsewhere?

2   How effective a speech do you think the source is? Identify any three statements Del Ponte makes which you consider to be particularly noteworthy. Explain your reasons for thinking this to a partner or small group.

3   Find out what happened to Ratko Mladic.

The final years of Milošević

Milošević called for presidential elections to be held in Serbia in September 2000 in order to reaffirm his grip on power. It was a gamble that did not pay off. In the first round of elections he was challenged by opponents on the grounds of his failures in the wars and was defeated by opposition leader, Vojislav Koštunica, who gained over half the votes. The Serbian people had finally grown tired of Milošević's rhetoric, combined with the hardships faced in the last decade, the defeats and the break-up of the Yugoslav federation. Mass demonstrations in Belgrade ensued when Milošević tried to call for a second round of voting.

Milošević, having lost the support of his army leadership, accepted defeat and conceded victory to his opponent. After almost 13 tumultuous years in power, Milošević was replaced as head of the Yugoslav state. In October 2000, Koštunica became president of Yugoslavia, declaring that cooperation with the ICTY would not be one of his main priorities. Nevertheless, in the interests of his country, Koštunica would be forced to come to terms with the demands of many around the world to bring Milošević to account for the crimes committed during his tenure from 1987 to 2000.

The indictment of Milošević

It would be inconceivable to allow Milosevic to walk away from the consequences of his actions.

— Carla Del Ponte, chief prosecutor

Milošević was indicted by the ICTY in May 1999, during the NATO bombing campaign. This was deliberately done, not only to send a message to him and the Serbian people, but also to show the determination of the international community that a serving head of state would not be able to hide behind diplomatic immunity from the charges being brought against him. His election loss in 2000 made it easier, but he still had to be apprehended and face charges in an open court. In September 1999, Del Ponte announced that the tribunal's top priority was the investigation and prosecution of Milošević and the other leaders indicted in May. Thereafter, indictments against other individuals in positions of political and military authority could follow. Del Ponte urged the UN to pressure the new Yugoslav authorities, particularly President Koštunica, to cooperate in securing Milošević's arrest and extradition to The Hague to face charges. It would not be easy to do; Koštunica himself repeatedly labelled the international body as an anti-Serb institution and, despite the Serbian people's opposition towards Milošević (outlined above), he was still popular with a significant percentage of the Serbian population. He also received support from Russia and several other leaders.

The arrest of Milošević

In January 2001, Special Prosecutor Del Ponte visited Belgrade to meet with President Koštunica and members of the Yugoslav government. She returned reporting that she was disappointed with the lack of cooperation that she had received. Ultimately, it was to be money that opened the doors to cooperation. This came in the form of aid promised by the USA, who had allocated $50 million to the Yugoslav government. This package was contingent on the cooperation of the government with the tribunal, including the surrender and transfer of those named by the ICTY. The Bush administration had set a deadline to decide whether to allow this payment to go to the Yugoslavs. Desperate for money, the Serbian police arrested Milošević on 1 April. One day later, US aid was approved and, four days after that, the Federal Republic of Yugoslavia served an arrest warrant on behalf of the ICTY on Slobodan Milošević. This was organized by the prime minister of Serbia, Zoran Djindjić – a charismatic Serb leader who encouraged his country to reintegrate with Europe and was assassinated in 2003 by radical Serb nationalists who saw him as a traitor. Djindjić then helped to organize Milošević's transfer to The Hague in the summer of 2001.

Milošević was the first former head of state to stand trial for crimes against humanity. The "Butcher of the Balkans", the man many hold responsible for the bloody wars that destroyed Yugoslavia and brought war, misery and a decade of bloodshed and vengeance that resulted in the deaths of more than 200,000 people, was finally under arrest.

▲ Milošević at the ICTY in The Hague

In June 2001, Milošević was transferred into the custody of the ICTY in The Hague. On 2 July, he appeared in court for the first time, refusing defence counsel and denouncing the proceedings as a political trial. He dismissed the court as "victor's justice", refused to cooperate with the tribunal and declared that he would conduct his own defence.

The trial of Milošević

The trial was to be the longest war crimes trial ever held and ended inconclusively with his death in March 2006. He faced charges of violating the laws of war, breaching the Geneva Convention in both the Croatian and Bosnian wars, genocide in Bosnia and crimes against humanity. He was also charged with genocide and complicity in genocide, murder, persecutions on political, racial and religious grounds, of committing inhumane acts including forcible transfer (ethnic cleansing), unlawful deportation, torture, killing, the plunder of public or private property, attacks on civilians and the destruction of historic monuments. These charges related not only to what Milošević did in Kosovo but also to crimes committed in Croatia and Bosnia. He was deemed responsible for the murder of hundreds of non-Serbs in Croatia and Bosnia.

The trial began at The Hague on 12 February 2002. Milošević, a lawyer by training, defended himself. At the beginning, he refused to recognize the authority of the Tribunal because it had not been established with the consent of the United Nations General Assembly, but through the Security Council. On those grounds, he refused to appoint counsel for his defence and would conduct his own. He often spoke for hours, summoning witnesses including the former President Bill Clinton, who declined to attend. Already suffering from hypertension and a heart condition, Milošević attended court on only three days a week following advice of medical specialists.

Some of the proceedings were pure drama. Milošević retained a core of loyal supporters and, taking the stand, presented himself as a Serbian nationalist, adopting the role of martyr for the Serbian cause until the end of his life. The prosecution took over two years to cover the charges against Milošević. During that time he consistently attempted to delay proceedings, scolding the West and questioning the legitimacy of the court.

The death of Milošević

As his health deteriorated, his advisers asked permission for Milošević to go to Moscow for medical treatment. This was refused on the grounds that sufficiently good medical treatment was available in The Hague. At the beginning of 2006, his health took a turn for the worse and on the morning of 11 March 2006 he was found dead in his bed. The autopsy revealed that he had died from a heart attack.

Reactions to Milošević's death were mixed: some lamented that he had cheated justice and remained unpunished, while his supporters blamed the tribunal for bringing on his ill health and refusing him adequate treatment. As Milošević had died before the trial could be concluded, he was therefore not found guilty of the charges brought against him.

▶ A cartoon by Martin Rowson entitled "The Dutch anatomy lesson" published in *The Guardian* in 2006

However, the evidence presented to the tribunal and the world left little doubt of Milošević's moral guilt for the crimes.

Following his death, there was even some controversy about where he should be buried. Some did not want him in Serbia, and a burial site was offered in Moscow. In 2006 the Serbian government granted permission to his family and friends to bury him in Serbia and they held a private funeral service in his hometown of Požarevac. This followed a large ceremony in Belgrade attended by tens of thousands of his supporters.

The legacy of Milošević

Milošević's legacy left an indelible mark on the history of late 20th-century Europe. Vilified by his critics and deified by his supporters, a critic in the Belgrade weekly *Vreme* wrote, "*he turned Serbia into a colossal ruin*". Another summed up Milošević's legacy when testifying against him in The Hague in 2002, saying, "*You brought shame upon the Serbian people … You brought misfortune on the Croatian people, on the Muslim people*" and "*orchestrated*" the Balkan conflict (http://www.nytimes.com/2006/03/12/international/europe/12milosevic.html?_r=0&pagewanted=print).

Milošević was the most dangerous figure in post-Cold War Europe. In 1989, with the fall of the Berlin Wall and the beginning of communism's decline in Europe, the rise of Milošević took that corner of south-eastern Europe in a different and bloody direction. Misha Glenny, a British expert on the Balkans, said:

> At a time when there was real optimism in Europe, Milosevic almost single-handedly – with help from some Croats and some Serbs – managed to plunge Europe into a profound crisis. There will be few people mourning his death because he did great damage to Serbia, as he did to other Yugoslav republics.

http://www.nytimes.com/2006/03/12/international/europe/12milosevic.html?_r=0&pagewanted=print

However, there are those who worshipped the man and still value his legacy. How was he able to retain his hold over so many? In 1991, before the conflicts started, Warren Zimmerman, the late US ambassador in Belgrade, said *"Milošević is a Machiavellian character for whom truth has no inherent value of its own. It's there to be manipulated."* Milošević manipulated people into believing what he wanted them to believe. CIA psychiatrists who profiled the Serbian leader during the crises of the 1990s concluded that he had *"a malignant narcissistic personality … strongly self-centred, vain and full of self-love"* (http://www.theguardian.com/news/2006/mar/13/guardianobituaries.warcrimes).

For a long time, Milošević seemed to hold Serbia in the palm of his hand and the rest of Yugoslavia in his thrall. Kosovo had brought him to power and losing the war the war in Kosovo was one defeat too many. The legacy of his years in power fostered the mutual estrangement of Serbs, Croats, Bosnians and Albanians that will haunt the region for generations to come.

The achievements of the ICTY

The court has been criticized for being a politically motivated and very expensive body to run. Other criticisms point to its ineffectiveness but, as we have seen in the case of Rwanda, the price of administering justice not only involves soul-searching and compromise but can also be expensive and time-consuming. In South Africa, justice was served through a Truth and Reconciliation Commission (which had its own detractors). In Rwanda, the slow progress at the International Criminal Tribunal for Rwanda (ICTR) made way for the local Gacaca courts. Following Milošević's fall from power, Vojislav Koštunica created a Truth and Reconciliation Commission in Serbia. One of his reasons for doing this was to demonstrate that Serbs could administer their own justice to their own people. However, it was disbanded within two years as it dealt with only low-level crimes and would not handle the complicity of the Serbian government in any crimes. The international community was even less impressed with this commission than the ICTY and continued to use the international tribunal.

During its tenure, the ICTY dealt with 91 cases, 20 more than were managed in Rwanda. There will always be critics of a system established to try those accused of war crimes – especially when the system is set-up by the so-called "winners". Milošević claimed that the court had no legal authority because it had not been created on a broad international basis. Other critics have argued that the tribunal exacerbated tensions rather than promoting reconciliation. The alternative to not having an international tribunal is surely more problematic. Certainly, the majority of those sentenced were Serbs: fewer sentences were handed down to other ethnic groups accused of crimes, such as the Croats and Kosovar Albanians – but that surely represented the reality that Serb aggression was much more widespread.

Milošević, the media and political cartoons

Milošević was keenly aware of the value of propaganda, taking control of Belgrade television and the authoritative Belgrade newspaper Politika. As noted in Kosovo in 1987 and 1989, television was central to establishing his power. In the years that followed, Milošević recognized that the manipulation of television could be vitally important. Under his rule, the party machine, the army and the media were Milošević's main instruments for maintaining his power. In the early years he was seen everywhere, displaying a formidable talent for public oratory. He was not alone in this of course. Like other great despots of the 20th century, he established a cult of personality that struck fear into non-Serbs in Yugoslavia.

Leaders throughout history have used a cult of personality, but in the 20th century the development of mass media has enabled those with power to exercise a formidable and persuasive influence over millions of people. We have seen in Rwanda, how Hutu "hate" radio, the RTML and the magazine Kanguru were able, in a short time, to ruthlessly exploit latent feelings within the Rwandan people and further the political aims of the government. Milošević was not alone in using latent nationalism, and the hero-worship he received after his death, as well as his continued status among some Serb nationalists, bears testimony to the esteem in which he is held.

In his television addresses, he emphasized the negative impact of "the enemy" and the threat this group posed to the existence of Serbia. He played on the dangers of the Ottoman past and on Serbia's glorious handling of itself since 1389. In the 1990s he portrayed the Catholic Croats as fascists bent on destroying the Serb nation, as had been shown in the Second World War. He portrayed the Muslims of Bosnia as Islamic fundamentalists, and the Albanians of Kosovo as little more than rapists and terrorists. As for the Americans, they were imperialists: anxious to secure more influence in the Balkans. Much of this nationalist appeal stemmed from a Serbian persecution complex, but Milošević was able to harness it as a vehicle for his ambition through the use and control of the media.

In Western eyes, his media image was different. It is worth examining how the Western press often portrayed Milošević through political cartoons; look at the ones provided here to further your understanding of the political bias that can be used, and the power of image and symbolism.

Source A

A cartoon by Chris Riddell published in the UK newspaper *The Observer* on 28 March 1999.

Source B

A cartoon by Peter Brookes published in the UK newspaper
The Times on 21 April 1999.

Source C

A US cartoon of Milošević.

International reaction and the impact of the Kosovo war

The NATO campaign was hailed by many as a victory for democracy, the rule of law and for the rights of oppressed minorities. This type of selective thinking allowed Western leaders to bask in the success of their stance against the aggression which took place in Kosovo. For others, though, it was less clear-cut. NATO's war against Yugoslavia over Kosovo was a precedent of sorts in international law, breaking a new dawn for the principle that aggression should not be allowed against defenceless minorities. However, many of the wars in the 20th century were fought over similar issues; indeed, Hitler was able to justify his aggression against the Sudetenland of the former Czechoslovakia by claiming that ethnic Germans were being persecuted.

The NATO campaign against Yugoslavia was strongly opposed by both China and Russia, and, to a lesser extent, by India too. Their reaction to this war was based, in public at least, on the premise that the Western powers bypassed the UN in going to war. More cynical observers might note that China and Russia (and India) were alarmed because of the precedent it set, and that having a number of triggers for ethnic and regional conflicts within their own borders might be turned on them in the future. The Russians were dealing with the Chechens at the time, and the Chinese have long suppressed any Tibetan or Uighur calls for self-determination.

The war in Kosovo shows the importance of the principle of national sovereignty, which has largely governed nation-state relations for much of the last century. Sovereignty and self-determination were often cited as reasons for fighting wars in the first half of the 20th century. The intervention in Kosovo (and not in Rwanda) sent the signal that there might be new rules in the post-Cold War world. In facing situations of humanitarian disaster and instability provoked by internal conflict in places such as Rwanda, Bosnia and Kosovo, the USA and its allies found themselves having to redefine the limits and circumstances regarding intervention and their own interests. However, in the case of Kosovo, it seemed as though consensus among the major powers was impossible, and that the moral imperatives and their own national and humanitarian interests outweighed the question of sovereignty. Following the Kosovo conflict, UN Secretary-General Kofi Annan endorsed this position in a speech in Stockholm, Sweden.

> *There is an emerging international law that countries cannot hide behind sovereignty and abuse people without expecting the rest of the world to do something about it.*

— Kofi Annan

Reflections

In the final analysis you should reflect upon the case studies of Rwanda and Kosovo and contemplate some of the similarities and differences between them – the conflicts and the interventions. For example, consider the following:

- Both conflicts were caused by ethnicity merged with nationalism; in Rwanda, an ethnic minority won, largely on its own and, importantly, on the battlefield.

- In Kosovo, the causes were similar and the minority won this contest too; but they were grateful victors as opposed to conquerors. They had not won the war themselves but depended on the international community for their victory.

- In Rwanda, the UN was slow to intervene; none of the major powers had enough at stake or wanted to risk their own troops until late in the conflict.

- In Kosovo, dissension among the major powers meant that the UN was unable to act effectively until after the conflict had been won – and by another international agency: NATO. Intervention in this case had been crucial, though; it is conceivable that, left alone, the Tutsi would have triumphed in Rwanda; it is inconceivable that the Kosovars would have done the same.

- The aftermath of the Rwandan genocide contributed towards instability in central Africa for a decade after the conflict in 1994; in Kosovo and the Balkans, the region has benefited from being at peace.

- The UN was a central character in the diplomatic situation in both case studies, playing a more passive role until the conflicts had largely been resolved; the UN and the international community undoubtedly learned from the lessons of Rwanda; but it did not prevent other similar genocides taking place; the situation in Darfur, for example, has been largely ignored in the 21st century.

- Finally, the impact of Kosovo demonstrated that there is no cheap and easy way to prevent genocide.

There are questions of morality which you could address as you draw conclusions on these two case studies from different regions of the world. Some of these may have been addressed in the case study of Rwanda; some questions remain the same.

ATL Thinking, social and communication skills

Debate on conflict and intervention

Part of the argument about the morality of intervention has to do with international law but also, essentially, what one thinks is the right thing to do. Consider some of the debates elicited by the arguments below. They can be used as starting points for a debate on conflict and intervention in either or both case studies.

Work in a pair or small group to discuss the statements below and to answer the questions.

1 NATO Secretary General Javier Solana asked the question: Are human rights and the rights of minorities more important than sovereignty? What do you think?

2 *"There are occasions when if force is not used, there is no future for international law"* (Robert Skidelsky). Do you agree?

3 *"Armed intervention can only be justified in two instances: first, when human rights abuses rise to the level of a systematic attempt to expel or exterminate large numbers of people who have no means of defending themselves; second, where these abuses threaten the peace and security of neighbouring states"* (Michael Ignatieff). Do you agree?

4 *"Force can't be justified simply to punish, avenge or signify moral outrage. It must be a credible way to stop abuses and restore peace"* (Michael Ignatieff). What do you think?

5 The slogan of the ICTY has been "Bringing war criminals to justice: Bringing justice to victims". Of the two parts to this slogan, which do you consider is the most important? Which do you consider may be the most difficult? Explain your reasoning.

6 Is there any such thing as a "just war"?

References

Cohen JL. 2000. "Living an Illusion: Political transition in Kosovo". *Canadian Military Journal*. Spring issue. http://www.journal.forces.gc.ca/vol/no1/doc/41-48-eng.pdf

Davis, P. 2013. *Corporations, Global Governance and Post Conflict Reconstruction*. London, UK. Routledge.

The Economist. 2000. "Ibrahim Rugova, Kosovos's awkward survivor." 2 November 2000. http://www.economist.com/node/413320

The Economist. 2006. "Ibrahim Rugova". 26 January 2006. http://www.economist.com/node/5436910

Elsie, R. 2011. *Historical Dictionary of Kosovo*. 2nd edition. (*Historical Dictionaries of Europe No. 79*). Plymouth, UK. The Scarecrow Press.

Glenny, M. 1999. *The Balkans*. Harmondsworth, UK. Penguin.

Hall, RC. 2000. *The Balkan War 1912–1913*. page 132. London, UK. Routledge.

Human Rights Watch, 2001. Report: "Under orders", executive summary, page 5. http://www.hrw.org/reports/2001/10/26/under-orders-war-crimes-kosovo

Jackson, M. 2007. *Soldier: The Autobiography*. London, UK. Transworld. Extract reproduced from: http://www.telegraph.co.uk/news/worldnews/1562161/Gen-Sir-Mike-Jackson-My-clash-with-Nato-chief.html

Judah, T. 2008. *Kosovo: What Everyone Needs to Know*. Oxford, UK. Oxford University Press.

Malcolm, N. 1998. *Kosovo: A Short History*, page 324. London, UK. Macmillan.

Nation, C. 2003. War in the Balkans 1991–2002. Carlisle, PA, USA. Strategic Studies Institute.

Roukanis, S. 2007. "Development in post-conflict Kosovo". *Southeastern Europe Journal of Economics*. http://www.asecu.gr/Seeje/issue09/sklias.pdf

Silber, L and Little, A. 1995. *Yugoslavia: The Death of a Nation*. Harmondsworth, UK. Penguin.

The World Factbook: https://www.cia.gov/library/publications/the-world-factbook/geos/kv.html

Writing the internal assessment for IB History

"Doing history": Thinking like a historian

The **internal assessment (IA)** is an engaging, inquiry-based **2200 word investigation** that provides teachers and students with the opportunity to personalize their learning. You will select, research and write on a historical topic of individual interest or curiosity.

The IA is an essential component of the IB History course. Students in both standard level (25%) and higher level (20%) will complete the same task as part of their course mark. Your teacher will evaluate your final draft, but only a small, random sample of your class' IAs will be submitted to the IB for moderation.

The purpose of the historical investigation is to engage students in the process of thinking like historians and "doing history" by creating their own questions, gathering and examining evidence, analyzing perspectives, and demonstrating rich historical knowledge in the conclusions they draw. Given its importance, your teacher should provide considerable time, guidance, practice of skills and feedback throughout the process of planning, drafting, revising and submitting a final

copy of the IA. In total, completing the IA should take **approximately 20 hours**. This chapter is designed to give both students and teachers some guidance for approaching these tasks.

What does the IA look like?

The IA is **divided into three main sections**. Each of these sections will be explained and approached in more detail later in this chapter. Below is an overview of each section:

1. Identification and evaluation of sources (6 marks)

- Clearly state the topic in the form of an appropriate inquiry question.

- Explain the nature and relevance of two of the sources selected for more detailed analysis of values and limitations with reference to origins, purpose and content.

2. Investigation (15 marks)

- Using appropriate format and clear organization, provide critical analysis that is focused on the question under investigation.

- Include a range of evidence to support an argument and analysis, and a conclusion drawn from the analysis.

3. Reflection (4 marks)

- Reflect on the process of investigating your question and discuss the methods used by historians, and the limitations or challenges of investigating their topic.

Your history teachers can use the IA for whatever purposes best suit the school context, syllabus design or the individual learning of students. Nevertheless, you should be encouraged to select and develop your own question. The IA can be started at any point during the course, however the task is most effectively introduced after students have been exposed to some purposeful teaching and practice in historical methods, analysis and writing skills.

The IA is designed to assess each of the following History objectives:

Assessment objective 1: Knowledge and understanding

- Demonstrate understanding of historical sources.

Assessment objective 2: Application and analysis

- Analyse and interpret a variety of sources.

Assessment objective 3: Synthesis and evaluation

- Evaluate sources as historical evidence, recognizing their value and limitations.

- Synthesize information from a selection of relevant sources.

Assessment objective 4: Use and application of appropriate skills

- Reflect on the methods used by, and challenges facing, the historian.

- Formulate an appropriate, focused question to guide a historical inquiry.

- Demonstrate evidence of research skills, organization, referencing and selection of appropriate sources.

Beginning with the end in mind: what does success look like?

ATL Self-management skills

Throughout the process of planning, researching, drafting and revising your investigation, you should be continually checking the criteria. Ask your teacher and other students to provide specific feedback using the criteria. Continually ask yourself if your work meets the criteria.

Before getting started, you should look carefully at the assessment criteria to appreciate what each section of the IA demands. Teachers will **use the same criteria for both SL and HL**. It is important to have a clear understanding of what success will look like before you invest the time and hard work that this task will require. Teachers will use the criterion found in the IB History Guide to provide feedback to teachers and to assess the final draft. The assessment is based on "positive achievement", meaning that teachers will try to find the best fit according to the descriptors in each criterion. Students do not have to write a perfect paper to achieve the highest descriptors, and teachers should not think in terms of pass/fail based on whether scores are above or below 50% of the 25 marks in total.

To simplify the criterion and to provide some fixed targets for what success looks like, consider using the assessment tool provided on the next page.

Teacher, Peer and Self-Assessment Tool

Criterion A: Identification and evaluation of sources (6 marks)

Suggested word count: 500

Criteria for success	Strengths	Improvements needed
• Does the investigation have an **appropriate question clearly stated?**		
• Has the student selected, identified, and referenced (using a consistent format) **appropriate and relevant sources?**		
• Is there a **clear explanation of the relevance** of the sources to the investigation?		
• Is there detailed analysis and evaluation **of two sources** with explicit discussion of the **value and limitations**, with reference to their **origins, purpose and content?**		

Criterion B: Investigation (15 marks)

Suggested word count: 1,300

Criteria for success	Strengths	Improvements needed
• Is the investigation **clear, coherent and effectively organized?**		
• Does the investigation contain **well-developed critical analysis clearly focused on the stated question?**		
• Is there evidence from a **range of sources** used effectively to **support an argument?**		
• Is there **evaluation of different perspectives** (arguments, claims, experiences etc.) on the topic and/or question?		
• Does the investigation provide a **reasoned conclusion** that is **consistent with the evidence and arguments provided?**		

Criterion C: Reflection (4 marks)

Suggested word count: 400

Criteria for success	Strengths	Improvements needed
• Does the student **focus clearly** on what the investigation revealed about the **methods used by historians?**		
• Does the reflection demonstrate clear **awareness of the challenges** facing historians and/or the **limitations of the methods** used by historians?		
• Is there an **explicit connection** between the reflection and the rest of the investigation (question, sources used, evaluation and analysis)?		

Bibliography & formatting (no marks applicable)

Suggested word count: Not included in total

Criteria for success	Strengths	Improvements needed
• Is the **word count clearly stated** on the cover? *(2200 maximum)*		
• Is a single bibliographic style or format **consistently used**?		
• Is the bibliography **clearly organized** and **include all the sources** you have referenced or used as evidence in the investigation?		

Getting started: Approaches to learning history

To start generating ideas for a topic and to help you focus your question, use a research-based thinking routine such as **Think-Puzzle-Explore** (see Ritchhart, Church and Morrison, 2011. *Make Thinking Visible*, Jossey-Bass).

Think: What topics do you **think** might interest you?

Puzzle: What **puzzles** you about these topics?

Explore: How can you **explore** more about each of these topics?

Ideally, you will have opportunities throughout the IB History course to explore and develop understandings about the methods and the nature of history. This will prepare you to better develop the skills necessary for the IA and the other assessment papers in the IB History course. Additionally, these kinds of learning activities provide clear links to TOK.

- Debate controversial historical events and claims.
- Compare and corroborate conflicting sources of evidence.
- Take on, role play or defend different perspectives or experiences of an event.
- Discuss the value and limitations of historian's arguments and evidence.
- Develop criteria for selecting and comparing historical sources.
- Gather and analyze a variety of different kinds of sources (photos, artwork, journal entries, maps, etc.) focused on the same event or issue.

- Co-develop good questions and carry out an investigation of a historical event as a entire class.
- Read an excerpt from a historian's work and identify which parts are analysis, evidence and narrative.

If students better understand that history is more than simply memorizing and reporting on facts, dates and chronological narratives, then they are more likely to be curious, engaged and motivated learners of history. Accordingly, they will more likely develop appropriate questions for their investigation and have a better understanding of how to organize and write effective analysis.

Selecting a topic and appropriate questions

ATL Self-management skills

Before beginning, ask your teacher to find some examples of student IAs with examiner's feedback. These can be found on the **IB Online Curriculum Centre** or in the **Teachers' Support Materials** for History. Examine the formatting and layout of each component to visualize in advance what your IA might look like, and the steps that will be required to complete them.

Once you have some general understanding of the IA components and are familiar with the assessment criteria, it is time to select a topic focus. Students often do not know how to begin selecting a topic. Identify a historical topic of interest and get to know it well by conducting some background reading from a general history textbook or an online encyclopaedia. You may find some information that will help you narrow the topic focus quickly. These kinds of sources often outline the differing perspectives, interpretations and controversies

that make for an engaging investigation. Well-written textbooks and articles will also include references, annotated bibliographies and footnotes of additional, more detailed sources that will help in the research stage.

After selecting a topic, formulating an appropriate research question can also be very challenging. It is essential that you take the time to carefully think about what kinds of topics help produce good questions for investigations. Before you begin any writing, **you should submit a proposal** to your teacher to ensure that the investigation will be successful.

Some teachers recommend that students write about a topic related to their course syllabus, but there are a countless number of possible topics and you are better off choosing topics that interest you and motivate you to learn. The topic must be historical however, so students **may not investigate any topic that happened within the last ten years.** All investigations will take one of three forms:

1 **An investigation of a historical theme, issue, person or event based on a variety of sources.**

2 **An investigation based on fieldwork of a historical building, place or site.**

3 **An investigation of a local history.**

When selecting a historical topic, students often fail to select a topic that is manageable. For example, examining all of the causes of the Second World War is too broad for the purposes of a 2200 word investigation. Many students also select topics that cannot be researched in depth because there are not enough readily available primary and/or secondary sources.

Investigating a historically-themed film or piece of literature can be very engaging; but many students write better papers when they focus the investigation on a particular claim, portrayal or perspective contained in the work, rather than the entire work itself. Students who choose to investigate a historical site, or to investigate local or community history, often have an opportunity to engage in experiences that are more authentic to the work of professional historians, but these can also produce a lot of challenges when looking

for sources. Whatever the topic that you select, it is essential to formulate a good question.

One of the most common errors students make when planning and writing the IA is formulating a poor question about their topic. Formulating a good question is essential for success and helps ensure that the IA is a manageable and researchable investigation. Consider the following criteria when formulating a good question:

1 The question is researchable.	• There is an adequate variety and availability of sources related to your topic. • The sources are readable, available and in a language that is accessible.
2 The question is focused.	• Questions that are vague or too broad make it difficult to write a focused investigation limited to 2200 words. • Questions that are too broad make it difficult to manage the number of sources needed to adequately address the topic.
3 The question is engaging	• Interesting, controversial or challenging historical problems make better questions. • Questions with obvious answers (i.e. Did economic factors play a role in Hitler's rise to power?) do not make good investigations.

Using the concepts to formulate good questions

The IB History course is focused on **six key concepts: change, continuity, causation, consequence, significance and perspectives**. Each of these concepts shape historians' thinking about the kinds of questions they ask and investigate. Therefore, they are helpful to students as a framework for formulating good IA questions. Using the historical thinking concepts, you may be able to generate several good questions about any historical topic that can be eventually focused into successful investigations.

Concepts	Possible investigation prompts

change
- What changes resulted from this topic?
- To what extent did this event, person or issue cause change?

continuity
- To what extent did the topic remain the same?
- Did this event, person or issue cause progress or decline?

causation
- What were the long term, short term and immediate causes?
- What were the factors that caused the event related to the topic?

Student's topic

consequence
- How has this topic had immediate and long-lasting effects?
- How significant were the effects of this topic?

significance
- To what extent is this topic significant? Is the significance of this topic justified?
- What events, people or issues are important to know about this topic?

perspectives
- What different perspectives or interpretations are there about this topic?
- How did people experience this topic?

To illustrate, a student interested in the Russian Revolution might use the concepts to brainstorm the following possible investigations:

Change: *In what ways did the Russian Revolution change Russian society?*

Continuity: *To what extent did Stalin's regime resemble the Tsarist system?*

Causation: *How significant were long term factors in causing the February Revolution?*

Consequence: *To what extent did Stalin's purges affect military preparedness?*

Significance: *How important was Lenin's role in the October Revolution?*

Perspectives: *To what extent did Doctor Zhivago capture the experience of upper class Russians during the Revolution?*

After generating some possible questions, students can bring greater focus to their topic. For example, a student interested in how women experienced Stalinism may narrow the focus to a particular place or event. A student investigating long-term causes of an event may have more success if the question is focused on the significance of a specific, singular cause. For good examples of historical questions, you should consult past Paper 2 or Paper 3 examination questions.

You should notice that many of the questions above include more than one concept. Most good historical investigations will require students to think about perspectives because there will likely be multiple accounts of the issue under investigation, or there will be some controversy between historians. Here are some question exemplars showing how they capture more than one key historical concepts:

- *How significant was Allied area bombing in reducing German industrial capacity during the Second World War? (significance; consequence)*

- *To what extent did Gandhi's leadership achieve Indian independence? (significance; perspectives; causation)*

All successful IAs begin with a well-developed, thoughtful and focused question that is based on one or more of the historical concepts.

Internal Assessment skills

Categorize the following questions (Good – Needs Improvement – Poor) according to their suitability as a historical investigation according to the criteria provided above. Suggest ways the questions might be improved.

1   Which Second World War film is the most accurate?

2   To what extent did ethnicity play a role in bringing about the Rwandan genocide?

3   How did women win the right to vote in the United States?

4   Did Hitler use film for propaganda?

5   Why did Ibrahim Rugova's policy of passive resistance fail in Kosovo?

6   What were the most important reasons for the launching of Operation Amaryllis by France in July 1994?

Common problems when selecting a topic and question:

- Poorly focused question – too broad and unmanageable.
- Obvious question.
- Question is not researchable.

2 Researching	• Gather information sources and evidence. • Carefully read and evaluate information.
3 Organizing and processing	• Create notes. • Record references using a standard citation format. • Create a bibliography. • Organize ideas into an outline. • Formulate an argument.
4 Drafting	• Write each section of the IA. • Revise and edit. • Check assessment criteria.
5 Sharing	• Submit a draft for feedback.
6 Revising	• Revise based on feedback from your teacher.
7 Publishing	• Submit final copy to your teacher. • Evaluate using criteria.

Getting organized: making a plan of investigation

ATL Self-management skills

Create your own plan for completion with target dates and goals. Submit this with your proposed topic and question. Include some initial sources of information you will use.

Completing the IA successfully requires that students **create a plan for completion** that includes several important steps of the inquiry process. Some of the steps may overlap, but it is important that you organize your tasks and stay on track for completion by setting goals and due dates. Your teacher should read at least one draft and give some feedback to ensure that the IA is not plagiarised. A plan of investigation should include the following steps:

1 Planning	• Select a topic and formulate a question. • Submit a proposal to your teacher. • Identify information sources.

Getting organized: researching

ATL Communication skills

When supporting historical claims, it is important to make your evidence visible to your reader. Make sure you use a standard bibliographic format to show the reader where your evidence was found. In the discipline of history, the University of Chicago style or MLA style is most commonly used because it provides significant information about the origins of the source, and the endnotes or footnotes format allows the historian to insert additional information about the source where necessary.

Take good notes during the research stage.
Post-it notes are helpful to record thoughts and ideas next to key passages as you read and think about the information in relation to the question. Using different coloured highlighters to identify different perspectives on the question as you read can also be helpful. If using borrowed books, take a photo of important pages on a tablet device and use a note taking application to highlight and write notes on the page. Students who make their thinking visible as they read will have a easier time writing later in the process. Create a timeline of the event you are researching to ensure the chronology is clear in your mind.

It is strongly recommended that you record the bibliographic information and page numbers where you find important evidence and analysis. Many students wait until the very end of the writing process to compile their bibliography, but this is much more easily accomplished if the information is recorded throughout, instead of as an afterthought when the draft is finished. There are several easily accessible web sites that provide the most up-to-date versions of **MLA** (www.mla.org), and **Chicago Manual of Style** (www.chicagomanualofstyle.org), which are the two most common formats used for bibliographies in university history departments.

> **Common problems when planning and organizing an IA:**
> - Lack of general background knowledge of the topic.
> - No feedback on proposed topic and question.
> - No plan for completion.
> - Inaccurately recording page numbers and references.
> - Poorly organized notes; or no notes at all.

Internal Assessment skills

Create a proposal for the IA using the template shown.

Topic:	Student:
Research question:	
Proposed sources:	
Sources (2) proposed for evaluation in Section A:	

Section A: Identification and evaluation of sources

Section A is worth 6 of the 25 total marks. It is recommended that the word count does not exceed much more than 500 words. While this section does not count for a substantial portion of the marks, most students will not be successful without a strong Section A. There are three key aspects of this section.

1 **Clearly state the topic of the investigation. (This must be stated as a question).**

2 **Include a brief explanation of the two sources the student has selected for detailed analysis, and a brief explanation of their relevance to the investigation.**

3 **With reference to their origins, purpose and content, analyse the value and limitations of the two sources.**

> **Common problems with Section A:**
> - Question is not clearly stated.
> - Relevance or significance of selected sources not explained.
> - Student summarizes the content of selected sources.
> - Limited analysis.
> - Discussion of origins, purpose and content is in isolation to value and limitations.
> - Poorly chosen sources.
> - Speculates vaguely about the values and limitations of sources.
> - Reference to origins, purpose and content is not explicit.

Thinking about evidence: origins, purpose, value and limitations

Because it is built on a foundation of evidence, history is by nature interpretive and controversial.

This is not something many people understand – to them history is simply a long list of dates and dead people. While there are a great many things historians agree upon, there are countless historical questions that are enshrouded in debate and controversy. Since relatively few people personally witness the events they study, how one understands the past depends largely on which sources of evidence are used, and how they are interpreted. Even facts that historians generally agree upon can change over time. Philosopher Ambrose Bierce once said, *"God alone knows the future, but only a historian can alter the past."* Though the past cannot actually be changed, historical memory and understanding is always changing as each generation brings forward new questions, new evidence and new perspectives. This process of changing historical interpretations is referred to as **revisionism**. Revisionist historians are those who challenge **orthodox**, or generally accepted arguments and interpretations.

Besides revisionism, another reason why history is controversial is that accounts or evidence from the same events can differ drastically. People record events from different **origins and perspectives**, and for different **purposes**. Historical evidence might come from a limitless number of possible kinds of sources. Sources that all originate from the same time and place that we are investigating are typically referred to as **primary sources**. The interpretations and narratives that we find in documentaries, articles and books created by historians are called **secondary sources**.

Students often make the error of thinking that primary sources are more authentic and reliable, and therefore have more **value**, and fewer **limitations** than secondary sources. This isn't always the case. Being there does not necessarily give greater insight into events, and indeed, sometimes the opposite is true. Historians can look at events from multiple perspectives and use a wide range of evidence not available to the eyewitness. Students often speculate that a primary source is valuable and significant to their investigation, but

have poor reasons in support of this beyond the fact that it is a primary source.

It is important that you understand how to evaluate the value and limitations of sources with reference to the origins, purpose and content of the source. Discussing the origin, purpose and content outside the context of the value and limitations will result in a poor assessment.

Origins	• Where did the source come from?
	• Who wrote or created it?
	• Whose perspectives are represented? Whose are not?
Purpose	• Why was this created?
	• What purpose might this document have served?
Content	• What does the source mean?
	• What does it reveal or contain?
	• How useful is the information? Is it reasonable to believe it is accurate? Can it be corroborated?

Generally, the closer in proximity (place and time) the origin of a primary source is, the more **value** it has to historians. If students can find ways to **corroborate** (support, confirm) a source by other sources, then the source likely has greater value to the investigation. **Limitations** may include any factors that cause someone to question the truthfulness, validity or value of a source.

Keep in mind, that using the term **bias** is not always useful in history – it is important to be able to identify bias, but bias does not necessarily limit the value of a source. Students often make the error of assuming a source is unreliable because they detect bias. Remember that most people will have biased perspectives that are unique to their own experiences, time and place. This does not mean that you should blindly dismiss the evidence they offer us. You should ensure that you explain clearly how the bias affects the value of the content in the source used.

Internal Assessment skills

Use this template for taking notes from each of the sources used in the investigation.

Research Question:		
Source (bibliographic information):		
Primary or secondary source?	How is the source relevant/significant to the investigation?	Origins/Purpose? Value/Limitations?
Page#:	What evidence does the source provide? (quote, paraphrase, describe)	What is your interpretation? How does the content of the source relate to your question? What perspective does it add?

Selecting sources for the IA

One of the challenges to students writing a successful Section A is making sure that they choose two appropriate sources to evaluate. You should be able to clearly and effectively explain why the chosen sources are relevant and important to the investigation.

Often students make the mistake of relying too heavily on non-scholarly sources such as online encyclopaedia articles and general history textbooks. As stated, these are good starting points for finding a topic, but they are not good sources to build your investigation upon. They are especially poor choices to use for detailed analysis in this section. Before selecting sources consider the following:

- You will be expected to discuss as much detail about the origins and purpose of the source as possible. Be sure to choose sources where you can identify as much of the following as possible: when it was created; who created it; why it was created; where it was created. If much of this information is not readily identifiable, you will have difficulty evaluating value and limitations with explicit reference to the origins and purpose.

- Select sources or excerpts of sources that have clear significance to the question. You should be able to clearly, and explicitly explain why the content of the source is important to the investigation. Some students choose sources that are largely irrelevant or vaguely related to the question.

- The investigation should include an appropriate range of sources. As a general rule, you should include both primary and secondary sources, but this may not work with some types of investigations. While secondary sources on a topic are likely to be easily obtained, they often provide less to discuss in Section A. Interviews, personal correspondence, newspaper articles, journals, speeches, letters, and other primary sources often provide students with much more meaningful material to evaluate in Section A. Ideas about origins and purpose come more readily with primary sources than they might when using secondary sources which generally, but not always, strive to present balanced arguments and perspectives.

- Choose secondary sources that reference the evidence the historians used to support their arguments. You will find it less difficult to

assess the validity of the evidence the historian uses, or how the evidence is interpreted in the arguments, if the historian has documented the evidence clearly.

- Consider using periodical articles. Many historians write excellent, concise articles on historical topics for peer-reviewed journals. These articles often have rich footnoting and bibliographies that you can use to find additional sources for the investigation.

- Be careful about relying too heavily on general web-based sources. Many online sources are not referenced or footnoted properly so it is difficult to validate information about the origins, purpose and authorship. On the other hand, a great number of rich primary sources can be found online, as well as articles written by respected historians.

- Consider using interviews. Some students have written exceptional IAs based on people's experiences, or by interviewing historians or other people with extensive knowledge and experience. When using interviews, record them as an audio file for reference and accuracy.

Analysing the selected sources

After stating the research question and explaining the two selected sources and their relevance to the investigation, the largest portion of Section A should focus on analysing the two sources. Depending on the sources chosen, they can be discussed simultaneously and comparatively, or they can be discussed separately. Discussing them separately is often more advantageous because you can make the origins, purpose, value and limitations more explicit.

- It is important that any arguments about the value and limitations make specific references to the content, origins and purpose.

- Be careful that the value of a source is not dismissed on the basis of bias without a strong argument about why the bias limits the validity or reliability of the content.

- You should avoid summarizing the content too much. Summarize and describe content only to the extent necessary to construct a strong analysis about the source's value and limitations.

- You should be thorough in examining all aspects of the source's origins including date of origin, cultural context, author's background, publisher or other important details. If little information about the origins is identifiable, it is likely a poorly chosen source for analysis.

Internal Assessment skills

Use the Section A assessment criteria to discuss and evaluate this excerpt of a student's work. Identify where the student has explicitly discussed origins and purpose, and value and limitations.

This investigation will seek to answer the question **"What did the Tiananmen Square protest reveal about the democratic sentiments in China between 1980 and 1989?"** *Democratic sentiments are defined as people's attitudes toward democratic ideals. This investigation will analyze factors that influenced democratic sentiments from multiple perspectives, but will not assess the ethics and justification of the Chinese government's response to the protest.*

In order to take into account the opposing views on this event and keep the scope of the investigation manageable, I have made use of a variety of carefully selected sources. Two primary sources will be evaluated …

Source 1: Prisoner of State: the secret journal of Zhao Ziyang[1]

The origin of the source is of great value because the author is Zhao Ziyang, the General Secretary of the Communist Party during the Tiananmen Square Protest (the Protest). Zhao attempted to use a non-violent approach to resolve the protest and spoke against the party's hardliners. After a power struggle, Zhao was dismissed and put under house arrest until his death in 2005. The content of the journal is translated from thirty audiotapes recorded secretly by Zhao while he was under house arrest between 1999 and 2000. The book is published in 2009 by Simon & Schuster, one of the largest and most reputable English-language publishers. The reputation of the author and publisher increases the reliability of this source.

Zhao's purpose for recording these tapes is to publicize his political opinions and express his regret for failing to prevent the massacre. This is valuable because Zhao was not allowed to publicize his opinions while under house arrest, so this source is the only surviving public record of Zhao's opinions and perspectives on the Protest. This source is also valuable because its author, Zhao, was directly involved in the government's decision-making process during the protest. It reveals the power struggle

within the Communist Party through the lens of the progressive bloc.

However, its exclusivity may limit its value because there are no counterparts to compare with and to verify its claims. As a translated material, the source may not accurately present Zhao's intentions and may have lost some cultural expressions. In addition, this source may be biased in that Zhao speaks in favour of political reform and democracy, which does not represent the Party's position ...

[1] Zhao, Ziyang, Pu Bao, Renee Chiang, Adi Ignatius, and Roderick MacFarquhar. *Prisoner of the state: the secret journal of Zhao Ziyang.* New York: Simon & Schuster, 2009.

Section B: Investigation

Common problems with Section B:

- Too much narrative.
- Poor referencing of sources.
- Limited awareness of different positions or perspectives.
- Listing of evidence instead of integrating analysis and evidence.
- Overuse of quotations.
- Plagiarism.
- Poor organization and arguments that are difficult to follow.
- Few connections to the question and purpose of the investigation.
- Conclusions are not evidence-based.

It is essential that you keep Section B focused on the purpose of the investigation and construct an argument using all of the sources you have listed in the bibliography. No marks are awarded for the bibliography, but an incomplete treatment of your sources, or inaccurate referencing will cost you marks in this section. **Evidence must be integrated** with **very clear critical commentary** that leads the reader to an eventual **evidence-based conclusion** that addresses the question posed in Section A. Students often make the error of simply listing facts they researched, without explaining how they are relevant or relate to their question. The following points should be considered when writing this section.

- The investigation should be carefully organized. The synthesis of evidence and critical commentary should be carefully planned to ensure that there is logic and flow to the section, and that your argument is very clear.

- The type of question you pose for the investigation will determine how you organize your writing. For example, a question that invites comparisons (for example: whether a film portrays an event accurately) will require you to discuss both similarities and differences. "To what extent" questions will require you to discuss both perspectives of "ways no" and "ways yes".

- As you gather evidence and document your thinking in your notes, keep in mind you may need to adjust or change your question. You should give some consideration to planning and writing Section B before writing Section A.

- Where appropriate, discuss different perspectives of the topic. Historians may offer different interpretations, or there may be multiple experiences of an event.

- Quotes should be used sparingly. Most of your writing should summarize and paraphrase the evidence collected and explain explicitly how it relates to the investigation. Too many student papers read as long lists of quotes from sources. Quotes must be explained, or integrated as evidence in support of an argument, and add something specifically and convincingly to your argument.

- Any references to sources, or ideas that are not your own, should be referenced appropriately using endnotes or footnotes. If this is not completed carefully, you risk plagiarizing others' ideas as your own.

- You should avoid writing significant amounts of narrative. Retelling a historical narrative or sequence of events is not the purpose of the investigation. On the other hand, you should demonstrate a clear understanding of the chronology and historical context of the events you are analyzing.

- Your conclusion is essential. The conclusion must offer possible answers or solutions to the question identified in Section A. It should not read simply as a summary of points, but rather as a well-reasoned, convincing, evidence-based closure to the investigation.

- There is no suggested number of appropriate sources required for your investigation. The number of sources you should use depends entirely on your topic and the kind of investigation you are doing. Local or community history, for example, might offer a limited numbers of sources. Interviews or community archives that this kind of IA might require could yield fewer, but very rich primary sources. Wherever possible your sources should be varied and specific, rather than few and general.

Submitting your bibliography

The bibliography – an **alphabetically ordered list of sources** – should be inserted at the very end of your paper. It is mentioned here with Section B because it should be created as part of the writing process, not simply thrown together at the last minute before submitting the paper. This bibliography is not worth any marks but it is an essential component of the paper that is often overlooked or poorly completed. Any sources referenced as evidence in Section B must be included in your bibliography.

Internal Assessment skills

Use the Section B assessment criteria to evaluate an excerpt of this student's investigation. Has the student effectively integrated evidence and critical commentary?

…Sentimentality played a key role in the events leading up to the protest in 1989. Western democracy and parliamentary system were believed to be the panacea for China's social problems. As Zhao Ziyang stated in his memoir: "in fact, it is the Western parliamentary democratic system that has demonstrated the most vitality. It seems that this system is currently the best one available."[1] The death of Hu Yaobang, the former General Secretary of the Party who advocated strongly for democratic reform, created a unified sense of democratic sentiments that united both ideological and practical groups.[2] Hu's successor, Zhao Ziyang, an even more progressive leader, spoke publicly in favour of political reform. Zhao's rise in power gave people an optimistic belief in democracy, and encouraged other progressives to act more openly.

However, contrary to the revolutionary attitudes later in the protest, the democratic sentiment under Zhao's leadership was relatively constructive. Based on the Seven Demands[3] drafted by the protesters, it was clear that, in the beginning of the Protest, protesters did not intend to be anti-governmental or anti-communist; they merely demanded that the Party take actions to end corruption and grant citizens more political freedom.[4] As the leading figure behind the Party's progressive bloc, Zhao was generally in line with the protestors. Internally, he attempted to persuade hardliner party officials, particularly Deng, into making concession with the protestors.[5] He also allowed the media, such as the People's Daily and the China Central Television to bypass censorship and broadcast the protest…

---

[1] Zhao, Ziyang, Pu Bao, Renee Chiang, Adi Ignatius, and Roderick MacFarquhar. "Preface." In *Prisoner of the state: the secret journal of Zhao Ziyang.* New York: Simon & Schuster, 2009. xv.

[2] Meaning the intellectuals and the working class.

[3] Liang, Zhang. "The Tiananmen Papers." The New York Times. https://www.nytimes.com/books/first/l/liang-tiananmen.html (accessed May 26, 2014).

[4] Ziyang, op. cit.

[5] Zhao, Dingxin. *The power of Tiananmen state-society relations and the 1989 Beijing student movement.* Chicago: University of Chicago Press, 2001. 156.

Section C: Reflection

In Section C (approx. 400 words) you have the opportunity to reflect on what the investigation revealed to you about the methods used by historians and the challenges they face when investigating topics like your own. This section is worth the fewest marks (4), but it could make the difference between a good and an outstanding paper. You should no doubt already have an understanding that the study of history is beset with a number of challenges and limitations, some of which have been discussed earlier in this chapter. Section A is designed to give you an opportunity to reflect on this understanding, but it must be focused specifically on the nature of your topic and/or the kind of investigation you undertook, rather than a reflection on the nature of history in general.

> Common problems with Section C:
> - Limited understanding of the nature of history and the challenges facing historians.
> - Limited understanding of the methods historians use to examine and study history.
> - Poorly focused on the challenges specific to the student's topic.

Throughout your IB History course, your TOK and History teachers should provide opportunities for you to think about and discuss the challenges of determining historical truth and understanding.

History can often be determined largely by who writes it, his or her purpose, and the methods he or she decides to use. Consider also that where there is scant evidence, historians often make very authoritative sounding **speculations** – essentially educated guesses – where they fill in gaps in the historical record with judgments they think are reasonable to believe. But often we cannot with absolute certainty verify or prove beyond doubt that their accounts are correct.

Many of the inherent challenges of history stem from problems related to its evidence-based nature. History is also challenging because of how it is used for so many different purposes including political slogans, national narratives, personal and group identity, entertainment, advertising and countless other ways. The past the historian studies is not a dead past. History is living, changing and visible in the present. Therefore, there is no shortage of questions to consider in your reflection section.

- What is history? Is it more creative and interpretive as opposed to scientific and objective?
- How did the nature of your investigation present specific challenges to finding reliable evidence?
- What methods did historians use? How were they limited by time and place? How are they limited by ideology or world views?
- Is it possible to capture the entirety of an event?
- What are the challenges of causation? How far back in time should the historian search for causes? Can immediate causes ever be separated from long term causes?
- How might national identity, cultural norms, values or beliefs affect one's ability to reason and arrive at an understanding of history?
- How might mass culture, the entertainment industry or other powerful forces influence historical understanding?
- Who decides what topics and issues are important to record and study?
- How does bias and editorial selection impact what is recorded and reported on, and what is not?
- In what ways does the outcome of an event determine how it is recorded in history?
- How does technology affect understanding of history, or the methods the historian uses?
- How are value judgements in history determined? For example, how are terms like atrocity, terrorism or revolution treated now compared to the period under investigation? Should historians make moral judgements?
- In what ways does the idea of progress and decline affect our treatment of some historical events?
- What is the role of the historian? Can the historian ever be objective?
- Are all perspectives of history equally valid? If not, how do we determine which have greater value?
- How might knowledge of your investigation be used to solve complex problems in the present? How might it be abused?

In would be far too ambitious for you to consider all of these questions in Section C. It is essential however that you give considerable thought

to what you learned about history from your investigation. You should demonstrate clear awareness of the challenges facing historians, and the limitations of specific methods used in investigating topics like your own. In other words, there should be a clear connection between the nature of history as a way of thinking, and your own investigation. For a greater understanding of the nature of history, the following books are very useful.

> E.E. Carr, 1961. *What is History?* Penguin Books. London, UK
>
> M. MacMillan, 2008. *The Uses and Abuses of History.* Viking. Toronto.
>
> J. L. Gaddis, 2004. *The Landscape of History.* New York, Oxford University Press.

Final touches: Wrapping up the IA

The Internal Assessment is arguably the best opportunity IB History students have to maximize their overall course mark. The final assessed mark is entirely in your hands because you control the process of topic selection, research, planning and writing. Before submitting to your teacher for final assessment, make sure you have completed the following:

- Select and thoroughly research a question of personal interest.

- Complete all sections fully, according to the criteria.

- Compare your IA to examples posted on the OCC or in the Teacher Support Materials.

- Include all relevant sources in your bibliography.

- Reference all sources using a consistent, standardized citation format.

- Edit and proofread your work carefully.

- Submit a draft for effective feedback from your teacher.

- Include a title page with your question, name, candidate number and total word count clearly listed.

- Include a table of contents.

Internal Assessment skills

Discuss and evaluate the student example below using the criteria for Section C:

Ever since Deng declared martial law on May 20th, 1989, the Tiananmen Square Protest had been a taboo topic in Mainland China. There are no public records of the Protest, and any discussion regarding the Protest is immediately censored. In the educational system, particularly, the Protest was considered "non-existent". The Party's illegitimate historical revisionism illustrates the extent to which history can be manipulated to influence public opinions. Therefore, historians have the morally imperative role to present a balanced account of the Protest.

However, historians hoping to investigate the Protest face a dilemma: most primary sources are not made public by the Chinese government, and most available sources are from the protestors' perspectives. Historians either have no primary sources to work with, or have a disproportionate number of pro-protest sources. This dilemma is a common problem caused by illegitimate historical revisionism, which made it difficult for historians to remain objective. Government records are not available. Media coverage during the Protest is censored. Government and military officers who gave orders during the Protest are not permitted to publicize their narratives. On the other hand, a large number of sources originate from political dissidents, protesters who sought asylum overseas, and families of protestors who were killed

on June 4th. These sources, although highly valuable to historians, can be biased and unreliable. Therefore, historians should exercise caution when evaluating these sources.

In order to counterbalance the aforementioned dilemma, I purposely limited the number of sources originated from the protestors. I also took advantage of my Chinese proficiency by looking through Chinese newspaper archives and talking with former protestors and former Party officials during the protest. These methods of acquiring evidence should have helped me gain a more balanced understanding of the democratic sentiments during the protest.

Apart from balancing different perspectives, historians who investigate this issue are under social and ethical pressures. If they suggest that there were democratic sentiments within the Party and the Army executing the martial law, many former protesters (especially families of victims who were killed during the June 4th incident) would accuse the historians of downplaying the Party's crime. In addition, the Western world almost unanimously agrees that the June 4th incident was a massacre and that the Party was the antagonist. Historians who propose otherwise are under significant ideological pressure. Therefore, historians should prevent these pressures from influencing the investigation. Any conclusions should be re-examined by other historians to ensure a higher degree of objectivity.

Index

William J. Clinton: 'Address to the Nation on the Military Technical Agreement on Kosovo', June 10, 1999, 'Public Papers of the Presidents of the United States', found here: http://www.gpo.gov/fdsys/pkg/WCPD-1999-06-14/pdf/WCPD-1999-06-14-Pg1074-2.pdf.

Prof. Lenard Cohen: 'Living in Illusion: Political Transition in Kosovo' from *Canadian Military Journal*, Vol. 1, No. 1, Spring 2000, reprinted by permission.

Romeo Dallaire: From *Shake Hands with the Devil: The Failure of Humanity in Rwanda,* (Arrow), copyright © 2003, Dec 21 2004 Roméo A. Dallaire, LGen (ret), reprinted by permission of The Random House Group Ltd., Random House Canada, a division of Penguin Random House Canada Limited, a Penguin Random House Company, and Da Capo Press, a member of the Perseus Books Group.

Anne-Marie de Brouwer and Sandra Ka Hon Chu (Eds.): *The Men Who Killed Me* (Douglas and McIntyre, 2009), reprinted by permission of the publisher.

Ambassador Swanee Hunt: Letter dated 30 July 1999 to President William J. Clinton,

FOIA 2006-0325-F, from Clinton Presidential Records, NSC Records Management [Wesley Clark], 9905915, OA/ID 2744, part of the William J. Clinton Presidential Library.

General Sir Mike Jackson: *Soldier: The Autobiography* (Bantam Press, 2007), copyright © General Sir Mike Jackson 2007, reprinted by permission of Penguin Random House UK and Christopher Little Literary Agency LLP.

Tim Judah: *Kosovo: What everyone needs to know* (Oxford University Press, 2008), copyright © OUP, 2008, reprinted by permission of Oxford University Press, USA.

Fergal Keane: from *Season of Blood: A Rwandan Journey* (Penguin Books 1995, 1996) Copyright © Fergal Keane, 1995, reprinted by permission of Penguin Books Ltd.

Elizabeth King: *From Classrooms to Conflict in Rwanda* (CUP 2013), copyright © Elizabeth King 2014, reprinted by permission of Cambridge University Press.

Arthur Koestler: Extract from *Janus: A Summing Up*, reprinted by permission of Peters Fraser & Dunlop (www.petersfraserdunlop.com) on behalf of the Estate of Arthur Koestler.

Catherine Larson: extracts from *As We Forgive: Stories of Reconciliation from Rwanda* (p.15, p.16, p.18), copyright © 2009, reprinted by permission of Zondervan, all rights reserved.

Noel Malcolm: *Kosovo: A Short History* (Macmillan, 1998), copyright © Noel Malcolm, 1998, reprinted by permission of Pan Macmillan.

National Security Archive: extract from 'The Rwandan crisis seen through the eyes of France. Part one: Lead-up to the genocide', French documents available in English for the first time, National Security Archive Electronic Briefing Book No. 461, 20 March 2014, edited by Arnaud Siad, translations by Christina Graubert, reprinted from www.nsarchive.org by permission of the National Security Archive.

Bill Neely: 'Serbs rewrite history of Račak massacre', *The Independent*, 23 January 1999, reprinted by permission of The Independent (www.independent.co.uk).

United Nations: quotation from UN Resolution 808, 1993 (http://daccess-dds-ny.un.org/doc/UNDOC/GEN/N93/098/21/IMG/N9309821.pdf?OpenElement) © 1993, United Nations, reprinted by permission of the United Nations.

United Nations: quotation from 'Letter dated 15 December 1999 from the Secretary-General addressed to the President of the Security Council (http://www.securitycouncilreport.org/atf/cf/%7b65BFCF9B-6D27-4E9C-8CD3-CF6E4FF96FF9%7d/POC%20S19991257.pdf), © 1999, United Nations, reprinted by permission of the United Nations.

United Nations: quotation by Colin Keating from article 'Rwandan genocide: Security Council told failure of political will led to 'cascade of human tragedy', 16 April 2014, found here: http://www.un.org/apps/news/story.asp?NewsID=47596#.VVmp4EKDnww © 2014, United Nations, reprinted by permission of the United Nations.

United Nations International Criminal Tribunal for Rwanda: 'The Hutu Ten Commandments' December 1990 and 'A cockroach (Inyenzi) cannot bring forth a butterfly', July 1994, originally published in *Kangura* magazine, © 1990 and 1994, United Nations, reprinted by permission of United Nations.

Keith Somerville: *Radio Propaganda and the Broadcasting of Hatred* (Palgrave, 2012), copyright © Keith Somerville 2012, reprinted by permission of Palgrave Macmillan.

Ian Traynor: quotation from 'Slobodan Milosevic', 13 March 2006, *The Guardian,* copyright © 2006 Guardian News and Media Ltd, reprinted by permission.

Carl Wikens: quotations reprinted by permission.

Laura Silber and Allan Little: *Yugoslavia: Death of a Nation*, published by BBC books. Reprinted by permission of The Random House Group Ltd. and the author.

Slobodan Milošević: Translation by Associated Press, reprinted by permission.

Western news agency: *Two Serb Orthodox churches destroyed in Kosovo*. Reprinted by permission of Associated Press.

M. Simons and A. Smale: *Slobodan Milosevic, 64, former Yugoslav leader accused of war crimes, dies*, published in New York Times. Reprinted by permissions of PARS Intl.

L. Melvern: *Conspiracy to Murder: the Rwandan genocide*. Reprinted by permission of Verso.

P. Gourevitch: *We Wish to Inform You That Tomorrow We Will Be Killed With Our Families: Stories from Rwanda*. Reprinted by permission of Farrar Straus and Giroux.

Donatella Lorch: *Heart of Rwanda's Darkness: Slaughter at a rural church*, published in *The New York Times*. Reprinted by permission.

UNHCR: Quotation from Refugees magazine, 2004, vol.2, no.135, p.22; Figure 10.2 'Rwandan refugees in the Great Lakes region, end-August 1994' from http://www.unchr.org/cgi-bin/texis/vtx/home/opendocPDFViewer.html?docid=3ebf9bb60&query=the%20rwandan%20genocide%20and%20its%20aftermath, Chapter 10 'The Rwandan genocide and its aftermath'; extract from Refugees magazine, 1994, Issue 97, 1 September 1994, 'Cooperation crucial in Rwanda crisis', hhttp://ww.unchr.org/3b5402fa1.html, reprinted by permission of UNHCR.

Jean Hatzfeld: extract from A Time for Machetes: The Rwandan Genocide – The killers Speak (Serpents Tail, 2008) / (Machete Season: The Killers in Rwanda Speak (Farrar, Straus and Giroux, LLC, reprinted by permission of Farrar, Straus and Giroux, LLC and Profile Books.

Anne-Marie de Brouwer and Sandra Ka Hon Chu (Eds.): *The Men Who Killed Me* (Douglas and McIntyre, 2009), reprinted by permission of the publisher.

National Security Archive: extract from 'The Rwandan crisis seen through the eyes of France. Part one: Lead-up to the genocide', French documents available in English for the first time, National Security Archive Electronic Briefing Book No. 461, 20 March 2014, edited by Arnaud Siad, translations by Christina Graubert, reprinted from www.nsarchive.org by permission of the National Security Archive.